Inventing a republic

Politics, culture and society in early modern Britain

General Editors

PROFESSOR ANN HUGHES
DR ANTHONY MILTON
PROFESSOR PETER LAKE

This important new series publishes monographs that take a fresh and challenging look at the interactions betwen politics, culture and society in Britain between 1500 and the mid-eighteenth century. It seeks to counteract the fragmentation of current historiography through encouraging a variety of approaches which attempt to redefine the political, social and cultural worlds, and to explore their interconnection in a flexible and creative fashion.

All the volumes in the series will question and transcend traditional interdisciplinary boundaries, such as those between political history and literary studies, social history and divinity, urban history and anthropology. They will thus contribute to a broader understanding of crucial developments in early modern Britain.

Forthcoming

Sixteenth century courtship DIANA O'HARA

Ambition and failure in Stuart England: the career of John, 1st Viscount Scudamore, 1602–43 IAN ATHERTON

Londinopolis MARK JENNER AND PAUL GRIFFITHS

Cromwell's Major Generals CHRIS DURSTON

Inventing a republic

The political
culture of
the English
Commonwealth
1649–1653

SEAN KELSEY

Manchester
University Press

Published by Manchester University Press
Oxford Road, Manchester M13 9NR, UK

British Library Cataloguing-in-Publication Data
A catalogue record is available from the British Library

ISBN 0 7190 5057 x *hardback*

First published 1997

01 00 99 98 97   10 9 8 7 6 5 4 3 2 1

Typeset in Scala with Clairvaux display
by Koinonia Ltd, Manchester

Printed in Great Britain
by Biddles Ltd, Guildford and King's Lynn

Contents

Plates

Acknowledgements

For their logistical support I owe thanks to a number of organisations and their helpful staff. At the Bodleian Library, the British Library, the Centre for Kentish Studies at Maidstone, the Greater London Record Office, the Institute of Historical Research, the House of Lords Record Office, the Public Record Office in Chancery Lane, Shropshire and Gloucestershire Record Offices, and the library of Worcester College, Oxford, I have received invaluable assistance measuring the dimensions of the beast in question. The British Academy generously funded the first three years of research. A research grant from the University of Wales, Cardiff, was but the smallest token of the generosity with which I was received there during the year of teaching in which this book was completed.

Justin Champion, John Miller, Henry Roseveare and Ian Roy have given me invaluable opportunities to try out ideas in the amiably testing environment provided by their Seventeenth-Century British History Seminar at the Institute of Historical Research. My thanks, of course, to the editors of this series, for the very great honour of inviting me to sail under their flag; and, at Manchester University Press, to Vanessa Graham for her guidance, and Carolyn Hand for all her help.

I am extremely grateful to Toby Barnard, not least for the generosity of his support, but especially for having inspired in me as an undergraduate an interest in a topic which became the subject of my doctoral research. The seeds sown in Oxford's glasshouse germinated in the clement surroundings of the Department of History at Manchester. It is inconceivable that they would have ever come to fruition without the thoughtful criticism and constant encouragement of Ann Hughes.

It is impossible to quantify the debt I owe to my family, and to my wife, Ali Moore. Without their unerring conviction in me, and sacrifice along the way, I could never have dreamed of taking the path I have chosen, let alone reached this particular staging post.

FOR MOLLY

Judge not the appearance, but judge righteous Judgment

John 7:24, cited by Francis Rous, MP
The Lawfulness of Obeying the present Government, 1649

Introduction

Reviving the Rump

THIS book aims to repair the reputation of the parliamentary republic which ruled England between 1649 and 1653. It takes issue with a conventional wisdom which depicts the Rump Parliament as a feckless, shallow and unconvincing expedient, committed to little more than blindly obstructing the goals of progressive reformers. It re-examines the republican regime in the light of the public image and imagery by which it represented itself and its authority. It demonstrates that the Rump not only successfully restored the norms of civil government, but also invented novel means for its expression. The Rump improvised a new adornment for civil authority. Its visual and verbal discursive strategies replaced the 'trappings' of the regal polity with an imagination and verve which bely common assumptions about the regime's reactionary character and lack of ideological commitment.

This post-revolutionary raiment was essentially conservative. Its strands recast old forms and reinvented traditional pomp in order to restore an edifice of civil governance rocked to its foundations by civil war and revolution. Some of the ideas from which it was woven were also of a piece with elements of the 'country' ideology of the early seventeenth century which had sustained opposition to the growth of royal absolutism. And yet the rule of the Rump, like the revolution which created it, inherently contradicted many aspects of that ideology, such as respect for legal and property rights. It erected arbitrary courts that it might execute its enemies judicially; it was more ruthless than any king in its exaction of taxes from the nation; it deliberately brought hundreds of gentle families to the brink of financial disaster; and it meddled incessantly in corporate politics up and down the country. This ambiguity was the central feature of an experiment in turning popular rights into popular sovereignty by casting a unicameral Parliament as a sovereign body – it was conservatism at its most radical.

It also reflected some of the deeper ambiguities of early modern English politics. The Rump was no Roman Senate, and rarely expressed an overt

1

commitment to an ideology of kingless republicanism. But the Common-wealth was effectively the embodiment of a 'gentry republic' which had always provided the bare bones of a structure of authority over which was draped the surface gilding of early modern monarchy.[1] Between 1649 and 1653 the quasi-republicanism implicit in Englishmen's beliefs about the duties of magistracy and virtuous civic responsibility helped fill the gaping hole torn in the fabric of order and authority by the revolution. Not for the first time, the 'acephalous body politic' which had shouldered an endless succession of monarchs to supremacy was forced to reveal itself. But revolution and the regime's claims to *de facto* authority had thrown up entirely unprecedented challenges which threatened to strip the English state of almost all its gilded fictions. Out of the tattered remnant, the Commonwealth leadership improvised a covering with which to hide the naked power by which they ruled. The mixture of imagery and spectacle they cooked up buried the armed revolution beneath layers of respectability which, with time, began to take on the patina of legitimacy. Ultimately this complex and sophisticated confection proved no match for the logic of the catalytic events which marked its inception. If the Commonwealth was a pearl, then the power of the sword was the piece of grit around which it formed, the grain of truth which sceptical early modern Englishmen were only just beginning to learn how to cope with – the fact that might made right.

'TRADITIONAL' HISTORIOGRAPHY

The Rump Parliament no longer attracts quite the degree of condemnation it used to. Historians have done much to mitigate the view that its members were uncommonly corrupt, and to prove that they did not conspire to keep themselves in power to the exclusion of all others.[2] However, there remain a number of substantial criticisms. The Rump is commonly described as an expedient which acted without conviction or ideals. Regicide and the abolition of the Crown and House of Lords were pragmatic solutions to temporary political problems. The reactionary regime which ruled by default thereafter saw its mission as no more elevated than keeping the lid on chaos, and, in the absence of any more substantial motivation or justification, 'most of the time did not know whether it was coming or going'. It suffered from 'ideological lameness' and the profound 'moral weakness' of its own shallow pragmatism. Its members saw the business of government as 'primarily a matter of sur-vival' – they lacked both the inclination and the imagination to change society. Their 'blinkered vision' frustrated the real revolutionaries in the army who had expected so much more. After the victory at Worcester on 3 September 1651 the royalist threat receded, but so too did the unity of purpose between MPs and the army. '[T]he alliance which had been cemented by danger was dissolved by victory.' Soldiers were now free to 'stir up the rather stagnant mill-pond at Westminster'. Spiritually cleansed by the fire and bloodshed of battle, the military men were disgusted by what they found – amongst the bootless civilians 'the arts of backroom politics, power broking, compromise and deals' were valued more highly than social justice. When it furthermore appeared that they had no intention of letting go the wheel, but were instead preparing to invite the enemies of the cause to join them at the helm, the soldiers lost patience altogether. The Rumpers were forcibly ejected from the palace of Westminster on 20 April 1653, and the army resumed its providential duty of leading God's chosen people to the promised land.[3]

The strength of modern prejudices against the Rump owes a great deal to the enduring influence of Thomas Carlyle's characterisation of Cromwell as the great Puritan hero and the New Model Army as a congregation of saints in arms. Carlyle drew a stark and romantic contrast between the men of action, animated by God's word, and the vacillating civilians who were deaf to the call. Attracted to Cromwell by his sympathy for the General's heroic spiritual beliefs, Carlyle's depiction of his religious idealism and 'tormented sincerity' single-handedly reversed a historiographical tradition which had stood virtually unchallenged since the Protector's death.[4] But his edition of Cromwell's letters and speeches also turned the 'Puritan Revolution' into a vehicle for his own personal and political philosophy. In Carlyle's platonic *Weltanschauung* the physical world was a representation of the deeper truths of a transcendent spiritual order. During the English civil war and revolution, the Real irrupted into the shadow world of reality, its spirit taking human shape in the form of the Lord General.[5]

Carlyle rescued Cromwell's corpse from the filthy ditch into which it had been cast, stitched his head back on and reanimated him with his own philosophical and political prejudices. This is the Cromwell which has dominated ever since.[6] Carlyle's solipsism and his vitriolic denunciations of the 'Fag-end of a Parliament' remain unique. So too his disdain for 'Dryasdust' methodology. Never one to let the matter of evidence disturb his analysis, Carlyle preferred to scythe through the complexities of the story in which he located his hero. He grimly dismissed the vast collection of tracts built up by George Thomason as 'huge piles of mouldering wreck, wherein ... lie things memorable'.[7] But if Carlyle's method was distinctive, some features of his analysis have become commonplace.

Having unlocked the Thomason treasure chest, and much more besides, Samuel R. Gardiner's 'scientific' history took over from Carlyle's morality play. Carlyle's condemnation of the parliamentarians was mitigated to a considerable extent, out of respect for the nineteenth-century liberal establishment for whom the mid-seventeenth-century struggle against tyranny was an ideological touchstone. 'The little group which ... found itself in possession of authority' after the revolution may not have succeeded, but 'their strivings to loose the fetters of dynastic interest' were the sign of 'honest endeavour', which 'even when it fails to clothe itself in external fact, ... contributes somewhat to the energy, and thereby to the ultimate vigour, of the race'. The Rump, 'doing the business of a more distant posterity', was, nevertheless, 'predestined to failure'. Its members were 'no more than instruments in the hands of the men of the sword' who could only 'wait for better times, contenting themselves with some makeshift constitutional arrangement'.[8]

The scale and scope of Gardiner's scholarship remain unchallenged even today. But it was a very specific kind of scholarship, tailored to fit the figure of Cromwell, who continued to occupy the centre of the stage. Gardiner's account also had its rhetorical turns. The revolutionary minority had had plans which 'were often such as to commend themselves to men of the nineteenth, perhaps even to the men of the twentieth century, rather than to those of the seventeenth'.[9] Such views are not as popular today. The Whig history of the revolution has been swept away in the last twenty-five years.[10] But the new histories of the post-revolutionary period are often still dominated by the intensely spiritual, highly sympathetic and sensitive appraisal of the General's personality which characterises Carlyle's and Gardiner's analyses. Cromwell remains 'the architect' of the Commonwealth, a regime fatally flawed by its creator's 'ideological schizophrenia'.[11]

Despite its merits as an analysis of the Cromwellian psyche, it is unsatisfactory to seek to personify so momentous a passage of English political and constitutional history in the image of one man. For our present purposes, it is as well to remember that the breaking of the parliamentary republic was also the making of Oliver Cromwell. We still await an appraisal of the Lord General's career which will place in context this defining moment in his reputation for revolutionary vision, a moment which cannot be understood fully until it is seen in the light of one man's rise from humble beginnings to a position of vast personal power and wealth.[12] The Lord General's story was shared to a lesser extent by many of his colleagues, many of whom also happened to be his blood or marital relatives – their careers, too, as much as their beliefs, have a bearing on the fall of the Commonwealth. Cromwell was the head and centre of some of the most significant groups within the revolutionary coalition, and continued to wield a weighty influence over the nation's affairs even when he was in the field. He may have seemed to contemporaries the archetypal *novus princeps*, but that was just a poetic way of describing a military commander whose office had some pretty prosaic functions. A substantial portion of Wilbur Abbott's massive edition of Cromwell's life records is made up of letters and communications written on behalf of relatives, friends and allies, and a whole range of matters relating to the General's personal and public 'business management'. Moreover, Blair Worden's microscopic structural reconstruction of the complex political and factional relations which crisscrossed the floor of the House itself testifies eloquently to the fact that there was a great deal more to Commonwealth politics than just Cromwell.

More than any other before or since, Worden's monograph has established that the Rump Parliament was not just a mercifully brief passage in the life story of one man, but a fascinating chapter in the history of English Parliaments. Amongst his numerous perceptive insights, uppermost, if also the most understated, was the acknowledgment that, as England's first full-time politicians, members of the Long Parliament in some sense enjoyed the experience of governing. If revolution knocked much of the gloss off that experience for many, the rule of the Rump provided an opportunity to reamplify all the positive lessons that came out of the 1640s, especially the realisation that it was perfectly feasible to get by without a king. Winning a degree of global power unprecedented in English history, some of these men also came to see some of the positive attractions of a 'free state'. Whether or not they were won over to some theoretical justification of kinglessness, the invigorating experience of self-rule had a dramatic effect on the deportment of many government members. Much of what follows testifies to the fact that most of them did not behave as if they were ruling simply because somebody had to: they ruled in a way which suggested they wanted to.[13] In the pages that follow, the republic will be treated as it was brought forth by its protagonists rather than as the hapless victim of its antagonists. The Commonwealth will be permitted to speak for itself, in its own terms, with a view to dissolving some of the more persistent and distorting tropes of the regime's historiography. The politics of reform, traditionally described as *the* bone of contention during the Commonwealth, will be interpreted as just one of those representational features of the parliamentary government with which this book is principally concerned. These are media with the power to subvert one particular convention (that there was a distinct lack of avowed republicanism within the republic) by rendering it irrelevant. On the one hand, the suggestion that a republic whose citizens exercised their God-given reason in virtuous self-government was somehow not a republic because it failed to follow precepts laid down by foreigners, dead or alive, must be mistaken. On the other hand, regardless of the relative lack of republican theory and polemic, the regime simply *was* republican. If it did not say so as often as it might, that was because it did not need to draw attention to the fact that it was inventing a republic, a fact which became more obvious by the day. Every tax paid, every subscription of the Engagement oath and every resort to law in the republic's courts was, like every diplomatic address, or every submission to 'the Honorable Members of the Supreme Authority', an implicit acknowledgment of the free state's *de facto* kingless legitimacy. Furthermore, these genuflections to the legitimacy of the regime came more and more to be couched in terms of set ritual, order and pattern. De factoism, once imbued with its own chants and formulas, ceremony and show, becomes something very different from a pragmatism which has become a cliche of Commonwealth historiography.

In contemporary terms, it was far more important for the Rump to contain the problem of its novelty than to worry about finding a coherent progressive ideology which dovetailed neatly with the great republican civilisations of classical antiquity, or modelled itself on the trade republics of early modern Europe. The progressive standard by which *de facto* theory is often judged is somewhat anachronistic. Although *de facto* conservatism became the mainstay of the regime's self-justification, it is rarely acknowledged how radically that creed 'grasp[ed] the nettle of change'.[14] It is still less common to acknowledge that the rulers of the republic successfully rose to the challenge that de factoism posed to ancient patterns of collective responsibility for the preservation of that due process in law and politics which characterised civil authority in England. Englishmen had had the meaning of 'necessity' drummed into them throughout the 1640s. The act of regicide demonstrated that there was simply nothing sacred any more. But at that moment, as the king's blood soaked the scaffold, England's floodgates finally began to close. This book credits the members of the Rump with seizing the initiative by creating a new kind of civilian regime. By doing so it also aims to destabilise a pernicious historiographical consensus, whose likeness has been so well captured recently by Richard Tuck. Given the perpetual disagreements about everything else early modern, it is remarkable that 'English historians of both a more and a less conservative cast of mind' consistently unite to dismiss the radicalism of the revolutionary mainstream, 'conservatives because they are attracted by the idea that revolutionary politics had weak roots in England, and repelled by the use made of 1649 by later political activists; and non-conservatives because they like to see the revolution as represented by the Levellers and betrayed by the "grandees"'.[15] A case will be made, instead, for interpreting the political culture of the Rump Parliament within the conservative norms of men who embraced radical change as the only guarantor of continuity. In turn, echoing Mark Kishlansky's appraisal of the revolutionary agenda of 1647-49, the political culture of the Commonwealth illustrates that 'conventional ideas newly perceived may be the ultimate source of radical ideology and the best preconditioning of radicals may be a tenacious hold on tradition'.[16]

REPRESENTATION AND POLITICAL CULTURE: RESTORING CIVIL GOVERNMENT

Prior to the revolution of 1648-49, London was gripped by wildly exaggerated fears that the army aimed at nothing less than 'the utter extirpation of all Law,

Government and Religion'.[17] With the occupation of London in November 1648, the levelling nightmare seemed at hand. Newswriters reported aghast the occupation of palaces and noblemen's town houses by the rude soldiery.[18] St Paul's Cathedral was turned into 'a most filthy stable, and filled ... with hay and horses etc.'. As one horrified writer remarked, Christians terrorised by Turks 'did always hold as their greatest affliction to see the accursed infidels put their horses into their churches, and turn the Houses of God into stables'.[19] Moreover, 'that sacred temple ... is become a den of thieves' – lead was stolen from the roof; the soldiers quartered there made a bonfire of the scaffolding, tearing up the pews for fuel until the Lord Mayor propitiated them with the City's supplies of coal.[20] Not only God's worshippers, but Mammon's, too, underwent their trials. Despite the commander-in-chief's reassurances that his men would respect property, citizens were robbed, their businesses declined with the mass exodus of gentle society, and bills of exchange plummeted in value.[21] The Lord General ordered the apprehension and punishment of criminals who were posing as soldiers, using the invasion as well as the obvious expectations of the terrified populace to take advantage of the chaos.[22]

The army's occupation of the capital also caused major disruption to the course of ordinary administration. Nearly £30,000 was removed by soldiers from the treasury at Weaver's Hall, and the treasuries of the committees for compounding and advance of money were also forced.[23] The occupation of Camden House distressed the committee for sequestrations which sat there, whilst members of the compounding committee petitioned Fairfax for the removal of the soldiers quartered at Haberdashers' Hall, who were making life impossible for them.[24] The purge itself, which effectively created the Rump Parliament, had a deeply embarrassing and demeaning impact. The prestige and self-respect of the parliamentary institution and the Long Parliament's claim to authority were damaged almost beyond repair by the sheer violence of this affront to parliamentary privilege.[25] To many contemporaries, those MPs who continued to sit after the purge were the army's puppets 'and their votes are but the echoes of the military junto'.[26]

Added to the insulting constitutional impropriety of the purge, 'to put the greater scorn on the Parliament' those MPs who felt the wrath of the army were forced to spend the first night of their detention sleeping on bare boards in the shabby surroundings of a Westminster tavern known as 'Hell'.[27] Five of those arrested, Browne, Waller, Massey, Clotworthy and Copley, were removed to St James's, where they were 'shut up in a foul room where the soldiers had lain some nights before, without hangings or bedding to rest their heads upon, where they must lie all night on boards, as they did in Hell'. This provision of 'inconvenient places without any fitting accommodations' was included in a list of the evils of the army which, one writer urged,

7

disobliged Parliament, people and even God from supporting the swordsmen any longer.[28]

When, in 1651, Ephraim Elcock wrote a pamphlet in defence of the Engagement oath of loyalty, in a dedicatory preface he urged the republic's governors to carry on their providentially blessed management of the nation's affairs, 'that your memorial in after ages may be, These are the repairers of the breach, the restorers of paths to dwell in'.[29] This motto, taken from the Old Testament Book of Isaiah, was a common refrain in the thoughts of men and women picking up the pieces after the catastrophe of civil war and revolution.[30] To the parliamentarians who had found themselves at the helm in December 1648 it must have had a special resonance. At that time the Rumpers were looked to as 'relics of the old Form', who must now rule, 'for some kinde of government the people must have'.[31] These men had stood in the breach, maintaining order against those who threatened 'the destruction and dissolution of all bonds of Civil Government'.[32] Ironically, their greatest hope of success lay with those military grandees who needed Parliament, especially those with seats there. The army was going through the motions of subjection to parliamentary authority before too long.[33] The 'junto' at Westminster, 'running all upon wire', had already reasserted its right to control its own membership by then. In February 1649 the Rumpers gave a Council of State executive power for a year, ignoring the army's demand that it should sit no longer than April.[34]

A civilian settlement had been created within two months of the purge. Even before the king's trial had opened, preparations were made for altering the form by which justice would be dispensed and the quondam 'king's peace' preserved in the aftermath of his demise. Writs, seals and terminology were all altered. Although term was delayed, the courts eventually reopened to countersign the guarantees of civility,[35] the judiciary having been assured that the old laws would continue to run in the old channels – only the names of things would change.[36]

The revolution had been launched on the strength of a tactical alliance between military commanders and convinced radicals which had appeared to make fundamental and long-lasting change to the balance of power within political society a realistic prospect. One of the supposed evil consequences of the *Agreement of the People* voiced in December 1648 was that it would 'tend to the utter subverting and taking away magistracy and government out of the kingdom ... and thereby that distance and reverence that God hath put upon his ordinance of magistracy being removed, it is like to fall into contempt', thus spelling the dissolution of civil society.[37] An ideological attack never materialised. But that was no excuse to let magisterial standards slip. Many years before, Henry Savile remarked that 'the mass of people is guided more by ceremonies or show than matter in substance'.[38] This book concerns the 'ceremonies or show' with which the Rumpers sought to reorganise and gild anew the institution of civil authority.

After the revolution, critics of the new regime complained loudly when the traditional pomp of Lord Mayor's day was curtailed, for

> You shall alwaies find every age, and sort of governours, adorning and exemplifying their severall authorities by anniversary shewes and pomps, to the people, who are naturally pleased with such gleames and irradiations of their superiors, and gaines at once honour to the magistrate, and effects content to the people ... Take away the fasces and the consuls are no more fear'd, but scorn'd; let fall the noble sword of the City in any place, and you are sure the mayor has there no privilege; ... no robes, no judges; no maces, no magestrate.[39]

One of the new regime's civil servants, George Wither, suggested ways in which it might conjure up a dignified outward aspect. Wither's aim was the 'supply / Of things pertaining to the Majesty / Of Supreme Senates', for

> though the dignity of Governments
> Consisteth not in outward ornaments,
> Or neat accomodations; yet, the wise,
> Having regard to mans infirmities,
> Did in all ages, by their joint consents,
> Add to essentiall things, such accidents,
> As might to those men make their worth appear,
> Who could not see, what in themselves, they were
> And, that they who discern'd it, might not find
> Discouragements in that which is enjoyn'd.[40]

Hence a plan, to which we shall return, whose salient features included rebuilding Whitehall, accommodating the people's representatives in suitable luxury, dressing them in ceremonial robes, badges of office and gold chains, and all manner of other means of achieving the appearance of 'magnificency, ... to further / The preservation of respect and order'.[41]

But the collection of statesmen, soldiers, courtiers and lawyers now assembled as a republic needed no prompting in order to make a song and dance about their authority. Some made a great virtue of the visibility of the regime and its actions. The revolution of 1649 was trumpeted as the first time Englishmen had done away with a bad king in public, rather than leave it to his peers to hustle him off to some dark corner of the realm to do him in. England's first popular revolution was no hole-and-corner affair. In the teeth of his condemnation in 1660, Major General Thomas Harrison proclaimed a characteristic refrain from the litany of revolutionary apology – 'the things that have been done have been done upon the Stage, in the sight of the Sun'. In *The Tenure of Kings and Magistrates* Milton justified tyrannicide 'by authorities and reasons not learnt in corners among schisms and heresies ... but fetched out of the midst of choicest and most authentic learning'.[42] John Cook, the Commonwealth's solicitor-general in Ireland, wrote that the High Court of Justice was 'erected for the most comprehensive, impartial and glorious piece of justice that was ever acted and executed upon the theatre of England'.[43]

The principal objective of this book is to describe how members of the republican regime shaped their own politico-theatrical environment rather than merely serving their turn as the painted flats on a stage dominated by a godly praetorian caricature. Their aim was to reconfigure the contemporary English political landscape. In the process they made the despised parliamentary remnant at Westminster into the chief physical as well as ideological landmark, three-dimensional, self-conscious and highly assertive.

The topography of the regime's palatial hub at Whitehall and Westminster reveals a 'court-based' polity where the unitary focus of a single, if diffuse, household was replaced by a collection of oligarchs and bureaucrats. It is beyond the scope of this monograph to attempt to track the eccentric and complex orbital paths followed by these courtiers without a king. Their choreography may only be hinted at in matters such as access and its control at court. If the Commonwealth lacked the illumination of a regal presence, the politics of the period were certainly still bathed in limelight, thanks to the commonplace iconic and ritual aspects of Commonwealth government. A novel vocabulary of political imagery supplanted regal symbols. The political spectacle of the republic provided the outward appearance of a unitary authority and advanced its claims to legitimacy. The conflicts just beneath its surface reveal the illusory nature of this hegemonic facade. The political culture of the Commonwealth was also the sophisticated medium through which were played out some of the struggles over power and patronage which racked the republic. All these representational discourses expressed and shaped the creation of a *de facto* republic conjured from the deeper ideological underpinnings of the early modern English political nation. For example, the iconography of the free state's great seal represents the minority appropriation of reasonably majoritarian, 'ancient constitutional' ideas about law and due process as well as parliamentary collectivism and multilayered community, from the nation down. In the light of this and many other examples, the claim that the republicanism of the Commonwealth was 'a language, not a programme', rather than implicitly condemning the lack of ideological commitment, actually begins to do some justice to the conservative idealism of the period.

Where possible the connections between the style and the substance of Commonwealth politics are established, or at least suggested. Commonwealth politics were court politics. The free state's measurements of degree, its titles and codes of honour were important linguistic features of its political culture. At crucial moments they could also constitute an important discursive battleground between the civilian and military arms of the post-revolutionary re-gime. Conversely, political conflict also had its representational features. In-deed, the whole notion of fundamental conflict between civilians and soldiers was a rhetorical construct. Described in terms of reportage, rhetoric and propaganda, a case can be made for describing military reformism as 'a language, not a programme'.

I have tried to describe the Rump as a living entity, to render the Common-wealth in its true colours, as a regime animated by a genius for conserving order in a radically imaginative way; and to show how successfully England's unwilling revolutionaries clothed their endeavours in Gardiner's 'external fact'. The intention, above all, is to revive for the 1650s the kind of subtle historiographical revolution, long since begun yet unaccountably abandoned, which has wrought such a dramatic change in our appreciation of early Stuart politics. Hopefully the effort will also reinforce the emergence of a different way of exploring the rich fertility of traditional English political ambiguities by putting flesh on the dry, dusty bones of England's republican past.

SOURCES

Of course, by comparison with the rest of seventeenth-century parliamentary history, the Interregnum suffers from obvious limitations in terms of mate-rial. The 'lack of sources' for the Commonwealth is, however, a commonplace with some substance but far less significance than is often supposed.[44] It is quite likely that Bulstrode Whitelocke was not the only person whose private papers were thrown into the fire on the eve of the Restoration.[45] It is also true that Interregnum patent rolls have not survived in very great numbers.[46] But a lack of certain kinds of source material need not deter us.

Like the precedents from which the republic and its apologists justified the execution of the king, the sources from which this book is written were not found 'in dark corners'. Relatively new sources, such as the eye-witness ac-count of foreign visitors to the seat of Commonwealth government, provide novel perspectives.[47] But plenty can be had from those well-thumbed tools of the Commonwealth historian, the *Journal* of the House of Commons, and the excellent calendars of state papers, monuments to historiography conceived on an imperial scale. Historians of the period also have the inestimable advantage of being able to capitalise on George Thomason's foresight in collecting together so many of the printed tracts and newsbooks of the day. All these sources have already been mined exhaustively by numerous hard-cal-loused hands. Yet surprisingly little use has been made of material about diplomatic receptions, or the fascinating details of Commonwealth iconogra-phy, for example. Much of this readily available information has a decidedly liberating impact on the historiographical conventions by which the Rump has become bound. Best known by a derogatory nickname which has passed into the political lexicon as 'a small, unimportant, or contemptible remnant or remainder of a body', the Rump in fact not only adopted the grandiose title of *Parliamentum Reipublicae Angliae* for itself in January 1650, but also refused to deal with the representatives of any state which failed to adopt the proper form of supplication.[48]

There is a massive amount of material for Commonwealth history. And yet excessive concentration on one particular piece of paper, the Bill for a new representative, has become one of the most common features of Rump historiography. This is quite ironic, as the Bill has not been seen since Cromwell snatched it from the Clerk of the House on the morning of 20 April 1653. Nevertheless, it has been raised to almost iconic status in many accounts of the Rump and its demise. Amidst a forest of paperwork, historians remain obsessed by a fragment of the record no longer extant.

This convention has bolstered many of the features of that 'traditional' historiography described above. It is generally acknowledged that the Rumpers had not contrived to perpetuate their own power. Military propaganda justifying the spring 1653 *coup* has been exposed as a sham. Yet historians continue vindicating the actions of the essentially heroic Cromwell, most commonly by attributing the Lord General's action to his 'misapprehension' of the Bill's uncontroversial contents. Blair Worden described the General as 'a devious politician, but ... not a cold-blooded one. His art was in deceiving himself, not others.' The lack of evidence for a recruiting clause did not rule out the possibility that Cromwell mistakenly *thought* there was one.[49] Austin Woolrych explored a range of possible areas of 'misapprehension', in the end plumping for an elaborate hypothesis with 'slender evidential foundations', and arguing that the Cromwellian propaganda was justified because the Lord General had thought there was a recruitment clause which would keep Rumpers in their seats. The main virtue of this explanation was that it 'reconcile[d] much of the apparently conflicting evidence rather nicely' (despite the fact that the most contradictory aspects of the evidence appeared within the high command's very own tenuous and unconvincing attempts to justify their leader's behaviour).[50] More recently, Ian Gentles has followed Woolrych, upholding the probity of the soldiers' case and even going so far as to say that the army must have believed that the Bill for a new representative contained a clause for the recruitment of members to vacant constituencies, for 'otherwise [the officers] were guilty of deliberate lying'.[51] Although they stick out like rather conspicuous sore thumbs in substantial and rightly respected accounts of much bigger subjects, there is remarkably little in the historiographically dubious assumptions underlying these two conclusions about the Rump's dissolution to distinguish them from the military propaganda on which they are based.

So apparently hypnotic are the mantras about the Bill for elections and what it may or may not have contained to so incense the army that the whole story of the Rump has come to hinge around its demise. Arguing that 'one is constantly driven back to the Bill because all other explanations of the dissolution seem in themselves deficient' is in effect to consign the Rump to a secondary role in its own story, one in which it simply awaits the inevitable.[52] Its vital signs have become almost secondary to the evidence for a 'collective death wish' amongst MPs, exemplified by the Bill and its 'faults'.[53] Ronald Hutton has faced the fact that the perpetuation story was untrue, but ultimately, since 'the crucial piece of evidence' is missing, he concluded that the motivation for the Rump's dissolution would therefore have to remain mysterious.[54]

Much as one might prefer an air of mystery to the palpable certitude which surrounds so many verdicts on the fall of the parliamentary republic, it dodges questions no less significant than those ignored by latter-day military apologists. As Professor Worden made clear, there is a far simpler explanation for the dissolution of the Rump. All that the Bill really showed was the Rumpers' desire to hold elections in order to keep authority in civilian hands. Of course, it can be argued that the army had swung decisively against the idea of elections because it feared the return to Westminster of former enemies. But it will be argued here, implicitly and explicitly, that the Rump was dissolved largely in order to prevent the successful transition to an electorally mandated free state in which the commander-in-chief of the armed forces would remain little more than an important employee of the state, albeit the most important one. The key to the downfall of the republic lies less in its failure by standards hypocritically pious than in the success of the Rump's restoration and preservation of civilian governance. The Rump had not done too little – it had gone too far.

Having negotiated the rocks of revolution and let the storm spend itself around them, the Rumpers had brought the ship of state back into safe waters, somewhere calm to drop anchor. In the chapters that follow I shall describe the extraordinary distance covered, in the fifty-three months of the republican state's short life. My avowed intent may be summed up naively as a wish to let the republican regime tell its own story. So many accounts have tried to understand the Rump backwards, as it were, by starting at the end. This study of republican political culture uses fragments of the vast institutional record from the period to describe how the regime was 'lived forwards'. It takes the republican government on its own terms, in the sanguine flush of rude health rather than as a chilly corpse to be anatomised *post mortem*. The men who built this new state may have remained relatively immune to demands for sweeping social reform, but they had considerably more vision about their role than is commonly allowed. To share that vision is an exercise in suspending the historical prerogative of hindsight, to see through the eyes of men who knew nothing of the 'inevitability' of their 'failure'.

The materials from which their story has been reconstructed are themselves, in a sense, a part of the political culture which they record. Literature, such as the poetry of Andrew Marvell and George Wither, the political prose of John Milton and Marchamont Nedham, and the reportage of newsbooks have all been studied as features of the interregnal political landscape.[55] State papers make up another category and constituted another landmark helping the navigation of political pioneers. The Rump's creation, collation and storage of records were integral and exemplary elements of the political culture of the English Commonwealth.[56] The day after declaring the supremacy of the Commons, on 5 January 1649, the Rump ordered a new book of vellum 'for entering all the public acts of this House'. In readiness for recording the first ever Act passed by the Commons alone, the Act for a High Court of Justice to try the king, the Rump literally prepared to turn over a new leaf in the history of Parliaments.[57] And as it prepared the declaration announcing the new form of government in March 1649 the Rump paid particular attention to 'the Orthography and Pointing thereof'.[58] In matters of such substance, form mattered more than ordinarily. It was precisely this attitude which epitomised the invention of Commonwealth political culture.

Paperwork, the symbol and substance of bureaucracy, was the defining feature of the development of centralised English governance, symbolically from Domesday on, as well as the indispensable medium of early modern government.[59] When talking of Parliament in the early modern period, Englishmen were accustomed to the idea that it was 'the highest and most authentical court of Englande', the most important court of record.[60] In the sixteenth century Parliament became increasingly conscious of the importance of preserving its records. These had normally been laid up in Chancery as records of that court. By the end of Elizabeth's reign the Parliament Office, bureau of the parliamentary secretariat, was increasingly independent of Chancery and 'had begun to take on many of the characteristics of a Record Office'. By the end of the reign of King James, Parliament had an archive, and the preservation of its records was one of the key functions of the Clerk of the Parliament.

The House of Lords, to which this officer was attached, was in effect the originator of the archive. It had a purpose-built repository, in the Jewel Tower at Westminster, wherein Parliament rolls were lodged at the end of sessions. Its contents were still prey to alienations made by Clerks who treated public records like private property. The Privy Council exercised a proprietary interest over them at times, too. But the establishment of the archive, 'perhaps the Lords' most enduring achievement during this period', was a crucial aspect of the growth of parliamentary institutional autonomy. It was also an area in which the House of Commons showed interest. Just as both chambers took equal care to have their Clerks commit a true account of their sessions to the record, so too did the lower chamber concern itself with the preservation of that record. The Commons first moved for a permanent home for their own papers in 1614, and the idea re-emerged in 1621, the year the Lords set up their archive in the Jewel Tower.[61]

The handling of public texts took on more than ordinary significance in the first decades of the seventeenth century. When the king had the Protestation torn from the *Journal* in 1621, he effectively decided what constituted an acceptable record of parliamentary business.[62] The issue of record-keeping was politicised further at the end of the Short Parliament, when the Clerk of the Commons, Henry Elsyng, handed over his sessional records to the Crown, whilst Thomas Crewe refused, in the king's presence, to hand over to Elsyng the records of the committee on religion, where he had the chair. When the Long Parliament opened, one of the first committees it appointed was ordered 'to peruse the Journals and Records of this House and see what state they are in', and 'to consider of some certain place for [their] constant keeping' and 'what the duty of the Clerk is, in the safe-keeping of the Records of this House'.[63] Once it had established its own executive role, the House of Commons was able to exploit the considerable talents and almost instinctive antiquarianism of its members to assume with confidence the governmental function of record-keeping. In 1643 the Tower Record Office was put under the supervision of John Selden, who had been amongst the first Englishmen to use state papers as historical sources. His *Mare Clausum* had been prefaced by remarks on state archives and their keepers, and included one of the first guides to public records.[64]

During the civil war, the symbolic significance of written records became even sharper. The public reading, publication and display of the king's correspondence captured at Naseby illustrated the immense political sensitivity of incriminating written records.[65] An interesting incident which occurred during the army's first occupation of London will also serve as just one illustration of the symbolic import vested in individual documents by the ancient constitutionalism of the era. At that time, custody of the Tower stronghold was taken from the citizens of London, and handed over to the Lord General of Parliament's army, who was appointed Constable. Fairfax went to the Tower, and, calling in on the Record Office there, having been shown the records of the kingdom, he asked to see Magna Carta. On seeing it, he is supposed to have remarked that 'This is that which we have fought for, and by God's help we must maintain.'[66]

Of course, for others, this charter of Englishmen's liberties was no more than a 'mess of pottage', Magna Farta, the lynchpin in the yoke of Norman tyranny. For such hot spirits, the archives of all the courts of record bore testimony to nothing but oppression, worthy of no more respect than that system of injustice which seemed at last to be on the brink of destruction. Now was the time to return to scriptural law, to reject the statute books and Chancery rolls, even to burn all those 'monuments to tyranny' stored up in the Tower record repository.[67]

Yet, amidst the clamour of the zealots, the Rump paid consistent attention to the storage, supervision and further compilation of state archives. On 1 January 1649 the Commons had appointed a committee to locate and inventory 'the Books and Records of this House'. A few days later, the committee was ordered 'to fit the room for the safe-keeping of the Records of this House'.[68] Another such committee was appointed in December, and in 1651 the Clerk of the House was explicitly linked with the storage and preservation of parliamentary records when the Rump ordered that he was to have the keys to the rooms over the Parliament House and to use the presses and tables there for laying up the records of the House.[69] Having abolished the House of Lords and vested the responsibilities of its secretariat in their own, the Commons were also quick to appropriate its records. The committee for Commons records was ordered to look into those of the Lords on the very day the Rump resolved to abolish the upper House.[70]

In 1651, acknowledging 'the Usefulness of the Office of Records in the Tower, not only to particular Men, but in general, also to the Commonwealth', the Rump accepted a proposal from the Council of State to retain the services of William Ryley, Norroy king-at-arms, assistant to the former Keeper of the Records, John Selden. The Rumpers allowed him the traditional perquisite of the job, Bowyer's House, next to the Record Office, and ordered him to calendar all state papers as a safeguard against loss and embezzlement. Ryley was allowed to demand 2s 6d from anyone requiring information from the records, instead of the former search fee of 10s. The Rump agreed to pay him £200 per annum in lieu. He was also to leave a calendar of state papers in the hands of the Clerk of Parliament. The Speaker, in his capacity as Master of the Rolls, was appointed as the new keeper of the records pro tempore.[71]

There was an obvious practical interest in the preservation of state paperwork. Parliamentary records were an important source of material for the Council of State, and there are frequent orders given for passing records to the Council, especially in connection with negotiations with foreign states.[72] In January 1652 the Council also undertook to pay Ryley's wages out of its own contingency fund 'until such time as the public Treasuries of this Commonwealth shall be freed from Anticipation'.[73] Other bodies also relied on Parliament as a central repository, a court of record in the administration of the republic. The commissioners for soldiers' arrears at Worcester House were given permission to search House records for orders given there for the payment of individuals' arrears claims, in order to avoid paying them twice.[74]

The attorney-general was allowed to borrow parliamentary records pertaining to the confessions of Thomas Cook, further to the High Court prosecution of Presbyterian plotters in the summer of 1651, and the Hale Commission on legal reform was given more general freedom to call for papers.[75] The keeper of the Whitehall Paper Office, the Council's own repository, Ambrose Randolph, was ordered to let the ambassadors going to The Hague take copies of records relevant to their mission; and state papers were used in similar fashion by the conciliar commissioners appointed to negotiate with the Danish representatives in London in 1652.[76] It was not just government agents who made practical use of the state's archives. Miles Woodshaw wrote to Lord Conway regarding some aspect of his master's private business, telling him that 'I have spoken to a clerk at Whitehall and he will endeavour to obtain me the copies you require', and, for any royalist put through the mill of sequestration, state records provided essential source material in the fight to hang on to property.[77]

Some aspects of republican record administration suggest a rationale beyond simple utility. Several new accessions to the record repositories of the Commonwealth are quite striking. There were important accessions by conquest.[78] In April 1652 the Rump ordered Major General Richard Deane to seal up the public records of the Kirk, found hidden away on the Isle of Basse, which he had recently captured, that they might be sent to the Tower 'there to remain under the same Custody [as] the other Records, which came from Scotland'.[79] Another important document commemorated the military defeat of armed Scottish opposition to the revolution and the inception of the Commonwealth. In September 1650 Parliament ordered its Clerk, Henry Scobell, to draw up an inventory of Scottish regimental colours captured at Preston and Dunbar.[80] Ryley had a hand in its compilation and it was when he presented the completed inventory to the Rump on new year's day 1651 that Parliament had first considered him for the post of state archivist, as well as telling the Council to give him a £20 gratuity. After Worcester, Ryley was appointed to update the list of colours by adding those captured at the crowning mercy.[81]

In December 1650 Parliament was presented with an account of the trial of the king. At that time it declared itself pleased with those involved in the trial, who had 'discharged their Trust in them reposed with great Courage and Fidelity', and with the account of the proceedings, which it ordered to 'be recorded, to remain among the Records of Parliament, for the Transmitting the Memory thereof to Posterity'.[82] (There is an interesting comparison here with the record of the trial of Mary Queen of Scots in 1586. At the end of that session, the Commons had requested that the proceedings 'might be entred of recorde in the rolls of the same parliament', to which the House of Lords agreed.[83]) The Rump also ordered that a copy of the trial record be kept in all the great courts, and that one be transmitted to each of the *custodes rotulorum*, to be held amongst the records of every county.[84] Several Rumpers were themselves county *custodes*, for example William Heveningham (in Suffolk), Sir Henry Mildmay (in Essex), and the fifth earl of Pembroke, Parliament having ordered the Lords Commissioners to install him as his Rumper father's successor in that capacity for the counties of Derbyshire and Wiltshire.[85]

Parliament certainly exhibited a sense of occasion. The Rump also asserted its institutional authority by ensuring the tight control of public texts, and by setting limits on the use and availability of records, thus circumscribing the political sphere at an ordinary level. Parliament set up committees charged with ensuring that *Journal* entries were correct, an essential job, considering the confusion amidst which committees were themselves appointed, and the complexity of the debate and amendment of legislation.[86] It also gave order that the Clerk was not to allow anyone to read through parliamentary orders and proceedings unless he was himself present.[87] When Oliver St John and Walter Strickland returned from The Hague in the summer of 1651, the details of their abortive negotiations with the States General were ordered to be written up in a book, which was 'to be entered and kept as Records of Parliament' by the Clerk. Non-members were to be allowed access to it only by special permission from the House. Parliament had declared itself satisfied with its ambassadors' efforts at the States General on behalf of the Commonwealth, and had even called in their entire entourage to give them their thanks (not unwarranted, judging from what they had had to endure from exiled cavaliers and their Orangist sympathisers). Printed accounts of the ambassadors' progress at The Hague had dwelt on the great dignity with which they had been received by their hosts in the States General, but made little reference to the frustration of their mission. The whole affair was clearly not thought to be a matter fit for the public domain in quite the way the king's trial had been.[88]

The Rump's treatment of state records demonstrates the fundamentally preservationist impulse of Commonwealth political culture. According to John Streater,

> Some of our Saints or white Devils have that horrid, damnable and wicked impudence to design that the Records of the Nation should be burned ... to prevent further contests and quarrels by suits of law ... [T]his is the only way that these Israelites will come by the goods and lands of the Egyptians at advantage.

The result would be legal decisions taken purely at whim.[89] This did not happen, in part because of the Rump's successful reassertion of the rule of law, the authority of the courts, and all the features of a complex bureaucratic state.

But the Rump's archival impulse had a deeper significance, too. A long time ago, Wallace Notestein described how English antiquaries 'read the rolls [of Parliament] in manuscript and out of them forged chains to bind fast Stuart kings'.[90] This view has been successfully challenged by historians who have demonstrated the confusion surrounding the issue of precedent and parliamentary privilege in the early seventeenth century.[91] But archives still had considerable political significance. The attention paid by the Rump to their preservation was a very clear indicator of where responsibility for government and executive authority now lay, and therefore of just how far the Commons had come towards the status of institution. In 1607 members of the lower House had humbly stood and listened while the Lords told them that they were no court of record.[92] Now they began building their own collection of state papers, attempted to appropriate the old one, and fleshed out their archive with new accessions which provided an index of political, military and diplomatic endeavours and achievements. By contrast, it seems quite likely that the Bill for a new representative was committed to the flames at the dissolution. Here was one piece of evidence Cromwell thought it best for posterity to do without.[93]

In 1659, when the Rump was restored, it immediately set about reasserting its authority over the archives and *Journal*. Aghast, it discovered that its Clerk, Henry Scobell, had recorded that on 20 April 1653 Parliament 'was dissolved by his Excellency the Lord General'. Under examination, Scobell admitted that he had not had permission to record any such entry.[94] The Clerk excused himself by saying 'that for the word dissolved, he never at that time did hear of any other term; and desired pardon if he would not dare to make a word himself what it was six years after, before they came themselves to call it an interruption'. Not satisfied with this answer, the Rump set up a committee to decide whether or not Scobell's 'crime' came within the Act of Indemnity.[95] The Interregnum is, by definition, a blip in the rolling continuity of English monarchy's long history. It is as well to remember that the men who ran the country during much of that short interlude were so self-possessed as to see their ejection in 1653 as little more than their own temporary difficulty.

NOTES

1 P. Collinson, 'The Monarchical Republic of Queen Elizabeth I', *Bulletin of the John Rylands Library* 69 (1986), 394–424; *idem*, *De Republica Anglorum, or, History with the Politics put Back* (Cambridge, 1990).

2 Blair Worden, *The Rump Parliament, 1648–1653* (Cambridge, 1974).

3 Worden, *The Rump Parliament*, pp. 18, 185; Derek Hirst, *Authority and Conflict. England 1603–1658* (1986), pp. 292, 301; Ronald Hutton, *The British Republic, 1649–1660* (1990), pp. 21–2; Austin Woolrych, *From Commonwealth to Protectorate* (Oxford, 1982), pp. 5, 8;

Ian Gentles, *The New Model Army in England, Ireland and Scotland, 1645–1653* (Oxford, 1992), pp. 416, 437; Thomas Macaulay, *History of England* (1906 Everyman edition) i, 98.

4 The condemnation of Cromwell owed as much to a tradition within the revolutionary party as it did to Restoration reaction. This tradition was much more sympathetic towards the Rump. See C. H. Firth ed., *Memoirs of the Life of Colonel Hutchinson, Governor of Nottingham* (2 vols, 1885) ii, 156, 190–1; *idem* ed., *The Memoirs of Edmund Ludlow* (2 vols, Oxford, 1894) ii, 349; Ruth Spalding ed., *The Diary of Bulstrode Whitelocke* (Oxford, 1990), pp. 286–7; William Godwin, *History of the Commonwealth of England from its Commencement to the Restoration of Charles II* (4 vols, 1824–28); J. Morrow, 'Republicanism and Public Virtue: William Godwin's *History of the Commonwealth*', *Historical Journal* 34 (1991), 645–64; W. C. Abbott ed., *The Writings and Speeches of Oliver Cromwell* (4 vols, Oxford, 1988) ii, 652–3; Worden, *The Rump Parliament*, pp. 86, 365–8.

5 A. L. Le Quesne, *Carlyle* (Oxford, 1982), pp. 9–11, 67.

6 J. Morrow, 'Heroes and Constitutionalists: the Ideological Significance of Thomas Carlyle's Treatment of the English Revolution', *History of Political Thought* 14 (1993), 205–223; Roger Howell junior, '"Who needs another Cromwell?" The Nineteenth-century Image of Oliver Cromwell', in R. C. Richardson ed., *Images of Oliver Cromwell. Essays by and for Roger Howell* (Manchester, 1993), pp. 98, 104.

7 Morrow, 'Heroes and Constitutionalists', p. 206.

8 S. R. Gardiner, *History of the Commonwealth and Protectorate* (4 vols, Moreton-in-Marsh, 1988) i, 1–2; ii, 265, 267, 269.

9 *Ibid.*, i, 2.

10 David Underdown, *Pride's Purge. Politics in the Puritan Revolution* (Oxford, 1971); J. S. Morrill, 'The Army Revolt of 1647', in C. A. Tamse and A. C. Duke eds, *Britain and the Netherlands* (The Hague, 1977); M. Kishlansky, *The Rise of the New Model Army* (Cambridge, 1979); *idem*, 'Ideology and Politics in the Parliamentary Armies, 1645–9', in J. S. Morrill ed., *Reactions to the English Civil War, 1642–1649* (1982); Worden, *The Rump Parliament*, especially part 5; Woolrych, *Commonwealth to Protectorate*; *idem*, 'The Calling of Barebones Parliament', *English Historical Review* 80 (1965) 492–513.

11 Worden, *The Rump Parliament*, pp. 19, 68–9.

12 See the editor's essay, 'The Making of Oliver Cromwell', in J. S. Morrill ed., *Oliver Cromwell and the English Revolution* (Cambridge, 1990), pp. 19–48.

13 Worden, *The Rump Parliament*, pp. 3, 174, 176, 378–9; cf. Woolrych, *Commonwealth to Protectorate*, p. 9.

14 J. Scott, 'The English Republican Imagination', in J. S. Morrill ed., *Revolution and Restoration* (1992), especially pp. 39 and 41.

15 Richard Tuck, *Philosophy and Government, 1572–1651* (Cambridge, 1993), p. 221.

16 Kishlansky, 'Ideology and Politics', p. 165.

17 *The Parliament under the Power of the Sword; with a Short Answer thereunto by some of the Army* ([11 December] 1648), p. 2.

18 *Mercurius Elencticus* 29 November–6 December 1648, pp. 523–4; *Mercurius Pragmaticus* 5–12 December 1648 p. [4]; C. H. Firth and G. Davies, *The Regimental History of*

Cromwell's Army (2 vols, Oxford, 1940) i, 340.

19 *We have brought our Hogs to a fair Market* (1648), pp. 3–4.

20 *Mercurius Elencticus* 5–12 December 1648, p. [532]; *The Moderate Intelligencer* 7–14 December 1648, p. 1787.

21 *Ibid.*, 30 November–7 December 1648, p. 1768; *ibid.*, 14–21 December 1648, p. 1790; *The Kingdom's Weekly Intelligencer* 19–26 December 1648, pp. 1197–8; *We have spun a fair Thread, or, London's Recantation upon Fear of her approaching Miseries* ([December] 1648); C. H. Firth, *Cromwell's Army. A History of the English Soldier during the Civil Wars, Commonwealth and Protectorate* (third edition, 1921), p. 290 n.; *idem*, 'London during the Civil War', *History* 21 (1926), 33; B. Lib., Thomason Tracts, 669 fo. 13, 59.

22 *The Perfect Weekly Account* 20–7 December 1648, p. 326; cf. B. Lib., E475(9).

23 *The Kingdom's Weekly Intelligencer* 5–12 December 1648, p. 1183; S. R. Gardiner, *History of the Great Civil War* (4 vols, Moreton-in-Marsh, 1987) iv, 273–4.

24 P.R.O., SP 16/516,136; *The Moderate Intelligencer* 14–21 December 1648.

25 Hirst, *Authority and Conflict*, p. 293.

26 *Mercurius Pragmaticus* 12–19 December 1648, p. [1]; *The Second Part of the Narrative concerning the Army's Force and Violence upon the Commons House* ([23 December] 1648), p. 8; Gardiner, *History of the Commonwealth and Protectorate* i, 1; Worden, *The Rump Parliament*, p. 85.

27 *The Parliament under the Power of the Sword*, p. 1.

28 *The Second Part of the Narrative concerning the Army's Force and Violence upon the Commons House*, pp. 5–7.

29 *Animadversions on a Book called, A Plea for Non-scribers*, sig. Av.

30 The text, taken from Isaiah 58:12, was adopted by Anne, Countess of Clifford, widow of Philip Herbert (d. 1650), the Rumper fourth earl of Pembroke and Montgomery, when she set about repairing and restoring the castles and houses of her estate in the 1650s. C. M. L. Bouch, *The Lady Anne, Hereditary High Sheriffess of the County of Westmorland and Lady of the Honour of Skipton-in-Craven* (Penrith, 1954). I am grateful to my grandmother, Mrs Molly Adams, for this reference. Cf. J. Mayer ed., 'Inedited Letters of Cromwell, Colonel Jones, Bradshaw and other Regicides', *Transactions of the Historical Society of Lancashire and Cheshire* 13 (Liverpool, 1861), 62–3.

31 Anon., *The Life and Reign of King Charles, or, The Pseudo-martyr Discovered* (1651), pp. 223–4, 225.

32 *The Cryes of England to the Parliament, for the Continuance of Good Entertainment to the Lord Jesus his Embassadours, collected as they came up from the severall Counties* ([27 April] 1653), p. 3.

33 *CJ* vi, 122; B. Manning, *1649. Crisis of the English Revolution* (1992); Worden, *The Rump Parliament*, p. 76.

34 Worden, *The Rump Parliament*, pp. 24, 177.

35 Alan Cromartie, 'The Rule of Law', in Morrill ed., *Revolution and Restoration*.

36 See below, chapter 3.

37 *Reasons against Agreement with ... The Agreement of the People* ([26 December] 1648), p. 6.

38 Quoted by Malcolm Smuts, 'Court-centred Politics and the Uses of Roman Historians, c. 1590–1630', in K. Sharpe and P. Lake eds, *Culture and Politics in Early Stuart England* (1994), p. 28. This was little more than the conventional wisdom of politics in the Renaissance European state. Cf. Blair Worden, 'Ben Jonson among the Historians', in Sharpe and Lake eds, *Culture and Politics*, p. 73; M. A. Screech trans., *Michel de Montaigne. Four Essays* (1995), p. 51.

39 F. W. Fairholt, *Pageants*, pp. 170–1, cited by M. J. Seymour, 'Aspects of Pro-government Propaganda during the Interregnum' (Cambridge Ph.D., 1986), chapter 7, n. 168.

40 George Wither, *The Dark Lantern, ... whereunto is annexed a Poem concerning a Perpetuall Parliament* ([24 April] 1653), p. 67. Hereafter cited as *Perpetuall Parliament*. Wither's poetics are treated amply in an important article by David Norbrook, 'Levelling Poetry: George Wither and the English Revolution, 1642–1649', *English Literary Renaissance* 21 (1991), 217–56.

41 *Wither, Perpetuall Parliament*, p. 70.

42 M. Y. Hughes ed., *Complete Prose Works of John Milton* (8 vols, New Haven, 1953–82) iii, 198, 222–7 and notes.

43 Walter Scott ed., *A Collection of Scarce and Valuable Tracts ... of the late Lord Somers* (13 vols, 1809–15) v, 215.

44 Worden, *The Rump Parliament*, pp. 16, 398–404; Woolrych, *Commonwealth to Protectorate*, p. 4.

45 Blair Worden, review of Spalding ed., *The Diary of Bulstrode Whitelocke*, in *English Historical Review* 108 (1993), 122–34.

46 R. B. Pugh, 'Patent Rolls of the Interregnum', *Bulletin of the Institute of Historical Research* 22 (1950), 178–81.

47 A. G. H. Bachrach and R. G. Collmer trans. and eds, *Lodewijck Huygens. The English Journal, 1651–1652* (Leiden, 1982); Leo Miller, *John Milton and the Oldenburg Safeguard* (New York, 1985).

48 *Shorter Oxford English Dictionary*. See below, chapter 4.

49 Worden, *The Rump Parliament*, p. 371.

50 Woolrych, *Commonwealth to Protectorate*, pp. 84, 100. The 'misapprehension thesis' appealed to Worden for similar reasons.

51 Gentles, *The New Model Army*, p. 435.

52 Woolrych, *Commonwealth to Protectorate*, p. 98.

53 Gentles, *The New Model Army*, p. 417; cf. Worden, *The Rump Parliament*, p. 377.

54 Hutton, *The British Republic*, p. 24.

55 David Norbrook, 'Marvell's *Horatian Ode* and the Politics of Genre', in T. Healy and J. Sawday eds, *Literature and the English Civil War* (Cambridge, 1990); N. Smith, *Literature and Revolution in England, 1640–1660* (New Haven, 1994); Blair Worden, 'The Politics of Marvell's *Horatian Ode*', *Historical Journal* 27 (1984), 525–47; Joseph Frank, *The Beginnings of the English Newspaper, 1620–1660* (Cambridge, Mass., 1961); A. N. B. Cotton, 'London Newsbooks in the Civil War. Their Political Attitudes and Sources of Information' (Oxford D.Phil., 1971); Joad Raymond, *Making the News. An Anthology of the Newsbooks of Revolutionary England, 1641–1660* (Moreton-in-Marsh, 1993); Seymour,

'Pro-government Propaganda', also has a useful chapter on the subject of newsbooks.

56 Sarah Lambert, 'The Beginning of Printing for the House of Commons, 1640–1642', *The Library* sixth series, 3 (1981), 43–61; *idem, Printing for Parliament, 1641–1700*, List and Index Society special series 20 (1984).

57 *CJ* vi, 111, 117.

58 *Ibid.*, 166.

59 M. T. Clanchy, *From Memory to Written Record, England, 1066–1307* (second edition, Cambridge, Mass., and Oxford, 1993)

60 L. Alston ed., *De Republica Anglorum* (Cambridge, 1906), p. 58; R. L. Rickard ed., 'A Brief Collection of the Queens Majesties High and Most Honourable Courtes of Recordes', *Camden Miscellany* 20 (1953), 11.

61 M. F. Bond, 'The Formation of the Archives of Parliament, 1497–1691', *Journal of the Society of Archivists* 1 (1955), 151–8; S. Lambert, 'The Clerks and the Records of the House of Commons, 1600–1640', *Bulletin of the Institute of Historical Research* 43 (1970), 215–31; E. R. Foster, *The House of Lords, 1603–1649. Structure, Procedure and Nature of its Business* (Chapel Hill and London, 1983), p. 209.

62 Hirst, *Authority and Conflict*, p. 130.

63 Lambert, 'Clerks and Records', pp. 218, 225.

64 Paul Christianson, 'Selden and Europe', a paper given at the Institute of Historical Research, London, June 1994.

65 Gardiner, *History of the Great Civil War* iii, 258; R. E. Maddison, 'The Kings Cabinet Opened: Case Study in Pamphlet History', *Notes and Queries* 211 (1966), 2–9.

66 Gardiner, *History of the Great Civil War* iii, 345–6.

67 Underdown, *Pride's Purge*, p. 259.

68 *CJ* vi, 108, 111.

69 *Ibid.*, 333, 542.

70 *Ibid.*, 132, 168, 262, 430, 508.

71 *Ibid.*, 617–18; cf. *ibid.*, 548, for the records of the former Court of Wards.

72 E.g. *ibid.*, 595; vii, 136, 191, 194, 223.

73 *Ibid.*, 63.

74 *CJ* vi, 518.

75 *Ibid.*, 518, 604; vii, 74.

76 P.R.O., SP25/17, 26; cf. SP25/65, 18.

77 P.R.O., SP18/37, 106; *A True and Perfect Narrative of the Several Proceedings in the Case concerning the Lord Craven* (1653), p. 4.

78 On the Scottish Registers captured in Edinburgh, and the efforts of their keeper, Sir Archibald Johnston of Wariston, to regain control over them, see Abbott ed., *Writings and Speeches* ii, 372, 374, 377, 387, 407, 412–14, 419, 421.

79 *CJ* vii, 6, 127.

80 *CJ* vi, 465; *Mercurius Politicus* 14–21 September 1650, p. [189]; I am grateful to Dr Ian

Roy for bringing this inventory, and another, compiled by Payne Fisher, to my attention.

81 *CJ* vi, 517; vii, 15.

82 *CJ* vi, 508.

83 Foster, *House of Lords*, pp. 54, 55. For the account of the trial see House of Lords Record Office, Parchment Collection, 3 March 1651.

84 *CJ* vi, 508.

85 J. G. A. Ive, 'The Local Dimensions of Defence. The Standing Army and the Militia in Norfolk, Suffolk and Essex, 1649–1660' (Cambridge Ph.D. 1986), p. 38; *CJ* vi, 360.

86 *CJ* vi, 217, 297; cf. *ibid.*, 308–9, 407; Worden, *The Rump Parliament*, p. 400.

87 *CJ* vi, 117.

88 *Ibid.*, 595.

89 *A Further Continuance of the Grand Politick Informer, discovering the Wickedness and Mysteries of the Present State iniquities on foot* ... ([31 October] 1653), p. 39; cf. R. P. Stearns, *The Strenuous Puritan* (Urbana, 1954), p. 376.

90 Wallace Notestein, *The Winning of the Initiative by the House of Commons* (1924), p. 51.

91 See the editor's 'Introduction: Parliamentary History 1603–29: in or out of Perspective?', in K. Sharpe ed., *Faction and Parliament* (Oxford, 1978).

92 S. Lambert, 'Procedure in the House of Commons in the early Stuart Period', *English Historical Review* 95 (1980), 768.

93 It was commonly assumed that Cromwell had destroyed the Bill. In 1659 a search ordered by the restored Rump failed to locate it. Worden, *The Rump Parliament*, pp. 365, 370.

94 *CJ* vii, 805.

95 R. Latham and W. Matthews eds, *The Diary of Samuel Pepys* (9 vols, 1970) i, 12–13.

Chapter 1

Court

I n the winter of 1648–49, the collapse of regal dignity symbolised the catastrophe about to befall the Stuart dynasty. Charles I had once maintained a household whose formality and decorum were the very 'image of virtue'.[1] Whilst a parliamentary majority remained committed to coming to terms with their king his captors kept him in reasonable comfort. Old formalities had been observed throughout his confinement.[2] But at the end of December 1648 the Council of Officers purged the king's retinue, ended traditional ceremonies of state and ordered that their prisoner was no longer to be served upon the knee.[3] Brought to London, Charles's last days were spent uncomfortably close to the smoking, drinking, swearing soldiery who guarded him.[4] England's greatest royal connoisseur, whose image had been captured by the finest artists of the age, was painted as a living, breathing subject for the last time from sketches made as he stood trial for his very life.[5] At the appointed time of execution the king was marched across St James's park from one royal palace to another. Arriving at the Banqueting House at Whitehall, architectural and artistic symbol of the sublime perfection of regal authority, he passed beneath Rubens's depiction of his father's apotheosis and was led out through a window on to the scaffold to his death.[6]

The English revolution was replete with such ironies, pregnant with symbolic meanings. In December 1648 Nedham described its premonitory rumblings in terms of the subversion of old regal forms. Coming to London, 'his Excellency [Fairfax] took up his quarter at Whitehall, as if he meant to king it, and brought along with him 4 Regiments of Foot, part of which became courtiers, and the rest were dispersed into York House and other noble houses'. The Sunday prior to the purge he 'took state at home, and would not admit so much as one member [of Parliament] to kiss his hand'.[7] Nedham, the master of the dismissive turn of phrase, called the revolutionaries 'mad Sainted Elves' who 'Boast [that] when the Royall blood is spilt, they'll all be kings themselves'.[8] Looking back later, royalists dramatised the revolution in similar terms. The eleventh book of Clarendon's *History of the Rebellion*, which

25

recounts the final chapter in the king's defeat and subsequent destruction, is prefaced epigrammatically with the seventh verse of the second chapter of the Book of Lamentations – 'The Lord ... hath given up into the hand of the enemy the walls of [Israel's] palaces.'

Once the king had been executed, the civil governors at Westminster made it clear that they were determined that the walls of the chief of those palaces, Whitehall, would fall into their hands. After the way their colleagues were treated following the purge, the Rumpers, even those who had supported the action, were not about to let Fairfax and his 'courtiers' get too comfortable. This chapter examines how the civil government refurbished this traditional focus of English politics and used it to serve the needs of its own members. The material restoration of the palace from 1649 on, and the establishment there of a kind of republican 'household', tell us a lot about the nature and intentions of the new regime. Almost instinctively, members of the gentry republic recreated a court environment at Whitehall as the setting for their rule. As we shall see, there were limits to the security and splendour of the republican occupation of the palace. But all through its short life the civil regime showed a consistently enthusiastic and increasingly confident commitment to restoring the charismatic focus of civilian government, bringing back some of the gloss to traditional patterns of authority tarnished by revolution.

The positive effort to restore some grandeur and civic sheen to the corridors of power reinforces the argument that 'we are sometimes too quick to dismiss the Interregnum as a period of philistinism'.[9] After the regicide itself, and the Irish massacres, no aspect of the Interregnum is more infamous than the sale of Charles I's vast collection of tapestry, statuary and paintings.[10] However, this diaspora, frequently condemned as the greatest ever loss to the artisitic heritage of the country, was checked to some considerable extent by the desire of the republic's governors to preserve a reasonable amount of magnificence in the places where they lived and worked.

The cataclysm which befell England in the winter of 1648–49 was no palace-storming revolution. It was the pragmatic solution to a state of civil chaos. Parliament had fought the Stuart tyrant in the name of the English Crown, and remained deeply committed to the rights of property, including that which belonged to the royal family. During the war, it went to great lengths to protect the royal estate. In August 1643 the House of Lords gave order that none of the king's houses was to be searched 'nor any goods carried out of them belonging to the king or queen but in the presence of one peer and two of the Members of the House of Commons'.[11] Initially it was committed to the care of the earl of Northumberland, but in 1644 the earl of Pembroke took over responsibility for Whitehall.[12] There were those who disapproved of this kind of diligence. But bouts of iconoclasm were rare, marking temporary radical ascendancies within the parliamentary coalition; and even radicalism had its limits. The vote of no addresses was passed in January 1648 after the Commons had called in the military to overawe the opposition of their noble colleagues. On the 18th of that month, units from Colonel Berkstead's regiment occupied Whitehall.[13] The same day, both Houses jointly resolved to move the palace library to the relative safety of St James's, there to remain 'for a public use'.[14]

After the revolution, the Rump declared an end to the days of courtly excess, bringing to a rhetorical climax the antipathy towards the court which had been mounting throughout the seventeenth century.[15] It claimed that one of the advantages of 'the late Alteration in the Government' was that the people would now be spared 'the vast expence of the Court, in ways of Luxury and Prodigality'. No longer would they have to pay for the parasites of the royal household, 'Drones and unprofitable Burdens of the Earth', nor their 'chargeable feasts and vain-glorious Masques and plays'. The moral fibre of the nation would be tainted no more by 'the great Nursery of Luxury and Intemperance'.[16] Measures for the sale of crown assets spelled the liquidation of Caroline grandeur. The announcement of the intention to sell the king's goods provoked angry royalist reaction. 'Was ever king thus martyred and marketed, by such hellish bloodbrokers? ... I wonder they do not make dice of his bones and fling them for his garments,' barked one newswriter.[17] But with ironic prescience he also commented that 'they might have reserved the hangings for themselves'. In the event, that is precisely what the rulers of the English Commonwealth did. Parliament's proprietorial attitude towards royal property continued beyond the regicidal watershed, but it was no longer held in trust for the royal family – like the palaces it had once adorned and furnished, it became the property of the Commonwealth itself.

Wandering through the deserted palace of Whitehall in 1642, an anonymous writer recalled how 'Majesty had wont to sit inthron'd within those glorious walls, darting their splendour with more awfull brightnesse then the great Luminaries in the Firmament, And with the same life and vigour Cherishing the hearts of their admiring followers.' Just as in masquery, so in life, the way in which the monarchs' presence gilded the palace was mirrored in the effect their presence had had on the courtiers around them,

> creating to those Favourites on whom their beames of grace reflected, names of honour, and estates to Maintaine it till the worlds end, and now all things as in a Chaos, involv'd and wrap't up in the black mists of confusion, and desolation ... and all as silent as midnight ... as if it were the decay'd buildings of ruin'd Troy ... The very walls as if they were sensible of this calamitie, doe weepe downe their plaister in griefe.[18]

The republican government spent a considerable amount of time, energy and money reversing the effects of neglect. Once more the palace became the stage on which the 'beames of grace' glorified the nation's political leaders. In the process, the guardians of the old court became the new courtiers themselves.

A decade on, in 1652–53, Major George Wither, poet, soldier and state servant, wrote a verse tract advocating the institution of a perpetual Parliament.[19] Part of his scheme for the monthly rotation of one-twelfth of a constantly sitting Parliament involved the creation of a fine palatial setting for the new republican regime. His idea was to lodge the senators of his parliamentary state at Whitehall, but only after it had been

> new model'd out;
> With Tow'rs adorn'd, with strong walls, fenc'd about;
> With buildings, having much variety
> Contriv'd into a neat conformity
> Of fair aspect, and duly beautifi'd
> With Gardens, walks, and with what els, beside
> Did render it magnificently fit
> For their abode, who did inhabit it.[20]

He proposed that twelve mansions should be built there to accommodate the people's representatives, grouped by county,

> that for conveniency they might be neer
> On all occasions; and that ev'ry Shire
> Might thereby find the easier addresses,
> And, quick dispatches in their businesses.

Meals would be provided,

> That none might be compelled to stray forth
> To places unbeseeming men of worth
> And all things pertinent to preservation
> Of health, with ev'ry fit accommodation
> Was there contrived, so as that they might
> Pursue the Publike Service with delight.

Significantly, he imagined that

> Nothing uncomely, or disorder'd there
> Could I behold; no noyses did I hear,
> Or such loud clamors, as have oft been heard,
> Among the rude Incommers and the guard;
> But such an awfull silence as if there
> The Turks Grand Signior, always present were
> By Mutes attended. To offend the eye,
> Or smell, no dung, or sinks, did open lye.
> I saw not there a despicable shed;
> No Coach hous'd there, or any Coach horse fed:

No little children in the garden sprawling,
Or in the Galleries, or Chambers yawling:
No Bakers Boy went tooting of his horn:
No Milk pails there, from place to place were born,
As in those Courts, and Allies which we see
Pester'd with Inmates, and poor lodgers be,

but only 'what the honour of the place befitted'.[21]

In his poetic guise, at least, Wither was unconstrained by a reality which clearly fell short of the grandeur he thought the republic should adopt. He imagined a regime and people so at ease with each other that the government compound did not even require the presence of guards. Although some of his ideas were already a reality in 1652, the creation of a glittering government compound at Whitehall was only ever imperfectly achieved by the Rump. It was not until Cromwell made it the seat of his personal monarchy that the palace was returned to something approaching its former splendour. After a visit to Whitehall in 1656, John Evelyn noted that, to his surprise, the palace was 'very glorious and well-furnished'.[22] An earlier visitor to Whitehall, the young Lodewijck Huygens, who accompanied the embassy of the States of Holland in 1651, was not so impressed by the palace, which had some decidedly tatty edges at that time.[23] But, despite dilapidation, the intrusive presence of soldiers and squatters, and the paranoia over security fostered by the republican regime's isolation, despite the clutter, mess and confusion, the continual coming and going of councillors, their servants and hordes of suitors, thanks to the Rumpers, Whitehall lived again.

I

On 17 February 1649, four days after it set up the Commonwealth's first Council of State, Parliament ordered that the palace of Whitehall be prepared for its executive body, 'and that the committee of Whitehall may be appointed to see it accommodated for that purpose'.[24] Extensive preparations were needed before the Council could take up its new offices. The palace needed a lot of repairs after periods of use as a garrison, armoury and military headquarters, and even longer periods of neglect – the palace was already filled with 'the raw scent of moist walls' just months after the flight of the court in 1642.[25] But work clearly went on quite quickly, as the Council was able to move into its new location on 28 May.[26] Cornelius Holland was ordered to ask the revenue committee to advance £500 to Edward Carter, surveyor of the works, or his clerk, Thomas Stevens, for the repairs carried out so far. Holland, along with Sir Henry Mildmay, also recommended that the revenue committee pay £100 to the wardrobe official, Clement Kynnersley, 'towards his charges in making ready Whitehall for the sitting of the Council'. Despite their best efforts, it seems likely that government was still being conducted from a location which resembled a building site. In August the Council ordered that 'the surveyor of the works do take care that the several lodgings appointed for the members of the council of state be made fit for their lodging in them'.[27]

Repair work continued, gradually becoming an institutionalised function of the government. At the end of August the Council ordered that those of its members who also sat on the revenue committee procure a warrant for £1,000 to be paid to Carter, for repairs he had made hitherto and to enable him 'to go on with that work'.[28] In January 1650 the Council recommended that Carter be paid £1,500 for his expenses.[29] As the Council's remit was extended to the guardianship of numerous properties reserved from the sale of crown real estate, the large repair bill grew even larger, and in July 1650 it was ordered that £4,215 be set aside 'for the repair of the Houses belonging to the Commonwealth between this and Michaelmas'.[30] Carter was by now overseeing work on the Parliament House and courts of justice at Westminster, the palaces of Whitehall (including the Cockpit and the Mews), St James, Hampton, Lambeth and Greenwich, as well as Somerset House, the Tower of London and the Mortlake tapestry works. At the beginning of 1651 the Council appointed a committee to consider the payment of arrears owed to Carter's workmen, and 'the settling of a constant allowance of money for ye future for the carrying on of public work'. It is not clear how well this idea went down with the more parsimonious members of Parliament. Around the same time, Carter received £2,415 paid out of the Council's own exigency funds at Gurney House.[31] A further £500 was ordered for his expenses in June.[32] In 1652 the Council became increasingly concerned by the cost of maintaining Whitehall. Cornelius Holland was instructed to recommend to Parliament that a financial comptroller be appointed to oversee the 'great sums' being spent on the repair of state property.[33] In April 1653, one week before the Rump's dissolution, Carter was paid £1,307 2s 3d for his expenditure on repairs to Whitehall, the Parliament House, the Mews and Somerset House in the six months to 31 March, presumably on the petition handed in by himself and Stevens the previous month.[34]

Responsibility for the palace seems to have rested primarily with Parliament. But it was the Councillors of State who, as the occupants, not surprisingly oversaw its repair. A report produced by one of the Council's *ad hoc* committees for Whitehall demonstrates the kind of work going on at the palace. It was recommended that passages such as the stone gallery and privy galleries be repaired and matted, 'the pavement made up with peble stones', and good doors and locks provided. The plumbing was to be fixed, 'the conduit heads, cisterns and pipes that convey the water to Whitehall … speedily repaired and so maintained for the future', and all sinks and drains 'cleansed and made good for the passage of water into the Thames'.[35] The chapel was repaired, and officials were appointed to maintain it and the privy chambers of the palace with 'the best frugality they can'.[36] By September 1652 the Council's interest in repairs even extended to fixing the weather vane.[37]

Considerable effort also went into the restoration of the privy garden at Whitehall. In March 1650 the Council wrote to the revenue committee, telling them that 'we have appointed that the Garden at Whitehall be trimmed up and repaired', and asked for £10 per week to be paid for six weeks to whomever Sir Henry Mildmay appointed in that connection. Ten weeks later, the same committee was asked to continue paying for the repairs at the same rate 'until the garden be finished'. In September 1650 it was ordered 'that such turf as is necessarie for the turfing of ye Quarters of the Garden in Whitehall be taken out of tuttle Fields and from such place there where it may be best spared'. The following December, Sir Henry Mildmay, Colonel Stapley and Sir James Harrington were appointed to examine the accounts 'as to ye charge of garden keeping at Whitehall', whereafter order was given for a letter to be written to the revenue committee asking it to pay £48 8s 11d for the repairs.[38]

By February 1651 the garden was getting back to normal, and the Council ordered Carter to see to placing there twelve statues from St James's 'proper for that use'. In all likelihood, these were the statues so offensive to the zealots who attacked the pieces erected in the privy garden at intervals throughout the Interregnum. One Mary Netherway addressed Cromwell on the subject, writing to him to demand that he

> demolish those monsters wich are set up as ornaments in [the] privy garden, for whilst they stand, though you see no evil in them, yet there is much evil in it, for whilst the crosses and altars of the idols remained untaken away in Jerusalem, the wrath of God continued against Israel.[39]

The garden was repaired from Council funds, and was apparently kept as an exclusive resort for the members of the Council, all of whom, along with their chief secretary, Walter Frost, were to be allowed keys to the garden.[40] (In December 1649, Sir William Masham and Colonel Valentine Wauton were assigned Brake Yard 'for the accomodating them with a garden'. But it is not clear what came of this plan after the repair of the privy garden.[41]) The Council ordered Captain Henry Middleton to keep the garden 'in good order and decently, avoiding curiosity, or superfluous charge', presenting his bills monthly.[42] His efforts seem to have paid off. One Sunday in 1652, after chapel at the palace, some of the Dutch ambassadors' party 'walked for a time in the private garden at Whitehall, which is rather nice'.[43]

Once repaired, Whitehall returned once more to the status of a government household whose maintenance employed a number of servants and staff. They were headed by the Whitehall housekeeper, (Captain) George Vaux. Richard Scutt, who kept the Council of State's rooms, was paid 16s a day, 7s for himself, 3s for an assistant, David, 2s apiece for two men and 1s apiece for two women. He was also empowered to pay somebody £12 per annum for 'the setting up and tending of lights in the galleries about Whitehall'). Keepers of the privy lodgings, Edmond Winstanley and Edward Jollie, long-standing servants of the Whitehall household, continued to act in that capacity. Captain Henry Middleton kept the garden and Long Gallery. Henry Jobson and Hugh Griffith served as Grooms of the Chapel. Henry Chadwell, clock-keeper, to-gether with Richard Thomas, bell-ringer, ensured that the republic's busy governors made it to sittings of the House on time. By the summer of 1652 the bell and clock were the responsibility of one man, Henry Shotwell (possibly Chadwell), who apparently also served as doorkeeper at the parliamentary committee responsible for Whitehall. John Hendrick was employed as keeper of the lower orchard. After Hendrick's death, Antony Hutton, 'ye gardener', was paid £40 per annum for keeping the privy garden, orchard 'and that part of Spring Garden where the bowling green was'. William Spittlehouse, a deputy to the Council's sergeant, also had a claim to the job of orchard keeper, clashing with Hutton over the post. John Sherife, or Shrieve, 'alias Doctor', received £12 per annum for keeping the privy garden door and one of the chapel galleries. Other passages were looked after by Ambrose Leech and Ambrose Tooth, who were paid the same as the Doctor. Stephen Sawyer, or Soters, and Thomas Pinckomb acted as Whitehall porters, receiving £30 per annum, the latter being replaced in September 1650 by 'Mr Bury'.[44] Govern-ment officials could take their meals at the palace. A cook was provided with a kitchen to dress meat for the councillors' table. Venison was a regular dish, judging by the Council's orders for stocking St James's park with a plentiful supply of deer. On one occasion, a trio of Medway fishermen presented the Council with an 8 ft sturgeon, a symbolic moment, for sturgeon were a tribute traditionally reserved for ruling monarchs.

Finally, two groups of officers served a dual purpose in both quotidian and ceremonial capacities. Edward Dendy, the Council's sergeant-at-arms, whose primary responsibilities were maintaining the physical security of the govern-ment as well as bearing a gilded mace before the Lord President of the Council of State, headed a team of assorted security men, armed guards and Whitehall police, as well as the ushers and doorkeepers who served in the Council chamber and its various lobbies and antechambers at the heart of the govern-ment's inner sanctum.[45] Richard Nutt was the Commonwealth's bargemaster, in charge of a team of liveried watermen, and was paid £60 per annum, 'as hath been formerly given'.[46]

Besides the officers of the works and the 'below stairs' household, the most important officers at republican Whitehall were those of the Commonwealth wardrobe, who looked after the vast array of furniture and fittings which turned the palace from a great house into a home for so many of the regime's members and officers. The leading inspiration for this undertaking came from the Council of State itself, which right from the off took a very proprietorial stance towards the stocks of goods and furniture which came into its hands on the abolition of the monarchy and dispossession of the dead king's heir.[47] As with the office of works, so with the wardrobe, successive Councils relied on the head of the former office, Clement Kynnersley, without whom it is unlikely that so much could have been achieved. By December 1651 the new republican state office over which he presided was becoming increasingly organised as an institution in its own right, Carter being instructed to fix up storage rooms for laying up the goods and furnishings of the 'Commonwealth Wardrobe'. Kynnersley's assistant, William Legg, was to be supplied with full records of government property and belongings, with details of their location, so that he 'may know where to repair for them'.[48]

Our anonymous guide to the palace in 1642 described the poignant emptiness which symbolised the crisis of regal splendour. '[T]hose rich and costly hangings of Persian Arras and Turky worke' had been '(like the Bishops) for their pride taken downe, And some (like the Bishops) thrown in the Tower, and the rest clapt close Prisoners in the Wardrop, unlesse it was those that (like the Bishop) made escape to York before the wars began'. Progressing through the empty palace, the author wrote that he 'would lead you into the Bed Chamber, but ... it may be a question whether there be a bed left there or no, for the Chamber to be call'd so by'. The palace had been stripped not only of its greater furnishings but of its lesser fittings too. In the guard chamber, 'where His Majesties great Beefe-eaters had wont to sit in attendance on their places ... [there is] nothing left but the bare Walls, and a cold Harth, from whence the Fire-irons are removed too, and as its thought converted into shooes for light Horses'. Not all the fixtures had been converted to such public uses. 'The drinking Dishes being pocket carriage you cannot but divine their fate.' Clearly Whitehall was not stripped bare, and its periodic repopulation by soldiers and others during the 1640s meant that there was still some furniture there when the Commonwealth assumed control in 1649. The previous December it had been reported that, when Fairfax had set up court there, Cromwell 'lay in one of the king's rich beds' at the palace on his return to the capital.[49] Thereafter, the palace was systematically restocked with the furnishings necessary to make the occupation as comfortable as possible.

In 1649 and 1651 the Rump passed Acts for the sale of the huge amount of movable goods which had furnished the numerous households of the late king, his wife and their children.[50] Forfeited by right of their 'several delinquencies' and 'having been of old belonging to the Crown and not to the persons' of the royal family, this property now belonged to the Commonwealth. Parliament, fearing the embezzlement of this vast booty 'for want of a certain accompt', decided to inventory, value and sell it, 'except such parcels thereof as shall be found necessary for the uses of the state'.[51] The Council of State would decide which goods ought to be set aside. A maximum value of £10,000 in the first Act was extended to £20,000 in the second.[52]

It was argued that the proceeds of the sale of what was now Commonwealth property 'might justly be disposed of for public uses'. But instead the Rump thought fit to use the money raised to settle the many debts, contracted before the wars, owed to the creditors, servants and provisioners of the royal house-holds who 'had constantly adhered to the Parliament and suffered for the same', as many of them were now 'so necessitous as that their condition cannot bear the want of their said debts'.[53] Unfortunately, these good inten-tions were never realised in practice. The sales foundered during a period of economic depression. The administration of the compensation scheme was blighted by corruption, malpractice and interminable delay.[54]

One critic pinned most of the blame for the scheme's failure on 'men in authority who had not only power, but occasion to the use of the goods'.[55] Having moved into the king's palaces and houses, not surprisingly, the gov-ernment came to feel just as proprietorial about their contents as their fabric. From the greatest artworks of the Caroline collections right down to the humblest furnishings of the royal households, England's republican rulers could not resist the temptation to raid the stock of courtly fixtures and fittings in order to furnish the buildings from which they ruled the country.

The government avidly exploited opportunities created by elements of the sale legislation which pertained to the reservation of crown property. The Council of State simply ignored the upper limit of £20,000, which it was entitled, with parliamentary approval, to lay by for the use of the state. By September 1651 the government had reserved goods to a value of £54,375, almost one-third of the Crown's personal estate, which, for the purposes of the sale, had been valued at about £185,000.[56] Other acquisitions made after September 1651 do not show up in the copious inventories compiled between 1649 and 1650. In 1651 a group of creditors had contracted for several statues but were unable to collect their goods, as these were the same ornaments which the Council had ordered to be set up in the privy garden at Whitehall.[57] In 1657 another creditor, George Wilson, petitioned the Protector's Council, complaining that he had been apportioned a parcel of goods, part of which was a piece of tapestry that had somehow remained ever since in service with the government at Whitehall.[58]

The Council earmarked for reservation from sale or distribution great swathes of the royal family's personal estate. Carpets, rich arras hangings, tapestries, bedlinen, furniture, paintings, statues, two whole libraries besides the one at St James's, plate and tableware, plus miscellaneous artefacts and regalia of English monarchy, all drawn from most of the metropolitan royal houses and palaces, and many of the provincial ones were all laid by.[59] The reserved goods ranged from the mundane – fireplace irons and equipment, curtains and close stools – to the more obviously ornamental, such as the agate and crystal cups set in gold and silver, four great gilt flagons, two gilt pots, twelve silver candlesticks and 'an old Bible with a silver and gilt cover' set aside in October 1649, and the bust of the Roman emperor Severus (it is not clear which one) set up at the Banqueting House.[60]

Numerous orders were made for furnishing the lodgings of individual government members. In November 1649, Colonel Valentine Wauton, MP and Councillor, was allowed a pair of brass andirons, four window curtains, two large carpets, two feather beds and bolsters, blankets and counterpanes, all to be taken from the government's stock of royal property, as well as six pieces of tapestry hangings, one set depicting the story of Elijah, an Old Testament prophet, scourge of King Ahab, who had set up a temple to Baal at Samaria and seduced the Israelites; the other the story of Hermes, herald of Zeus, god of dicing, and the inventor of the lyre.[61] Similar orders were made for furnishing the apartments of Lord Grey, Lord Commissioner John Lisle, Sir William Masham, Sir William Constable (for whom the trustees for the sale of the king's goods were ordered to provide a nine-piece suite of hangings from Hampton Court depicting Venus and Cupid), Sir William Armyne, Cornelius Holland and Colonels John Hutchinson, Anthony Stapley and Herbert Morley.[62] Hugh Peters's lodgings at Whitehall consisted of 'three or four decent and well-furnished rooms at the front of the House'.[63] Secretary Milton was also given the same privilege of furnished chambers.[64]

It is not possible to detail in every instance exactly what items each government member was provided with. But there was clearly considerable pressure on stocks available in London, as in March 1650 the Council ordered Kynnersley to have the contents of the removing wardrobe at York sent down to London.[65] Keeping a keen eye on what was available, the Council wrote to the trustees in January 1651 about 'certain Hangings' still at Ludlow Castle 'and are there wholly useless', which 'if they were brought up hither would be serviceable for accommodating of some rooms appointed for public service in Whitehall'.[66]

Tapestries, hangings and furnishings were needed in Parliament itself, for MPs' lodgings in the Mews and at Somerset House as well as Whitehall, in the courts of justice, the inner Court of Wards, the Speaker's chamber, and the High Court of Justice in Westminster Hall.[67] A number of committees of both Parliament and the Council had their chambers furnished from royal stocks. In April 1650 the committee of Whitehall was asked to provide forty-eight new chairs for the Council of State's use, and an additional dozen velvet stools were requisitioned in September.[68] A year later, new chairs were provided for the hard-working Admiralty, Irish and Scottish committees – which suggests that, if nothing else, the Rump's 'government by committee' took a heavy toll of furniture.[69] In July 1651, hangings and other furnishings were requisitioned for the use of the committee of examinations, which sat in a room near the palace chapel.[70] It is interesting to note that in 1650, as the Rump began to show greater interest in matters of trade and diplomacy, it ordered to its own use various books of charts and maps, including a copy of the famous nautical atlas published by the Dutchman, Lucas Janssen Waghenaer, as well as 'one large booke being the description of ye Empires and Kingdoms of the World'.[71] Costly tapestries adorned the antechamber of the late king's bedroom, which had been appointed for negotiations between the Dutch and Council commissioners, as well as a room in which a Dutch deputation met Sir Oliver Fleming, Master of Ceremonies, to discuss some details of diplomatic formalities.[72]

Three rooms at Somerset House were furnished and kept for state uses. Other rooms there which accommodated yet more members of the government, and the residence of Sir Abraham Williams, which served as a short-stay *pied-à-terre* for visiting foreign dignitaries, had to be furnished, too.[73] The Dutchmen who stayed there in December 1651 'were lodged in very beautifully furnished apartments and slept in new velvet beds with big silver and gold fringes. These belonged to the Republic, and it is believed that they were from the king's goods.'[74] Meanwhile, whole palaces and houses were reserved for the state's use fully furnished, for example Greenwich, and Hampton Court, where hangings and carpets viewed *in situ* by a Council committee were expressly reserved for use at the palace.[75] Council further ordered that the hangings in the wardrobe at Windsor castle should remain in use there, and that the governor, Colonel Whichcote, should detain the banners of the Garter knights, the pulpit cloth, cushions and the Bible 'belonging to the collegiate church' until the trustees for the sale 'have satisfied the Council that those things are by the Act to be disposed of by them'.[76] Clearly no such satisfaction was given, as the author of an appeal on behalf of the king's servants and creditors, the supposed beneficiaries of the trustees' labours, was left vainly asserting that the Garter regalia surely counted as the personal estate of the king.[77]

As the ward of the king's younger children the Commonwealth also furnished their household as they were shunted between a succession of guardians.[78] And, as Commonwealth property, the estate of the Crown could also serve the purposes of gift, patronage and reward. The Council's decision to present Dutch ambassadors with books from St James's in February 1649 first prompted their discussion as to how the library there might be disposed of to the Commonwealth's use.[79] Both Colonel Michael Jones and Lord General Cromwell were rewarded for their service in Ireland with gifts of horses hand-picked from the king's breed at Tutbury.[80] Cromwell also received one of the king's richly ornate gilt suits of armour by order of the Council of State.[81] A bed, bedclothes, carpets and two sets of hangings, one depicting 'Amazoones', another the story of St Paul, were inventoried in July 1649. A note appended to one of the inventories of the king's goods remarked that they were being kept 'in order to a present supplye for the Right Honourable the Lord Lieutenant of Ireland', presumably meaning Cromwell.[82]

II

One of the obvious distinctions between the court culture of the monarchy and that of the republic was the elimination of a dignified family home which served as a playground for the hordes of courtiers who crowded round the honeypot, and its replacement by a dignified extended office compound which served the needs of a large bureaucracy. This is a crude characterisation, however, for the change was more a matter of degree. The implied distinction between a culture characterised by play and one characterised by work is not as simple as it may seem (on both counts, as Whitehall had long been the very hub of regal governance, not least during the rather hectic 1630s). As we have seen, the republic maintained a reasonably well appointed household. But, even in the pokier corners of the Commonwealth administration, bureaucratic bodies were creating quasi-household structures. For example, the committee for taking the public accounts employed its own household staff, including doorkeepers, porters and cleaners. The committee also kept full accounts of its expenditure on food, drink and tobacco. In the year from December 1651 the members of the committee sat down to dinner together with increasing regularity, first monthly, then weekly, spending nearly £30 on dishes such as capon and sampheir, loin of veal, leg of mutton, lobsters and artichokes, and green goose in sauce. They had oranges, lemons, strawberries and cherries delivered. By the close of this period the committeemen were permitting themselves almost daily expenditure on tobacco and other necessaries.[83]

Yet change there undoubtedly was. Compared with the vast complement of men and women who had serviced the household of Charles I, the Commonwealth seems to have survived with something of a skeleton staff, many of whom appear to have had more than one job at the palace.[84] For occasional purposes, the regime made do by making its lesser officers double as household staff. Six of the Council's messengers and six of its sergeant's deputies were appointed to wait on the guests at diplomatic dinners.[85] In August 1649 a committee considered 'how the barge cloths reserved may have the arms of the Crown taken out and the arms of the Commonwealth put in'.[86] This illustrates the adaptive thrift which characterised the regime's court-building endeavours. The household at Whitehall maintained by the Commonwealth was never as lavish as those which went before or came after, as is clear from frequent instructions to employees emphasising frugality and the need to avoid 'superfluous charge'. There was clear reluctance to spend large sums on a particularly conspicuous government centrepiece. Much of the regime's thrift can no doubt be explained by the growth of hostility to the slightly *avant-garde* Stuart attitude, so at variance with Elizabethan policy, that a king should spend huge amounts of money advertising his cultural refinement. But it also reflected the severe financial restraints imposed on the regime by massive military expenditure and an overburdened fiscal infrastructure. In the light of government policy, it is nevertheless tempting to speculate that, if they had had greater financial and political leeway, the regime's leaders would have used it to create grandeur something nearer the level George Wither later prescribed.

The regime went to lengths to see that the taxpayer was not burdened by its policy of repairing Whitehall. Some of the costs were mitigated by shrewd estate management. Timber was brought from Windsor forest 'for the repairing of the houses of ye Commonwealth, and other public works', and Carter was given a warrant to bring large amounts of stone from Tower Hill to the same end. Order was also given for bringing lead from Windsor castle to repair the pipes which carried water from Hyde Park to the palace. Trees felled at Windsor were also used by Carter.[87] The tarras, an elaborate pulpit-like construction in Whitehall's inner courtyard, was demolished and the proceeds from the sale of its materials were ploughed back into the upkeep of the palace. This was the place where Latimer preached before King Edward and huge crowds in 1547–48, although by 1642 it was more famous in common parlance as 'that Exchange of Projectors ... where th' Attendants upon the Councell Table had wont to coole their toes' than as one of the birthplaces of the Reformation.[88]

In other respects the Commonwealth government showed itself committed to the preservation of the legacy left by monarchy. In October 1651 the Council ordered Carter to provide two engines to cast water in case of fire, fifty leather buckets and four ladders to be kept in readiness against all events.[89] On 30 March 1650 Parliament ordered the trustees for the sale of the king's goods not to 'meddle' with the royal horses at Tutbury, and asked the Council of State 'to take care for the preservation of the race and breed'.[90] Accordingly, the Council set up a committee to see that the Tutbury horses 'may be so disposed of that the breed may not be lost'. This decision could be taken to symbolise the fundamentally preservationist attitude of the Commonwealth to the whole issue of what to do with the legacy left behind by the Stuart monarchy. In point of fact the Council ran Tutbury as a stud farm, and sold a number of horses, mares and colts from there.[91]

The Commonwealth's rulers may not have shared the Stuarts' pretensions to grandeur, but their policy went further than careful stewardship.[92] When choosing furniture for public uses from the wardrobe, there are signs that the governors of the Commonwealth selected carefully, becoming increasingly sophisticated and imaginative as their efforts to create a dignified set of spaces gathered momentum. In January 1651 specific order was given to reserve the great tapestries depicting the defeat of the Spanish Armada, which Parliament ordered to be rehung 'in the late Lords' House'.[93] This was the famous set of hangings which Charles I had banished to the Tower wardrobe in the 1630s as part of the deliberate purge of martial bombast from his court. From the first meeting of the Long Parliament, and every day thereafter, MPs had begun the day with a prayer recalling 'our great deliverance from the Spanish invasion'.[94] In 1644, 'in a gesture laden with symbolism', the parliamentarian House of Lords assumed the mantle of their glorious forebears, who had faced down the last great Popish threat to English liberties, by rehanging the suite in their chamber at Westminster in time for the trial of William Laud.[95] After the abolition of the upper House, this was the location Parliament commonly chose as the venue for receiving foreign diplomats, its decor suitably suggestive of the glories of England's recent history and the potency of her modern navy.[96]

In the 1649 legislation for the sale of the king's personal estate, it was stated that some of the items were 'of such nature as that though by reason of their rarity or antiquity they may yield very great prices in foreign parts, where such things are much valued, yet for particular mens use in England they would be accounted little worth'.[97] Yet in the spring of 1651 the then Council of State wrote to the trustees ordering them not to sell 'certain statues at St James's House' precisely because they were 'worthy to be kept for their antiquity and rarity, and as they would yield little if sold, we desire you to deliver such of them as Mr Carter, surveyor of the works, may select to be set up in the garden at Whitehall'.[98] Busts, pedestals and other statuary were also ordered to be set up in the long gallery (over the stone gallery, its ceiling painted by Holbein), 'where they formerly were', until sold.[99] It was also apparently conciliar intervention which saved that masterpiece of the Italian Renaissance, Mantegna's *Triumphs of Caesar*, for the state (though the historical record usually associates these paintings with the protectoral court at Hampton rather than the pioneering work of the parliamentary republicans).[100] The regime also reserved for the state precisely those fine artworks it is accused of wilfully dispersing to the four corners of the art world. The Rumpers held on to works by Titian, del Sarto, Gentileschi, Pordenone, Mantegna, Bordone, Romano and Raphael, to name a few, which hung in private suites as well as in the committee rooms at Westminster.[101]

The connoisseurship of the regime and its members should not be overstated, however. The Whitehall library is a case in point. The Council acted too late to prevent the plunder of the king's cabinet, part of the library treasures, which Peter Young, royal librarian since 1609, alleged had been rifled by

Hugh Peters.[102] Young was less than blameless himself. Manuscripts he was permitted to borrow for the preparation of the Alexandrine text of the Septuagint were not returned after his death, and recovered for the library only after the Restoration.[103] Despite the appointment of Bulstrode Whitelocke as its keeper, and his employment of the noted irenic intellectual and library theorist, John Dury, the royal library was caught up in endless bureaucratic wrangles, apparently never returned from the palace of St James's to its rightful place at Whitehall, and was left instead to the mercy of rats and the elements.[104] Nevertheless, keepers continued to be appointed, and although in composing his account of his own appointment Whitelocke emphasised how little he relished the responsibility (and how relieved he was to have it lifted from his shoulders by the Council's appointment of Dury), the post does seem to have had some honorific appeal. The Lord Commissioner's successor after the dissolution of the Rump was Henry Lawrence, president of the new Council of State.

The example of the library suggests how important the appearance of proper form was to the Commonwealthsmen. These were no philistines, but their failure properly to safeguard, let alone (apparently) use the facility suggests that (apart from the fact that they were extremely busy men) they were more interested in making the right kind of impression.

III

The reasons for creating a government compound at Whitehall went beyond the impulse to preservation and the necessity for office space and accommodation. Another motive was to supplant and outshine the Stuarts. Orders were given for expunging all the dynasty's insignia from the palace.[105] The revival of Whitehall allowed the regime's propagandists to disparage the pretender's court after his coronation in Scotland in 1651. His chances of selling beer across the border, in Nedham's phrase, were not improved by the impoverished spectacle of his threadbare court in Scotland. Whitehall may have left something to be desired, but at least it wasn't a Scottish palace 'of as royall a structure as an English alehouse'. 'All ceremonies even from manners to cleanliness, are an abomination in the country,' Politicus claimed of Scotland, 'and to take down all the pride and vanity of kings, none but six-legged courtiers are allowed to be Guards of the Body.'[106] From France it was reported that Prince Rupert had taken apartments in the royal palace in Paris furnished by an official of the French king's bedchamber 'but the less willingly in regard he knows how basely Charles Stuart's people are wont to spoile whatsoever comes into their hands'.[107]

Governments create courts in order to provide a dignified and, where possible, comfortable environment for governing. They also aim to create clearly defined spaces over which they can exert a degree of control (of access, of occupancy) which itself symbolises the government's authority. The symbolism of the palace's fate in 1642 was all the more dramatic because its desertion meant that one could wander into the private apartments of the king wearing hat, sword and spurs without let or hindrance.

Turning Whitehall into a household proved a lot easier than turning it into a secure government compound, which was apparently something of an uphill struggle. Not the least of the government's problems was the constant press of petitioners who inundated the Council of State almost daily, seeking patronage, reward or redress of private grievances. A number of measures were taken in an effort to relieve the hard-pressed Councillors from such distractions from their public duties.[108] However, the lodgings of residents at Whitehall were also often thronged with suitors seeking their assistance in a private capacity.[109]

Squatters were one of the biggest headaches at Whitehall. In May 1649 the Council issued warrants to both Dendy and one Mr Collins 'to make your repair to all those families now lodging in Whitehall ... not being of the Council of State or belonging unto them, and require them to remove themselves, families and goods, and leave the rooms for the use of the said Council and their attendants'. If any refused or delayed, Dendy and Collins were to inform the Council, 'that warrant may thereupon be given to remove them by force'.[110] However, despite the escalating tone of exasperation with which the Council repeated this kind of instruction, it proved utterly impossible to dislodge all unofficial residents. By 1651 the Council had apparently given up all hope of clearing the palace of those living there unofficially, instructing the committee for Whitehall to keep them under surveillance, considering 'who are fit to be discharged from abiding in the House any longer, and ... who they are that are to remain'.[111] The problem with squatters is easier to understand if one bears in mind the scale and labyrinthine construction of the palace. One survey counted well over a thousand rooms, fifty-five closets, seventy-five garrets, twenty-six cellars and thirteen kitchens.[112] This layout had made the palace a resort for many fleeing justice. In 1642 it was said of the vacant palace that 'there is no body ... to stop a pursuing Bayly, if you should take that for your Sanctuary'. A vaguely criminal element could indeed be found at Whitehall in the 1650s. The Council received a petition 'complaining that Richard Jennings Esq. doth shelter himself in Whitehall from arrest for debt', and gave him three days to remove himself along with his family.[113]

The Council took great pains over controlling physical access in the area around Whitehall. Doors leading on to St James's park from most private houses were nailed up 'for the safety of the Council that there may be no attempts upon the garrison'. (Mrs Hamden was asked 'to have a care' who used the access she was allowed.) Colonel Pride and Major General Harrison, successive commanders of the garrison at St James's, were put in charge of the park's security, and assisted by Colonel Berkstead, commander of the units appointed to the guard of Parliament and the City.[114] Efforts to close the society haunt at Spring Garden, 'that the concourse usually thither may be prevented', excited a certain amount of activity.[115]

The riverside jetty known as Whitehall Stairs was locked at sunset, and only councillors and their agents were admitted thereafter.[116] But the palace itself was in fact never more than reasonably secure. In 1651 a conciliar subcommittee was set up to confer with Carter about changing the locks on certain passage doors around the palace; another committee was set up to consider 'some orders fit to be observed about locks and keys, and the passage through rooms in Whitehall'.[117] Orders for preventing 'idle persons', who caused 'many inconveniences', from coming into the garden and long gallery; orders to improve security to prevent the theft of lead and locks, and the breaking of windows; orders for fixing up broken-down doors which gave undesirables 'opportunity to act any villainy at any hour in the night so that at present they are so noisome that men cannot without annoyance pass through them' – all indicate the problems that the Council had to deal with. Whitehall was dark, a place of shadows and dangers, the Council ordering as late as February 1650 that the sergeant set up lamps around the galleries of the palace 'for making the passage convenient for the members of the Council'. Samuel Pepys recorded that he had fallen in a ditch on a visit to the palace not long before the Restoration, 'it being very dark'.[118]

Occasionally, security was breached. In April 1653 Allen and Love were sent by the Council of State to confer with Parliament's committee for Whitehall about preventing the problems arising from the great number of duplicate keys to the palace's various portals, possibly in direct response to the burglary of Secretary Frost's apartment at the end of March. In future the Council's exigency funds were to be kept in a strong chest guarded by a man in a secure room with a sentinel posted at the door.[119] The extent of any real danger always has to be weighed against the Council's sometimes excessive caution. In March 1652, Colonel Berkstead was ordered to examine a young boy caught cutting gold braid from hangings in the palace 'concerning that and other like misdemeanours'.[120] This was a breach of security but hardly a threat to the state. It also helps to confirm the impression of a world of attractive opulence at the heart of the republic.

Anxiety meant a continued military presence in Whitehall after its occupation by the government. This in turn created its own challenges to the regime's symbolic authority over its central 'official space', which was threatened by the incivilities of the loafing soldiery, and the not unnatural desire on the part of officers to live in the kind of grandeur which their civilian paymasters had cornered for themselves.

Early in its tenancy at Whitehall, the Council asked Fairfax to provide guards to be relieved every twenty-four hours by men quartered at St James's. It also made numerous orders for the provision of coal, candles and guard houses for soldiers on duty at the palace.[121] But on a number of occasions the Council ordered the military presence at the palace to be reduced. The Lord General's regiment had to remove before the government could move in.[122] In July 1649 Mildmay and Holland were ordered to confer with the Quartermaster General 'how the soldiers in Whitehall may be quartered in Scotland Yard so as the rest of the House may be free'. Carter and Colonel Saunders were also ordered to survey the stabling facilities in the Mews, 'to see with what convenience a regiment of horse may be quartered there, the accommodations of stabling wherewith the Council are accommodated being reserved for their use'.[123] As Whitehall was gradually demilitarised the Council took steps to see to it that 'all officers of what condition soever' left behind all property 'of the wardrobe of the Commonwealth'.[124] In April 1651 Council reclaimed hangings that had been used in the chamber where army officers had their regular meetings (as well as those which had hung in the newly deceased Sir William Armyne's chambers).[125]

A few days after being asked to remove from Whitehall, Fairfax was given the lodgings occupied recently by the Prince Elector Palatine at Somerset House, which was also appointed as the new site of army headquarters. On 18 August the Council wrote to Fairfax to complain that 'many officers of the army and others remaining here still ... the members of the Council are kept from their accommodations which cannot be delayed at this time of year when they are to lay in their stores of fireing and other conveniences'. Those now quartered in Scotland Yard could stay, but they asked that Fairfax 'give ... positive order' for the removal of all others.[126] But at the end of the month the Council hardly hastened the soldiers' departure when it asked the Lord General to delay setting up camp at Somerset House until the sale of crown goods from rooms there had been completed.[127] In February 1651 the Council was still trying to make alternative arrangements for the accommodation of soldiers quartered at Whitehall, who now included members of Harrison and Berkstead's regiments. George Vaux, the housekeeper at the palace, received £20 'for so much spent removing soldiers', and it is tempting to assume he had resorted to bribery.[128]

The Council also ordered the removal of the Marshal General's prison from the palace, 'those rooms in his possession being appointed for some of the Council who must presently remove thither', offering instead 'some convenient place' at St James's. In this instance the Council had to enlist the assistance of the commander-in-chief, for, when served with the order for his removal, the Marshal General expressly refused to obey 'with so much contempt as we think not fit to repeat nor is comely for us to bear'.[129] But it would seem that Farfax was unwilling to help out unless the Council could indeed find his Marshal alternative accommodation. The following February, the Council ordered Carter to prepare the granaries in the Mews, close to White-hall, 'for the receiving of the prisoners which are in the Marshal's custody in Whitehall, those quarters being assigned to him by the Quarter-Master General to the end Whitehall may be freed of them'.[130] The suggestion is that the Marshal would only obey a commanding officer in the army, as there is no other indication that the Quartermaster General, or any other officer, had any jurisdiction over accommodation at the palace.

There was, however, a certain irony in the choice of soldiers to oversee its security. First Pride, then Harrison, was commander of the garrison at St James's palace, both of whom, at one time or another, had a reputation as the scourge of the civilians (although Harrison's assumption of responsibility for security in the area coincided with his appointment as commander-in-chief of the forces remaining in England during Lord General Cromwell's campaign in the north). The Major General had certain discretionary powers in the matter of access to the park, as well as 'power to shut up all the doors opening into St James' park of which he cannot have assurance that they shall not be made use of to the prejudice of ye peace'. Subordinate, in this respect, to the Council (of which he was not a member until February 1651), Harrison was, however, empowered to direct the surveyors of the works regarding the use of doors and passages into and out of St James's park and Spring Garden. It was also referred to him whether or not Lady Nanton and Francis Pierrepoint might keep their doors on to Spring Garden open.[131]

By necessity, successive Councils effectively shared jurisdiction over the palace and its precincts with soldiers. But the civilian regime also acted to forestall certain other unwanted intrusions. The destruction of the tarras was perhaps intended to prevent any repetition of the scene in December 1648 when Hugh Peters came to Whitehall and revived the practice of public sermons in the palace's outer courtyard, 'where the Bishops were wont to preach before the king, and many people flocked from the Cities of London and Westminster and had free liberty to come in and hear him'. Peters's sermon allegorised the military *coup* with a story in which a younger son had broken down the door to rescue his mother from captivity because the elder son had refused to surrender the key to his sibling.[132] This was not the sort of thing the Council of State would have wanted to encourage. Hugh Peters did preach at Whitehall again, and on many occasions in his capacity as preacher to the Council of State, but he did so in the far more staid atmosphere of the refurbished chapel royal at the palace, which became quite a popular social resort.[133] In 1651 committees were appointed to consider how the chapel could be ordered for the best convenience of the Council and other MPs to sit there. It certainly seems to have attracted a large number of government members –

the Council sent one of the Frosts to the committee of Whitehall to recommend its enlargement.[134] Again, however, with its spiritual offices as with its material needs, the governors were unable to maintain strict control over their surroundings. On one occasion in 1652, whilst Peter Sterry was preaching in the chapel, a woman reportedly stripped naked and ran through the congregation, shouting 'Welcome the resurrection!'.[135]

IV

There are signs that, despite difficulties, the Commonwealth government became increasingly confident about its tenancy of Whitehall, seemingly 'growing into' the fabric of the palace. The Council of State had a Horse Chamber committee, named after its Whitehall location, and from 1652, it also had a 'Treaty Chamber', the room where diplomatic negotiations were held. After the Restoration, Whitehall reverted to regal use, and its return to normal service was marked by the production of one of the first detailed plans of the palace. This plan, a copy of which hangs in the ground-floor corridor of the Institute of Historical Research in London, depicted every gallery, chamber, nook and cranny, and ascribed each and every room to the suite of members of the royal family or to certain courtiers. In a sense, the restored Stuart regime was rewriting the palatial landscape. The plan clearly demonstrates who was now in possession of the palace. But in some sense it also indicates how strong the need was to expunge the palace of the memories of the 1650s.

Although England's monarchs had made the palace their home well over a century before their ejection in the 1640s, the history of Whitehall's royal occupation was not dissimilar to the brief period of usurpation in the 1650s. In 1529 Henry VIII had appropriated the palace, which had been the archbishop of York's, abandoning charred and dilapidated Westminster, which had never recovered after the fire of 1512. Elizabeth had done little to add to Cardinal Wolsey's fine construction, and despite the pretensions of her Stuart successors, Inigo Jones's grand design for an edifice to rival the Prado had resulted in just the Banqueting House, which cost James I over £15,000 to build. The Commonwealth spent very little on state building projects, but it seems likely that the Council of State spent at least as much on a more conservative policy of maintenance.[136]

Despite the reinstallation of statues in the privy garden, and busts in the long gallery, for example, this policy precluded a return to the full glory of regal Whitehall. But in essence there was little to distinguish the attitudes of monarchs from those of the republic's governors when it came to visual display. A visitor after the Restoration commented that externally Whitehall appeared as 'nothing more than an assemblage of several houses, badly built, at different times and for different purposes, [with] nothing from its exterior from which you could suppose it to be the habitation of a king'.[137] It has been said that 'it was indeed the tapestries and other furnishings that did most to transform the complex of interconnecting chambers and galleries into a display of royal opulence that owed more to the painter, the gilder, the carver and the embroiderer than it did to formal architectural design'.[138] Where possible, the Commonwealth's rulers certainly saw to it that a suitable level of opulent display was maintained by hanging acres of arras and tapestry. It was not until England's government returned to something like the old form of personal monarchy in 1653 that politics again came to centre on the courtly magnificence of the country's ruler.[139] However, it was the Rumpers who had saved Whitehall 'for the use of the Commonwealth'. Indeed, their efforts were in some sense the *making of* the Commonwealth.

The eye-witness account of the deserted palace written in 1642 lamented 'A Pallace without a Presence! ... A Court without a Court! These are misteries and miseries, which the silken ages of this peaceful Island have not been acquainted with ... !'[140] As well as describing its transformation in the absence of the royal household, the author made the state of the palace into a symbol of England's descent into civil disorder. Anthropomorphically, the walls wept down their plaster to see such decline. When the Rump was reinstalled in 1659, in reaction to rumours that it intended to sell the palace to raise desperately needed cash, the fabric of the palace spoke once more, imploring that the state's governors

> Disgrace me not by such opprobrious sail.
> Although on kingship was my true entail
> My splendid luster is only fit for you,
> And for Embassadors of me to take a view.
> ... gladder should I be if it would be my fate,
> To be preserved for the Council of our State,
> That they may sit there by your full consent,
> And keep me in repair, although they paid no Rent.
> The Premises taken to due consideration
> Will much redound to the Honour of our Nation.[141]

In many respects, after the revolution Whitehall became the court of the Commonwealth, the centre of its political life. As we have seen, it was not only the location of the Council of State and its numerous committees, but also provided accommodation for a large number of government members and their officers. There they lived, worked, prayed, ate, slept and when possible, perhaps, strolled in the garden to which they had privileged access.

But, as we have also seen, 'the court of the Commonwealth' was far from being the unitary entity created by the presence of one key individual and his retinue, as it had been under monarchy. The office of works was responsible for a great many locations where other limbs of the administration lived and worked, other courts with their own households. The Commonwealth wardrobe was also responsible for stage-dressing what was, in many respects, the real centrepiece or focal point of the republican court, the floor of the House of Commons. There the government acted out some of the most important features of state ceremonial, events orchestrated by the final key member of the Commonwealth household, the Master of Ceremonies, Sir Oliver Fleming.

NOTES

1 Kevin Sharpe, 'The Image of Virtue: the Court and Household of Charles I, 1625–1642', in idem ed., Politics and Ideas in Early Stuart England.

2 For the conviviality of Charles's treatment at Holdenby in 1647 see Thomas Herbert, Memoirs (1702), p. 11. Cf. J. Ashburnham (groom of the bedchamber), A True Coppie of a Letter ... concerning [his] Deportment towards the King in his late Attendance ... at Hampton Court and the Isle of Wight (1648).

3 Gardiner, History of the Great Civil War iv, 286.

4 Colonel Tomlinson, officer in overall command of his captivity, was thanked by Charles for insisting that he be shown proper respect, and for guarding him 'as far as he could from annoyance or incivility'. F. A. Inderwick, Sidelights on the Stuarts (1888), p. 236. Another of his captors, Colonel Hacker, was less sympathetic, but at his trial in 1660 he claimed in his defence that even he had tried to ensure the king got some peace and quiet before his execution. Gardiner, History of the Great Civil War iv, 318.

5 O. Millar, The Age of Charles I. Painting in England, 1620–1649 (1972), p. 109; plate 175 reproduces Edward Bower's famous portrait of the king seated, wearing a cloak bearing the insignia of the Order of the Garter.

6 Gardiner, History of the Great Civil War iv, 320–1.

7 Mercurius Pragmaticus 5–12 December 1648, p. [4].

8 Ibid., 19–26 December 1648, p. [1].

9 Blair Worden, 'Classical Republicanism and the Puritan Revolution', in H. Lloyd-Jones, V. Pearl and B. Worden eds, History and Imagination (1981), p. 191.

10 M. Whinney and O. Millar, English Art, 1625–1714 (Oxford, 1957), p. 7.

11 Journal of the House of Lords vi, 181.

12 Ibid., 415.

13 Gardiner, History of the Great Civil War iv, 53–4.

14 CJ v, 436.

15 The Parliamentary or Constitutional History of England xix (1763), 63–82. For hostility to the court see Hirst, Authority and Conflict, pp. 30, 42, 125, 144, 150–1; for the link between that hostility and specific policies and administrations see Alastair Bellany, '"Rayling Rymes and Vaunting Verse": Libellous Politics in early Stuart England, 1603–

1628', in Sharpe and Lake eds, *Culture and Politics*.

16 *Parliamentary or Constitutional History* xix, 74–5.

17 *Mercurius Elencticus* 21–8 February 1649, cited by Abbott ed., *Writings and Speeches* ii, 17.

18 Anon., *A Deep Sigh breath'd through the Lodgings at Whitehall, deploring the Absence of the Court and the Miseries of the Pallace* ([4 October] 1642), sig. A2v. Hereafter cited as *Miseries of the Pallace*.

19 Wither, *Perpetuall Parliament*.

20 *Ibid.*, p. 68.

21 *Ibid.*, p. 69.

22 E. S. de Beer ed., *The Diary of John Evelyn* (6 vols, Oxford, 1955) iii, 166.

23 Bacharach and Collmer eds, *Huygens' Journal*, pp. 41–2.

24 P.R.O., SP25/87, 14.

25 *Miseries of the Pallace*, sig. A3.

26 Gardiner, *History of the Commonwealth and Protectorate* i, 57; Abbott ed., *Writings and Speeches* ii, 75; Worden, *The Rump Parliament*, p. 195.

27 P.R.O., SP25/62, 355, 374, 379, 642.

28 P.R.O., SP25/63, 32.

29 *Ibid.*, 540.

30 P.R.O., SP25/62, 355; SP25/64, 502; C. H. Firth and R. S. Rait eds, *Acts and Ordinances of the Interregnum* (3 vols, 1911) ii, 188–9.

31 P.R.O., SP25/16, 42; SP18/15, 9 and 10.

32 *CSPD 1651*, p. 252.

33 *CSPD 1651–52*, pp. 216, 316.

34 P.R.O., SP25/29, 78; SP25/40, 50, 81; *CSPD 1651–52*, pp. 4, 316, 412, 505, 593, 615, 620.

35 P.R.O., SP25/63, 176; cf. SP25/64, 415, 480.

36 P.R.O., SP25/63, 176, 211, 242–3.

37 P.R.O., SP25/32, 81.

38 P.R.O., SP25/10, 20; SP25/14, 78; SP25/15, 45; SP25/63, 176, 211; SP25/64, 54, 331; SP25/95, 26.

39 J. Nickolls ed., *Original Letters and Papers of State, Addressed to Oliver Cromwell ... 1649–1658* (1743), p. 115 (not dated; spelling modernised); G. S. Dugdale, *Whitehall through the Centuries* (1950), p. 60; R. Hutton, *The Restoration. A Political and Religious History of England and Wales, 1658–1667* (Oxford, 1985), p. 77. Cf. similar incidents such as the destruction of the earl of Essex's funeral monument at Westminster Abbey in 1646.

40 P.R.O., SP25/17, 81; SP25/19, 131; SP25/63, 80; SP25/65, 84.

41 P.R.O., SP25/63, 390.

42 *Ibid.*, 176.

43 Bachrach and Collmer eds, *Huygens' Journal*, p. 65.

44 P.R.O., SP25/9, 68, 90; SP25/15, 45; SP25/16, 16; SP25/17, 80; SP18/15, 11; SP25/63, 176, 486, 538, 580, 608; SP25/64, 26, 409; *CSPD 1649–50*, p. 466; *CSPD 1650*, pp. 221–2; *CSPD 1651*, pp. 3, 7, 219, 463, 466; *CSPD 1651–52*, pp. 41, 120, 175, 231, 349, 365, 395, 462, 494; *CSPD 1653–54*, p. 73; Bachrach and Collmer eds, *Huygens' Journal*, p. 68; G. E. Aylmer, *The State's Servants. The Civil Service of the English Republic, 1649–1660* (1973), pp. 84–5.

45 *CSPD, passim*. Members of Dendy's team often doubled up in more than one capacity. One of his sergeancy assistants was Henry Middleton, noted above as the keeper of the garden at Whitehall. Another, William Spittlehouse, kept the orchard. For the mace of the Council of State see below, chapter 3.

46 P.R.O., SP25/62, 348; SP25/63, 33, 486.

47 P.R.O., SP25/62, 158–9, 403–4; *CSPD 1651*, p. 149.

48 P.R.O, SP25/66, 138.

49 Gardiner, *History of the Great Civil War* iv, 283.

50 Firth and Rait eds, *Acts and Ordinances* ii, 160–8, 546–7.

51 *Ibid.*, p. 160.

52 *Ibid.*, pp. 163, 547.

53 *Ibid.*, p. 160.

54 *A Remonstrance Manifesting the lamentable Miseries of the Creditors and Servants of the late King, Queen and Prince* (London, 23 May 1653). The sale will be considered in more detail in chapter 5.

55 *Ibid.*, p. 9.

56 O. Millar ed., 'The Inventories and Valuations of the King's Goods, 1649–51', *Walpole Society* 43 (Glasgow, 1972); A. MacGregor ed., *The Late King's Goods. Collections, Possessions and Patronage of Charles I in the Light of the Commonwealth Sale Inventories* (Oxford, 1989), p. 16.

57 *Remonstrance ... of the Creditors and Servants*, p. 4.

58 P.R.O., SP28/282, 9; SP18/157, 25; *CSPD 1657–58*, pp. 129, 240.

59 *H.M.C. Seventh Report*, Appendix pp. 88–93.

60 P.R.O., SP25/87, 14; SP25/63 121, 520; SP25/10, 51; SP25/64, 238. Millar ed., 'Inventories', p. 155, for the bust of Severus. It was during the reign of the Severan dynasty that imperial Rome first felt the tensions which ultimately destroyed the empire. *Oxford History of the Classical World* (Oxford, 1993), p. 859.

61 P.R.O., SP25/64, 240.

62 P.R.O., SP25/63, 517; SP25/64, 16, 52, 54, 110; SP25/66, 87.

63 Bachrach and Collmer eds, *Huygens' Journal*, p. 59.

64 P.R.O., SP25/64, 441, 460.

65 *Ibid.*, 110.

66 P.R.O., SP25/96, 8.

67 *CJ* vi, 421, 534, 572; P.R.O., SP25/63, 32; Millar ed., 'Inventories', pp. 327–9.

68 P.R.O., SP25/10, 20; SP25/63, 520; *CSPD 1650*, p. 95.

69 P.R.O., SP25/8, 68; SP25/9, 9; SP25/14, 9; SP25/87, 103, SP25/96, 275; *CJ* vi, 239, 421; *CSPD 1651*, p. 149; Millar ed., 'Inventories', p. 251.

70 *CSPD 1651*, p. 282.

71 P.R.O., SP25/10, 20; SP18/13, 14.

72 Bachrach and Collmer eds, *Huygens' Journal*, pp. 45, 66.

73 P.R.O, SP25/64, 238; Bachrach and Collmer eds, *Huygens' Journal*, p. 60.

74 *Ibid.*, pp. 43–4.

75 P.R.O., SP25/63, 32, 322; SP25/64, 238, 331.

76 P.R.O., SP25/63, 556; Millar ed., 'Inventories', pp. 294–5.

77 *Remonstrance ... of the Creditors and Servants*, p. 6.

78 P.R.O., SP25/8, 25–6; Millar ed., 'Inventories', pp. 220–3.

79 P.R.O., SP25/62, 7, 10; B. Lib., Add. MS 12,098.

80 P.R.O., SP25/8, 25–6; SP25/64, 499; *CJ* vi, 278.

81 *H.M.C. Seventh Report*, Appendix p. 88; Abbott ed., *Writings and Speeches* ii, 494.

82 Millar ed., 'Inventories', p. 54. For Cromwell's assumption of the traditional title see below, chapter 4. It is possible, however, that the note referred either to Charles Fleetwood or to Henry Cromwell.

83 P.R.O., SP28/259, 205–16.

84 Gerald Aylmer, *The King's Servants. The Civil Service of Charles I, 1625–1642* (1961), Appendix pp. 472–5.

85 *CSPD 1651–52*, pp. 33, 248.

86 P.R.O., SP25/63, 33. The bargemen also wore a livery which bore the arms of the Commonwealth. See below, chapter 3.

87 P.R.O., SP25/9, 67, 68; SP25/15, 7; SP25/16, 23; SP25/64, 245; *CSPD 1652–53*, p. 15.

88 Dugdale, *Whitehall*, p. 15, as recorded in Foxe's *Monuments*; *Miseries of the Pallace*, sig. A3.

89 *CSPD 1651*, p. 494. In 1684 a huge fire destroyed most of the palace.

90 P.R.O., SP25/88, 15.

91 P.R.O., SP25/64, 138. See below, chapter 5.

92 However, it is worth noting that Carter was instructed to build a guard house in the Tilt Yard 'for the better accommodating the soldiery who attend upon the service of Whitehall', which was supposedly the forerunner of Horse Guards. Dugdale, *Whitehall*, p. 57.

93 P.R.O., SP25/88, 58–9; *Remonstrance ... of the Creditors and Servants*, p. 4.

94 B. Lib., Harleian MS 162, fo. 4*v.

95 John Adamson, 'Chivalry and Political Culture in Caroline England', in Sharpe and Lake eds, *Culture and Politics*, p. 188.

96 See below, chapter 2.

97 Firth and Rait eds, *Acts and Ordinances* ii, 165.

98 P.R.O., SP25/64, 246; SP25/96, 124.

99 P.R.O., SP25/96, 246; Dugdale, *Whitehall*, p. 14.

100 P.R.O., SP25/64, 238; *H.M.C. Seventh Report*, Appendix p. 91

101 Millar ed., 'Inventories', pp. 66, 72, 190, 265, 267, 272, 316, 327–8.

102 B. Lib., Add. MS 29,547, fo. 28.

103 G. F. Warner and J. P. Gilson eds, *Catalogue of Western Manuscripts in the Old Royal and King's Collections in the British Museum* (4 vols, 1921) i, xxiii.

104 *Ibid.*, xxii, xxiv; P.R.O., SP18/16, 56; Spalding ed., *The Diary of Bulstrode Whitelocke*, p. 243; John Dury, *The Reformed Librarie Keeper* (1650).

105 See below, chapter 3.

106 *Mercurius Politicus* 4–25 July 1650, pp. 74, 83, 108.

107 *Ibid.*, 14–21 April 1653, p. 2377.

108 *CSPD 1649–50*, p. 145; *CSPD 1651*, pp. 52–3, 57, 70, 142.

109 Bachrach and Collmer eds, *Huygens' Journal*, p. 66.

110 P.R.O., SP25/62, 341–2, 351–2.

111 P.R.O., SP25/15, 45; SP25/16, 43; SP25/62, 460, 527, 542, 641; SP25/63, 80, 127.

112 MacGregor ed., *The Late King's Goods*, pp. 21–2 n.; B. Lib., Lansdown MS 736.

113 P.R.O., SP25/15, 77; *Miseries of the Pallace*, sig. A2.

114 P.R.O., SP25/8, 36, 45, 80; SP25/14, 13; SP25/63, 29, 31, 80; SP25/64, 188, 245.

115 P.R.O., SP25/8, 35; SP25/63, 31; SP25/64, 98, 118, 122. For Spring Garden as a popular summertime resort see Bachrach and Collmer eds, *Huygens' Journal*, p. 108.

116 P.R.O., SP25/63, 331.

117 *CSPD 1651*, pp. 158, 396.

118 P.R.O., SP25/63, 176, 580; Latham and Matthews eds, *Diary of Samuel Pepys* i, 26.

119 *CSPD 1652–53*, pp. 246, 273.

120 P.R.O., SP25/66, 518.

121 P.R.O., SP25/10, 37; SP25/63, 127, 193, 557; SP25/64, 128; *CSPD 1649–50*, pp. 182, 303, 398.

122 P.R.O., SP25/62, 184.

123 P.R.O., SP25/64, 495.

124 P.R.O., SP25/62, 158–9, 403–4.

125 P.R.O., SP25/65, 267.

126 P.R.O., SP25/94, 394–5.

127 P.R.O., SP25/62, 193, 517, 600; SP25/63, 33, 52.

128 P.R.O., SP25/17, 81; SP25/62, 184, 547; *CSPD 1651*, pp. 187, 209.

129 P.R.O., SP25/63, 19; SP25/94, 437.

130 P.R.O., SP25/64, 26.

131 P.R.O., SP25/8, 35, 36, 45, 80; SP25/14, 13; SP25/63, 31, 331; SP25/64, 98, 118, 122.

132 *A Declaration collected out of the Journals of both Houses of Parliament* (13–20 December 1648), p. 20; Stearns, *The Strenuous Puritan*, p. 329.

133 Bachrach and Collmer eds, *Huygens' Journal*, pp. 42, 65.

134 P.R.O., SP25/11, 32; SP25/62, 565; SP25/63, 193, 331; *CSPD 1651*, pp. 396, 466.

135 Gardiner, *History of the Commonwealth and Protectorate* ii, 95.

136 J. Newman, 'Inigo Jones and the Politics of Architecture', in Sharpe and Lake eds, *Culture and Politics*, p. 233.

137 *Travels of Cosmo III, Grand Duke of Tuscany, through England, during the Reign of Charles II* (London, 1821), quoted by MacGregor ed., *The Late King's Goods*, p. 22 n.

138 R. A. Brown, H. M. Colvin and A. J. Taylor, *The King's Works* iv (1982), 304.

139 Roy Sherwood, *The Court of Oliver Cromwell* (second edition, Cambridge, 1989).

140 *Miseries of the Pallace*, sig. A2.

141 *Whitehall's Petition to the Parliament that he may enjoy his former Priviledges* ([22 June] 1659).

Chapter 2

Spectacle

THE previous chapter showed how Whitehall was used by the Rump to provide the new republic with the physical locale of a court, and that appearances clearly did matter to members of the regime, their supporters and their detractors. This chapter considers further aspects of republican presentation and representation. It looks at how individual Rumpers had their own images recorded in oils, stone and metal as an introduction to the wider question of representing the regime. By looking at hitherto neglected aspects of the public ceremonial appearance of the state in all its forms after the revolution, it describes a collective political self-consciousness which stood in the place of regal pomp, fulfilling the objectives of political spectacle at least as well as the old order had.[1] Regal pageantry had served as a vehicle of royal charisma. The earl of Newcastle asked, 'what protects you kings more than ceremony ... Aye, even the wisest ... shall shake off his wisdom and shake for fear of it, for this is the mist is cast before us and masters the commonwealth.'[2] If anything, the parliamentary Commonwealth marked a return to this attitude of wilful mystification. Charles I paraded publicly only twice during his seventeen years: Rumpers went on show on at least eight occasions in less than one-third of that time.[3]

Commonwealth funerals and processions may not have impressed contemporaries – it is no easier to gauge their impact than it is with earlier periods – but they have certainly not impressed previous historians. There was no real innovation, it has been argued – spectacle continued to 'focus the attention of the audience on one man – admittedly often a dead one'. Cromwellian entries virtually mimicked their royal equivalent. Moreover,

despite a rich heritage of civic and corporate pageantry, independent of the pageantry of royalty, the Commonwealth saw no state or civic pageantry at all, and even its spectacles were of a limited kind. Further, there was never any attempt to deploy the republican images of classical antiquity nor even those of Venice or the United Provinces.[4]

As will become clear, the first claim as to the absence of state pageantry is incorrect. And in the next chapter we shall see that the Commonwealth in fact had no need to import signs and symbols, having invented its own. For now, the main focus is on the contention that ultimately the failure of the Rump's efforts showed that 'there was, perhaps, no convenient way to advertise the merits of a political collectivity'.[5] This chapter argues that, between them, the politicians and soldiers of the Rump scripted and directed spectacles which did precisely that, which affirmed the practical fusion of civil and military arms of the regime, which sought to impress both domestic and foreign audiences, and which aimed to replace the gorgeous mythology of regal authority with a more forthright expression of the grandeur of the state.

I

Commonwealth history has always had its stock-in-trade of cameo performances – thus Sir Arthur Haselrige with his coach-and-six, attended by page boys with silver buckles on their shoes, or John Lambert's well attested dandyism.[6] There is rarely much importance attached to such matters beyond their satirical potential. Hugh Peters's friends joked that his grandeur made him the new archbishop of Canterbury; less kindly opinion derided the pretensions of the jumped-up revolutionaries, or abhorred the shameless display of wanton rebels.[7]

But appearances did matter in more serious ways. In the sixteenth century Thomas Elyot wrote that 'we be men and not aungels, wherefore we know nothing but by outward significations'.[8] People 'read' clothing, for example, as a positive public statement. In 1652 Henry Ireton was buried at Westminster Abbey. Colonel John Hutchinson, who was related to the dead commander, felt snubbed when Cromwell failed to invite him to be one of the pall-bearers. At the funeral he purposely dressed in brightly coloured clothes to draw attention to this neglect.[9] Mrs Lambert wrote from Scotland in the summer of 1651 asking to be sent a yard of 'French lawne ... for I have nothing to weare about my neck and I dare not go bare for fear of offending tender saints'.[10] It is not clear how these 'tender saints' reacted to the gallant appearance of Mrs Lambert's husband, who had a pronounced taste for the fashionable.[11]

Appearance was one way in which the tensions between conservatives and radicals were dramatised during the revolution. But there was no clear-cut contrast between radicals and conservatives. In December 1650 Major General Harrison upbraided his fellow MPs for the ostentation of their appearance at the time of the Spanish ambassador's mission, warning that 'now the nations sent to them, they should labour to shine before them in wisdom, piety, righteousness and justice, and not in gold and silver and worldly bravery, which did not become saints'. This they took to heart, according to Mrs

Hutchinson, turning up at the audience in the Parliament House on 26 December soberly attired. The Major General 'came that day in a scarlet coat and cloak, both laden with gold and silver lace, and the coat so covered with clinquant that scarcely could one discern the ground, and in this glittering habit set himself just under the Speaker's chair'.[12]

Honest russet may have become one of the idealised images of the good old cause, but it was not a style favoured by commissioned officers, even those with roots in the radical van of the revolution. Immersion in the martial culture of the republic worked a conversion on some individuals strange to other men's eyes. In 1651 William Coddington returned to America as the Commonwealth's governor of Rhode Island and Connecticut. He had been away for two years, and occasional references in his American correspondence refer to the appearance of things in England under the republic. On one occasion, after delivering a letter from John Winthrop senior, governor of Massachusetts, to his son, Major Stephen Winthrop, Coddington remarked that 'we met at a book-binder shop ... I knew him not, for he was in scarlet etc., till I heard him named'.[13] Thus one American, returning to the homeland, left behind the puritan affectation of plain dress and adopted the garb of the military gallant.

These cameos and tales may seem quite peripheral. However, there is more to them than mere illustrative colour or curious verisimilitude. Given the widespread attention to appearances, it is not surprising to find that *representation* of appearance was just as significant for some republican governors. Politicians' self-consciousness about status and reputation is the preserve of neither left or right, old or new men. Recent criticism of a hard-and-fast 'court–country' polarity has demonstrated that royalists and parliamentarians patronised the same artists, and were rendered in the same styles.[14] The portraitist's art did not depend on royalists for its survival after the revolution. A number of the new political leaders were painted by the likes of Peter Lely and Robert Walker. Walker's well-known portrait of Cromwell was turned out in copy from his studio for several years.[15] Statues and busts were made of both Fairfax and Cromwell.[16] During the 1650s England's greatest miniaturist, Samuel Cooper, established his name and reputation in the service of the new courtiers. In seventeenth-century Europe miniatures were private tokens or gifts, and they were also a defining element of the Renaissance court sensibility, and in this sense they have been compared with other aspects of baroque illusionism such as ceiling paintings.[17] Although the portrait was the acceptable face of painting in the eyes of men whose Protestant sensibilities were offended by the superfluity of narrative or genre painting, this particular form might not be thought quite the medium for men who supposedly wanted to reverse the cultural tendencies of Stuart decadence. Still, whilst those with a more pronounced taste for the *avant-garde* continued to patronise miniaturists, they often had to queue. In 1650 Miles Woodshawe told his master, Lord Conway, that 'I spoke to Mr [Samuel] Cooper, the painter, who desires you to excuse him one month longer as he has some work to finish for Lord General Cromwell and his family'.[18]

There were a number of miniaturists at work in London in the 1640s and 1650s. Samuel Cooper was the most important ('Van Dyck in little' as far as contemporaries were concerned), but there were also his master and uncle, John Hoskins, his brother, Alexander Cooper, and a number of followers after the Samuel Cooper style, notably Thomas Flatman, the Gibson family and Richard Gibson's daughter, Susan Penelope Rosse.[19] Cooper painted Colonel Robert Lilburne in 1640, thereafter numerous parliamentarians, including Henry Ireton, George Fleetwood, Robert third Lord Brooke (all in the 1640s), Fairfax (1649), Charles Fleetwood (1651) and William Lenthall (1652).[20] The portrait medal also found considerable popularity among military and civilian members of the republican elite. The secretaries, Scobell and Thurloe, the Speaker, the Lords Commisioners of the Great Seal, Sir James Harrington and numerous soldiers, from John Lambert to John Lilburne, all had commemorative medals struck.[21] The design of that commissioned by Henry Ireton combined a portrait on one side with an attempt to justify some of the most horrific passages of the British wars on the other. It depicted graphically the destruction of the Irish, a soldier firing the roof of a cottage whilst a battle rages in the background, under the motto *Iustitia necessitasq[ue] iubet* ('Justice and necessity commanded it'). The Lord Deputy appeared to be making an effort at self-exculpation, perhaps in the eyes of mainland radicals, or of those in the army itself who expressed serious reservations about the savage treatment meted out to Irish rebels.[22]

This representational milieu is one context in which we can place a fascinating proposal to commemorate the civil wars, in a series of paintings, made some time in 1652–53 by three leading figures in the world of English and European art, Peter Lely, George Geldorp and Sir Balthazar Gerbier.[23] They lobbied the Rump 'Concerning the representing, in Oil, Pictures of all the memorable Achievements since the Parliaments first sitting'.[24] They proposed erecting at Whitehall a large-scale visual depiction of the military achievements of the parliamentary regime, based explicitly on the famous suite of hangings, commissioned by Lord Howard of Effingham, depicting the defeat of the Spanish Armada in 1588, which, as we have seen, hanging in the old Lords' chamber, provided the graphic backdrop to the conduct of aggressive republican diplomacy.

The premise of the proposal was that 'it hath been practised in most parts of the world to expose such objects unto the people's view, whereby the memorable acts of their general welfare, or those of their deliverances from some eminent danger may be extant'. The mural which they proposed to have hung in 'the great Room, formerly called the Banqueting-house' would depict battles and sieges of the British wars, from 1642 to 1651. Its would be sur- rounded by a border of portraits of the military commanders who won the victories. Such a mural would be made 'for the satisfaction of the present time, as also for posterity, and for an encouragement to all such as are in authority and command'. In similar vein Ben Jonson had remarked of Rubens's ceiling paintings of King James's apotheosis, executed earlier in the century at the Banqueting House (ironically procured through the agency of Sir Balthazar Gerbier, a friend and associate of Rubens), 'Look up to read the king in all his actions.'[25]

But the consortium went further than proposing a grand celebration of the founding and securing of the republic. For, 'as the great Room at Whitehall is very spacious' and could accommodate a number of large paintings, they proposed that

> there also be placed therein the representation of the [whole assembly of the Parliament], by [whose] directions the said great Achievements have been wrought. The said representation of the whole assembly in one large piece to be placed at the upper end of the great Room, ... as also the portraitures of the several members of the Council of State in another great piece, to be placed at the other end of the said great Room, both of them being adorned with a comportment answerable to the saying in the 85 Psalm, ver. 11, viz 'Truth shall spring out of the earth and Right- eousness shall look down from Heaven, etc.' All which may be most completely performed by choice Artists, expert both in the representing of personages, battles and landscapes.[26]

Gerbier, Lely and Geldorp's proposal was never put into effect. It has been convincingly suggested that the mere idea of such a permanent and public monument to the rebellion against the king was enough to put off the more conservative-minded majority in the house. The commemoration of 'all the memorable Achievements since the Parliament's first sitting' was an issue in itself. The idea of depicting the achievements of the Long Parliament as a historically continuous whole may have seemed too much of a distortion after war had split it in two, and after the experiences of 1647 and 1648–49. It was certainly not an idea designed to promote the goal of healing the breaches which had riven the parliamentary camp since the beginning of the wars.[27] Few MPs would have been won over by the suggestion that they pay out of their own pockets to save the public the expense.[28] The proposal took little account either of practicalities, such as the turnover in the Council of State, the composition of which changed every year,[29] or indeed of politics. If the scheme could be counted on to do little to promote national unity, it also made a highly insensitive incursion into the realm of the future settlement. The status of the civilian assembly which it would have depicted was far too contentious for the idea to commend itself within revolutionary circles.

Nevertheless, the proposal resonates strongly with the visual priorities of the regime. It probably had at least some appeal to a group of men many of whom were not the slightest bit averse to being depicted in oils. As we shall see in the next chapter, they had made just such a group portrait the centre-piece of their public iconography. The Parliament had published histories of itself since 1642, and had accounts of its army's victories read out in churches all over the country.[30] It even had prints made depicting those victories.[31] There certainly were depictions in oils of the battles of the civil wars in existence (although when Hugh Peters showed a pair he claimed to have commissioned to Lodewijck Huygens and friends the Dutchman recorded that 'we had great difficulty in looking at them without laughing'!).[32] The wars were already dramatically commemorated at Westminster, where hundreds of Scottish regimental colours captured in battle at Preston, Dunbar and Worcester hung proudly in the great hall until 1660.[33] It is quite possible that this particular project failed because events conspired against it.

But, if the scheme never became reality, some of the spectacle which surrounded Commonwealth politics did have a group portrait quality, provid-ing a succession of *tableaux vivant* which, rather than looking back to the founding of the republic, reflected the current pretensions to grandeur of the republican rulers. The revolution had been deplored on the Continent not least for 'those horrid things done against the only visible authority that is left among you in the kingdom and the unparalleled affronts done to them and the City of London'.[34] After the revolution, radical voices urged that 'all costly pomp and state hereafter be suspended until the desolations and spoils of the poor people be repaired'.[35] But spectacle was an expected part of any state's self-legitimisation. After 1649, however much radicals might complain,[36] it was still the case that for the Commonwealth 'to avoid all forms of display would be to deny the authority of the new regime to act as all states acted'.[37]

II

The Rump used ceremony to lend it the 'occasional' aspect required of any early modern regime. Between 1649 and 1653 the regime mounted a number of set-piece spectacles, including banquets, state funerals and the public cel-ebration of Cromwell's victories on his return to London in 1650 and 1651.[38] Less well known but equally important were the occasions made out of ship-launching on the Thames, military reviews in and around London, and an honorary degree ceremony held at Oxford in May 1649. It is also seldom stressed just how often ritual was used by the Rump to dignify political processes, most notably its diplomatic relations.

Any early modern court included an international element made up of residential or visiting diplomats. This was no different during the rule of the

Rump. The post-revolutionary government was quick to consider the quality of its future relations with foreign states. In March 1649 Lords Commissioners Whitelocke and Lisle, Sir Henry Vane junior, Viscount Lisle, the earl of Denbigh and Henry Marten were appointed to a committee of the Rump's first Council of State to consider 'what alliances this Crown had with foreign states', whether to continue them and on what terms. But even before then the government was looking into the ritual aspects of its executive function as the body responsible for conducting foreign relations. The question of diplomatic protocol first arose as the Rump sought to establish a *modus vivendi* with the foreign dignitaries in London at the time of the revolution. After Charles's death it was 'commonly reported and believed' in London that the French and Spanish representatives had been ordered to withdraw from England 'with instructions not to take any ceremonious farewell'.[39] But other diplomats were less concerned to snub the Commonwealth publicly in this way.

The day before the king's execution Parliament had received the extraordinary embassy of the United Provinces sent to plead for mercy at the behest of the condemned man's son and heir. The urgency of their mission meant that the Dutch envoys had dispensed with ceremony.[40] After its failure, with the king's execution, the tone changed, and the regime took pains to treat the representatives with 'civility'. Pauw was dined by the Lord President and, according to one no doubt touchy royalist informant, reciprocated the respect he was shown 'somewhat too ceremoniously and cheerfully'.[41] Parliament decided it would be fitting to mark the embassy's eventual departure by dispatching Oliver Cromwell, Sir Henry Vane junior, Thomas Harrison, Henry Marten, Philip Skippon, Sir Henry Mildmay and Michael Livesey to wish Pauw a safe journey and to present him with a gift of books selected from the royal library.[42] A few weeks later, Parliament was informed of the Prince Elector's decision to leave England, and considered whether 'the usual civilities' ought to be extended to him at his departure.[43]

Within a week of the Council of State's first sitting it had set up a committee (composed of the earls of Denbigh and Salisbury, Henry Marten, Sir James Harrington, Sir Henry Mildmay, Robert Wallop, Luke Robinson and Sir Gilbert Pickering) which was to look into the conventions of ambassadorial dignity and precedence, and which was advised to seek the opinion of John Selden.[44] Although apparently unable to take advantage of the antiquarian's wisdom, the Council did have at hand the practical experience of many of its members, as well as the expertise of Charles I's master of ceremonies, Sir Oliver Fleming, who had served Parliament in a similar capacity in the 1640s. Since the revolution Fleming, Cromwell's cousin, had showed no sign of wanting out, and he served as an important diplomat in his own right throughout the Commonwealth, with a particularly well developed sense of the regime's strengths.[45] In February 1649 he was in charge of seeing to the preparations for the Dutchmen's departure.[46] In April he submitted a report to the Council of State on the subject of how the republic ought to conduct its diplomatic business with foreign nations.[47]

Fleming considered the way the Commonwealth should seek to present itself to its European neighbours as well as detailing the manner in which their representatives should be received at Westminster. He suggested the provision of state barges and coaches and the appropriate livery for them, discussed seating arrangements for parliamentary receptions of dignitaries, as well as the question of how best to control access to ambassadors. Interestingly, he also suggested that some of the royal wardrobe be set aside to supply the state's decorative ceremonial needs. Most of his report is taken up with examples of how other 'free states' comported themselves in the conduct of their foreign affairs. Principally he concentrated on Venice and Switzerland, omitting the United Provinces, whose practices were 'sufficiently known'. The implication was perhaps that the Commonwealth would more naturally adopt the mannerisms of an existing republican regime than those of a monarchy. He did not consider examples of the protocols observed at the courts of European monarchs, as they were so similar to those used in England 'during the regal government'.

There were clear reservations in Fleming's mind on the subject of certain republican protocols – for example, he could not commend the Swiss practice of heavy drinking at diplomatic receptions, 'which causes aching heads next morning to those that are not used to such cup skirmishes'. And there may be an implicit reservation about Dutch practices, since the existing Orange supremacy at The Hague at the time, and its natural alliance with Stuart interests, made the United Provinces a slightly ambivalent object of English republican affections.[48]

Fleming's report gives an interesting insight into post-revolutionary political culture, indicating the awareness in England of the importance of maintaining or rewriting the familiar fictions of political theatre which were so important to diplomatic relations. Looking at the theatre which surrounded England's diplomatic relations under the Commonwealth, it would certainly seem that Rumpers needed little reminder of the importance of protocol and ceremony. And it is clear from the frequency with which they found themselves arranging the formalities for the reception of foreign ambassadors that the rulers of Europe rapidly came to appreciate the importance of wooing the Commonwealth. In its first two years the Rump remained isolated, with no state recognising its existence, whilst its first tentative steps towards diplomatic relations ended in the murder of two representatives, Isaac Dorislaus in the Netherlands and Anthony Ascham, its first proper ambassador abroad, in Spain. But whatever shock waves the regicide sent through the Continent, by the end of 1652 most major European powers had acknowledged the supremacy of the Commonwealth government in the affairs of England and its empire, and had extended some kind of formal recognition in the form of diplomatic legations.

The process began at the end of 1650, when Philip IV of Spain ordered his ambassador, Cardenas, to recognise the Commonwealth.[49] Accordingly, Cardenas came to Parliament on 26 December that year and was received 'with very great honour'.[50] It was an exciting moment for the republic, and Parliament pulled out all the stops (as did certain individuals such as the commmander-in-chief in England, Major General Thomas Harrison, as we saw above).

The manner of Cardenas's reception at Westminster laid down the basic form of all subsequent receptions of foreign ambassadors. (The audience held a few days later for the Portugese minister who arrived around the same time as Cardenas set down the basic principle for the reception of representatives below ambassadorial rank.) The earl of Salisbury, Sir Henry Mildmay and Sir Peter Wentworth were sent to fetch him from the residence prepared for him at Sir Abraham Williams's house in Westminster in 'the State's owne coach, with the armes thereupon'; the delegation brought Cardenas to the Parliament House, accompanied by 'diverse gentlemen with thirty or forty other coaches'. At the palace of Westminster, two troops of horse 'in compleat armes', and Colonel Berkstead's Tower regiment, 'made a guard for him, through the Palace Yard, and Westminster-hall to the Parliament door'. Arriving at the palace of Westminster, he was escorted to the Court of Wards ('a place prepared and appointed for all Ambassadors, and others under that degree, to withdraw, till the time of Reception and Audience'), where he waited whilst the House was informed of his arrival. Parliament then despatched the serjeant-at-arms, with his mace, to bring him to the House, which he entered flanked by the serjeant and the master of ceremonies. 'The whole flore of the House was covered with a rich Persian carpet, and in the midst of the House, something on one side, stood a very rich chair of state, with cushions and a foot stool.' The ambassador and his attendants entered and approached the bar. Cardenas saluted the Speaker, 'and in a manner every member of the House', then sat, whilst Fleming presented his credentials to the Speaker. After the exchange of salutations, and 'the usuall Ceremony', Cardenas was seated in an armchair placed 'in the midst, with a table before him on which were two velvet cushions, with two others at his feet'.[51]

According to the Venetian ambassador in Spain, after receiving Cardenas, Parliament resolved that all ambassadors of crowned heads would be received in like manner, while those of 'inferior powers were not to enter the House but only to treat with commissioners. They deal in the same way with ministers of kings below the rank of ambassadors.'[52] (As the Rump's treatment of

Dutch representatives was to demonstrate in 1652, the republic did not discriminate against the representatives of non-monarchical states.) The experience of the Portugese minister who arrived around the same time as Cardenas demonstrated the reality of this two-tier ceremonial approach. He was received by a parliamentary committee in the former House of Lords, to and from which he was escorted by the same officials who had accompanied Cardenas from the Court of Wards to the bar of the Commons' House.[53] This became the basic pattern for the reception of all representatives below the rank of ambassador, and as such involved correspondingly less spectacle.[54] Nevertheless, even at this humbler level the regime clearly kept in mind the spectacular imperative, for instance by adorning 'the place called the House of Lords' with the famous tapestry hangings depicting the defeat of the armada in 1588, a clear indication of national strength and prestige; and by seating these lesser representatives in chairs without arm-rests – a small point, but a significant indicator of the lowlier degree of the humble agent.[55]

In terms of press coverage, the Spanish mission and its reception were pushed into the background by events in Scotland, where Edinburgh Castle had just fallen to Cromwell's besieging forces. In certain quarters this was cause for patriotic celebration.[56] Cardenas's reception was noted not so much for its splendour as for the fact that he had been induced to address the Rump in the manner they themselves had chosen, a line followed by most newsbooks.[57]

A year later, when the Dutch sent an embassy to Westminster, the press paid far more attention to detail. Again the embassy coincided with another, that of the Swede, Spiering, Queen Christina's representative at The Hague, whose mission was effectively to counterbalance any possibility of Anglo-Dutch amity which might prejudice Swedish Baltic interests. News came from The Hague that the Dutch and Swedes 'not only strive, who shall come soonest, but vie who shall fayrest. Monsieur Spiering's equipage is scarlet with gold and silver lace; ours [the Dutch] about 120 persons in gray liveries.'[58] Nedham's correspondent added that 'To shew their confidence in you, Monsieur Schaep brings his wife with him, and Monsieur Catz his daughter', perhaps a sign of trust in the republicans' awareness of how to behave in the presence of high-ranking ladies.[59]

The Dutch and Swedish parties arrived at the same time, taking and returning cannon salutes from the English shore, and landing at Gravesend, where they were met by Sir Oliver Fleming (having been greeted in the first instance by the governor of the fort at Tilbury, Colonel Compton). They then passed by water up to Tower Wharf, whence they processed through the City 'in great pomp being accomodated with above forty English Coaches, the richest that of late dayes have been seen together in England'. They were thus brought to Westminster, to Sir Abraham Williams's house in Old Palace Yard, the usual accommodation provided by the Commonwealth for visiting dignitaries. There 'they were triumphantly entertained'.[60]

A few days later the Dutch had their audience. The earl of Salisbury, Sir John Danvers and Sir Henry Mildmay accompanied them to the House, and they were also attended by Fleming, about thirty gentlemen of their retinue, a like number of 'their Laquies' and 'many Gentlemen that attended our Councel of State'. A double row of pikemen and musketeers stood as guard of honour along the route from Williams's house to the Court of Wards, and a troop of horse was drawn up at the palace. The ambassadors were attended from the Court of Wards to the Commons chamber in regular fashion, flanked by Fleming and the serjeant 'with the Golden Mace on his shoulder'. For the occasion 'the Parliament-house was beautified with extraordinary rich hangings, and very rich Chaires and Foot-Clothes, set on the North part of the House for the said Ambassadors'.[61]

In May 1652 it was the turn of a Danish extraordinary embassy to be received by the republic. This was a particularly sensitive moment, as the royal house of Denmark was related to the Stuart dynasty. English trade interests were also closely tied up with the handling of relations with the Danes and Dutch. The Venetian, Paulucci, described the formalities of what had become routine procedure. The Danes made a 'state entry' into London, and were met by a parliamentary deputation in their state coaches. The party proceeded to the embassy's Westminster lodgings, followed by a convoy of other coaches.[62] Newsbooks reported similarly the arrival of Rosencranz and Reed and the convoy of coaches which brought them to Abraham Williams's. But, as to accounts of the reception itself, events again limited the amount of space deemed necessary by editors. The clash in the Downs between Blake and Tromp overshadowed the official reception, which received universally laconic treatment, and was largely described in the formulaic manner with which the newswriters had become accustomed to dealing with such occasions.[63] Uncommonly, the Danes had subsequent audiences in Parliament.[64] (A Venetian commentator later remarked on an 'extraordinary' audience granted to the Spanish ambassador in December 1652, saying that Parliament 'usually only receives the foreign ambassadors on their arrival and departure. On other occasions, unless there be some exceptional reason, it refers them to the Council of State.'[65])

Around the same time a Dutch deputation made an emergency trip to London to try to forestall impending hostilities at sea. Almost the only thing said of this hurried and abortive piece of diplomacy was that the Dutchmen had arrived and received audience 'very formally', although it seems their arrival had been at least as grand as any seen hitherto, involving state coaches and long convoys bringing them up to the usual Westminster residence. The laconic reporting of the audience granted at this time may have reflected hostility to the Dutchmen, whom the government wished to portray as the aggressors in the coming war, and it is interesting to note that the only aspect of their embassy given detailed attention was the manner of their departure. This involved a leave-taking ceremony which repeated exactly the dance steps of the official audience given to ambassadors on their arrival at Westminster. Thereafter they went in state coaches to the riverside, the Commonwealth's barges conveying them from the Tower Stairs, twelve miles down river, where they took ship for home.[66]

Republican diplomatic ceremony reached its height with the arrival of a Portugese mission in September 1652, thanks to the splendour with which Rodriguez de Sa e Menezes, count of Peneguiao, made his official *entrée*. Having once paid the price for helping the Commonwealth's enemies, the Portugese must have been fearful of the growing amity between England and Spain, which had already seen Blake destroy the French ships sent to relieve the siege of Dunkirk. Accordingly, they went to some lengths to make the most of the considerable distance that still remained between London and Madrid over the rights of Protestants trading in Spain, in an effort to get on the right side of the Rumpers.[67] Paulucci anticipated a very grand show, as the ambassador was 'of the highest rank and fortune'. For their part, the rulers of the Commonwealth naturally took great pleasure in the prospect of so honourable a visitation.

After making land, the count was lodged in a mansion 'prepared for him by Parliament' outside London. This may have been Sion House, near Brainford, used as a stopping-off point by the Dutch on their departure in June. But it was possibly Greenwich palace, where *The Perfect Diurnall* reported he had dined before taking to the Thames. Arriving at the Tower, he was met by Fleming with forty to fifty state and private coaches. Making his entry into the capital, the count travelled in a Commonwealth coach, accompanied by two MPs. They were preceded by twenty Portugese attendants in rich liveries on horseback, and three coaches, one with its roof let down to show off the silver and gilt plate the ambassador had brought with him, the coachmen wearing velvet and silver passment; twelve packhorses carried the count's luggage, all under rich coverings of crimson velvet which bore his arms in silver. The whole entourage was followed by sixty coaches, 'forming a fine show'. This level of grandeur was unprecedented and the embassy 'was correspondingly popular'. The Rumpers received the count 'with all possible honour, to the increasing vexation and jealousy of the Catholic ambassador [Cardenas]'.[68] They also defrayed his expenses for three days out of the public purse prior to his official reception in Parliament.[69]

The Venetian account claimed this was the first full state entry made by an ambassador, 'and consequently the first to be observed'. This may mean that it was the first time republican diplomacy had attained the kind of spectacular heights it had reached under the rule of the Crown. However, in terms of popular reception, it is interesting to note the virtual absence of interest in the usual formalities of the reception in the House which the press showed. The count's entry was made, wrote one reporter, 'with such magnificence as I have not seen the like', and his entourage was described in some detail in another newsbook. His parliamentary reception was 'honourable and magnificent', and he 'went in greater state than any ambassador that came yet to the Parliament'.[70] Yet the press tended to omit all details of the latter occasion, not even employing the stock formula about being conducted from the Court of Wards by Fleming and the serjeant. Interestingly, one newswriter commented that 'that which wise men do look upon was not the show, but the busines of his Embassy'.[71]

After the execution of the king, all Europe was shocked; after the victory at Worcester and the assertion of English maritime power, all Europe was humbled. But the English Commonwealth also sought to make a more civil impression on European powers. Hence the brilliant polemic of Milton, but also the care and cash expended on presenting Commonwealth representatives to the courts of Europe. At the end of 1650 the French agent, Croulle, commended the English civilians to Mazarin for their lack of pomp and pretension.[72] However, the embassy of Lord Chief Justice Oliver St John and Walter Strickland to the United Provinces in the spring of 1651 demonstrates how seriously the regime took the task of holding forth the Commonwealth's potency by means of show.

The ambassadors could expect a mixed reception. The States General was in The Hague, an Orangist bastion. However, with the decline of the Orange ascendancy after 1648, and the death of stadtholder William II in 1650, Holland's power grew correspondingly. Hearing that an embassy from the fledgling republic was intended, the states of Holland and Zeeland persuaded the Great Convocation to resolve to give them an honourable reception, and in the weeks before it left English newswriters confidently expected that the embassy would be received 'with as much honour and respect as the Ambassadours of any Prince whatsoever'.[73]

In the previous autumn, the funeral of the Prince of Orange had been marred by a violent clash over precedence between the retinues of the Duke of York and a Portugese prince. Nedham mused that 'One would have thought sorrow should have choaked the humour, but that we know in Princes, Pride takes the place of all other Passions'.[74] The manner of the Commonwealth's embassy reminds us, however, that humility was not necessarily one of the virtues of a free state either. In the context of Dorislaus's bloody end, it was imperative for the mission to make a big impact, as much for its own safety as anything else. But also at stake was the honour and repute of the regicide regime. Having decided to despatch the embassy, Parliament ordered that it was to be sent 'with due respect to the honour of this Commonwealth'.[75] £1,000 was advanced for the ambassadors' preparations, £3,000 provided in cash and the like sum in bills of exchange, and £2,000 spent on silver plate tableware which bore the arms of the Commonwealth.[76] 'The young English Republic was resolved on doing its embassy bravely.'[77]

The retinue set out from London by state barge to Gravesend on 8 March 1651. When it set sail a few days later, with no fewer than three ships to carry all the baggage along with a state coach, two frigates carried the ambassadors and their three preachers, Nye, Dingley and Goodwin, and nearly 250 men, forty of whom 'were gentlemen that came out of England out of respect to the persons of the Embassadors'.[78] Some of their would-be companions were a lot less desirable, the Council issuing a warrant on the 10th for the arrest of a London pickpocket gang 'who endeavoured to go over with the Lords Ambassadors'.[79]

The party made quite an impression on the Dutch. News of the magnificence of the embassy soon spread from Rotterdam, where the ambassadors first came ashore. After their arrival at The Hague, crowds gathered to watch their procession through the principal streets of the city in twenty-five Dutch carriages flanked by Englishmen in livery, each carrying a drawn rapier.[80] The retinue was far too vast to be accommodated in the residence set aside for the ambassadors ('which', Nedham complained, 'is very mean for such a receit, though the entertainment in all other particulars were very noble'[81]), and the larger part had to seek private lodgings. At the residence, the ambassadors were banqueted on their first night in the company of a representative from each of the six provinces, and every night thereafter dined with two members of the States General, who 'entertained my Lords Ambassadors very civilly and gallantly'.[82]

On the day of their audience with the States General (20 March) the retinue really turned on the style. Nedham reported with delight: 'For my Lords Gentlemen, who were all as brave as the sun, the like hath not been seen for these many years. The French Ambassadour's retinue is not to be compared to their Lordships: the Dutch blessed themselves to see so much gallantry.'[83] St John and Strickland came garbed in black velvet, St John wearing a mantle of the same, lined with cloth of gold, and a waistcoat adorned with tinsel loops. A gilt rapier hung at his side and his broad-rimmed 'puritan' hat was set off with a band of diamonds.[84]

At their reception by the Great Assembly, its president thanked the English Parliament 'for haveinge honored them with their first embassage, and with an Embassage soe splendid as this was'. At this early stage, the ambassadors felt confident enough to inform the Council of State back at Whitehall that they could win agreement on the idea of a closer union, which proposal, the manner in which it was made and 'ye greatnesse of ye Retinue you sent us over with' had, they claimed, made their embassy 'of general acceptation'.[85]

As it turned out, there was far less 'acceptation' on the part of the Dutch state than there was recrimination on the part of the community of aggrieved exiles at The Hague and their Orangist confederates. In a piece of its own pointed political theatricality, the Stuart retinue daily rode slowly past the ambassadors' official residence, glaring in silence at the house 'in a manner to encourage the rabble'.[86] Their many enemies showered the Commonwealthsmen with invective and worse throughout their stay. There were assassination attempts. On occasion, there were moments of relief. The States of Holland gave the ambassadors sumptuous entertainment at Amsterdam. Nedham reported that many of the young blades of the retinue were trotting about the country with an eye to the fashions of the place. On a day off, the ambassadors went for a turn round a park to take the air in two coaches-and-six attended by another two-horse coach, a dozen horsemen and twenty to thirty footmen.[87]

This kind of safety in numbers should not be taken as proof of a great sense of republican dignity. And the dangers to which the Commonwealth's diplomats constantly fell prey are testimony to the fact that no amount of decorum would erase the stain of regicidal guilt for which many felt they must suffer. But that is hardly the point. Republican officials themselves clearly thought it was important to act with a gravity and grandeur befitting the supremacy of the regime they served, and the legitimacy of that regime's claim to authority rested at least in part on the notion of an honourable manner in public dealing. 'The Honour of Parliament' and its preservation and enhancement was an idea which saw wide currency in republican government during the Commonwealth. Conjured by the Rump itself, the Councils of State, parliamentary committees, the army, individual soldiers, suitors and writers, the honour of Parliament was again a concept not alien to Englishmen before the Commonwealth, but one which the experience of the Interregnum added new depth to.[88]

Newsbooks generally bear this out. Occasionally, one must speculate as to how much people like Nedham, or indeed Commonwealth ambassadors themselves, sought to exaggerate, or at least accentuate, the respect shown by foreign powers, and we can never know how much of an impression the *gravitas* of the Commonwealthsmen made on either ambassadors or, more importantly, the wider public. However, when dealing with questions of representation through literary sources, one is dealing with the same materials from which the vast majority of the contemporary 'audience' consumed spectacle. What is important is that spectacle was deemed worthy of the not inconsiderable coverage the contemporary press gave it.

Some negative impressions do survive. In February 1652 the Venetian Senate first considered making its own approaches to the English government, 'which has now established and consolidated itself in authority and considerable power', seeing the advantage in striking up 'a good understanding' with so formidable a sea power. Accordingly, it ordered its ambassador at Paris, Morosini, to send his secretary, Lorenzo Paulucci, to England. On the pretext of hiring ships and negotiating levies, Paulucci was to strike up a relationship with leading republican politicians, and to take note of the manner in which foreign representatives were treated and the formalities observed at public audiences in the matter of titles.[89] After experiencing the kind of thumb-twiddling which representatives of lesser states usually had patiently to suffer, he complained of 'punctiliousness', and blamed the delay on the fact that 'the government is new [and] its forms are defective in many respects'.[90] It was in just such terms that the German, Herman Mylius, representative of the count of Oldenburg, complained to John Milton about how long it was taking to complete some basic paperwork. Milton excused his masters by telling Mylius that they were 'mechanics, soldiers, home-grown, strong and bold enough, [but] in public political affairs mostly inexperienced'. This was a bit rich coming from Milton, and a blatant misrepresentation of the men he served. Of course, we are relying on Mylius's telling of it, but it is also possible that Milton said something like this just to get the German off his back.[91]

Similarly, Paulucci was having to make excuses for delays which were basically caused by his failure to submit proper credentials to Parliament.[92] On Paulucci's arrival in May 1652, Salvetti, the Tuscan agent, instructed him in the basic form of the parliamentary and committee reception styles, saying 'everything [is] done with wonderful order and decorum'.[93] It has recently been suggested that Milton's description of the republicans was about right, and that 'their inexperience can be seen in the elaborate instructions for the reception of Gerard Schaep [in 1649], arrangements that established governments carry out as a matter of routine'.[94] Maybe so, but the Commonwealth was, from very early on (and even before looking into foreign treaties), establishing its own routine, which required a big break with precedent; by 1650 it was sufficiently conversant to differentiate between diplomatic ranks, and to make the Portugese minister undergo interview in a chair without arms; and by 1652 Parliament was giving orders for the reception of the numerous deputuations coming to England which were to be received 'according to the Rule', occasions greeted by the press with an increasingly formulaic response.[95] The Rump rapidly settled into its diplomatic function on an international stage, and the public rapidly got used to the idea.

III

Public edification was provided in more domestic circumstances, too. As will have been clear from the foregoing, Commonwealth spectacle combined both civilian and military elements – from the involvement of leading soldiers in diplomatic ritual to the provision of a very prominent guard of honour. This fostered the appearance of a spirit of co-operation symbolised by the Speaker and Cromwell riding together in a coach as part of the post-Worcester celebrations. In a host of other contexts, too, an attempt was made to combine civilian and martial cultures.

In the spring of 1649 the army of the English Commonwealth stood at a crucial point in its history. Lots had been drawn for the service in Ireland, and the operation to avenge the bloody rebellion of 1641 was in a forward stage of planning. It was at this moment that the ranks were racked with the biggest crisis since 1647, a mutinous rebellion rising up around the standard of the Levellers. In desperation at the impending break-up of the army as a coherent whole committed nominally to the enforcement of a new constitution in the form of the army's Agreement of the People, the radical remnant in the rank and file kicked one last time.[96]

After their defeat at Burford in May 1649 the government and the army high command were free to continue preparations for the imminent Irish expedition. But before returning to the capital to see to final arrangements, leading military commanders first fetched up in nearby Oxford, where for three days they were feted by the dignitaries of the university.[97] A parliamentary visitation two years earlier had expelled the dominant royalist Anglicans from the university, and their places had been taken by staunch Commonwealthsmen such as Jerome Sankey (or Zanchy) who was made sub-warden of All Souls in place of Gilbert Sheldon in 1648, and proctor of the university the following year, before riding with Cromwell in Ireland as the colonel of a horse regiment there. On their arrival from Burford on Thursday 17 May, Fairfax and Cromwell were lodged in the quarters of All Souls' warden, Dr John Palmer, a recruiter member of the Rump. They came, so Wood claimed, 'to the end that they might see what reformation or alterations had been made, and be entertained by their creatures with such ceremonies and solemnity as great persons formerly had been'.[98]

The officers did service to their hosts, writing to Parliament to ask for the endowment of three lectureships in scripture.[99] They also made nominations to the new posts, recommending Dr Reynolds,[100] one Carroll (probably Joseph Caryl, government preacher on the conciliatory right wing of the independents, who later served as a preacher in the army which invaded Scotland[101]) and Thomas Goodwin (the president of Magdalen College, another 'safe divine'[102]).

The day after their arrival, the vice-chancellor, proctors and college heads donned their gowns to welcome the Lord General and wait on him.[103] He was treated to a speech – 'bad, yet good enough for Soldiers' – from one of the new fellows at All Souls, Master John Rowse or Rous. Wood also reported a speech made in reply by the Lieutenant General, saying 'that they knew no Commonwealth could flourish without Learning, and that they, whatsoever the world said to the contrary, meant to encourage it, and were so far from substracting any of their means, that they purposed to add more, etc.', to which the academics listened thankfully, 'the Poor spirited Presbyterians believing him'.

The General and his commanders were then dined and 'entertained with much freedom' and more bad speeches on the Saturday at Magdalen, at the invitation of the president. After a quick post-prandial game of bowls with the vice-chancellor, the officers proceeded to Convocation. Rigged up in the scarlet gowns and caps of doctors of civil law, Fairfax and Cromwell were granted their degrees at the proposal of Sankey, who presented them to the assembly. After a speech in which the proctor expressed 'the greatnesse of that honour and respect which was given to Learning, tryumphing in all their former and latter successes', and gave thanks that 'the University have such eminent Patriots to countenance them', the two took their seats on either side of the vice-chancellor. Beadles then conducted a bevy of commanding officers into Convocation to receive the degrees of master of arts, again after Sankey's formal proposal. Sir Hardress Waller and Colonels Thomas Harrison, John Okey, Richard Ingoldsby, the governor of the city, and John Hewson were amongst the soldiers newly decked out in the appropriate gowns.[104] The speechifiers on this occasion strove 'to out-vie one another, who should give the greatest honour to the present proceeders, and expresse the greatnesse of their favour in countenancing the university'.

After the soldiers had been 'dismantled of their Academic Formalities' they were dined once more, 'a sumptuous banquet' being served up in the library at the university's expense. Then after some sermons on Sunday by leading university figures, who 'prayed hard, if not heartily, for the Army and their blessed proceedings', thanking God for the defeat of the Levellers and encouraging the army 'to goe on with alacrity to relieve Ireland', and the induction of the army's principal secretary, John Rushworth and a number of lesser lights on the Monday, Fairfax and the generals took their leave of the chief members of the university at a solemn farewell.

This 'curious interlude' is a reasonably well known tale, which deserves more attention than it usually gets.[105] The conferring of honorary degrees, proceeding naturally enough from Parliament's purge of royalist academics, also added to the lustre of the commanders' personal glory, and almost consciously seemed to confirm their own civic character as scholars and promoters of learning rather than mere swordsmen. And this came on the day the Rump officially declared England a free state.[106] The following year, Cromwell became chancellor of Oxford. In 1651 Hugh Peters voiced the hope that the universities could be reformed by the removal of 'those ornaments ... the monuments of idolatry, viz. gowns, caps, Matriculations, with the many ceremonies about Commencements; but let scholars live as other men for apparel etc."[107] But however sympathetic Cromwell and his colleagues may have been to the religious principles of their preacher and fellow-traveller, they could not let pass a public relations opportunity such as this.

Their reluctance to forgo formality can also be explained by the attempt to turn the occasion into another moment of public edification. A week before Fairfax and Cromwell arrived in Oxford, the parliamentary universities committee had given order that, 'upon considerations that great meetings and extraordinary expenses in these times were not convenient, ... the public Act of the university, and the public commencement of Cambridge should be put off for this year'.[108] For the ceremonial on the 19th, however, a rail was set up in the assembly room, 'that the youth of the university may be encouraged in the sight of such a solemnity, who against the custom of that House, were admitted thereinto'. It was reported that 'the Solemnity and exercise of that day more resembled a publick act then private Convocation'.[109]

Ceremony was also used on the other wing of the republican armed forces. On the occasion of the launching of the frigates *Speaker* and *President* in April 1650, *Mercurius Pragmaticus* offered a disdainful commentary on the Rump's maritime policy.

> You presse men, build new ships, and make great feasts at their lanching and christning; eighteen Chines of Beef, besides other meat; on the kingdom's score, was the States dinner at the lanching, and these great ships are called Speaker and President, names of dishonour to England.[110]

In another number, *Pragmaticus* returned to the same event, declaring that

> We have something else to speake of the great Maying, the Saints in Triumph rode coached; no feare can disswade them from their pleasure. Six rich coaches loaded with states-men took fresh air *in pontificalibus*, and on the same day ... the great Don Quixote, or the Thymble-maker Backstead, marched to rendezvous for recreation of their Rebell-ships ... bestrid a gallant gray Horse ... prancing before a regiment of Redcoate-Janizaries, and looking big as bull beefe, use[ing] a complementall civilitie to such as reverenced his Collonellship.

The royalist was snobbish about the enthusiasts among the crowd lining the colonel's way – 'the best I saw was a chandler, scarce any of better sort stirring their hats till he came to Westminster'.[111]

Barkstead was regularly to be seen at the head of his Tower regiment, which performed guard duties for the government on state occasions, such as the reception of ambassadors. In October 1650, a fortnight after the thanksgiving day of prayer for the victory at Dunbar, he was at the centre of another 'gallant appearance' in the metropolis when he drew up his regiment in Hyde Park along with the City and Middlesex horse, and newly raised units from London commanded by the two supremos of the Tower of London under the Commonwealth Major General Thomas Harrison, commander-in-chief of all forces in England during the Scottish campaign of 1650–51, and alderman Colonel Robert Tichborne. In all, about 8,000 men had marched from the City with their train and newly acquired brass artillery. 'Colonel Pride and many eminent commanders and souldiers of the trained bands of the City, and other Gents and clerks (in honour of the Company) trailed pikes this day.' At the park, the assorted commanders and dignitaries gave the salute to members of Parliament, led, as always, by Speaker William Lenthall. The air was then filled with the roar and smoke of the cannon, and there rose up

> a general shout of the souldiery throughout the Field. The Trumpets and Drums made a sweet harmony, when also with their great and small shot they made the fields rebound with their Ecchos for a long season. The whole daies exercise was carryed on with a great deal of gallantry, and there appeared among them all aboundance of love and sweetnesse.[112]

A similar public military muster was held in London prior to Worcester, again attended by the Speaker and 'many members of Parliament', on which occasion the king of Scotland's declaration was burnt at the head of every regiment.[113]

The principal occasions for martial parading during the Commonwealth were the entries into Westminster and London which marked Cromwell's victorious returns from Ireland and the battlefield of Worcester.[114] On the former occasion the celebrations began at his putting into Bristol, where he was greeted by a triple cannonade. 'Many vollies of shot' marked his arrival at Windsor two days later with a small retinue of his own servants and a few officers and gentlemen of the army. There he was met by his wife

> and many persons of eminency, Members of Parliament, and of the Councel of State, and chief Officers of the Army; after much time spent in expressing civil respects one to another, they had some discourse on the affaires of Ireland, and of the prosperous success wherewith it hath pleased God to crown his undertakings.

That evening, some of Colonel Rich's regiment arrived to welcome the Lieutenant General; 'most of the Innes in towne are full of guests, which come from London on purpose to attend him in his way tomorrow. They tell us that a great number wil also meet him by the way, in his passage to London.' The dignitaries then accompanied him on his route into London, as did 'many hundred well-affected Gentlemen and Citizens'. Coming into London, he was saluted by great guns at Hyde Park Corner, and by a volley from Barkstead's regiment, 'drawne up in the way for that purpose'.[115]

After Worcester, Cromwell was formally received amidst considerable pomp and ceremony on 12 September. The City corporation met in the morning at Guildhall in their robes and gowns of office, then rode out in a dozen coaches to meet the Lord General around Acton, where the Recorder made a congratulatory speech. He was also met by many lords, the Speaker, members of Parliament and the Council of State, and many thousands of citizens, 'both horse and foot (yet the Trained-bands went not forth) which filled the ways and places best scituate for beholders four or five miles together'. In the procession that then set out for the capital,

first, came his Life-guard being a Comapany of as gallant Gent. as you have seen mounted, heroick and valiant; after them a troop of Col Rows horse belonging to the City, next unto them a great number of Commoners and Gent. of quality, then his Excellency and the Speaker of Parliament came in a coach themselves, and by estimation at least three hundred coaches close after one another.[116]

At Hide Park corner near Knights-bridge stood to receive him the blew Regiment of Volunteers lately raised and from thence to Piccadilly was placed Col. Barksteads Regiment of red-coats, the great guns were also drawn out of St Jameses, and about the time that his Excellency came to Charing-crosse they went off one after another once over which they had no sooner done, but there was a gallant volley of shot given by the souldiers that brake the air, and with a mighty shout of the people echoed again to the earth, with order in the manner aforesaid with great and small shot, and hallowing of the people was observed done severall times over.

As the Generall passed by, the people all along as he went put off their hats, and had reciprocal respects return'd from him again; his Excellency chose rather to come in as privately as he could in a coach then openly on horseback, to avoid the popularity and applauses of the people, desiring rather that the good he doth to this Common-wealth may be heard and felt then seen, that the people should attribute or ascribe too much unto him, who desires to carry on the work of the Lord in all meeknesse and humility.

The following day, in a complementary anti-spectacle, 4,000 Scottish prisoners were marched through the City and Westminster ('in a way', as *The Weekly Intelligencer* put it, 'quite contrary to their former expectation ... to testifie they had been Conquered'). The prisoners were marched through 'to shew the Cavaliers a true copy of their Kings countenance, in his gallant designe to over-runn the Nation at once with Barbarism and Tyranny'.[117]

IV

Although intended to reaffirm unity in both crisis and celebration, the spectacles orchestrated by the Commonwealth regime did not necessarily always work. There were always critical voices – radicals often deplored republican pomp as much as royalists did. Opinions clearly differed among the parliamentarians, and, as with Ireton's 1650 medallic *apologia*, representative milieux might serve to dramatise the fact. After defeating the Catholic Confederates at Dungan Hill in 1647, Colonel Michael Jones ordered that captured colours were not to be paraded on entering Dublin because it looked too much like 'ostentation and attributing unto man the glory of this great work due unto the Lord only'.[118] His righteous humility was not shared by a Parliament delighted by its army's successes over Scottish forces between 1648 and 1651, ordering their captured colours to be displayed in Westminster Hall. After capitalising on the foundations of conquest laid by Jones, Cromwell was typically brilliant in his accommodation of all points of view. At his return from Ireland, the official line on his own opinion of his reception was that he 'expresse[d] much humility', saying that it was

> not suitable to his desire to come up to London in great pomp and Glory, yet because men would not be thought guilty of that abominable vice of ingratitude, and for that worthy deeds are not to be requited with neglect, it may be decent and seemly for those that are well-wishers to the common good, to testifie their affections this way, which may be done without ostentation in the one, or ascribing more then is due by the other.[119]

Spectacle was a question not just of impressing the public, but also of allowing their participation in the glory of the republic's achievements. As we have seen, Cromwell was accompanied to London from Windsor by 'many Lords, and most of the Members of Parliament and Council of State, and many well-affected Gentlemen and Citizens'.[120] After the battle of Gabbard Sands, the interim Council of State mounted possibly the grandest Commonwealth spectacle, burying Admiral Deane with great ceremony and drama, a crowd-pleasing circus which was possibly also calculated to overawe the Dutch negotiators sent to sue for peace.[121] Some thought the regime's sensitivity to appearances did not go far enough. George Wither turned his own imaginative powers to the subject of dignifying the appearance of both the regime and its members. He imagined that, in his rhapsodical parliamentary republic,

> ... forasmuch as outward habits draw
> Respect unto men's persons, there I saw
> That custome which all Senators did hold
> In strict observance, though most times of old,
> The Knights and Burgesses who represent
> The Nation entered not the Parliament
> In common habits only; but each one
> A robe or upper garment did put on
> Peculiar to that Senate, differing neither
> In fashion, stuffe or colour from each other
> To signifie (as I conceive) thereby
> Their brother-hood and their equality.[122]

One of the 'Fundamentalls' by which he proposed to entrench the regime considered public spectacle. 'Let some appearance everday be made,' he wrote, 'That this great Body never want a Head / That's visible ...', for 'Venice hath by long experiment / Found that this caution might be pertinent.'[123]

These ideas were borrowed from other republican cultures which the rulers of the Commonwealth showed no interest in emulating. There is some indication of official suspicion of feting any one individual, least of all the single most obvious candidate for the role of visible head. Both *The Brief Relation*, licensed by the secretary to the Council of State, and *Several Proceedings*, the officially sanctioned version of events in Parliament, made absolutely no mention of either the Lord Lieutenant's return from Ireland or the Lord General's triumphal entry after Worcester, in which his triumph was quite deliberately shared with the Speaker. Walter Frost filled his weekly digest, as usual, almost exclusively with foreign news. *Several Proceedings* concerned itself exclusively, as usual, with the passage of business in the House. Others obviously felt a lot more open in their sympathies. On the latter occasion, the army's own *Faithfull Scout* pirated the official account printed as a separate, which its editor prefaced with a remarkable panegyric to the Lord General, 'to whom next to the Almighty, this Nation remains indebted for the preservation of their Freedom and Liberties'.[124]

There was an obvious difference between the entries in June 1650 and September 1651, celebrations which marked quite different phases in the onward, but often hard-fought, march to military supremacy in Britain. Although marked by silence in June 1650, as *The Man in the Moon* commented, most conspicuous by its absence from Frost's treatment of recent events was news of the English setback (albeit temporary) suffered at the siege of Clonmel, the ignominious final chapter in the Lord Lieutenant's personal involvement in Ireland, and the biggest military upset there, or indeed anywhere, for some few years.[125] Parliament had set aside 13 June as a day of fasting and humiliation for a blessing on the Commonwealth's troubled affairs; and the week before Cromwell's return from Ireland, officers of the army at HQ in Whitehall had circulated a call for setting apart 30 May, the day he entered Windsor, 'as a solemne time to seek [God's] face ... [w]herein (hoping you will joyne with us) we desire that both you and we may be humbled before the Lord'. Although this was directed specifically at the forces in England, who 'at ease' appeared to have 'contracted rest', it may explain why Cromwell himself betrayed an uneasy ambivalence about the whole affair.[126]

Still, the thrust of Wither's recommendation had long been realised in practice. Did Commonwealth spectacle 'work' as a political circus? This is a hard question, as we have very little evidence as to crowds and their reaction. The spectacle of the vanquished Scotsmen being herded through the streets of London in September 1651 certainly did not have quite the effect expected, as there were plenty of 'Scottified', or at least sufficiently humane, citizens on hand to distribute to them out of pity good white bread and money, as well as blankets and bandages for their wounds.[127] There are also some very negative impressions, as with Whitelocke's hair-raising experience at the burial of alderman Rowland Wilson in March 1650. This was not officially a state funeral, but it was attended by members, Councillors, citizens and officers of the army, with the Speaker 'taking precedence', followed by the Lord Mayor, the Lord General, the Lord President and Whitelocke himself, who were 'ranked together, and the rest in their order'.[128] The City regiment of which Wilson had been colonel, together with other companies of soldiers, 'were in arms to attend the corps of their officer', and 'great multitudes' crowded the streets round Bishopsgate to see the ceremony.[129] Whitelocke claimed there was an ugly atmosphere. Bradshaw was supposedly threatened by some in the crowd, who cursed him as 'the Rogue that judged the king' and made menaces 'as if they would presently have set upon him'. At one point, when 'the guards were far off', Bradshaw became so afraid of the crowd that 'he desired Whitelocke not to leave him, which Whitelocke thought dishonourable to do', and 'when they came to a Lane near the Church, they slipt down the lane, left the Company and got safe home again'.[130]

Interesting as it is, this story does not really ring true, given the military presence and the formation of processions so that senior figures would generally be towards the middle. And it certainly contrasts strongly with accounts of the public acclamation at Cromwellian entries, or even that of Colonel Berkstead in 1650. The usefulness of Whitelocke's story also hinges on the issue of its composition. A different version of the same event, in Whitelocke's *Annales*, referred to a caucus of royalist agitators; and despite the

> presse of people ... holding up their hands and their staves, ready to strike ... it pleased God to turne the raging and madness of the people, and to prevent the intended mischiefe. Neither Bradshawe nor I, nor any of the Company said a word to those bailing rude rabble, but went on our way taking no notice of them.[131]

Those who wished to see ceremonial as evidence of unity would see it so, those who did not would not. Of more than twenty newsbook accounts of a procession of government and military members through the City to a corporation banquet held in their honour, including royalist versions, only the Leveller-ish *Moderate* referred to the supposed sabotaging of Cromwell's coach, the abuse from spectators, and the deployment of soldiers all along the route to guard government members from violence.[132]

Whitelocke's story does, however, highlight the degree of unity between the government and the all-important City authorities, a relationship reaffirmed at every available opportunity throughout the Rump's reign, as it had been in the 1640s. The City dined Parliament, Council and officers after Burford, Dunbar and Worcester; it joined in all the Cromwellian acclamations and a number of Commonwealth funerals. In November 1641, Charles I had performed his first City entry, an event which helped to strengthen his position at a key moment, and it was claimed that 'the consideration of his majesty having the love of able citizens will conduce much to his affairs'.[33] There was an element of wishful thinking here – the occasion highlighted the distance between Charles and the people, too, with a mounted guard placed along the route. The possible ambivalence of the crowd during the Commonwealth was different, but neither 'worse' nor 'better'.

Nevertheless, it is important to note that the new state was mounting political circuses with considerable popular appeal. Large numbers came to watch the arrival and audience of ambassadors, who could always pull a crowd.[34] Huygens recorded how the Dutch ambassadors 'had many people coming to watch them eat, among others many young ladies. We usually had all the candied fruits from the table offered to the latter, who were not coy about accepting them.'[35] On the other hand, he himself was far from impressed by the state ceremonial which accompanied the mission of the ambassadors from Holland. The House was 'so crowded that the ambassadors scarcely had room to pass through'. Jacob Catz delivered an address in Latin that lasted the best part of half an hour. In response 'the Speaker ... answered briefly and so softly that none of us could hear it ... I must confess that I had imagined this meeting would be rather more majestic than I actually found it.'[36] But it was not the first time diplomatic spectacle had failed to live up to expectations. The Spanish ambassador's first public audience with Charles I and his queen had been marred because the Banqueting House was crowded with women 'ranked so close together' that they had 'many fallings out for spoiling one another's ruffs'.[37]

Two further aspects of the ceremonial described here are worth noting. First, in an age when state ceremonial is encapsulated by events like the changing of the guard and the trooping of the colour, it is of more than passing interest to note the role played in Commonwealth pageantry by England's first military full-timers. Secondly, in an age when state openings of Parliament are conducted in a very traditional manner (with the Commons squeezing into the House of Lords, despite the fact it can accommodate even fewer MPs than their own House), it is quite remarkable to see the Commons being used as a stage for the conduct of dignified political theatre. As Fleming pointed out in his report, here was another sphere in which the executive mantle, with its attendant responsibilities, had passed from a monarchy to the sovereign Parliament. In the matter of seating arrangements at diplomatic receptions, Fleming asked 'whether the ambassador's chair shall be set in the same place it was during the late troubles, when they looked upon the Parliament as subject to another power'. The political spectacle of the Rump marked one of the first confident steps down a road which would make the one-time parliamentary event a supreme institution.

It is not possible to reach a definitive conclusion on the merits of republican spectacle relative to its monarchical equivalent. But that is not really the point. Any regime's public appearances must always reflect the ambiguity inherent in activities whose objectives are rarely expressed explicitly and whose impact is beyond quantification. Charles I defaulted on his 'public duty' to parade himself. But then how significant was the sight of the king in arms at the head of an army in the 1640s? Charles's greatest moment as a king in the public eye came at the moment of his deepest personal crisis – *en route* from Windsor in December 1648, then in Westminster Hall and on the scaffold before the Banqueting House in the following January. All agree that this was Charles at his most charismatic; it was his greatest moment. But it did nothing to prevent his death, nor the abolition of the Crown. Hopefully this chapter has demonstrated that, given conventional wisdom about the Rump, it is unnecessary to assess how 'successful' its public image was before we take account of the simple, largely unacknowledged fact that it went to such extraordinary lengths to create one in the first place.

NOTES

1 Blair Worden mentions the fact that Rumpers 'immensely enjoyed' these activities. *The Rump Parliament*, p. 253.

2 Quoted by R. M. Smuts, 'Public Ceremony and Royal Charisma', in A. L. Beier, D. Cannadine and J. M. Rosenheim eds, *The First Modern Society* (Cambridge, 1989), p. 67.

3 Seymour, 'Pro-government Propaganda', p. 230. In fact, if one counts the numerous public and semi-public occasions not examined by Seymour, one could fairly argue that the Rumpers, or at least some of them, went on display up to two dozen times in fifty-three months.

4 *Ibid.*, pp. 228–9.

5 *Ibid.* He reaches this conclusion despite the illuminating suggestion in his account of Cromwell's entry after Worcester that it was 'a spectacle in praise of an abstract, the State'.

6 Maurice Ashley, *Cromwell's Generals* (1954), p. 105.

7 *Collections of the Massachusetts Historical Society* fourth series, vii (1865), 281.

8 Quoted by J. G. Marston, 'Gentry, Honour and Royalism, in Early Stuart England', *Journal of British Studies* 13 (1973–74), 26.

9 Abbott ed., *Writings and Speeches* ii, 504 n; Firth ed., *Memoirs of the Life of Colonel Hutchinson* ii, 186–8.

10 J. Y. Akerman ed., *Letters from Roundhead Officers written from Scotland ... 1650–1660* (Edinburgh, 1856), p. 36.

11 *Ibid.*, p. 21.

12 Firth ed., *Memoirs of the Life of Colonel Hutchinson* ii, 171; C. H. Simpkinson, *Thomas Harrison, Regicide and Major-General* (1905), p. 114. Mrs Hutchinson did not like Harrison, but his vanity is attested elsewhere, too – cf. Herbert, *Memoirs*, p. 97; Gardiner, *History of the Great Civil War* iv, 279–80.

13 *Collections of the Massachusetts Historical Society* fourth series, vii (1865), 281. Major Winthrop also served as a commissioner for the propagation of the Gospel, and was later promoted to a regimental command. *Ibid.*, pp. 115, 499.

14 J. C. Robertson, 'Caroline Culture: Bridging Court and Country?', *History* 75 (1990), 388–416.

15 D. Foskett ed., *Samuel Cooper and his Contemporaries* (1974), p. 131.

16 Fairfax's bust can be seen in the National Portrait Gallery, along with the Walker Cromwell, and portraits of John Lambert, Henry Ireton and Charles Fleetwood. Cromwell's statue, *CJ* vii, 51.

17 J. Douglas Stewart, 'Samuel Cooper: an English Baroque "Man of his Century"', in Foskett ed., *Samuel Cooper*, p. xv. Cf. Roy Strong, *The English Renaissance Miniature* (1983).

18 P.R.O., SP18/11, 81.

19 Foskett ed., *Samuel Cooper*, p. ix.

20 J. J. Foster, *Samuel Cooper and the English Miniature Painters of the Seventeenth Century* (1914–16), p. 44.

21 Edward Hawkins, Augustus W. Franks and Herbert A. Grueber eds, *Medallic Illustrations* (2 vols, 1885; reprinted 1969) i, 384–408.

22 *Ibid.*, p. 387; Gentles, *New Model Army*, epilogue; Norah Carlin, 'Extreme or Mainstream? The English Independents and the Cromwellian Reconquest of Ireland', in B. Bradshaw, A. Hadfield and W. Maley eds, *Representing Ireland. Literature and the Origins of Conflict, 1534–1600* (Cambridge, 1993); for republican attitudes far more sympathetic to the Irish than the average see Sarah Barber, 'Irish Undercurrents to the Politics of April 1653', *Historical Research* 65 (1992), 315–35.

23 Whinney and Millar, *English Art*, pp. 75, 81, 173. The proposal is treated at length by Maija Jansson, 'Remembering Marston Moor: the Politics of Culture', in S. D. Amussen and M. A. Kishlansky eds, *Political Culture and Cultural Politics in early modern England. Essays presented to David Underdown* (Manchester, 1995), pp. 255–76.

24 Stowe MS 184, fo. 283, undated. This is a printed single sheet, suggesting the possibility that the idea was circulated amongst the members.

25 O. Millar, *Rubens and the Whitehall Ceiling* (1958), p. 18. For Gerbier's involvement in arranging for paying Rubens and despatching his friend's finished work to London, see W. Noel Sainsbury, *Original Unpublished Papers Illustrative of the Life of Sir Peter Paul Rubens* (1859), pp. 183–6, 191–205.

26 The portions in square brackets are damaged.

27 Jansson, 'Remembering Marston Moor', pp. 268–9.

28 *Ibid.*

29 Seventy-nine Rumpers sat on the five Councils elected between February 1649 and November 1652. About a quarter of them served in all or almost all of them, and another quarter in only one.

30 Joshua Sprigge, *Anglia Rediviva* (1647); Thomas May, *History of the Long Parliament* (1647); *idem*, *Breviary of the History of the Parliament of England* (1650); George Wither, *Respublica Anglicana, or, The Historie of the Parliament in their late Proceedings* (1650);

Abbott ed., *Writings and Speeches* ii, 484.

31 See, for example, the engraving of the victory at Dunbar commissioned by Parliament in 1651, C. Carlton, *Going to the Wars. The Experience of the British Civil Wars, 1638–1651* (1994), plate 14.

32 Bachrach and Collmer eds, *Huygens' Journal*, pp. 50–1.

33 *CJ* vi, 465, 517; *CJ* vii, 15.

34 Letter from The Hague, 13 December 1648, *Mercurius Pragmaticus* 19–26 December 1648, p. [6].

35 *Mercurius Impartialis* 5–12 December 1648, p. 5.

36 See for example the response to Ireton's grandiose interment, Gardiner, *History of the Commonwealth and Protectorate* ii, 126.

37 Seymour, 'Pro-government Propaganda', pp. 188–9.

38 *Ibid.*, especially chapter 6.

39 T. Carte ed., *A Collection of Original Letters and Papers concerning the Affairs of England from the year 1641 to 1660* (2 vols, 1739) i, 276. The two representatives were rather late showing their respective masters' disdain for the rebels, as these rumours were circulating in April.

40 J. Geddes, *History of the Administration of John de Witt, Grand Pensionary of Holland* (2 vols, 1879) i, 101.

41 Carte ed., *Original Letters and Papers* i, 225, 231–2. This was of considerable significance to the partisans of the Stuarts, especially because of their suspicion of the 'cheap civilities' shown to Charles the younger in the Netherlands. It was vital that he establish his position as an alternative court to that being set up at Whitehall, and so royalists were heartened to learn that the king of Denmark had sent an ambassador to Charles at The Hague 'who comes in very great pomp'. A fortnight later, however, royalists were making excuses to each other to explain why, two weeks after arriving, the Dane had still not made any formal contact, despite having had a reception from the States General. *Ibid.*, pp. 231–2, 264.

42 Abbott ed., *Writings and Speeches* ii, 20.

43 *CSPD 1649–50*, pp. 10–11, 14, 37.

44 P.R.O., SP25/62, 16.

45 See for example his conversation with Paulucci, *CSPVen 1647–52*, pp. 226–8. For his kinship with the General see S. J. Weyman, 'Oliver Cromwell's Kinsfolk', *English Historical Review* 6 (1891), 53–4.

46 P.R.O., SP25/62, 7, 12.

47 P.R.O., SP18/1, 73.

48 Cf. Blair Worden's observation that Commonwealth admiration for the United Provinces may have been limited by the 'suspicion' that its improvised constitution would not last. 'English Republicanism', in J. H. Burns with M. Goldie eds, *Cambridge History of Political Thought* (Cambridge, 1991), p. 446.

49 Gardiner, *History of the Commonwealth and Protectorate* i, 308.

50 *CSPVen 1647–52*, p. 182.

51 Ibid.; *Several Proceedings in Parliament* 26 December 1650–2 January 1651, pp. 987–8; *Mercurius Politicus* 9–16 January 1651, p. 522; Nickolls ed., *Original Letters and Papers*, pp. 42–3.

52 *CSPVen 1647–52*, p. 186.

53 *Mercurius Politicus* 9–16 January 1651, pp. 522–3; *Perfect Diurnall* 6–13 January 1651, p. 764; *Severall Proceedings in Parliament* 9–16 January 1652, p. 1027. Cf. *CSPVen 1647–52*, pp. 234, 237, 239, for the committee reception given to the Swedish minister, Haroldus Appleboone, in May 1652.

54 *CJ* vi, 318, 321, 322, 517–18, 520; vii, 74.

55 *CSPVen 1647–52*, p. 225.

56 See below, p. 99.

57 E.g. *The Weekly Intelligencer* 24–31 December 1650, pp. 3–4. Titles of address will be considered in chapter 4.

58 *Mercurius Politicus* 27 November–4 December 1651, p. 1250.

59 Ibid., p. 1251.

60 Bachrach and Collmer eds, *Huygens' Journal*, pp. 33, 36–7; *The French Intelligencer* 16–23 December 1651, p. 35; *Several Proceedings in Parliament* [11–18] December 1651, p. 1804; *Perfect Passages of every Daies Intelligence* 12–19 December 1651, p. 338; *The Faithful Scout* 12–19 December 1651, p. 375.

61 *The French Intelligencer* 16–23 December 1651, p. 37; *A Declaration and Narrative* (1651), p. 5; *A Perfect Diurnall* 15–22 December 1651, p. [1750]; Bachrach and Collmer eds, *Huygens' Journal*, p. 41.

62 *CSPVen 1647–52*, p. 244.

63 E.g. *The Weekly Intelligencer* 25 May–1 June 1652, pp. 472–3; *French Occurrences* 24–31 May 1652, p. 23. *Mercurius Politicus* confined itself to noting the simple fact of the reception, 20–7 May 1652, p. 1624.

64 *Several Proceedings in Parliament* 1–8 July 1652, p. 2272.

65 *CSPVen 1647–52*, p. 326.

66 *The Weekly Intelligencer* 8–15 June 1652, p. 492; *Perfect Account* 9–16 June 1652, p. 607; *Perfect Diurnall* 28 June–5 July 1652, p. 1993; *CSPVen 1647–52*, pp. 249, 255.

67 Gardiner, *History of the Commonwealth and Protectorate* i, 181, 300, 303, 312; ii, 189–90, 243.

68 The first Portugese mission to Westminster came the month after Cardenas's initial reception, in January 1651, by which time 'the Rump felt strong enough to play off rival powers against one another'. Worden, *The Rump Parliament*, p. 253.

69 *CSPVen 1647–52*, pp. 284, 295; *The Perfect Diurnall* 27 September–4 October 1652, p. 2197; cf. Gardiner, *History of the Commonwealth and Protectorate* ii, 243.

70 *The Perfect Diurnall* 27 September–4 October 1652, p. 2195; *The Weekly Intelligencer* 28 September–5 October 1652, pp. 613, 619.

71 Ibid., p. 613.

72 Gardiner, *History of the Commonwealth and Protectorate* i, 312–13.

73 *The Weekly Intelligencer* 18–25 February 1651, p. 65; Geddes, *De Witt* i, 157–8; Worden, *The Rump Parliament*, p. 253.

74 *Mercurius Politicus* 13–20 March 1651, p. 669.

75 *CJ* vi, 529.

76 P. Aubrey, *Mr Secretary Thurloe. Cromwell's Secretary of State, 1652–1660* (1990), pp. 19–20.

77 Geddes, *De Witt* i, 158; *CSPVen 1647–52*, p. 172, Gardiner, *History of the Commonwealth and Protectorate* i, 323; Bachrach and Collmer eds, *Huygens' Journal*, p. 1.

78 Bod. Lib., Rawlinson MS C 129, Journal of the embassy, fo. iv; *Certain Propositions sent by the States of Holland to the Lords Ambassadors of the Commonwealth of England* ([15 April] 1651), p. 3.

79 P.R.O., SP25/65, 81, 88.

80 Geddes, *De Witt* i, 158–60.

81 *Mercurius Politicus* 3–10 April 1651, p. 716.

82 Bod. Lib., Rawlinson MS C 129, fo. 2v; Gardiner, *History of the Commonwealth and Protectorate* i, 323–4; *Mercurius Politicus* 27 March–3 April 1651, p. 697.

83 *Ibid.*, p. 695.

84 Geddes, *De Witt* i, 160.

85 Bod. Lib., Rawlinson MS C 129, fo. 6v; *Joyful Newes from Holland: shewing, The Royall Entertainment given by the States of the United Provinces to the Lords Embassadours of the Common-Wealth of England* ([7 April] 1651).

86 Geddes, *De Witt* i, 173.

87 *Mercurius Politicus* 3–17 April 1651, pp. 717, 726; Geddes, *De Witt* i, 165, 175.

88 This will be discussed further below, chapter 4.

89 *CSPVen 1647–52*, pp. 213–14.

90 *Ibid.*, p. 294.

91 Miller, *Milton and the Oldenburg Safeguard*, pp. 171–2.

92 *CSPVen 1647–52*, pp. 294, 314.

93 *Ibid.*, p. 225.

94 R. T. Fallon, *Milton in Government* (University Park, Pa., 1993), p. 28.

95 *CJ* vi, 517–18; vii, 96, 103, 129.

96 Manning, *1649*.

97 *Perfect Occurrences of every Daies Journall in Parliament* 18–25 May 1649, pp. 1063–4; *Perfect Diurnall of some Passages in Parliament* 21–8 May 1649, pp. 2531–2; Gardiner, *History of the Commonwealth and Protectorate* i, 54; Anthony Wood, *The History and Antiquities of the Colleges and Halls in the University of Oxford* (2 vols, Oxford, 1786–90) ii, pt. 2, 619–21; idem, *Athenae Oxoniensis* (2 vols, 1691) ii, 75–90.

98 Wood, *Antiquities of Oxford* ii, pt. 2, 619.

99 *Perfect Occurrences of every Daies Journall in Parliament*, the official newsbook, referred to their promotion of 'a good work for that City', 18–25 May 1649, pp. 1061–2.

100 Edward, the vice-chancellor. Abbott ed., *Writings and Speeches* ii, 73.

101 *Ibid.*, pp. 346, 355; Worden, *The Rump Parliament*, pp. 122–3, 191, 246, 395.

102 Abbott ed., *Writings and Speeches* ii, 59 n, 331 n, 522, 568 n; Worden, *The Rump Parliament*, pp. 122–3.

103 Wood says the university deputation was led by the pro-vice-chancellor, Dr Rogers, the vice-chancellor being away from Oxford until Saturday.

104 Others included Adjutant General George Sedascue, Quartermaster General Edward Grosvenor, Scoutmaster General Owen Roe and Lieutenant Colonel William Goffe.

105 Gardiner, *History of the Commonwealth and Protectorate* i, 54; Abbott ed., *Writings and Speeches* ii, 72–4. Gardiner was himself an honorary doctor in civil law at both Oxford and Edinburgh. The remark is Abbott's.

106 Firth and Rait eds, *Acts and Ordinances* ii, 122.

107 Hugh Peters, *Good Work for a Good Magistrate* (1651), p. 3.

108 Wood, *Antiquities of Oxford* ii, pt. 2, 619.

109 *Perfect Occurrences of every Daies Journall in Parliament* 18–25 May 1649, p. 1064.

110 *Mercurius Pragmaticus* 9–16 April 1650; *CSPD 1650*, pp. 87, 545; Nickolls ed., *Original Letters and Papers of State*, p. 8; Bernard Capp, *Cromwell's Navy. The Fleet and the English Revolution, 1648–1660* (Oxford, 1989), p. 52; *Perfect Diurnall of some Passages and Proceedings of and in Relation to the Armies* 18 September 1651, p. 1322, for an account of the launching of a frigate called *Worcester* (cited by Abbott ed., *Writings and Speeches* ii, 477).

111 *Mercurius Pragmaticus* 30 April–7 May 1650, fo. Fff2r.

112 *Perfect Diurnall* 21–8 October 1650, p. 577; *CJ* vi, 485.

113 *Mercurius Politicus* 28 August–4 September 1651, p. 1042.

114 *A Speech or Declaration of the Declared King of Scots upon the Death of Montrose ... Also some excellent Passages concerning the Lord Generall Cromwell, his Entertainment at Windsor Castle, and the Manner of his Coming from thence to London, the first of June, 1650* ([3 June] 1650); *Another Victory in Lancashire obtained against the Scots ... Together with the Manner of my Lord General Cromwells Comming up, and noble Reception by the City of London; and an Account of the Scots Prisoners which marched through the City on Saturday last* ([15 September] 1651).

115 *A Perfect Diurnall*, 27 May–3 June 1650, pp. 278, 280.

116 According to Nedham, the pair rode in a coach of state, *Mercurius Politicus* 11–18 September 1651, p. 1071.

117 *The Weekly Intelligencer* 9–16 September 1651, p. 286; *Another Victory in Lancashire obtained against the Scots*, pp. 3–4.

118 Gardiner, *History of the Great Civil War* iv, 106.

119 *A Speech or Declaration of the Declared King of Scots*; Seymour, 'Pro-government Propaganda', pp. 212–13.

120 *Some excellent Passages concerning the lord General Cromwell his Entertainment*, p. 6.

121 Seymour, 'Pro-government Propaganda', pp. 225–7. Cf. Woolrych, *Commonwealth to Protectorate*, p. 136.

122 Wither, *Perpetuall Parliament*, p. 70.

123 *Ibid.*, p. 71.

124 *The Faithfull Scout*, 12–19 September 1651, pp. 265–6.

125 *The Man in the Moon*, 29 May–5 June, 1650, p. [429].

126 *A Perfect Diurnall*, 20–7 May 1650, pp. 271–4.

127 *Another Victory in Lancashire obtained against the Scots*, pp. 3–4.

128 Spalding ed., *The Diary of Bulstrode Whitelocke*, p. 255.

129 B. Lib., Add. MS 37,345, fo. 54.

130 Spalding ed., *The Diary of Bulstrode Whitelocke*, p. 255.

131 B. Lib., Add. MS 37,345, fos 54–v.

132 Seymour, 'Pro-government Propaganda', p. 206.

133 Thomas Wiseman to Admiral Pennington, 18 November 1641, cited by Smuts, 'Public Ceremony'.

134 Bachrach and Collmer eds, *Huygens' Journal*, pp. 37 n, 41.

135 *Ibid.*, p. 44.

136 *Ibid.*, pp. 41, 53.

137 Sainsbury, *Original Unpublished Papers ... of Sir Peter Paul Rubens*, p. xix.

Chapter 3

Icons

*T*HE ceremonial events described in the previous chapter gave the republic an institutional character. When soldiers paraded or received honorary degrees, when MPs took the salute, launched new frigates or welcomed foreign diplomats, the new regime went on display, orchestrating a series of spectacular set-pieces. This chapter concerns a number of representational devices which institutionalised Rump authority by their regular appearance in the course of ordinary administration. These were the 'icons' of the English Commonwealth.

Just as monarchy was physically represented by the Crown, sceptre and orb, and by a host of regal images, the republican regime also had an iconic aspect. A variety of signs and symbols were invented and deployed by the Rump to replace the outmoded artefacts and images of regality. This chapter looks at the great seals of the English Commonwealth, the mace of Parliament, and the republic's key emblem, the arms of the English Commonwealth, which figured prominently in the designs of these and other objects, and which were also used in their own right as the decorative equivalent of the royal arms which they replaced in a number of public and governmental locations.

These republican symbols of authority help take us beyond the usual argument that revolutionary change was a matter of mere convenience or expediency, demonstrating the imagination with which the English republic was invented, as well as some of the ideals to which it gave expression. Moreover, as we shall see, this new republican style spread beyond the seat of government at Westminster and Whitehall during the rule of the Rump, when urban, educational and charitable corporations all across England had new maces made, and erected the arms of the state in town halls, on city gates, in school rooms and hospitals.

I

Early modern England's political landscape was mapped by a system of signs and symbols which represented authority. When the revolution destroyed monarchy, many of the traditional landmarks were cleared from that land-scape. In 1649 the Rumpers completed the liquidation of the most important regal icons which had begun in the 1640s. The Crown jewels and other insignia were broken up, the metal was coined, the stones were sold.[1] Images of monarchy, in all media, were defaced and destroyed. In London the king's statue at the Old Exchange was beheaded, removed and replaced with a heroic statement of England's liberation from tyrants.[2] Statues were also removed from St Paul's, Covent Garden and Greenwich, and the gilded images of the old king and queen were removed from Queen's Street.[3] The Rump and its Councils of State gave a number of orders for the removal of the royal arms from all public places.[4] Shortly after the king's execution, his arms were taken down from over the Speaker's chair.[5] In April 1649 Parliament ordered that the royal arms in the court of common pleas be removed and a carpet hung in their place.[6] In August, Henry Marten, Augustine Garland and Luke Robinson were charged with bringing in legislation for the removal of regal arms, statues and insignia from 'all publick Places'.[7] There were also specific orders for removing those royal arms still on display in London churches, on the sterns of ships of the Commonwealth navy and in shipyards.[8]

Although pubs even went so far as to replace their signs with ones that read 'Here *was* the king's head', there was no way the new regime and its support-ers could hope to annihilate the image of the dead king completely, even if the trappings of the institution of monarchy were easily eradicated.[9] In the popu-lar memory Charles lived on, of course, as the martyr whose personal credo and heroism were laid bare in the *Eikon Basilike* – making him the most prominent icon of the age.[10] A mythology grew up around the imagery of the king as animistic as it was anglican. Nedham reported that

> when the late kings statue was thrown down on Saturday last, from off the west end of Pauls, it fell upright upon the feet ... a Groan ... was heard (they say) when the head of his Statue was cut off at the Old Exchange. Admirable inventions all and may fit very well, being calculated for the Meridian of every Club and Ordinary and Alehouse.[11]

Attempts to mount a co-ordinated campaign against the image of the king were not very successful, and progress remained piecemeal, even in the highest circles of the administration. It was not until December 1650 that the Rump's Council of State ordered the removal of all royal insignia at Whitehall, or in any other 'public house'. In February 1651 it reiterated the instruction to the surveyor general, Edward Carter, stressing that he was to apply the order stringently to all insignia, 'whether they be in chambers *or windows of cham-*

bers, or any other public or private place'.[12] Even at the epicentre of republican authority, the Rump's 'court' at Whitehall, it proved impossible to expunge completely the memory of the Stuarts because it was written into the very fabric of the palace.

The dead king's presence lingered, too, in the form of the currency minted in his lifetime, a constant reminder of the regal polity. It is ironic that most of the huge sums paid to the regime in taxation, or in payment for land confiscated from royalists, bore the dead king's stamp. Most, but not all. In April 1649 Parliament accepted the Council of State's recommendations on the design of a new Commonwealth currency. One face of the coins would depict the cross of St George on a shield, with the motto 'The Commonwealth of England', whilst the other would bear the arms of the Commonwealth and the words 'God with Us'.[13] The arms of the Commonwealth incorporated the cross of St George and the Irish harp of Erin in escutcheons. They formed the most important device with which the Rump replaced regal imagery, and became the stamp of the republican regime's authority.

It is highly unlikely that the scale on which the new currency circulated ever swamped or drowned out the prevalence of the king's head (which, in the circumstances, may be thought an image of distinctly ambivalent connotation). But the Commonwealth coinage had considerable iconic significance. In the month it was adopted, royalists excitedly reported that the besieged remnant at Pontefract had proclaimed the succession of Charles II and struck their own coinage bearing his inscription.[14] The new regime had little to fear from this isolated pocket of resistance, but its symbolic defiance had to be countered as much as the military threat it posed had to be crushed. Issuing currency was a matter of the highest public discourse – the government could not afford to have its authority undermined in that way.

The creation of new visual discourses rapidly extended well beyond simply fulfilling the obligation to provide a suitable currency. There is evidence of a growing enthusiasm for replacing the old signs of the Caroline monarchy with the emblems of the new state. One of the earliest resolutions taken by the republic's first Council of State was to equip the ships of its fleet with flags bearing a red cross on a white background, and to have the twin arms of England and Ireland engraved on their sterns. It ordered the navy commissioners to see to this with all expedition, so that the summer guard would be properly turned out in the Commonwealth style.[15] Soon the Council began elaborating on the basic form set down for naval flags, ordering on 5 March 1649 that those flown by the admiral, vice-admiral and rear-admiral should bear the arms of England and Ireland in escutcheons set in a gold compartment, all on a red background.[16] In June 1650 the Council ordered the ordnance committee to provide Cromwell with standards 'agreeable to the arms of the Commonwealth'.[17]

The arms of the Commonwealth also featured in the peaceful conduct of the regime's foreign policy. In April 1649 Sir Oliver Fleming recommended that a state coach and barge be provided for the reception of guests, that they should bear the arms of the Commonwealth, and that those who manned them should wear state livery.[18] At the end of the following August the Council gave orders for picking out the royal arms from the barge cloths used on the old state barge and replacing them with those of the Commonwealth.[19] A few days later it ordered that Richard Nutt and the twenty-one other men chosen to be Council bargemen were to wear badges of the Commonwealth arms as part of their uniform.[20] Early in the following year the Council sent Lord Grey to Parliament to propose equipping the coaches and horses used in diplomatic business with liveries bearing the arms of the Commonwealth, in line with the practice of other states.[21] And in preparing to send Oliver St John and Walter Strickland as ambassadors to the States of Holland in 1651 the Council ordered that their retinue be provided with £2,000 of plate tableware engraved with the arms of the Commonwealth.[22] A similar republican dinner service was used at the reception banquet held in honour of the ambassadors of Holland who came to England the following year.[23]

During the rule of the Rump, domestic authority also bore the stamp of the Commonwealth regime in a number of more ordinary ways. The arms appeared on a host of parliamentary enactments, orders and declarations posted in the capital and disseminated all over the republic, ranging from Acts for the Engagement, the coinage, the militia, London elections, assessment and composition rates, the relief of poor prisoners and days of thanksgiving or humiliation to proclamations, resolutions and orders on subjects such as highwaymen, the press, the Excise, the apprehension of Charles Stuart, the price of coal and the postal system.[24] When the regime published Milton's *Pro Populo Anglicano* the tract bore a particularly smart version of the arms on its title page.[25] The device caught on in wider literary circles, even appearing on the title page of the 1650 edition of Walter Blith's agricultural handbook *The Improver Improved*, along with the motto 'Vive Le Republick'.[26]

These arms, then, rapidly became an important badge of England's new order. They were also deployed in public places, set up as the decorative alternative of the royal arms. Shortly after the king's execution, Henry Marten was asked to bring in legislation for replacing the king's arms with those of the state in the central courts at Westminster.[27] In February 1651 orders were given for the replacement of the royal arms in all public places with those of the Commonwealth, which alterations were to be paid for out of parish rates.[28] They were eventually set up in the Parliament House, over the Speaker's chair, but apparently not until after the battle of Worcester.[29] Still, by that time, orders had already been given that they be erected at the Tower of London.[30] And, where once the very fabric of the palace at Whitehall had preserved the memory of the old order, the arms of the Commonwealth started to appear in a decorative capacity at the seat of the republican executive. On new year's day 1652, prior to their audience with the Council of State, the Dutch ambassadors 'were first shown into a large tapestried room with a fire burning where Mr Peters told [Lodowijck Huygens] the Privy Council used to meet. Here was a beautiful chimney piece with sculptured figures and the coat of arms of the Parliament in the middle.'[31] The arms also replaced the king's in a number of prominent locations of a non-governmental nature, such as at Charterhouse (at the expense of the hospital) and Skinners' Hall in London.[32]

The arms spread well beyond the narrow confines of metropolitan official-dom. In November 1650 the Council of State ordered that they be set up in the town hall at Aldborough, in preparation for the formal tendering of the Engagement to the townsfolk.[33] This is a rare example of direct governmental intervention. Examples of the arms being erected voluntarily are more common. Leicester's corporation demonstrated its new loyalties by removing the dead king's arms from the town hall and common hall parlour and from all the gates of the town. In every instance they were replaced with the arms of the Commonwealth. The town's governors even paid 8s to have the state's arms put on the staves wielded by the borough's constables and bailiffs.[34]

This local dimension is significant. There is considerable evidence of voluntary participation in the reinvention of traditional political forms in corporations the length and breadth of the republic. It is most apparent in the scale on which civic regalia changed during the rule of the Rump. For example, at Gloucester, a city which took considerable pride in its role as a bastion of parliamentary authority in the largely royalist south-west during the 1640s, the corporation replaced the regal badges adorning the city's sword of state with the arms of the Commonwealth.[35] Moreover, in 1652 it employed a London goldsmith, Thomas Maundy, to make no fewer than four new maces bearing the arms of the free state.[36] This is only the most spectacular example of a remarkable phenomenon little noted by historians hitherto. The proliferation of republican maces is of fundamental significance for the way we understand the nature of England's short-lived republican experience.[37]

The civic mace has a long tradition as a symbol of authority in England. For a long time it was not so much a symbol as the implement for enforcing authority, the weapon wielded by sergeants of the military orders of the Holy Land, by Richard I's sergeants-at-arms, by Edward I's domestic bodyguards, then by medieval town constables, bailiffs or sergeants as the indispensable tool of their police duties and penal jurisdiction.[38] They gradually attained a more ceremonial quality as the emblem of the Crown sergeancy's administrative powers. The City of London was the first civic body whose bailiffs' or sheriffs' officers underwent the transition from catchpoles to sergeants-at-mace, entitled to bear silver or gilt maces as badges of their office from the first half of the fourteenth century. Hence the emergence of the great mace, carried before the mayor and aldermen of town corporations in civic processions. By the seventeenth century this was a well established aspect of English civic political culture. In his verses entitled *The Verry Merry Wherry-Ferry Voyage* of 1622 the 'water poet', John Taylor, wrote that 'A Sword, a Cap of Maintenance, a Mace / Great, and well gilt, to do the town more grace: / Are borne before the Mayor and Aldermen, on high days'.[39]

The mace was a symbol of authority deputed by the Crown. In effect, a sergeant-at-arms was a delegate with powers to execute regal authority on the behalf of civic governors. Not surprisingly, in the wake of the abolition of the monarchy in 1649 a large number of corporations adopted maces which bore the arms of the Commonwealth instead of those of the dead king. As we have seen, Gloucester had four such republican maces. Bridgwater had three, Coventry, Marlborough, Rye, Tenby, Weymouth and Wigan had two each. Other corporations with at least one republican mace included Banbury, Buckingham, Cambridge, Chipping Norton, Congleton, East Retford, Faversham, Leicester, Lincoln, Maidstone, Newtown (Isle of Wight), Portsmouth, Richmond (Yorkshire), Stratford-on-Avon, Wallingford, Warwick and Windsor, as well as the City of London and the wardmotes of Cripplegate Within and Aldersgate. Down to the late nineteenth century, over forty examples of republican civic maces survived in the collections of town and city corporations throughout England and Wales.[40] This figure accounts only for those maces re-adapted in line with the restoration of monarchy. As Jewitt and St John Hope remarked, most corporations made alterations in 1660 as only a temporary measure, and in the first few years of Charles II's reign dozens of new maces were commissioned by town corporations across the country. No doubt some of them were made to replace republican maces.[41]

The most important mace in the realm and the first to be altered was that of the House of Commons. The House got its own serjeant-at-arms in 1415, when Nicholas Maudit was appointed. Since then the mace has been the supreme symbol of parliamentary authority and privilege. The abolition of the monarchy destroyed the tradition of regal authority, and Parliament acted accordingly. On 17 March 1649, the day the Rump issued its justification of the regicide and subsequent constitutional revolution, a parliamentary committee was ordered to look into redesigning the mace used in the House. A few weeks later, on 13 April, it made a number of suggestions, one of which was accepted. Then, on 6 June, the new mace was brought to the House and delivered to the serjeant-at-arms, Edmund Birkhead.[42]

This was the first commission undertaken by the goldsmith Thomas Maundy, maker of the Gloucester maces noted above. He was paid £137 1s and 8d for making this parliamentary mace, the state footing the bill.[43] The republican government employed the goldsmith's services on a number of occasions thereafter. A week before the introduction of the new parliamentary mace, the Council of State ordered its own sergeant, Edward Dendy, to confer with Nicholas Love (a member of the parliamentary committee responsible for the mace's alteration) about providing the Rump's chief executive body with a mace of its own. In July the Council ordered that the mace they had now commissioned be gilded in the same fashion as the one made for Parliament, and later appointed Alderman Francis Allen to arrange paying Maundy for the Council mace 'out of the Revenue'. According to a warrant dated 4 September 1649, Maundy was paid £151 10s and 4d, which sum was charged on excise receipts.[44] In March 1651 another mace was ordered, this time for use in Ireland (which, John Evelyn records, was carried at the head of Henry Ireton's funeral cortege in 1652); in 1655 another was made for Scotland, as was a fifth which was carried by the sergeant-at-arms to the Lords Commissioners of the great seal and, from 1654, the Treasury Commissioners, Henry Middleton.[45]

When Maundy delivered the new mace in June 1649, Parliament ordered that 'all other great maces to be used in this Commonwealth be made accordingly to the same forme and Paterne', and 'that the said Thomas Maundy have the making thereof and none other'.[46] Parliament's favour to Maundy aroused indignation amongst his fellow London goldsmiths. In November 1650 there was a row at the company court over his privileged position, which ended with Maundy backing down from a claim to nationwide monopoly rights which had been too much for his colleagues to stomach.[47] Supplying civic maces must have been quite a lucrative market, and judging from the number of surviving republican maces their concern is not surprising.

Maundy clearly maintained a substantial stake in this national re-stocking of civic plate collections, providing new maces for the corporations of London, Leicester and Wallingford, for example, as well as Gloucester's four. But, just as clearly, his bid for a national monopoly was defeated. The goldsmith employed by the Convention to replace the Commonwealth mace in 1660, Thomas Vyner, seems to have been responsible for providing Congleton's striking example of a republican corporation mace, whilst Tobias Coleman made a pair for Marlborough in 1652.[48] Coventry's maces were altered by Richard Blackwell in 1651.[49]

Parliament's regulation of maces and their provision across the country was as unprecedented as the Rump's initial decision to adopt a mace of its own at the state's expense. The design it laid down was also innovative. The wide variety of different designs actually adopted is no doubt explained by the diversity of the institutions which adopted them, as well as by the eventual involvement of a number of metropolitan workshops in the restocking of civic plate collections. But there was a basic set of features common to all. The main differences between the old style of mace and the Maundy 'paterne' were the removal of the regal and religious insignia (the coronet, orb and cross on top;

the Stuart emblems on the shaft), their replacement with the arms and insignia of the free state, and, in a remarkable number of instances, the fashioning of an alternative to the coronet's bars and arches in the form of decorative branches of oak supporting escutcheons with more arms, with an acorn replacing the traditional orb and cross. The oak motif also sometimes replaced the floral emblems of the Tudor and Stuarts which decorated many mace shafts.[50] Although exact details varied, this design became the basis for the reinvention of the civic regalia in the regions. The maces of Banbury, Congleton, Coventry, Gloucester, Leicester, Maidstone, Portsmouth and Wallingford all featured this central oak motif.[51]

The novelty of the new design is obvious. Its political and cultural significance will be considered later. For the moment, we turn now to consider perhaps the most important, and undoubtedly the most familiar, reinvention of England's political icons conjured by the Rump – the creation of a brand new great seal.

Seals have existed almost as long as there has been a technology of written communication. As physical artefacts which gave visible evidence of authorship they straddled the divide between the literate and the illiterate. From the rise of ancient civilisation until the last century they were the crux of secure and reliably authenticated communication, from the bureaucratic to the purely personal, from public to private. In England the great seal of state was the ultimate expression of this mode of administrative communication technology, and it has figured prominently in English conceptions of legitimate authority for centuries. It was integral to all concepts of the proper form that the highest levels of administration should take. It has been used for centuries as a recognisable guarantee of the authenticity of the sovereign's appointment, gift or adjudication. In his *Constitutional History* Hallam noted that 'the Great Seal, in the eyes of English lawyers, has a sort of mysterious efficacy, and passes for the depository of royal authority in a higher degree than the person of the king'.[52]

Not surprisingly, then, the great seal became a bone of contention in the 1640s. After Lord Keeper Littleton had fled to York with the great seal in 1642 its absence 'put a stop to the regular course of the executive government, and to the administration of justice within Parliament's quarters. No employments could be filled up, no writs for election of members issued, no commissions for holding the assizes completed, without the indispensable formality of affixing the Great Seal'.[53] In January 1643 this great seal was invalidated by the Commons, and thereafter Parliament debated the introduction of a new one. The initial decision to supply Parliament with its own great seal was again taken on the initiative of the Commons. When the idea was put to the vote in May 1643 the war party won an important tactical victory which strengthened the factional divisions in the parliamentary cause, with eighty-six MPs in favour and seventy-four against. Many opponents of this measure were deeply concerned about its treasonable aspect, John Maynard arguing that there was 'no end in making a new Great Seal unlesse they intended making a new king'.[54] Opposition to the implementation of the Commons' decision remained strong, especially in the Lords, and even though the lower House set about preparing the new seal, which was eventually brought in by the engraver Thomas Simon in September, it was not until the following month that the Lords capitulated, finally passing an ordinance annulling the king's seal, authorising Parliament's and appointing its keepers on 10 November 1643.[55] The king was outraged, declaring that here was proof, were it still needed, that Parliament intended violence not only against his royal person but against the whole institution of monarchy. Counterfeiting the great seal was high treason, and amounted to the complete destruction of law; and, he asked 'what is it lesse then to depose us ... ?' By this action Parliament had taken away 'the three most glorious jewels in our Diadem, Our power to doe, Our justice to inforce, and Our mercy to pardon, three such inherent prerogatives that as without them We are no King'.[56]

After the capitulation of Oxford in 1646 the negotiated terms of settlement included the surrender of the great seal then in the custody of Lord Keeper Lane, despite the latter's efforts to keep hold of it. Fairfax sent it to Parliament, along with other seals and swords of state, where it was resolved on 3 July to have it destroyed. Accordingly, on 11 August, the same day as the installation of new parliamentary Lords Keepers, the king's great seal was ceremonially smashed up by a blacksmith 'amidst much cheering', and the fragments were divided between the Speakers of both Houses.[57]

Parliament's great seal was now the repository of royal authority. The only difference between it and the old one was the date. It bore the same portrait of the king and the royal arms of the Stuarts. When Pride's purge set in motion the revolution which would depose Charles from supremacy in the state, the regal symbolism became outmoded, and the declaration of Commons supremacy on 4 January 1649 logically required a new emblematic representation of state authority. Two weeks before the king's trial opened, the parliamentary clerk, Ralph Darnell, informed Bulstrode Whitelocke that Parliament was considering the revision of court proceedings 'upon the alteration like to be'.[58] In the week before the king's execution the Commons passed legislation altering the basic formula for the conduct of legal proceedings. Writs would run *Authoritate Parliamenti Angliae*, and 'instead of the Peace of the king, it shall be hereafter the Publick Peace'.[59] The stamp of the dead king's authority was also purged from the instruments of English justice. Within two months of his death the Rump had altered the seals of most courts, and settled new forms for various commissions and writs.[60] But the most fundamental of these revisions, and the first which had attracted the Rumpers' attention, was the adoption of a new great seal.

The Rump appointed a committee two days after declaring the supremacy of the Commons to consider 'the framing of a Great Seal'. The members of the committee were Nicholas Love, John Blakiston, Thomas Scott, William Purefoy, Gilbert Millington, William Lord Mounson, John Fry and Francis Allen.[61] It was headed by Henry Marten, who had been a leading proponent of the case for Parliament having its own great seal in the debates of the 1640s.[62] On the 9th the committee reported the design they had settled on. One face would depict England, Ireland and the Channel Isles, with the legend 'The Great Seal of England 1648'; the other would depict the House of Commons in session, and bear the motto 'In the First Year of Freedom by God's Blessing Restored 1648' around the border.[63] On the 26th the parliamentarians again appointed Thomas Simon to make their new seal, and offered him £200 for his costs, twice the amount he had received in 1643.[64] The seal was soon ready, and a week after the king's execution it was brought in, along with the old one, which now suffered the same fate as had befallen the king's great seal in 1646. It was smashed up and the pieces, along with its purse, were given to Whitelocke and Sir Thomas Widdrington to dispose of at their pleasure. The same day the new Lords Keepers were sworn in, and they were ordered to provide a new purse to keep the great seal in, and an Act authorising the new seal was passed.[65]

The seal made in 1649 was apparently not very hard-wearing, and in 1651 the Rump ordered its replacement.[66] Simon prepared the second great seal of the Commonwealth, which was identical to the first, except that it bore the new date and the motto was altered accordingly, denoting the third year of freedom.[67] The new seal was brought into use on 17 December, and handed over to the Lords Commissioners, who were also enjoined to make arrangements for the destruction of the old one.[68] At the same time the House ordered the Council of State to pay Simon £300 for the two great seals he had made for the Commonwealth, and a warrant was issued accordingly on 21 January 1652.[69]

The great seal of the Commonwealth was used in a variety of conventional ways. Immediately after its introduction, Parliament discussed reissuing commissions to sheriffs and local justices, other commissions such as oyer and terminer, and gaol delivery, as well as validating writs of assize and association which had been taken out during the previous legal term.[70] It is not explicitly stated whether the Commonwealth great seal was used in connection with these instruments of administration, though orders were given that the fees for changing commissions and patents 'to be renewed upon the late Change, by reason of the king's death' were to be defrayed out of the Hanaper, Chancery's own treasury, and that the new forms of writs be 'passed' by the Lords Commissioners.[71] More specifically, in October 1649 the Rump ordered the

Lords Commissioners to issue their commission under the great seal to Sir John Savile, who had been appointed high sheriff of Yorkshire.[72] State appointments were regularly passed under the great seal.[73] It was affixed to important diplomatic documents, such as the commissions issued to the republic's ambassadors.[74] The patents issued to the Cursitor Baron (an Exchequer revenue official), Admiralty judges and officers of the Mint, for example, were all passed under it.[75]

But it was not just judicial instruments and the patents appointing great officers of state which had the great seal affixed for authentification. In June 1649 John Richardson's presentation to the rectory of Settrington, Yorkshire, by the Lords Commissioners was denoted in an instrument sealed with the Commonwealth great seal, one of very few surviving documents relating to the hundreds of presentations made by the Lords Commissioners in the period.[76] A York charter, possibly issued as part of the reform of English corporations to bring their formal embodiment in line with the institutions of the Commonwealth, had the new great seal affixed to it.[77] The Admiralty committee of the Council of State also recommended that, as part of the reform of Trinity House, its charter be brought up to date by having the great seal affixed.[78] The parliamentary governors appointed to run Charterhouse petitioned to have its foundation confirmed under the great seal.[79] The Council of State issued its warrant to the judges of the Admiralty court on 4 June 1650, ordering them to issue a commission to be passed under the great seal authorising certain shipowners to conduct privateering operations against Irish shipping.[80] The Rump gave numerous orders for affixing the great seal to the hundreds of pardons it passed during its reign, for offences ranging from treason to horse theft, forgery to witchcraft, frequently ordering that the Lords Commissioners' fees for affixing the seal be waived in such instances.[81] George Vaux, Whitehall housekeeper, was even granted confirmation under the great seal of the patent given him by the king.[82] Given the extent to which the Commonwealth used its great seal, it comes as no surprise that Stephen Iles, chafer of the wax to the great seal, was allowed the nonetheless remarkable sum of £360 per annum to cover his expenditure on wax.[83]

Simple administration carried the striking parliamentary imagery of the new great seal all over the republic. It was broadcast in a number of other ways, too. The image of the House became a hallmark device of the new regime, used by Simon in a number of other designs. It featured on one of Parliament's own seals, as well as the Commonwealth seal of the court of common pleas (which was an almost exact replica of the Commonwealth great seal).[84] When Cromwell wrote to Parliament after receiving the engraver in Scotland, where he had been sent to make the likeness of the Lord General which would appear on the medal celebrating Dunbar, he noted that he had heard it was intended to represent Parliament on the other face of the medal, remarking that he thought such a device 'will do singularly well'.[85] Thus the image of parliamentary republican authority was struck in silver and gold, and distributed among the officers and soldiers of the republic's victorious army. But, even before this, Simon had incorporated the image of Parliament in the *Meruisti* medals for bravery and service distributed on a more regular basis to members of the Commonwealth navy (whose ships Nedham once described as 'king fishers').[86] In September 1651 Thomas Mackworth's refusal to open the gates of Shrewsbury to Charles Stuart was rewarded by the Rump with a gold chain worth £100 bearing 'the Medall of the Parliament'.[87]

A number of other Commonwealth devices used the motif of the Commons in session. In 1649, when undertaking the reform of Westminster school and almshouse, Parliament appointed a new board of governors, drawn almost exclusively from amongst its members, for whom Simon engraved a seal. Appropriately enough, this design again incorporated the image of Parliament in session, presumably to foster symbolically the closeness of the ties between the Rump and the school.[88] The Commonwealth seals of both the county palatine of Chester and Flint, and the county palatine of Lancaster, made in 1649, also incorporated the Westminster scene, complete with the 'First Year of Freedom' motto, in the design for their reverse faces. This version of the scene also bore the additional detail of the arms of England. This seal is of some interest. Formerly, palatinate seals had followed a standard pattern, depicting the monarch on one face and the relevant royal arms on the other. Under the Commonwealth, one face depicted Parliament, whilst the other showed a castle, with ornamental shields bearing the arms of England and Ireland on the right- and left-hand side-towers respectively, and carried the motto 'The Originall Seale for the County Palatine of Chester and Flint'.[89]

The other noteworthy feature of the Commonwealth great seal's reverse is its justly famous motto 'In the First Year of Freedom by God's Blessing Restored 1648', updated in 1651. Although it was a forthright revision of the old system of regnal dating, the state rarely used it to date its decrees or legislation. On occasion, however, the Rump might use the supposed date of the restoration of freedom as the defining limit for retrospective measures. For example, on 27 May 1651, Parliament resolved to cancel all recognisances, fines and amerciaments to keep the peace 'which are or may be levied as due to the Commonwealth, at any time before the thirtieth day of January, One Thousand Six Hundred Forty-and-Eight, when this Commonwealth was restored to its Freedom and Liberties'.[90] More dramatically, the statue of the king at the Old Exchange was replaced by an inscription which also echoed the great seal motto:

Exit Tyrannus, Regum Ultimus
Anno Libertatis Angliae Restitutae Primo ... 1648[91]

Again, the local evidence is quite interesting. The corporation of Congleton in Cheshire was just one of those which adopted the motto for incorporation in the design of its new mace, acquired in 1651, which bore the legend 'The Freedome of England by Gods Blessing Restored 1651' in a band at the top of the cup on which sat the republican oak coronet.[92] There is even fragmentary evidence for the use of the republican dating system, such as the dating of local election returns in Kidwelly, Wales.[93] And again, as with the arms of state, there was a small-scale literary fad for the new dating system. In 1652 Payne Fisher, a writer later closely associated with the Cromwellian Protectorate, published a volume of neo-Latin panegyrics to the republic's leaders, which he dated in both the conventional and the republican style: 'Salutis Humanae MDCLII' and 'Libertatis Angliae IIII'.[94]

II

An entirely new representational language of political signs and symbols emerged during the Commonwealth period. Its significance can be gauged by interpreting, where possible, what the language said to contemporaries, by assessing their response, and by locating the visual culture of the republic within the context of Commonwealth politics.

The imagery of republican iconography was unmistakably nationalistic. Arms, maces and seals all bore the stamp of English nationalism, articulated by the cross of St George, the oak motif, the map of the Commonwealth on the great seal and the use of the English language in the mottoes which appeared on it and on the coins issued by the new regime. None of these devices was the intellectual property of the post-revolutionary regime. St George was the patron saint of the highest expression of English chivalry, the royal Order of the Garter. The oak was a significant feature of both classical Roman and druidic British culture.[95] But the Commonwealth's use of these icons, and the rest of its symbolic repertoire, also had distinctly radical parliamentarian qualities. The image of the House assembled in debate certainly articulated the declaration of Commons supremacy, replacing the traditional regal portrait which usually featured on great seals. The vast differences between Tudor and Commonwealth depictions of Parliament are hardly surprising, but they are instructive nevertheless. In the earlier period the Commons was conventionally depicted as an anonymous lumpen mass huddled at the bar of the upper House, spectators of the important and dazzling ritual bonding between monarch and peers.[96] Nothing could express so clearly, therefore, the significance of the constitutional revolution than the great seal's depiction of the new supreme authority. There was, nevertheless, something rather idealised about the image of the Commons in debate. At least 100 MPs appear to be assembled in the chapel of St Stephen, a figure rarely attained in the course of the Commonwealth. The one event able to excite so much enthusiasm amongst the membership was the annual election of the Council of State.

The map of the Commonwealth on the reverse also suggests a sense of a community for whom decision-making had been collectivised by the assembled representatives.[97] The mainland isles were depicted in great detail. In England nearly 400 ports, castles, boroughs, towns, cities and counties were picked out, and about 100 similar topographical details make up the description of Ireland. Possibly taken from an atlas published by the Dutchman, Blaeu, in 1645, the attention to detail in Simon's rendering of the maps is impressive.[98] The lettering is tiny, and crammed into a space only a few inches across.

A cursory examination reveals it is no constituency map of the English Commonwealth, and so we can rule out the possibility that it was designed to reflect the representational basis of the Commons' new-found supremacy. A great many constituencies whose members were purged or withdrew voluntarily do not appear, including Weymouth, Devizes, Reigate, Bridport, St Ives and Evesham. But many constituencies no longer represented after December 1648 were still depicted, as were a number of places that had never been enfranchised. If there was a specific logic in the choice of locations depicted, it does not seem to have much to do with the prominence of individual Rumpers, either. There is no Malmesbury (Sir John Danvers), no Great Marlow (Bulstrode Whitelocke), no Aylesbury (Thomas Scott), no Wendover (Thomas Harrison), no Tamworth (Sir Peter Wentworth) and no Marlborough (Charles Fleetwood). None of the West Country constituencies of the three Ashes, Edward, James and John, appears, either (Heytesbury, Bath and Westbury, respectively). The greatest ports, towns and cities seem the natural choice for depiction, but there is no Lichfield, no Great Yarmouth, no Dover (the last two being the constituencies of another pair of leading Rump politicians, Miles Corbett and John Dixwell respectively).

One is driven to conclude that in fact there is no particular logic in the fine detail, no deliberate choice behind most of the inclusions and omissions. In some sense the form was clearly more important than all the details which made up its content. Nationhood was captured cartographically. In the 1640s, in order to counter the theory of divine right with their own convenient fiction, parliamentarians had 'invented the sovereignty of the people in order to claim it for themselves'.[99] The imagery of the great seal also represented an imaginative claim to dominion. The Commonwealth depicted on the great seal was equally fictional in the sense that large parts of it (principally Ireland, but also the Channel Isles, and the last bastion of mainland royalism, Pontefract castle) were not yet conquered, let alone loyal, when the seal was adopted. Even when the second version was introduced in December 1651, the image still represented an idealisation in that respect. As with the image of its rulers, the map of the Commonwealth had an imaginary quality. But the creative potency of this idealisation was compelling. It was later taken up by George Wither, whose perpetual parliamentarians would each wear a 'badge of honour', passed down to new members from year to year, in the form of a golden wreath surrounding an enamel pendant bearing the British Isles

> within the Ocean plac't;
> And with a verge of curled waves embrac't
>   ... to priviledge
> Their persons, whersoe're they were unknown;
> That due respect might ev'ry where be shown,
> And no affronts received.[100]

The conceit was apt, especially given the vigour with which the regime enforced its physical superiority, not only by land but also by sea. The regime's imagery also had an imperial, even jingoistic appeal. Both in the arms of the state and in the design of the great seal, Ireland was simply annexed to the authority of Parliament, even before the reconquest had begun. In a constitutional context, this reflected the unprecedented nature of the 1642 Act for the Irish Adventure, the first legislation of an English Parliament binding on Ireland. The depiction of the Irish realm was later echoed by William Petty's 'Down survey', one of the earliest attempts to map a territory whose cartographic dimensions had eluded generations of would-be conquerors. Meanwhile, Scotland's absence from the great seal map echoed the decapitation of a king with Scottish blood and the inauguration of a new era of violent conflict with England's northern neighbour.

The simplicity of the arms of St George also expressed a certain kind of nationalistic pride. Charles I had reinvented the device of the Order of the Garter, emphasising its sacred aspect by setting the cross within an aureole of silver rays in emulation of the French chivalric order, the Knights of the Holy Spirit.[101] Under the Commonwealth, the saint's arms were purged of this cosmopolitan affectation. It was in the context of military success that Englishmen took greatest pride in the achievements of the republic. And it was the arms of the Commonwealth which formed the emblem of success. When Edinburgh Castle was finally captured in December 1651, falling to hostile forces for the first time ever, an English newswriter wrote with relish of the English ensign which now flew proudly from its flagpole. 'The English colours are now planted on it, and the sun smiles on them as they dance before the wind, who courting them as they passe by, will carry the glory of our achievements into the furthest ends of the world.'[102] Under the Stuarts England's standard had advanced not one yard in forty years. In Rubens's famous allegory of Charles as St George slaying the dragon of war, the imagery of the nation's patron saint was used to serve the pacifism of the later Caroline court.[103] This ideal conflicted with (but may be explained by) the ignominy of Charles's previous attempts to conduct an aggressive foreign policy.[104] In the 1650s, after half a century of desultory European impotence, pan-pacifism and Spanish matches, Englishmen once more took pride in the geostrategic achievements of their nation. The language and symbolism by which it was expressed were the forerunners of rhetoric about an empire upon which the sun never set.

At sea, the Commonwealth also asserted its right to the recognition of English maritime dominion. Shortly after the naval victory at Gabbard Sands in June 1653, another newswriter warned the Dutch that they could expect more of the same if they 'do not come in and submit timely to our cross and harp, that now makes the sweetest harmony'.[105] Simon's seal placed the Commonwealth in the midst of its greatest strength, its watery defences. The republican regime adopted protectionist trade policies and an anti-piracy crusade which were enforced by the most powerful navy England had ever sent to sea. Under the republic, King James I's claim to dominion over the seas off England's coastline, and Charles I's grand vision of enforcing the same, actually became a reality. Indeed, in the aggressiveness of its maritime policies the Commonwealth seems almost to have had in mind monopoly control not only over its coastal seas but over the Mediterranean and even the Atlantic, too.[106] 'The British Seas' depicted on the great seal could even be seen as a dim and distant precursor of Britannia's defiant ocean-going reign.

The sophistication and complexity of Simon's engraving articulated a classical principle of virtuous self-rule in a vernacular English way. This was also reflected in the simplicity of the arms of the regime, shorn of the dynastic devices to which the national emblems had traditionally been hitched. The modernity of this sense of nationhood is also expressed by the use of the English language. In January 1649 Hyde was informed by one of his English correspondents that Parliament was to introduce a great seal which would bear the motto *Anno Primo Libertatis*.[107] The assumption would seem to be that, even for revolutionaries, the fitting style for rendering their absurd claims was Latin, the language of all official *sigillae*.

There was radical potential in the Commonwealth's imagery. However, the language of republican iconography also implied a commitment to authority, law and tradition. The new icons were a positive response which ruled out the anarchy many feared would follow the revolution, and as such may have had a somewhat wider appeal to basic conservatism. The great seal served wholly traditional judicial and executive purposes; its introduction was the iconic equivalent of the regime's reassurance of the judiciary that the ancient laws of the realm would continue to run in the traditional channels.[108] Its imagery idolised Parliament and nation. Even the dating may be read in a conservative light. There was possibly something quite deliberately anti-millenarian in calling 1648/49 'The First Year of Freedom'. Rather than stopping the clock of human history, the revolution had set time back in motion. It would now continue its linear progression forwards, when the zealots were holding forth that Englishmen should be counting down, through the last days, to the inauguration of Christ's reign on earth.

As for the maces, they are a reminder that 'considerable civic state was maintained during the Commonwealth', indicating no diminution in the contemporary sense of hierarchy, order and its adornment.[109] In 1649 a well-known print depicted Cromwell supervising the destruction of 'the Royall Oake of Brittayne'.[110] In the tree's boughs hung Crown, Bible and Magna Carta. To many Englishmen the revolution seemed to have dissolved an authority as ancient and deep-rooted as an oak. By a small stretch of the imagination we may almost see the republican maces as 'new growth', sapling oaks symbolising a resurgent civil authority.

Their adoption in the country at large seems to bear out Marchamont Nedham's assertion that 'the state hath a party in all countries and corporations', its bulwark throughout the nation.[111] It should be noted that Parliament did not positively require corporations to change their maces. The decision, taken, as we have seen, all over the country, was due largely to the discretion of individual town and city authorities. Their actions, and the way they acquired their new or altered maces, sometimes suggest strong support for the new style, and occasionally reflect their affinities with the new regime. Many bought brand-new maces. At Leicester the old mace, weighing 52 oz, was handed over to Maundy by a local goldsmith, John Turvile, to whom it had been entrusted by the corporation. In London, William Purefoy, MP for Coventry, supervised the making of the new mace, which weighed 87 oz.[112] The City of London was furnished with a massive new mace weighing more than 200 oz, supplied by Maundy at the cut-rate price of £81 12s.[113] Elsewhere, new maces were paid for by public subscription. At Maidstone, during the mayoralty of Andrew Broughton, clerk to the High Court of Justice, an old mace was sold for less than £4 and a new one purchased for £48, £10 of which was provided from the bequest of an ardent local roundhead, John Bigg.[114] In London, Sir John Wollaston, treasurer-at-war, made a gift of a new Maundy mace to Aldersgate ward, where he was an alderman.[115] The evidence from Banbury was slightly more equivocal. There, fourteen members of the corporation lent £32 between them towards a new mace, only £1 being 'freely given'.[116]

Many corporations, particularly the smaller ones, made do with simply having their old royal-style maces altered to conform with the institution of the Commonwealth. But, again, there is evidence that such changes were undertaken with some enthusiasm. At Wallingford the mayor gave £10 towards alterations which cost nearly £50, and an ex-inhabitant of the borough, Walter

Bigg, who now lived in London, contributed another £20. Again, the evidence may be slightly equivocal. One of two maces altered for Faversham apparently acquired the nickname 'the Rompe' in 1660, which was probably not a term of endearment.[117] But the evidence from Chipping Norton, where only the mace head was altered, or Newtown, Isle of Wight, where only the arms and other regal devices were changed, demonstrates that even boroughs of limited means undertook, unbidden, what alterations they could afford.[118]

Some evidence suggests a much more negative response, especially, and not surprisingly, in royalist quarters. The twin-arms device was said to resemble a pair of breeches, and was thus a fitting emblem for the Rump. It was also derided as 'the Fidlers Arms' (*The Man in the Moon* excitedly reporting that they would be 'razed out' from the stern of Commonwealth warships falling into the hands of the royal party, and replaced with Charles Stuart's).[119] It was also said of the coinage that it was unwittingly honest of the republicans to have 'The Commonwealth of England' on one side, allowing that God was on the other side.[120] *The Man in the Moon*'s uncharacteristic outburst may also be taken to be humorous: describing the naval insignia, he wrote that

> they carry top and top gallant, a Crosse, O profane! Superstitious idolatry in the superlative: Are we not like (thinke ye) to have the Victory, when the Devill carries the Crosse? The Irish harp too! Now by Saint Patrick, a Relique too: How is it possible that these sincere tender-conscienc'd Dopp-chickens should brook such raggs of Rome? Surely the Whore of Babylon and the Brethren are in conjunction.

It may be that the iconography of the regime did indeed disconcert radical Protestants. The adoption of George's cross, an emblem closely associated with the papal reward of Henry VIII's staunch if short-lived defence of the Roman Catholic faith against Luther's onslaught, and the widespread use of the oak motif, with its obvious pagan associations, might almost have been calculated to offend a certain cast of mind. Perhaps Commonwealth iconography testifies to the success with which the public image of the revolution, at least, was 'captured' and thereafter defined by the likes of Marten, Chaloner, Scott and the rest of 'those wits' assailed by their godly critics as amoral atheists.[121]

The great seal was referred to by one hostile newswriter as 'the Great Butterprint of State'.[122] More seriously, in February 1649, the peers of the realm denounced the Rumpers as traitors, not only for killing the king, but also for altering the great seal.[123] Sir John Stowell, brought before the Upper Bench and put on trial for murder and treason in March 1649, refused to acknowledge Lord Chief Justice Rolle's commission, 'it being counterfeit and the seal also'.[124]

Such hostility must be taken into account when we weigh up the significance of republican imagery. Interpretation is not made any easier by the fact that, although they used them widely, republican politicians made few explicit statements on the subject of the republican images. The regime's public image was dreamt up by only a handful of MPs – most notably the regicides Henry Marten, Thomas Scott, Nicholas Love and John Blakiston. One much more conservative member, Francis Rous, prefaced his assertion of the legality of obeying the Rump with the New Testament verse 'Judge not according to the appearance, but judge righteous judgement.'[125] Other commentators were not sure what to make of the new style. Addressing the Rumpers, Isaac Penington junior told them that 'Yee have made a change in the forme of Government, and put a new image and superscription upon it, which is like to be of great concernment one way or other, but which way it will be is yet somewhat doubtfull'.[126]

The only explicit statement about the mace made by any Rumper was Cromwell's disparaging reference to 'that fooles bable', made as he dissolved the Parliament in April 1653.[127] The size of the new great seal gives another indication of ambivalence, or at least suggests that the Rumpers' veneration of their political fetishes was qualified to some extent. The two Commonwealth great seals were only 5½ in. and 5¾ in. in diameter respectively, whereas regal ones were traditionally 6 in. across. During the original debates over the introduction of a new great seal in 1643 Sir Simonds D'Ewes recorded that John Glynn argued in favour,

> but soe weakly as I did wonder such light and impertinent matter should come from him who usually spake with weight and reason, for one Argument that hee used for to make a great seale was that it needed be neither soe thicke nor soe broad as that the king used.[128]

Nevertheless, the fact that the regime deployed its signs and symbols as widely as it did is at least suggestive of their significance for members of the republican executive, legislature, judiciary and military. Despite the impotent accusations of the secluded peers, Parliament clearly intended the great seal to be taken seriously as the iconic embodiment of the Commonwealth's authority. Counterfeiting it was deemed a treasonable offence in May 1649.[129] An early example of Rump ceremony attended its formal adoption, the swearing-in of its new keepers and its handing over to their care.[130] As well as wielding the traditional rights of appointment to vacant ecclesiastical benefices, and controlling the composition of the county benches, just as their predecessors had done under monarchy, the Lords Commissioners of the Commonwealth great seal were made responsible for the appointment of new central court and circuit judges and sergeants-at-law after the resignations amongst the judiciary which followed the revolution. They also appointed a new solicitor-general, and were authorised to grant commissions of sewers and charitable uses 'as any Lord Chancellor, Lord Keeper or Lords Commissioners have and ought to have Power to do'.[131] It was fitting that their importance should be acknowledged in the outward form of things. Two of the commissioners – Whitelocke and Lisle – were awarded the lease on the Duke of Buckingham's palatial residence at Chelsea, chambers at Whitehall were set aside for their use, and their headquarters at Westminster were set up in two rooms belonging to the former Court of Wards.[132] They played occasional ceremonial roles which also featured the great seal itself. They attended the swearing-in of Thomas Andrews as the mayor of London in April 1649, bringing the seal with them, 'with usual ceremonies'. By 1652 the seal was being kept and carried in a rich purse embroidered with 'the best double refined gold and silver upon a rich crimson velvett ingraine, with the armes of the Commonwealth of England at large'.[133]

The Rump's mace had an exclusively ceremonial role. Serjeant Birkhead's job was to carry it before the Speaker as he passed to and from the House. Maundy delivered it in time for Birkhead to perform this function at the head of the procession of Rumpers which made its way to the City the following day for the banquet referred to in the previous chapter.[134] Thereafter the mace played a central role in all Rump ceremonial. When Birkhead escorted visiting foreign dignitaries into the chamber, or formally called MPs conducting business in Westminster Hall to attend the House, he always carried the great gilt mace on his shoulder.[135] On one occasion it was damaged by a half-brick aimed at Speaker Lenthall.[136] This apparently caused considerable offence to some Rumpers.[137] Another instance certainly suggests the fetishistic quality of the parliamentary mace as perceived by some contemporaries, if not appreciated by all. In April 1650, during one of the regime's periodic bouts of anxiety about pro-Stuart conspiracy in the capital, a royalist newspaper reported that the Presbyterian minister Thomas Juggard had been arrested on charges of treason, and imprisoned at Newgate. He was visited by parishioners, who were perplexed by the idea that there could be such an offence as treason when there was no king to betray. Juggard observed sardonically that '"there is a great Mace which is worse and they that at the Sound of their Drum and Trumpet will not fall down and worship it are to be put into Cromwell's Copper" (meaning their Prisons)'.[138]

The dissolution of the Rump provides further evidence for the importance of the mace. There are numerous accounts of this key event of the Interregnum, and though most of them are second-hand they more often than not pay some attention to the detail of what happened to the parliamentary mace.[139] Even Hyde described to Rochester, at third hand, how Cromwell ousted the Rumpers, 'himself brought up the Reare, ... [and gave] the mace to a Colonell to carry to St James's'. An account given by the Genoese ambassador, Bernardi, suggests the symbolic importance of the moment. Having fulminated against the House, Cromwell, he recounted, first took off his hat, then picked up the mace from the table in front of the Speaker, handed it to Harrison, who then handed it to a subordinate, the General then putting his hat back on. His version of the event may be a little imaginative, but it certainly captures his own sense of the importance of the mace. The account of the Venetian ambassador also suggests the symbolic significance attached to it. He reported that the Speaker left the House

> without the mace, which always used to go before him as a mark of authority, and of the session of Parliament, whose arms it bore ... the whole city perceiving that he had been deprived of the public badge, which remained in the hands of the troops, and so the authority of the Parliament was entirely dissolved and abrogated.[140]

Finally, the significance of republican iconography is demonstrated by the fact that, unlike the abolition of the monarchy, the dissolution of the Rump was not followed by a purge of the old order's signs and symbols. The Rump's great seal remained in use, even after the establishment of the Protectorate, which did not have its own seal until 1656.[141] The arms of the Commonwealth remained in use as the 'masthead' device used on orders and ordinances issued by Protectors, and even by the 1659 Committee of Safety. Remarkably, just before the Restoration, when William Prynne was making a bonfire of the Commonwealth's arms in Lincoln's Inn Fields, the king's arms began reappearing all over London, and the English navy was hurriedly replacing republican emblems with the regal insignia of Charles II, the Convention voted to continue using the Rump's great seal, simply because it was the only available instrument of authority which commanded any respect.[142] After the Restoration, despite orders for recoining the currency of the Commonwealth, much of it remained in the public domain, according to Pepys, and as we have seen, many republican maces survived at least down to the end of the nineteenth century.[143]

III

Republican iconography is a potent and useful source for understanding the political culture of the English Commonwealth and parliamentary republicanism. Its existence does not in itself prove the supremacy of an avowedly anti-regal pro-republican ideology. The politics of the Interregnum show all too clearly the continuing attachment to monarchy in English politics. The cynicism fostered by the double-speak and propaganda deployed by Parliament during the civil war and later in justification of the revolution also warn us to beware assuming that members of the Rump overly venerated the 'baubles' which symbolised their rule.

But that does not mean it was impossible to take seriously the invention of a republican regime. England may have become a republic by default in 1649, but the inventive imagination which went into adorning the new regime's authority is a useful reminder of the fact that even 'mere necessity' can have radical implications. Taken as a whole, the iconography of the parliamentary republic displays an obvious conservatism, reflecting an attachment to the principles of law and dignified magistracy on which the ancient constitution was built. Serjeants-at-arms had borne maces as emblems of parliamentary authority for well over 200 years. However, the Rump's mace was the first made at the behest of 'the People', the first paid for by 'the State'. There was considerable hesitancy on the part of the wider Commonwealth, and the new style did not sweep the nation. But, in time, Parliament's early lead was followed all over the country.

Contemporaries may have seen the potency of the revolution in images in the same way that modern Europeans are alive to the significance of the removal of Communist symbolism. This is meant only as the broadest kind of analogy. Clearly England did not witness the kind of revolution which has swept away decades of ideological conformism and modern European imperialism. But it did experience a revolution which temporarily put paid not just to decades of Stuart rule but to centuries of monarchy. The scale is very different, but the significance is not. All over eastern Europe a thousand Lenins have toppled from their plinths. In the middle of the seventeenth century a handful of Englishmen were temporarily powerful enough to have statues of the late king torn down, putting in place of one the famous gilded motto commemorating the revolution, 'Exit tyrannus Regum ultimus'. This statue was only one of many depicting the kings and queens of England which presided over the merchant community which did business at the Old Exchange in London. For eleven years they continued as before, but were reminded daily of how times had changed. Symbolism of this kind may have made infinitely less impression than the tax burden laid on the same men by the new regime. But symbols do count for something, in this case perhaps reminding the mercantile community of the titanic struggle to overcome an old and repressively exclusive commercial order.

Finally, it is worth noting that the symbolic languages spoken by the arms and great seal of the Commonwealth, the Rump's mace, its medals and currency and the plate and insignia of its urban corporations bore little discernible relation to the republican ideology of classical Greece or Rome. They can be understood only in the context of the veneration of traditional English civic government, the significance of English parliamentarism, and as propaganda for the policies of the Rump. But the new imagery also celebrated principles such as patriotic nationalism, corporate decision-making and representative government, principles which reflected one side of those slow-burning arguments which characterised the long-term causes of the civil war and revolution.[144] Invented by a revolutionary Parliament of commoners and soldiers, that imagery was an advertisement for the creation of a free state, the English Commonwealth, and gave visual expression to *de facto* republican positions about a nation, its people and their rulers. It was elaborate, coherent, and used extensively in all quarters of the republic throughout the eleven-year Interregnum. Above all, it used familiar, domestic motifs to make an aggressive statement of the Commonwealth's power, policy and ideals. It was nothing less than the language of a vernacular republicanism. The political imagery of the Rump republic should make us think twice before dismissing the regime as a half-hearted expedient.

NOTES

1 *CJ* vi, 276; Millar ed., 'Inventories', p. xx, and relevant inventories; R. Lightbown, 'The King's Regalia, Insignia and Jewellery', in MacGregor ed., *The Late King's Goods*, pp. 268, 272; M. Holmes and H. D. W. Sitwell, *The English Regalia. Their History, Custody and Display* (1972), pp. 3–14.

2 *Mercurius Politicus* 15–22 August 1650, p. 162; Norbrook, 'Marvell's *Horatian Ode* and the Politics of Genre', p. 151.

3 *Mercurius Politicus* 8–15 August 1650, p. 160; P.R.O., SP25/16, 78; *CSPD 1650*, pp. 261, 389.

4 *CJ* vi, 274, 394, 516, 531; Worden, *The Rump Parliament*, p. 219; *CSPD 1649–50*, p. 481.

5 *CJ* vi, 142.

6 *Ibid.*, 183.

7 *Ibid.*, 274.

8 P.R.O., SP25/62, 406; *CSPD 1649–50*, p. 481.

9 Bachrach and Collmer eds, *Huygens' Journal*, p. 109.

10 For the most recent, and illuminating discussion of 'the king's book' see K. Sharpe, 'The King's Writ: Royal Authors and Royal Authority in Early Modern England', in Sharpe and Lake eds, *Culture and Politics*, pp. 117–38. The king's image also continued to circulate on medals and in print. See Hawkins *et al.* eds, *Medallic Illustrations*; A. Globe, *Peter Stent. London Printseller c. 1642–1665* (Vancouver, 1985).

11 *Mercurius Politicus* 8–15 August 1650, p. 160. As *Pragmaticus* Nedham had taken a more tragic tone in December 1648, crying out against the rebels, 'Stamp, stamp! on Royal Majesty; and as you stamp him down, stamp your own image in his dust.' Cited by A. Fraser, *Cromwell, Our Chief of Men* (1973), p. 275.

12 P.R.O., SP25/15, 69; SP25/65, 22. My emphasis.

13 P.R.O., SP25/62, 222; SP25/87, 46. See plate 6 (a). 'God with us' was also the motto adopted by the earl of Essex, Parliament's original Lord General. Graham Seel, 'Cromwell's Trailblazer: Reinterpreting the Earl of Essex', *History Today* 45/4 (1995), 24.

14 Carte ed., *Original Letters and Papers* i, 274.

15 P.R.O., SP25/62, 8; SP25/94, 208–9. See plate 7.

16 P.R.O., SP25/62, 53.

17 P.R.O., SP25/64, 494–5.

18 P.R.O., SP18/1, 73.

19 P.R.O., SP25/63, 33.

20 *Ibid.*, 38.

21 *Ibid.*, 612; Bachrach and Collmer, eds, *Huygens' Journal*, p. 37 and n.

22 P.R.O., SP25/17, 35.

23 Bachrach and Collmer eds, *Huygens' Journal*, p. 40.

24 B. Lib., 669 f. 14, 15, 16 and 17, for a great many examples. Also P.R.O., SP18/1, 46 and 48.

25 See plate 5. This was the most prominent of a number of official publications which used the arms in this way. Cf. *A Declaration and Narrative*, regarding Parliament's dealings with the Dutch in the winter of 1651, printed 'by authority' by George Horton, [29 December] 1651, B. Lib., E651 (8).

26 Morrill ed., *Revolution and Restoration*, p. 108.

27 *CJ* vi, 142.

28 *Ibid.*, 531; *Weekly Intelligencer* 4–11 February 1651, p. 53.

29 *CJ* vii, 19. See plates 8 and 9.

30 P.R.O., SP25/89, 69.

31 Bachrach and Collmer eds, *Huygens' Journal*, p. 53.

32 A. Quick, *Charterhouse* (1990), p. 19; Latham and Matthews eds, *The Diary of Samuel Pepys* i, 106.

33 *CSPD 1650*, p. 430.

34 H. Stocks ed., *Records of the Borough of Leicester* (4 vols, Cambridge, 1923) iv, 384, 394, 397–8, 405–7, 411–13.

35 The people of Gloucester were dubbed 'the Conservators of the Parliament of England' for their staunch resistance to the king. John Dorney, *Certain Speeches made upon the Day of the Yearly Election of Officers in the City of Gloucester* (1653), p. 23.

36 Ian Roy, 'The English Republic, 1649–60: the View from the Town Hall', in *Schriften des Historischen Kollegs Kolloquien* II. *Republiken und Republikanismus im Europa dem frühen Neuzeit* (Oldenburg, 1985), pp. 213–237; L. Jewitt and W. H. St John Hope, *The Corporation Plate and Insignia of Office of the Cities and Towns of England and Wales* (2 vols, London and Derby, 1895) I i, li, I ii, 224.

37 For a notable exception, see Ann Hughes, 'Coventry and the English Revolution', in R. C. Richardson ed., *Town and Countryside in the English Revolution* (Manchester, 1992).

38 Lieutenant Colonel Peter Thorne (serjeant-at-arms in the House of Commons, 1976–82), 'The Royal Mace', *House of Commons Library Document* 18 (1990); Major General H. D. W. Sitwell, 'Royal Serjeants-at-Arms and the Royal Maces', *Archaeologia* 102 (1969), 203–50; Jewitt and St John Hope, *Corporation Plate*; National Maritime Museum, *Oar Maces of the Admiralty* (1966).

39 Quoted on the title page of Jewitt and St John Hope, *Corporation Plate*.

40 *Ibid., passim.*

41 *Ibid.*, I i, liii.

42 *CJ* vi, 166, 185, 228.

43 *Ibid.*, 275.

44 P.R.O., SP25/62, 378–9, 504, 573; SP25/63, 6, 38.

45 P.R.O., SP25/65, 93; Sitwell, 'Royal Sergeants-at-Arms and the Royal Maces', pp. 214–15; de Beer ed., *Diary of John Evelyn* iii, 57; *CSPD 1655*, pp. 61, 608. On Middleton see also Aylmer, *The State's Servants*, pp. 66, 118 n, and P.R.O., SP18/23, 98, schedule of his fees. Also P.R.O., E403/2523.

46 *CJ* vi, 226.

47 Thorne, 'The Royal Mace', p. 32.

48 *Ibid.*; Jewitt and St John Hope, *Corporation Plate* I i, li–lii. For the Congleton mace, see plate 3.

49 *Ibid.*, II ii, 386.

50 *Ibid.*, I i, liv. See plate 4.

51 *Ibid.*, I i, liii, 28; I ii, 224, 274, 344–5; II i, 57, 59–61, 254–5; II ii, 386.

52 Henry Hallam, *The Constitutional History of England from Henry VII to George II* ii (1872), 161–2. For the important general point about the symbolism of ordinary administration and its forms, see Clanchy, *From Memory to Written Record*, pp. 257, 311–12, 316–17; cf. Aylmer, *State's Servants*, p. 19, for the ritualisation of bureaucracy.

53 Hallam, *Constitutional History*, pp. 161–2.

54 B. Lib., Harley MS 164, fo. 389.

55 C. M. Williams, 'Extremist Tactics in the Long Parliament, 1642–3', *[Australian] Historical Studies* 15 (1971–73), 136–50, p. 143 n.; William Prynne, *The Opening of the Great Seale of England* (in *Somers Tracts*, third collection, 1643, i, 390–426), and John Taylor's reply, *Crop-Eare Curried* (1644). See also A. B. and A. Wyon, *The Great Seals of England* (1887), pp. 85–90.

56 *The Declaration and Ordinance of the Lords and Commons touching the Great Seale of England, 11 November; and His Majesties Declaration to all his Loving Subjects upon Occasion thereof* ([21 November] 1643), pp. 12, 14, 16.

57 Wyon and Wyon, *Great Seals of England*, p. 88.

58 Whitelocke Papers X, fos IV–2 (I.H.R. microfilm); Underdown, *Pride's Purge*, pp. 183–4 n.

59 *CJ* vi, 123, 124, 144; Firth and Rait eds, *Acts and Ordinances* i, 1262; ii, 6.

60 E.g. *CJ* vi, 130, 133, 136, 137, 151. The Rump was quick to order the replacement of seals used under the monarchical regime, but there were clearly delays in getting them all revised, as in mid-February Parliament ordered that the old seals might remain in use, for sealing the writs, process and proceedings of the courts, until 10 March 1649. *CJ* vi, 144.

61 *CJ* vi, 112–13.

62 Williams, 'Extremist Tactics', p. 143; *idem*, 'The Anatomy of a Radical Gentleman:

Henry Marten', in D. Pennington and K. Thomas eds, *Puritans and Revolutionaries. Essays in honour of Christopher Hill* (Oxford, 1982), pp. 118–38, p. 133.

63 *CJ* vi, 115; Underdown, *Pride's Purge*, p. 204; Worden, *The Rump Parliament*, p. 36.

64 *CJ* vi, 123.

65 *Ibid.*, 134–5.

66 The 1648/49 seal reproduced on plate xxx in Wyon and Wyon, *Great Seals of England*, is badly worn, its detail barely discernible. The authors suggest that this may have been due to the hurry in which Simon was required to make it.

67 See plates 1 and 2.

68 *CJ* vii, 47, 51; Wyon and Wyon, *Great Seals of England*, p. 92 and plate xxxi.

69 P.R.O., SP25/66, 236.

70 *CJ* vi, 136 and 141.

71 *Ibid.*, 140.

72 *Ibid.*, 314.

73 P.R.O., C54 and C66/2907, 2908, 2912–15 (close and patent rolls); C82/2233–44 (warrants for affixing the great seal, March 1649–March 1650); C.231/6 (Crown office docquet book for 1643–60).

74 *CJ* vii, 276; Bod. Lib., Rawlinson MS C 129, fo. 2v.

75 *CJ* vi, 140 and 142; cf. *ibid.*, 305, the Council of State asked Parliament for direction on what to do with Mint officials not prepared to hand over their old patents from the king in exchange for new ones from the Commonwealth; *CSPD 1649–50*, pp. 249, 334–5, 549 – Mint officials refusing new patents were to be thrown out of office and their official accommodation.

76 B. Lib., Add. Charter 27,326.

77 Wyon and Wyon, *Great Seals of England*, p. 90.

78 *CSPD 1652–53*, p. 29.

79 R. Ackerman, *The History of the Colleges of Winchester, Eton and Westminster, with the Charter-house, the Schools of St Paul's, Merchant Taylors, Harrow and Rugby, and the Free-school of Christ's Hospital* (1816), p. 18.

80 *CSPD 1650*, p. 547.

81 *CJ* vi, 127, 150, 204, 249, 375–6, 378, 379, 447, 456–7, 468, 477–8, 480, 482, 483, 524, 537–8, 585, 587, 595; *CJ* vii, 2, 9, 28, 97, 150, 156, 173, 265, 266, 274, 278 375–6.

82 *CSPD 1651*, p. 48; *CSPD 1652–53*, p. 29.

83 P.R.O., SP18/23, 81.

84 George Vertue, *Medals, Coins, Great Seals and other Works of Thomas Simon ...* (second edition, 1780), plates III and V.

85 Cromwell to the Army Committee, 4 February 1651. Cited by H. W. Henfrey, *Numismata Cromwelliana* (1877), p. 3. See plate 6 (b).

86 P.R.O., SP25/63, 262; A. J. Nathanson, *Thomas Simon, his Life and Work, 1618–1665* (London, 1975), p. 19. See plate 6 (c).

87 *CJ* vii, 6–7.

88 H. Farquhar, 'New Light on Thomas Simon', *Numismatic Chronicle* fifth series xvi (1936), 229–30.

89 Vertue, *Medals, Coins, Great Seals and other Works*, plate IV; W. de G. Birch, *Catalogue of Seals in the Department of Manuscripts in the British Museum* (1887) ii, 51–2.

90 *CJ* vi, 578.

91 *Mercurius Politicus* 15–22 August 1650, p. 162.

92 Jewitt and St John Hope, *Corporation Plate* I i, lii, 67–8. See plate 3.

93 D. and R. Hook 'More Light on John Davies of Kidwelly', *Carmarthenshire Antiquary* 15 (1979), 57–64. Cited by Roy, 'The English Republic', p. 226.

94 *Irenodia Gratulatoria*, cited by Norbrook, 'Marvell's *Horatian Ode* and the Politics of Genre', p. 151 n.

95 D. Brooks-Davies, *The Mercurian Monarch* (Manchester, 1983), p. 151; G. H. Bishop, *The History and Legend of the Oak* (Batley, 1975); R. A. Clarke, A. Wright and R. Barnett, *The Blasted Oak. The Oak Tree: Natural History, Art, and Myth in European Culture* (Batley, 1987), pp. 23–4.

96 David Dean, 'Representations of Parliament', in D. Hoak ed., *Tudor Political Culture* (Cambridge, 1995). The 1640s were an important benchmark on the way to the design of the Commonwealth's great seal. In April 1640 an engraved broadsheet, *The Platform of the Lower House of Parliament*, was printed at the start of the Short Parliament. See M. Corbett and M. Norton eds, *Engraving in England* (Cambridge, 1964) III, plate 206 (a).

97 Cf. Victor Morgan, 'The Cartographic Image of the Country in early modern England', *Transactions of the Royal Historical Society* fifth series 29 (1979), 129–54.

98 J. Blaeu, *Atlas Novus* (1645).

99 E. S. Morgan, *Inventing the People* (New York, 1988), p. 50.

100 Wither, *The Perpetuall Parliament*, p. 71.

101 I am grateful to John Adamson for his help on this point. See his 'Chivalry and Political Culture in Caroline England', p. 174.

102 *The Weekly Intelligencer* 24–31 December 1650, p. 8.

103 Carlton, *Going to the Wars*, p. 11.

104 *Ibid.*, pp. 14–17, 24–30, for the disasters of Cadiz and La Rochelle, and the humiliation of the bishops' wars.

105 *The Faithfull Scout* 10–17 June 1653, p. 1048.

106 Capp, *Cromwell's Navy*.

107 Bod. Lib., Clarendon MS 34, fo. 72.

108 Gardiner, *History of the Commonwealth and Protectorate* i, 9; Abbott ed., *Writings and Speeches* ii, 12, 33.

109 Jewitt and St John Hope, *Corporation Plate* I i, xlviii.

110 See plate 10.

111 P. A. Knachel ed., *The Case of The Commonwealth of England, Stated* (Charlottesville, 1969), pp. 60, 114.

112 Jewitt and St John Hope, *Corporation Plate* II i, 57, 59–61.

113 *Ibid.*, II i, 98.

114 *Ibid.*, I i, 344–5. See *CJ* vi, 222, for Broughton's appointment as Clerk of the Upper Bench.

115 Jewitt and St John Hope, *Corporation Plate* II i, 153.

116 *Ibid.*, pp. 254–5.

117 *Ibid.*, I ii, 331.

118 *Ibid.*, p. 273; II i, 260.

119 29 May–5 June 1650, p. 430.

120 R. Ruding, *Annals of the Coinage ...* (6 vols, 1819) iii, 240–1, cited by Nathanson, *Thomas Simon*, p. 14.

121 *Man in the Moon*, No. 26, April 1649, p. 7. The emblematic nationalism of the cross of St George dated back to the same epoch as the papal bestowal of the 'Fid. Def.' tag. I have found no evidence that the Commonwealth's use of the device excited the kind of emotion aroused in Massachusetts in the 1630s. See J. H. Adamson and H. F. Holland, *Sir Harry Vane. His Life and Times, 1613–1662* (1973), pp. 60, 70–1. The saints also seem to have had little to say about the incorporation of the heathen harp of Erin.

122 *Mercurius Pragmaticus* 7–14 May 1650.

123 P.R.O., SP18/1, 4.

124 *The Vindication of Sir John Stawells Remonstrance against a Pamphlet written by Mr John Ash* ([18 May] 1655), pp. 42–3.

125 Francis Rous, *The Lawfulness of Obeying the Present Government* (1649), frontispiece.

126 Isaac Penington junior, *A Word for the Common Weale* ([15 February] 1650), p. 2.

127 Spalding ed., *Diary of Bulstrode Whitelocke*, p. 286.

128 B. Lib., Harley MS 164, fo. 389.

129 Firth and Rait eds, *Acts and Ordinances* ii, 120.

130 *CJ* vi, 135; Spalding ed., *Diary of Bulstrode Whitelocke*, pp. 230–1; Wyon and Wyon, *Great Seals of England*, p. 92.

131 *CJ* vi, 187, 205, 246.

132 *Ibid.*, 266, 321; *CSPD 1649–50*, p. 239. In Whitelocke's 'History of his 48th Year', the Lord Commissioner muses at length on the delights of living at Chelsea during his period of political withdrawal in the summer of 1653 which followed the dissolution of the Rump. See below, chapter 4.

133 Spalding ed., *Diary of Bulstrode Whitelocke*, p. 236; Sir H. C. Maxwell–Lyte, *Historical Notes on the Use of the Great Seal of England* (1926), p. 319.

134 *Perfect Occurrences of every Daies Journall in Parliament* 1–8 June 1649, p. [1096].

135 *CJ* vi, 228, 541–2; *Mercurius Politicus* 9–16 January 1651, p. 523; *A Declaration and Narrative of the Proceedings of the Parliament of England touching the Message sent from the*

Estates General of the United Provinces (1651), p. 5; *The Weekly Intelligencer* 25 May–1 June 1652, pp. 472–3; *The Perfect Diurnall* 28 June–5 July 1652, p. 1993; *Severall Proceedings in Parliament* 30 September–7 October 1652, pp. 2473–4.

136 *CJ* vii, 209.

137 In modern British politics the mace is held in no less veneration. John Beckett, the 1930s radical socialist, and Michael Heseltine, in his capacity as maverick during Lady Thatcher's reign (quite distinct from the rather more grave demeanour of his perform-ance as President of the Board of Trade and Deputy Prime Minister), are just two MPs who have shown their outrage by violating the mace.

138 *The Royal Diurnall* 14–23 April 1650, p. [7].

139 C. H. Firth, 'Cromwell and the Expulsion of the Long Parliament in 1653', *English Historical Review* 8 (1893), 526–34, and 'The Expulsion of the Long Parliament', *History* new series 2, I (1917), 129–43, II (1918), 193–206.

140 *CSPVen 1652–53*, pp. 64–5.

141 Wyon and Wyon, *Great Seals of England*, p. 92.

142 M. F. Bond ed., *Sir Edward Dering's Convention Diary* (1976), pp. 40, 41. I am grateful to Dr Gerald Aylmer for bringing this reference to my attention. Cf. Latham and Matthews eds, *The Diary of Samuel Pepys* i, 113, 133–4.

143 The survival of Commonwealth imagery beyond April 1653 will be considered at greater length in chapter 5, below.

144 Ann Hughes, *The Causes of the English Civil War* (1991).

1 Obverse of the great seal of England, 1651

2 Reverse of the great seal of England, 1651

3 The Congleton
mace

4 Speaker Rous with the 'bauble' mace

5 Title page of John Milton's *First
Defence of the English People* (1651)

6 (a) Gold 20s piece, 1649

6 (b) Dunbar Medal

6 (c) Naval *Meruisti* Medal

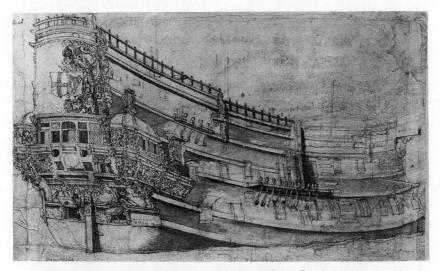

7 *The Garland*, by van de Velde the elder, after its capture
at the battle of Dungeness, 1652

8 Dutch engraving of the dissolution of the Rump, 1653

9 [Peter Stent,] Barebones Parliament, 1653

10 The Royall Oake of Brittayne

Chapter 4

ℌonour

ℌ O N O U R and its codes and languages were central to the dignity of early modern politics.[1] This was a further element of traditional English political culture which survived the revolution of 1649. The abolition of the monarchy and the House of Lords did not herald an attack on the most ancient traditions of the honour code. After the revolution, the earl of Leicester complained to a friend in exile that 'common Wealths be not ordinarily so well natured to particular persons, as Princes are'.[2] But despite the relative political isolation of the old peerage, felt by even the parliamentarian lords, old notions of the hereditary and titular honour of the nobility survived, whilst the Rump made no attempt to prevent this, or to create an alternative Roman republican idea of the civic virtues of the citizen.[3]

The regime established in 1649 was, by any measure, an overwhelmingly gentle regime. Its leaders numbered a handful of peers, and the majority were of good breeding and varying degrees of county standing. As ex-courtiers themselves, several were members of a socio-political elite steeped in the notions of honour and dignity which pervaded the thinking of the wider traditional political nation to which all Rumpers belonged. James Howell dedicated his edition of Finet's observations on diplomatic protocol to Councillor Philip Lord Lisle, commending his work to the viscount as a lover of both the theory and practice of honour espoused by his forebear Sir Philip Sidney.[4] In justifying the revolution, the Rump even implied it had acted to preserve gentry virtue, which had become corrupted by association with the royal court. The moral fibre of the nation would be tainted no more by 'the great Nursery of Luxury and Intemperance; the corrupter of the Manners and Dispositions of many otherwise hopeful branches, sprung from the Noblest families; and an universal Perverter of Religion and Goodness therein'.[5] The distinctly unvenerable history of English monarchs was laid bare by one historian who catalogued the instability created by the birth of illegitimate children fathered by intemperate kings, 'to let the world see what foundation these six-and-twenty Bastards have laid for honourable, noble and right worshipful Families of long continuance'.[6]

There was no real revolution in the theory of honour and its derivation in the period. Heredity had its critics during the Commonwealth. Milton attacked the 'empty and vain titles' of contemporary nobility. Nedham remarked that the marquis of Ormond '(according to the fate of all lords) is a thing that lives but by courtesie'.[7] But this was a common enough theme already in Renaissance thinking, given added edge by the 'inflationary' policies of the first Stuart king in the matter of titles, and strongly stated by Selden, Jonson and Camden earlier in the century.[8] Come the wars in England, there had been a 'remarkable reassertion of the aristocratic prerogative of leadership in war', and parliamentarians were attacked for being of humble standing in society. This was not a terribly accurate accusation, but it was a persistent one. Even Cromwell famously denounced Parliament's soldiers as serving men and tapsters, whereas the royalists had the support of gentlemen and 'men of quality ... that have honour and courage and resolution in them'.[9]

Still, the 1650s may be seen as a high point of the more pluralistic notions of honour and reputation which had been spawned by a century or so of English Protestant civicism.[10] Milton's famous remark that Cromwell had 'done in a few years more eminent and remarkable deeds whereon to found nobility in his house ... than Ormonde and all his ancestors put together' is a reminder of how years of warfare had promoted a stark contrast between the virtue of action and the presumptions of heredity.[11] Milton implicitly defended the notion of heredity, but clearly had no patience with the disavowal of its responsibilities by noble houses grown mossy for want of that active *virtu* with which fortune must be mastered. Blood was not the safest guarantee of honourable achievements, for inherited honour could be tainted by indolence and its vices. When Parliament gave Thomas Fairfax the lordship of the Isle of Man, James Chaloner wrote of his patron that he fully deserved the reward, which accorded him the same jurisdiction and title as the Stanley earls, 'for that as He in Vertue and Nobility of Blood is not inferiour to any of his Predecessors, Kings or Lords of Man; so in high Achievements of Arms he far surmounteth them all'.[12]

The parliamentary paragons of virtue were men like Fairfax and Essex who showed their breeding by action. But their actions were no longer the preserve of an aristocratic elite. A military training manual published in 1650 intended for use by England's amateur soldiers gave lengthy consideration not only to postures and exercises but also to the honour and dignity of every member of the soldiering body, from the high command right down to the ranks and files, which were to be ordered according to the individual virtue in arms of the private soldiers.[13] The author knew that this was the sugar coating the pill of square-bashing. For, having learned his postures, the soldier 'begins to look about himself, what next is needfull for to fasten upon, to make a further progresse in this Art. And straight he meets with some that whispers to him, that it were a gallant thing to know the Dignity of a file ... to which he answers, but where can it be found, the opinions of souldiers are so various.' The author then offers his own definitive account of what the raw recruit wants more than anything to know, 'to satisfie the longing desire of the young Souldiers request of every particular place of honour as they stand in dignity both in Rank and File'.[14]

The economy of honour in the 1650s was not affected by any fundamental shift away from blood towards virtue, even if emphases were altered. Nonetheless, the Commonwealth was different in one marked respect, for the revolution deprived the state and its institutions of their traditional regal topstone, an accepted paragon of honour who would give hierarchy its essential pyramidal conceit. Conventionally, it was argued that the honour of Parliament derived from the presence of the king, who was 'head and fountaine of honour'.[15] With the king's head cut off, from whence did Parliament's honour flow in the period of the Commonwealth? The question would have appeared impertinent at best to any cavalier, of course. But parliamentarians could clearly not make do without their own sense of the honour of Parliament and its officers.

Apologists of the revolution would later claim that, 'If a people be depraved and corrupted, so as to conferre ... power ... upon wicked men, they forfeit their power ... unto those that are good, though but a few'. This was first argued by John Goodwin in justification of the army's purge of Parliament. Milton soon 'civilised' the thrust of this new providential aristocratism by praising the 'men of noblest temper', those 'worthy men in Parliament', whose virtue made them peers of the king, and therefore fit to act as his judges.[16] Revolution, then, not only created a new set of rulers, but also, at least to its apologists, anointed them, giving the new elite a sacred, honourable cast. These were the new aristocrats, the 'most eminent and worthy Patriots' who had come to their nation's rescue.[17] Their elevation was not a matter of title. It was their heroism which entitled them to respect. '[F]uture ages, if they prove not too degenerate, will look up with honour, and aspire toward those exemplary and matchless deeds of their ancestors, as to the highest top of their civil glory and emulation.'[18]

This was a highly partisan point of view. In order to dignify the ordinary business of administration, the rulers of the republic looked to far more conventional arguments about the dignity of governing itself. At the first York assizes after the revolution, the circuit judge reminded the grand jury that

> all men in their Originall Creation are all of one and the same Substance, Mould and Stamp, yet for preservations sake, they finde a fitnesse in Subordinations and Degrees among them, for the better ordering of their affairs; and so they appoint rulers.[19]

This kind of conventional platitude prefaced any number of political homilies on obedience to the powers-that-be as an extension of the domestic obligation to 'honour thy father'. But there was a further dimension, too, built on the realities of *de facto* authority. Another apology for the new regime argued that 'they that possess the places and performe the duty *de facto*, must *de jure* and *ex debito*, receive the dignity annext to the publike authority'.[20] In his eulogy on the honour and dignity of Fairfax, Chaloner also argued that law and its execution were so important to human society 'that the Law-givers and Administrators of such, have been ever held, even with the most barbarous Nations, in very great veneration'.[21] The Rump was concerned not only to be obeyed, but to be *honoured* and obeyed. Efforts were made to ensure that the Commonwealth, its institutions and their officials were all located within contemporary notions of honour and so received the respect that was their due.

To some extent this was the logic behind each of the elements of Commonwealth political culture examined so far, the topography, spectacle and iconography of the regime. But, along with a simple desire to shore up order with as much of the old deferential ways as possible, there went a greater emphasis on the alignment of honour with the state and the nation. This was the basis of the Rump's solution to the problem of what to do about articulating a code of honour in the absence of a king. In August 1651 Charles Stuart summoned the surrender of Shrewsbury, which was under the command of Thomas Mackworth. The pretender commended the governor as 'a gentleman of an ancient house'. Mackworth addressed his reply 'to the commander-in-chief of the Scottish army', telling him, 'I resolve to be found unremovable the faithfull servant of the Commonwealth of England, and if you believe me to be a gentleman you may believe I will be faithful to my trust.'[22]

At the end of October 1646 the Long Parliament annulled all peerages and titles granted by Charles I since 20 May 1642, the day the great seal had passed from parliamentary control with the flight of Lord Keeper Littleton.[23] In accordance with this legislation, when it put George Goring on trial for his life in 1649, the Rump referred to him consistently by his baronial title alone, refusing to recognise the title of earl of Norwich granted him by Charles in 1644. The duke of Hamilton, on trial before the same High Court, was referred to consistently by his English title, the earl of Cambridge.[24] In February 1652 the Rump extended the Long Parliament's Act, annulling all titles granted under the king's great seal since 4 January 1642, because the king had conferred 'titles of Honour, Dignities and Precedencies' on 'such persons as he thought were or might be serviceable to him', and because nobody 'should presume to assume unto themselves any Titles, Honors, Dignities or Advantage, by a work so much contrary to the interest of the nation'.[25]

The Rump's measure extended annulment to all titles granted since the failure of the king's military *coup*. The attempted arrest of Lord Mandeville and the five MPs had effectively destroyed the conventional conception of government. Parliament thereafter claimed it had a right to appoint the king's councillors.[26] With the passage of this legislation against the titles granted by the king the Rump symbolically claimed an alignment between Parliament and the nation, and a strict association of honour with the service done to both. The king's revolt had ended his claim to be a fount of honour, and it was not long before Parliament made itself arbiter in the matter. Nedham harangued Ormond for continuing to use his 'fustian titles ... as if he were at Dice still before Dublin, and had never been cashiered out of his Excellency, and other evidences of the supreme Authority of the Nation'.[27]

I

Title and insistence on the proper form of address as a mark of deference were a primary feature of Commonwealth conceptions of honour. The Rump never assumed to itself the right to hand out traditional titles as rewards or marks of elevation, despite the support for such a scheme in some quarters. One author argued for the introduction of titles of honour for 'the eminent maintainers of the Liberties of the Commonwealth', which would be hereditary only if the heir to the title was 'thought worthy of the state'.[28] In June 1649 the Rump considered a proposal that it grant knighthoods because 'honour is a principall reward of virtue and hath bin in all times in this Nation of great incoragement to generous spiritts'.[29] In the event it rejected the measure, and it was not until the establishment of the Protectorate that the idea of bestowing titles of honour was revived.[30]

But the Commonwealth regime was not hostile to titles *per se*. As we have seen, what mattered was that they had credible provenance, and, given the gentry support for a regime which numbered peers, baronets and knights among its members, it is not surprising that there was reluctance to claim parity with the monarch's right to create traditional titles, or to add to the inflationary pressure which so many contemporaries felt had debased the honours system.[31] In the meantime, members of the government were keen not to let basic standards slip in such a way as to diminish their authority. We have seen how the adoption of a great seal provided a degree of continuity with previous executive, judicial and administrative practice, legitimising the practice of republican government whilst restating the terms of legitimacy. The officers of government, too, it seems, were the object of a similar exercise. One of the Commonwealth's new keepers of the great seal, Bulstrode Whitelocke, recorded a debate on the subject of the title and powers to be bestowed on him and his colleagues in that office, claiming that the Rump had decided that 'though the word Lords was less acceptable at this time than formerly' it was right that they be styled Lords Commissioners, 'that they [the Rumpers] might not seem to lessen their owne authority, nor the honour of their officers'.[32]

Aside from this retrospective account, there is apparently no evidence of a positive decision in the matter. Commissioners were appointed on 8 February, but by the time they were sworn into office by the Speaker later that day they were being styled Lords Commissioners, and Whitelocke and his colleagues were indeed known throughout the Rump period by that title.[33] Likewise, Cromwell was known as the Lord Lieutenant of Ireland, even though appointed only as commander-in-chief of the Commonwealth's forces in Ireland, and Bradshaw was known as the Lord President of the Council of State without any record of a formal decision to give him the lordly epithet.[34] The republicans simply recreated the gravity and dignity of traditional forms.[35] But it was not just a matter of mere words. It was reflected, too, in outward appearances, and by the deference with which the highest officials of the regime were treated.

At the banquet held by the City in honour of the government and the army commanders on 7 June 1649, Whitelocke again records, Philip Herbert, the earl of Pembroke, gave him precedence at table, he 'being the antient Commissioner of the great seal'. Whitelocke, declining, 'desired his Lp would be pleased first to sitt downe', but the earl, speaking 'aloude (as he used to doe) that all near him might hear, [asked] what doe you thinke that I will sitt downe before you? I have given place heretofore, to Bp Williams, and to my L. Coventry and my L. Littleton. And you have the same place that they had, and as much honor belongs to the place under a Commonwealth, as under a king, and you are a gentleman as well borne and bred as any of them, therefore I will not now sitt downe before you.'[36]

The story cannot be taken at face value.[37] The day before the banquet Pembroke had asked Parliament's permission to go to the country for the sake of his health, and it is not absolutely certain that he was still in London on the 7th.[38] But, even if he was not present, he, along with the earls of Salisbury and Denbigh and viscount Lisle, had been appointed to the committee of the Council of State set up to consider the arrangements for the banquet, a committee which did indeed recommend the precedence of the Lords Commissioners over the noblemen.[39] Whitelocke may have imaginatively reconstructed the basic gist, putting suitable words in the mouth of a peer who had submitted himself to election in order to gain his seat in Parliament. Possibly Whitelocke drew on the stereotype of the earl's bluff, straightforward manner, established in a number of satires of the period.[40] His account may also reflect Whitelocke's post-Restoration desire for self-vindication. Possibly he sought to defend himself retrospectively against the accusation that had been levelled by a remnant of the House of Lords back in 1649, that it was 'an act of the deepest treason to take our places as judges or Commissioners'.[41] In any case, whatever the factors prevailing in the composition of Whitelocke's account, there is at least no evidence that peers preceded leading officers of state in this or any other ceremony. On the other hand, there is considerable evidence to suggest that Whitelocke's elevation brought with it a kind of functional ennoblement.

Whitelocke's appointment to the pinnacle of the legal and judicial establishment made him one of the most powerful men in the Commonwealth, and his favour and assistance were courted accordingly. The earl of Northumberland approached him in November 1649, seeking his support for a suit for retrieving a debt soon to be presented to Parliament by the countess of Leicester (the earl's sister, and mother of Algernon Sidney, whom the earl had apparently 'entreated ... to acquaint your Lordship' with the particulars).[42] On other occasions the earl sought the Lord Commissioner's assistance, as when he asked Whitelocke if he would like to take up rooms in Sion House, the earl's London residence, in order to prevent its use as a military barrack.[43] Whitelocke accepted, and Northumberland wrote to thank him: 'the consideration you are pleased to have of me and of that house of myne is a very great favor, which shall thankfully be acknowledged and returned unto you if ever it be in the power of your very affectionate friend and servant'.[44] Whitelocke was so pleased with this sign of deference from one of the greatest nobles in the land that he later transcribed the letter into one of the volumes of his *Annales*.[45] He was similarly taken by the 'very respectful letter' he received in September 1649 from John Williams, in which the one-time archbishop of York, seeking a benefice for a dependant, declared himself 'very cautious in importuning my noble friends at this conjuncture of times, when I little understand what is fit for me to ask or fit for them to graunt'.[46]

Whatever doubts may have existed about the new patronage system, Whitelocke was not short of suitors who clearly recognised he had the power to help them and who were prepared to defer to his honour in order to win his support. A servant of the earl of Downe wrote to him to ask his assistance in the matter of his master's estate, which had been confiscated by the state. To prevent its falling into the hands of someone less scrupulous, the earl was clearly pinning his hopes on getting Whitelocke to procure legislation which would allow him to sell land to the Lord Commissioner. According to his servant, the earl 'esteems it for a great honour and happinesse that he may deal with a man of so much honor and iustice as your lordship is'.[47] At one time there was talk of a marriage between Whitelocke and Lady Hungerford.[48] His colleague in government, Lord Grey of Groby, took Whitelocke and John Lisle to visit his grandmother, the countess of Exeter, who 'highly entertained' them.[49] In his 'diary' Whitelocke also recorded the approaches he received from several other eminent members of the social hierarchy, noting that Lord Tracey was 'very civill' to him; and that the countess of Nottingham's brother had presented him with 'a fair English Bible richly bound, and an ingenious letter with it, praying its acceptance'.[50] Lord Broghill offered his services, mentioning those he had done the Lord Commissioner's son, James (who was serving in the army in Ireland), in gratitude for 'many Noble favours'.[51] The commissioners of the peace, militia and assessment in Berkshire petitioned the Lords Commissioners of the great seal for the removal of the earl of Kent from the post of county *custos rotulorum*, and asked Whitelocke to do them the honour and favour of taking his place, not only because of their regard for 'the nobleness of your Lopps disposition', but also because of their 'desires to promote the good of the County'.[52]

Whitelocke kept up the appearances on which the honour of his office depended. Lord Berkley and the earl of Suffolk both made their homes available to him. The latter put Audley End and his servants there at Whitelocke's disposal for his convalescence after a bout of illness in December 1649, and the next month the Lord Commissioner rode out from London 'in an Equipage suitable to his condition, hansom horses in his Coach and two handsom horses for his own saddle' accompanied by Dr Denton, serjeant Eltonhead, 'and his servants well mounted'.[53]

Out of office, Whitelocke was just as prone to the affectations of dignity. When he sat down to collate his thoughts on the traumatic events of his forty-eighth year, he concocted a retrospective vision of political retreat out of the idyllic surroundings of his palatial residence at Chelsea, one of the perquisites of his place at the centre of Commonwealth politics.[54] When Cromwell 'insolently and unwisely' dissolved the Parliament which had made him what he was, Whitelocke fell from power, and 'had not the least imagination of further employment'. This was a relief 'most wellcome to him in those times', allowing him to retire 'to the injoyment of the Comforts of his wife and family, which men in publique service cannot doe nor recreate their minds with those meditations which are farre more valuable then Cappes and knees, then fees and salaries'.[55]

The narrative of his retirement which he constructed focuses on a stylised account of how Cromwell's Council of State settled on Philip Lord Lisle as the Commonwealth's ambassador to Sweden, and how Lisle then went off the idea, leaving a vacancy in that post which Whitelocke was eventually called on to fill. Thus he recorded how Lisle was chosen, and eminently suited to the job, and how his preparations progressed. But he also wrote (in the third person, as was his wont), that 'Whitelocke enquired not after that buisnes, butt remained in the contentment of his privacy and retirement; and being att his house at Chelsey contemplat[ed] the wonderfull power and goodness of God appearing in the grasse herbes, plants and trees, fruit, and everything that comes within our view and meditation.'[56]

All the while, Whitelocke interspersed the details of a story to which he was supposedly not privy with the 'meditations' his withdrawal permitted him, his muse ranging across subjects as diverse as heredity and hawking, marriage and creation, patriarchy and rainbows, death and bereavement, preaching and travel. All this he intended by way of spiritual instruction to his children. He kept up his account of developments at Whitehall, recording on the day after his forty-eighth birthday that Lisle's preparations 'began to be slackened by him, and his mind to be changed, which yett he did not communicate nor did Whitelocke heare thereof'.[57] Instead he continued enjoying his retirement, walking in his Chelsea garden, 'meditating on the pleasures thereof, and the beautifull River of Thames running by it', opining that it was 'full of pleasure, fitt for a Duke, a great Prince on earth', but that it was 'as a dunghill' compared with the garden of Eden, the subject of his next lengthy meditation.[58] He tended his vines and his fruit trees. And, as required by the trope of country retreat, he mused on the vanity of earthly things. He was struck by the stateliness of his new home, 'and how the same was gotten by the great ones who formerly injoyed it', but saw in it, and their fate, 'the vanity and uncertainty of these earthly pallaces and mansions', all of which prefaced a lengthy meditation on the fate of all things 'built of earthly materialls, and by mortall hands'.[59]

Whitelocke wrote this piece of country retreat prose as the introduction to his account of his embassy to the Swedish court. Its idyllic rendering of a man sitting about doing nothing is the affectation of a gentleman with power and influence (or quite possibly the affectation of a gentleman quite wistful about power and influence long gone). It did not take him long to get back in the saddle, and before he left for Sweden he complained about the niggardly sum allowed him in order to deck himself and his entourage out in a style befitting his mission.[60]

Two other officers of the civil regime performed key honorific roles during the Commonwealth. At the City banquet, and on a number of other occasions, the position of honour went to the Speaker, William Lenthall, hero of January 1642, when he refused the king's demand that he be handed the five members on a plate, and the new figure head of the civil state. In June 1649 he took the kingly role in ceremonially receiving, then returning, the corporation's sword of state from the lord mayor, and he then sat at the head of the banquet. A satire on the event had alderman Thomas Atkins give a speech in which he told Lenthall it was 'mervilous in our eyes, to see you become our Supreme Head and Governour, now that we have cut off the king's head'.[61]

In October 1649 Lenthall was officially the first member of the Parliament to subscribe the Engagement when it was extended to non-conciliar MPs.[62] A warship was named in honour of the post, and when attending the chapel in the Rolls, Chancery Lane, Lenthall sat 'by himself in a separate place, and when he went out a gilt mace was carried in front of him'.[63] Lenthall shared in

Cromwell's glory in 1651 at the triumphal City entry which followed the victory at Worcester. As Protector, Cromwell rode into the City with the full pomp of Augustan regality. In 1651 he entered London in the Speaker's coach.[64] Indeed, in 1659, when the army reinstalled the Rump, it swore loyalty to Lenthall as 'the father of the nation'.[65] The Speaker had come a long way from disrespected partisan appointee.

Another official who came to perform an important function in the hierarchical arrangements of the Commonwealth was the chairman of its executive, the Lord President of the Council of State. Although this office was clearly based on the chairmanship of the king's council, it should be noted that there was no Lord President of the Privy Council between 1631 and 1679.[66] Again, the title bestowed tacitly on Bradshaw indicates how successfully the Rump overcame apparent scruples on the subject of the single person (having originally decreed that the Council should get by without a head). Despite bouts of in-fighting over his position, and even after the Rump had adopted the motion that the chairmanship of all committees should rotate on a monthly basis, thus ousting Bradshaw from his permanent headship, the Lord President continued in his designation and in being regularly reappointed to his position as chancellor of the duchy of Lancaster. In 1654 one newsbook account of the opening of the first Protectorate Parliament referred to 'Lord Bradshaw' as a candidate for Speaker.[67]

The Lord President's title and his ceremonial functions bespeak the dignity of his office, which also had a warship named after it, as well as the influence wielded by a chancellor of the duchy. Bradshaw was lobbied by the corporation of Leicester in its application for a new town lecturer, as 'the power of presenting another [is] clearly devolved to your Lordships hands'.[68] The position, like the Speakership, also entitled its holder to special parliamentary largesse, and to the kind of hyperbolic praise reserved for the greatest officers of state.[69] Nedham acclaimed the Lord President, 'to whose especial vigilance and indefatigable industry and care we owe much of our present peace and safety'.[70] George Walker commended a book of his 'to the Right Honourable Lord President', for 'though I may seem bold, I am not so blind, but that I perceive your Lordship taller by the head than most I can set by you, and so come for patronage in hopes of a favourable smile'.[71] A panegyric to the military achievements of Oliver Cromwell was dedicated to the Lord President as 'the All-Worthy, ... the Overseer of the Commonwealth, and Re-gained Liberty' and the rest of the patriots of the Council.[72]

Bradshaw, like Whitelocke, also seems to have adopted the affectations of dignity. At the end of 1650 he reflected on the coming Council elections phlegmatically. 'Some of us shall interteine our dismissions with much contentedness' – he looked forward to taking up a country residence, 'thereby to atteine to some fresh ayre to recover health somewhat impaired, and prevent more wastes and spoiles' on his new estate at Hanworth.[73] At times, the honour of the elevation given an ordinary attorney was apparently more than his humility could bear, to the irritation of some of his colleagues at the Council table, for, Whitelocke records, 'the President spent much of their time in his long speeches, a great hindrance to ... business'.[74] And he almost certainly did not entertain his eventual dismissal from the permanent head-ship with much contentedness. In February 1651 it was reported that a dispute had arisen at a committee customarily headed by the Lord President where Henry Marten had managed to assume the chair. Bradshaw retaliated, coming to the committee 'in state with a great guard before him'. It was even claimed that after he had secured re-election to the Council in the same month 'it was spoken by one of the Council of State that they kept him in for fear he should have hanged himself'.[75]

II

Civilian officers of the Commonwealth tried to present a dignified face to the world which reflected their position of authority. In turn, their honour was amplified by the supplications of suitors and petitioners. Honour was, as ever, closely related to issues of power. The Rump was in power, it called its officers honourable, and therefore they *were* honourable. As a linguistic feature of republican political culture, honour was, in consequence, a relatively unstable force within politics. Different limbs of the regime might argue over different interpretations of the honour of the Commonwealth. A dispute between the commissioners for compounding and sequestration and the indemnity committee over the respective privileges of the two bodies illustrates how conflict over honour could play a role in the day-to-day administration of the republic. It arose in the winter of 1651 in a jurisdictional wrangle caused by the different actions being pursued by each against the royalist colonel Richard Conquest.[76] In November 1651 the colonel attended a meeting of the commissioners at Haberdashers' Hall, where he was discharged fully from his composition and sequestration. However, as he was leaving the hall he was seized by deputy sergeant John King in execution of an indemnity committee warrant originally issued against him in May 1650 for contempt of that body's authority.[77] The committee had first attempted to arrest Conquest in December 1650, at which time the royalist had 'caused the persons whoe apprehended him to be beaten and wounded'. This time Conquest was taken away under armed guard.

On being notified of what had happened, the compounding commissioners took considerable umbrage, demanding Conquest be set free, and King arrested, to even things up. They sent their own messengers to the indemnity committee chamber to arrest the deputy sergeant and secure Conquest's release. The indemnity committee refused to comply, demanding instead the recall of the warrant for King's arrest. The compounding commissioners protested at this contempt of their authority, particularly the committee's detention of the warrant against King and their demand that it be recalled.

Thomas Hussey MP intervened on behalf of his colleagues, the committee-men, representing to the commissioners that they had acted 'with all respect to you and your privileges which they are really sensible ought for the honour and justice of the Parliament to be as well preserved as their owne', but were upset by this attempt to arrest their servant on a warrant 'which your officers were ready to serve in the face of the Committee'. The committee also argued that 'the Colonell being in so high contempt (as a person outlawed) cannott be capable of or in justice ought to receive any protection from you or any committee before whom he shall appeare untill he shall discharge and take off his contempt'. In the interests of conciliation the committee declared itself

> ready to doe what in honor and iustice is fitt to be done by them to prevent any the least violation of those priviledges which to you as to all acting under authority of Parliament is iustly due and to preserve a right understanding in this business for the honour of the Parliament and publique service of the State which is chiefly to be intended.

To this the commissioners replied with their own representation. They were, they said, concerned 'lest the world consider that we have not, as all courts have, power to protect in going and returning, whereby we were unable to fulfil our service', and noted that 'many persons, as the earl of Arundel and others, noticing this, refuse to appear before us'. Maintaining the tone of conciliation, the commissioners agreed with the justice of the committee's attempts to vindicate its jurisdiction, but could not accept the violation of its own in the process. 'In civility,' they argued, 'one court should not arrest a man attending another,' and, while conceding that the committeemen were 'absolute masters of your resolves', they asked that Conquest be freed and King punished 'for the honour of the Parliament and the service ... [and] that the world may see that we aim only at the public honour'.

The committee relented, and on 9 December they set Conquest free, 'in complyance with your desires for the service of the publique and the preserva-tion of your priviledges which they are willing to be as tender of as theire owne'. But the same day they issued a fresh warrant for the royalist's arrest on the same charge, on the grounds that another order had been made against Conquest since the original contempt, as a result of his violent escape from the committee's clutches the year before, an order against which no warrant had yet been drawn.

The politics at issue here are complex. As the commissioners eventually assumed responsibility for the business of the indemnity committee, it seems possible that the matter did not rest at the point where the records break off.

However, this dispute demonstrates the connection between notions of honour and realities of jurisdiction and authority. The interested parties consistently asserted that any disrespect for their own power derogated from the honour of their parent body, the Parliament of the Commonwealth of England, whose dignity, and its preservation, must remain paramount.

Politically, the most significant area of conflict prompted by the interpretation and vindication of the regime's honour arose over the issue of articles of war. These were the terms on which royalists had surrendered to commanders of the parliamentary armies in the 1640s. They took the form of a negotiated settlement agreed at the capitulation of individual garrisons and towns, under which the victors effectively guaranteed to constrain the degree of retribution by limiting sequestration and dictating the maximum composition fines payable on the lands of the defeated. They depended on parliamentary ratification for their validity, but were frequently contradicted by the execution of parliamentary policy on sequestration, compounding, oblivion, land sales and related aspects of the post-revolutionary settlement. Typically the issue has been described as a matter of principle involving the honour and self-respect of the army's commanders.[78] However, its dimensions were wider, involving the whole issue of the honour and justice of the parliamentary regime. In May 1648 Fairfax wrote to the House of Lords, asking for their confirmation of the articles granted at the surrender of Oxford, motivated by 'a deep sense of the Parliament's and Army's Honour (which cannot in anything suffer more than in the violation of the Public Faith which stands engaged for the making good all such capitulations)'.[79] Thereafter, political agitation by the army asserted that Parliament ought to respect and uphold the undertakings its commanders gave the enemy.[80]

In June 1649 the Rump passed an Act for the relief of persons who had been 'molested' at law contrary to the terms of their surrender. In its preamble this legislation stated that the Rumpers had acted on the 'divers complaints ... made touching the breach of Articles ... taking into account the Faith of their Armies and Forces by land engaged for performance of the same, and how much it concerneth them in Honor and Justice that the same be made good'.[81] A commission was set up to hear all disputes and empowered to rectify serious breaches in vindication of articles wherein 'the faith of the army, and honour and Justice of the Parliament and nation are concerned'. But, despite this measure, conflicts continued over the interpretation of where the honour lay in all such disputes. Problems arose, for example, when both plaintiff and defendant invoked the honour of the Commonwealth, the one to demand rectification, the other to demand that the sale of a delinquent's lands be upheld.

A good example is the case of Sir John Stowell, a Somerset royalist who fought a running battle with the state and the purchasers of lands confiscated from him in 1651, fending off first the threat of execution and, eventually, his sequestration on the grounds of his comprisal in the articles granted at the surrender of Exeter in April 1646.[82] Stowell argued that 'the Public Faith and Honour of the Parliament, Armies and whole Nation [are] ingaged for the performance of my Articles'.[83] Stowell having won the backing of the court for relief on articles of war, the purchasers of his lands were forced to defend what they considered their inviolable property right by mounting their own appeal to the justice and integrity of Parliament. They retorted that 'Touching Honour, it will reflect deeply on the Honour of the Parliament to retract their own sales ... And the Honour of God to justify Delinquents to destroy Innocents'.[84] They argued that 'pardon (tho' of grace) is grounded upon the compact and agreement of the whole Nation; but these Articles are but the agreement of certain persons thereof; of the Army with Traitors'. It was alleged that Stowell 'insinuates with the Army, suggests unto them the great dishonour if their faith should be questioned, that the highest security that the world affords is engaged for his Indempnity'. But, they claimed, 'whereas it is true, that the Faith of an Army is a high security, and the honour of it ought to be as pretious as the Apple of the eye', yet it was pledged only to facilitate compounding, to avert the worst excesses of the soldiery, not to protect the delinquency of confirmed enemies of the Commonwealth. Thus 'it will be a dishonour to them [the Army] now to support him'.[85] With the backing of the commissioners for lands confiscated for treason, they secured a parliamentary order confirming the sale of all lands confiscated for treason two months before the dissolution of the Rump.[86]

Stowell's case was an extreme example of a not uncommon phenomenon – the honour of nation and state becoming implicated in the myriad disputes which made up the post-war settlement.[87] But it is only the most dramatic illustration of the fact that, after the revolution, power was, in some sense, as it always had been, the power to put a definitive value on such undefinable entities as the honour of the state, of its institutions and of their officials. Not surprisingly, the most vociferous protagonist in the struggle for the meaning of the honour of the Commonwealth was Parliament itself.

III

The Rump was keen to maintain the honour and respect due to its officials and carefully patrolled the borders of respect and deference. Before he invaded Scotland the Council of State had given Cromwell the title of General of the forces of the Parliament of the Commonwealth of England, and instructed him to receive no communications from the Scots addressed any otherwise.[88] Nedham took the Scots to task for addressing themselves to Lieutenant General Cromwell, saying that title was 'just as current as one of their Scotch half-crowns in England', but felt that 'there is some hope they may alter the phrase, when his Excellency has taken his way through Edenburgh'.[89]

Sensitivity to honour, dignity and title was not just a matter of addressing individuals in the correctly deferential style – Parliament's title also became a matter of state under the Commonwealth. Parliament asserted the dignity of its commander in Scotland, and interestingly this was reciprocated by the invading force, which replied to a Scots communication saying 'we cannot endure to hear them called a Pretended Parliament; ... take notice ... if you write to us again ... speak more reverently of the Authority of our Nation'.[90] The whole revolution had been predicated on a rump House of Commons calling itself a Parliament and its public decrees Acts instead of ordinances. Thereafter, the Rump passed a number of resolutions on the manner in which it wanted to be addressed. The Speaker drew attention to an error in the style of an address made on behalf of Christopher Love in August 1651, requiring its amendment before bringing it to the House's attention. In June 1650 the government mouthpiece, Marchamont Nedham's *Mercurius Politicus*, reported with obvious distaste an address made to 'the Speaker of the House of Commons'.[91] A Leveller petition 'in the behalf of the Army', which was similarly misdirected to the House of Commons, also drew a stinging rebuke in the pages of the same newspaper, which was always careful to defend to the hilt the pretensions of the Parliament and its officers.[92]

But it is in the area of foreign policy that we see most clearly the seriousness with which Rumpers sought to underpin Parliament's claims to honour and prestige by enforcing a more or less rigid conformity in the manner in which it was addressed. The preservation of the regime's dignity was the rationale underlying much of the Rump's political theatre. The issue of title became just as important as mounting suitable spectacle in the conduct of diplomatic relations. The report submitted to the Council of State in April 1649 by Sir Oliver Fleming also considered matters of title.[93] He recommended that the new regime should adopt a title which would 'hold forth the supreme authority of this nation', which 'should be insisted upon, and no diminution allowed of honour due either to the Commonwealth or to persons they dignify with public employments abroad who should have instructions given to them in these matters'.[94]

Fleming suggested something along the lines of 'most excellent, most high, most mighty'. Before any formal decision had been made, John Milton seems to have taken his own initiative in the matter. His earliest letter of state, sent to the Senate of Hamburg in the same month as Fleming's report, was addressed from *Senatus Populusque Angliae* in obvious emulation of republican Rome.[95] The Rump, however, opted for something a little simpler, but not as simple as the Council of State recommended in January 1650, when the suggested *Ordines Reipublicae Angliae* was rejected in favour of the slightly grander formula, *Parliamentum Reipublicae Angliae*. This was in accordance with earlier resolutions, one empowering William Lenthall to sign all letters to foreign powers as 'Speaker of the Parliament of England', the other laying down that henceforth members would refer to themselves as the Parliament rather than the Commons assembled in Parliament, in recording their votes and orders.[96]

The point of Fleming's advice was that the Rump would never survive, England would never survive, if its rulers were too weak-willed to stand up and demand respect for their power. In applying his advice the Rumpers added further backbone to their resolve by demanding to be addressed in their chosen fashion and no other. Although in August 1649 Parliament had recorded in the *Journal*, with obvious pride, the gushing address by the Senate of Hamburg (which referred to the most illustrious, noble, excellent and magnificent Parliament[97]), the formula adopted in January 1650 was thenceforth to be the only acceptable manner in which Parliament was to be addressed by foreign dignitaries. Thereafter, a number of diplomatic missions to the court of the republic got off to false starts, ambassadors frequently assuming that the only way to conduct their business was to open with the usual flourishes of diplomatic flattery.

The startling growth of the English Commonwealth's maritime power and the success of its admirals off the Iberian coasts and in the Mediterranean made England's friendship increasingly highly prized amongst the nations of that region. The first full ambassadorial deputation sent to recognise the Commonwealth, the December 1650 embassy of the Spaniard, Cardenas, was temporarily delayed because he had addressed his desires 'To the Most Serene Republic of England'. (This despite the fact that the Spaniard had been in unofficial contact with the Council of State for well over a year already; and that even Ascham's murder in May 1650 did not weaken what was effectively an unofficial detente between the two powers.[98]) According to the Venetian ambassador in Spain, the Council of State had advised Cardenas that the parliamentarians 'rejected all epithets, possibly to avoid embarrassing punctilio at the outset of their career'.[99]

Parliament forcing Cardenas to alter the style of his address 'exactly as prescribed by themselves' caused a ripple in the diplomatic community.[100] Overshadowed as his reception was in an English press preoccupied with the recent capture of Edinburgh Castle, one of the few details which was reported was the fact that so potent an official had been made to do as he was told by Parliament. This was given as jingoistic a gloss as the capture of the castle itself. Thus *The Weekly Intelligencer* told its readers that

> you see now by what due titles Forreign Nations do learn to address themselves unto our Parliament: and no doubt but the other potentates in Europe will follow

their example, when either their necessity, or their interests shall instruct them in the way.[101]

The Spaniard's error would seem to have stemmed from an assumption that the Rump would adopt a formula along the lines of that used by the Venetian republic. As it was, even this latter, despite the assumption of an affinity, experienced its own difficulties arising from the scrupulous observation of protocols on the part of the English republic. Lorenzo Paulucci was sent to London in 1652 on the pretext of hiring ships and negotiating levies, but with the aim of a covert association with government members and the observation of the manner and formalities with which foreign representatives were received by the new regime. When officially upgraded by his government, Paulucci found himself unable to impress the regime with his credentials, which 'many of the [English] ministers consider ... derogatory to the dignity of the Parliament', as he had not been promoted sufficiently for their liking.[102]

Despite having been told of the 'wonderful order and decorum' with which the republic conducted its affairs, when Paulucci was still waiting for reception some months after the initial presentation of his credentials, he blamed the delay on the fact that 'the government is new, its forms are defective in many respects and foreign ministers must have patience'.[103] He was of course making excuses for the slowness of his progress in London, but he was also clearly experiencing the subtle statecraft of the all too wily republicans. When he first arrived in London in May 1652, his only permitted contact with an official was an informal meeting with Sir Oliver Fleming in St James's park. Reporting the meeting, Paulucci seemed thoroughly chided by Sir Oliver's complaint about the Venetian Senate's tardiness in recognising the Commonwealth, and described how

> this official, who has influence in the present government, and like many others, vaunts its power accordingly, represented the strength of England as warranting the highest hopes for any undertaking. Although in their hearts the English desire foreign alliances, they dissemble this outwardly and scorn all title, saying that the Roman republic, which ruled the world, merely aspired to that of SPQR ... I do not imagine the loftiest conceptions or the wisest reasoning will alter the the the dominant tone here, which is umbrageous, suspicious and self-sufficient in the extreme.[104]

There may have been much to be gained by this diplomatic gamesmanship with a nation of Venice's trading stature. At times, though, there seems something quite deliberately disruptive about the republic's treatment of its smaller suitors. The experiences of the representative sent by the count of Oldenburg read at times like a Kafkaesque nightmare of endless delay and fruitless application to the oracles of a mysterious bureaucracy dedicated solely to the baffling of even the tiniest request.[105] But greater states than

Venice and Oldenburg experienced the cost in delay and wasted time which could arise from not taking seriously enough the republic's scrupulous regard for matters of title and 'due honour'. Cardenas's mission of 1650 seems to have set the tone for the Rump's conduct of foreign affairs. Subsequent Swedish and French missions were also turned away at the first attempt. In December 1651 it was reported that Parliament was 'preparing to receive [the Swedish minister, Spiering] and give him audience with the ceremonies customary with royal ambassadors'. But all that changed when Spiering presented letters of credence incorrectly addressed to 'Serenissimae Reipublicae Angliae amicae nostrae'. As a result 'that minister experiences great difficulty in obtaining audience'. He was dead before it was ever granted.[106] In December 1652 the French representative, Bordeaux, applied to 'Parliamento Populi Angliae', and brought a letter from his king addressed to 'nos Treschers et Grands Amis les Gens du Parlement de la Republique d'Angleterre'. He was informed that 'the Parliament cannot take notice' of his address, and his improper accreditation meant he could be received only in committee.[107]

Degree was an issue of the greatest importance in the political culture of the early modern period. Failure to observe titles strictly could be used in a calculated way to hold up diplomatic proceedings. Bordeaux had come to scoop the Spaniard in the Commonwealth's affections, and to plead for the release of French shipping. The Rump's umbrage at the use of inappropriate language was no doubt the greater as it was its first impression of a lowly horse-trader, briefed to end France's long refusal to recognise the Commonwealth in return for a few thousand pounds' worth of shipping. But it is probably also significant that Parliament's rebuke was delivered on the same day the House received Cardenas once more. This was not partiality. The Commonwealth took advantage of how much both Paris and Madrid wanted a special relationship with London, flaunting its self-sufficiency in the face of both its powerful suitors.[108]

Foreign states also knew when to push their luck. In May 1650 the minister from Holland, Gerard Schaep, was informed by Parliament that his address, directed to 'Mons. Mons. William Lenthall, Orateur au Parlement de la République d'Angleterre, à Westminster', was unacceptable, as 'the Parliament cannot admit of any Address to be made to them, by any Foreign State or Prince whatsoever, in any other Manner or Form than they have already enacted and declared'. But a fortnight later the Rump accepted an address made in almost exactly the same way as the first, apparently without demur, arranging a reception accordingly (even granting Schaeph the privilege of a 'Chair with Elbows' to sit in whilst being received). Schaeph represented the minority sympathetic to the Westminster regime in the Netherlands – the Commonwealth could not afford to stand on the tiniest punctilio whilst the Orange faction was supreme at The Hague.[109] When the States of Holland went over the heads of Van Tromp and the other Dutch provinces by seeking peace in the spring of 1653, its members had less room for manoeuvre and were careful to address Parliament in the proper form.[110]

Formalities necessarily played an important role in the foreign policy manoeuvrings of the Commonwealth because the honour of an early modern state was intertwined with the maintenance of a position of international strength. Fleming, in the report cited above, addressed himself to the subject of titles as an essential ingredient in any attempt by the fledgling republic to gain the friendship, respect or at least the non-hostility of European rulers who looked on the example of the English revolution with considerable trepidation. 'It is to be expected,' he wrote,

> that we must wrestle with many difficulties incidental to a new government, now established in a more just and equal way; and that princes, looking upon their common interest, will apprehend the prosperity of the commonwealth may prove an allurement to their people to shake off the yoke, (whereof there are some symptoms in several parts) and to imitate so laudable an example.

Nevertheless, however reluctant foreign princes might be about giving the Commonwealth respect in the matter of titles, the republic had the right to insist on their due observance, not least because titles had been given the kings of England not in their capacity as 'particular men, but in relation to the greatness and potency of the commonwealth, from whence all their titles were derived'.[111]

Power and reputation were closely linked in Commonwealth naval policy. In 1649 the Council addressed one of its first maritime priorities, ordering the fleet to drive Prince Rupert off the sea to protect merchants and thus prevent 'our loss of reputation and their increase of it'.[112] Potency and honour went hand in hand in the most explicit fashion in the question of flag courtesy. English maritime power could only suffer if the newborn Commonwealth regime allowed even a moment's relaxation on the protocol of flag-breaking in the seas over which England claimed sovereignty. This was not the time to allow the diminution of England's maritime pretensions, and in 1652 the Rump took the country to war with the Dutch when a row over flag courtesy led to an exchange of fire between Blake and Van Tromp.[113]

The Commonwealth's international potency clearly had its limits. It failed to secure full satisfaction for the deaths of Isaac Dorislaus and Anthony Ascham. In these and other matters, such as the entitlement of the Rump's Hamburg representative, Richard Bradshaw, and the insults given its ambassadors to The Hague in 1651, it often turned out that, however vociferous and consistent the republic's demand for due recognition, its power to enforce those demands could be severely limited.[114]

The latter is a case in point. We have seen the elaborate preparations for the republic's first full-scale embassy in 1651, and the central importance of the honour of the mission, its members and the government they represented, in the calculations involved in staging the event. Although they had some close calls, St John and Strickland did better than their predecessor, Dorislaus, getting home alive. But they suffered some serious indignities at the hands of both Orange and Stuart supporters. Prince Rupert's brother, Prince Edward, insulted the ambassadors to their faces as they took the air in a park.[115] St John and Strickland immediately demanded that the authorities take appropriate action for the 'high dishonour and abuse ... done to the parleyment of the Commonwealth of England', insisting that the prince be brought to justice 'without which the honour of the parleyment of England cannot be repayred'. They also refused to supply information of the offence to the secretary of the Dutch ordinary court of justice, since they represented England's 'Supreme Authority' and 'would not submit to be judged in this case by an Inferiour Court, especially the matter complained of being matter of State'.[116]

It is not clear whether the ambassadors secured vindication in the affair. The prince was summoned to answer for his effrontery by the States General on pain of banishment and confiscation, albeit long after he had fled to Germany.[117]

IV

That the Parliament which ruled England between 1649 and 1653 is known universally by its derogatory nickname has not done much good for its reputation.[118] Ironically, however, the matter of titles neatly illustrates the fact that the Rump was a self-determining body, a Parliament quite unlike any that had gone before, one powerful enough to command respect for its own exercises in self-fashioning. As with the imagery of the House, the comparison with the Commons of the ancient constitution is instructive. In 1614 Lord Coke had referred to the 'lower House' of Parliament, 'for so I must call it, having the presidence so to do of former times, and not to term it as nowadays it is the Commons House, for I know no Commons House but the lower House of Parliament'.[119] Clearly even at that time tensions could arise over the creation of a Commons identity. After 1649 the commoners had no one to answer to any more. They coined their own name, became the Parliament of the Commonwealth of England, and denoted themselves members thereof. Individuals, too, mastered their own destinies in this way. For his East Anglian roots and his involvement in the issue of fen drainage, in 1643 the royalist press gave Cromwell the derisory title of 'Lord of the Fens' (i.e. 'a nobody').[120] Since then he had earned the more honourable epithets which went with military command, and it was said that he had even been offered a peerage by the king during the negotiations of 1647.[121] In 1649 Cromwell simply assumed to himself the traditional title of vice-regency in Ireland.

Such developments give the measure of the Commonwealth as a complex combination of the old and the new, of tradition and innovation. On 6 January 1649, the day the Rump passed its first Act as a unicameral Parliament, the Painted Chamber was chosen as the venue for the first meeting of commissioners appointed to try the king. Ralph Darnell, Commons clerk, informed Whitelocke of this decision, and the rejection of the Exchequer Chamber which some had proposed. He clearly sensed it was of some moment, perhaps related to 'a quarrel about drinking to Harry the Ninth' in the Lords' robing room. But he had to concede that 'I know not the weight of this argument', and thought his patron 'may perhaps conceive the meaning of it'.[122]

Whitelocke does not record his own conclusion, if indeed he drew any at all. However, the incident serves as a suggestive indicator of how the revolution in the winter of 1648–49 temporarily altered the nature of English politics. Within days of the execution of the king, the House of Lords would be voted down as 'useless and dangerous'. Two days after the Rump decided to abolish the Lords, the handful of peers who had continued to sit declared that those who had usurped power in the state were traitors, for killing the king and altering the form of government, but also because it was 'an act of the deepest treason to take our places as judges or Commissioners'.[123] Their description of the 'grand gentlemen' who had hatched this treachery conveys the indignant impotence with which the lords met their fate at the hands of their socially inferior successors. Yet, a month before that momentous piece of constitutional iconoclasm, the revolutionaries were hatching the execution of the king in the very chamber where the peers of the realm used to attire themselves in the garb of the king's equals. For the Painted Chamber was the room in the palace of Westminster, adjacent to the House of Lords, where the peers had in the past changed into their ceremonial robes prior to the official opening of Parliaments, or whenever they were to be attended on by the king.[124] It had also provided the venue for those countless, almost daily conferences between Lords and Commons during the wars, and already in some sense symbolised the accession of commoners to the highest counsels of the realm. That they might there encompass the death of a king, as their noble critics clearly sensed, marked their virtual accession to the offices of the peers. Similarly, the scheme for a group portrait and military commemoration described in an earlier chapter would appear to have been the direct descendant of Anthony Van Dyck's proposal to decorate the Banqueting Hall at Whitehall with a mural depicting the venerable history and honourable membership of the Order of the Garter.[125]

Apologists like Goodwin and Milton depicted the actions of that handful of 'good' men which tried and condemned Charles I in terms of a latter-day baronial revolt, in which the roles of the chief protagonists were taken over by untitled but virtuous men of noble disposition. By and large, the sense of honour that accompanied this new state of affairs was the traditional gentry virtue of magistracy writ large. But there was more to it than that, for the revolution itself and the regime it created was as far from the norms expected by the gentry as they could imagine, short of outright anarchy. Whatever their misgivings, much of conservative society, whether republican or not, played the game and deferred to the honour of their political superiors. The revolution was, both in portrayal and in effect, a new chapter in the history of the aristocratic constitutionalism which had long sustained English traditions of resistance to royal authority.[126] After the crisis of January 1649 it was the Rump which inherited this new mantle of republican aristocratism.[127] The appropriation of the Lords' record office was an assumption of the peers' mantle, too. The new government went further, colonising the very chamber of the upper House. It was used for receiving foreign agents, and was later appointed as the venue for meetings of the commission on legal reform chaired by Matthew Hale.[128]

To some, the 'worthy patriots' had done what was required of the traditional aristocracy, serving as a 'hedge' between a tyrant and his subjects, as well as mastering the nation's fortunes against foreign dangers. To many others, they were the only guarantee of an order founded on economic inequality, social degree and respect for its privileges. One group contrived, another connived in, a new order of honour. In March 1649, on trial at the court of upper bench, 'whither multitudes resorted to observe his deportment', Sir John Stowell decried the pretensions of Parliament and its judges.[129] Three years later, his life no longer in danger but his lands confiscated and sold, he submitted a petition to 'the Supreme Authority, the Parliament of the Commonwealth of England', begging the reversal of his fortunes 'by the mediation of your favour'. He hoped that he and his sons 'may be restored to your favours and good opinions' according to 'that benefit which the house was most honorably pleased to grant and allow to such persons as should claime reliefe by articles', and desired 'nothing more [than] to spend the residue of my days ... in such peaceable obedience to this Commonwealth, as by your Faith and Honour made good unto me, I hold myself obliged unto'.[130]

In the charged atmosphere of the 1650s, one man's honour was another man's hypocrisy. The government and its supporters battled back and forth with presbyterian critics over the meaning of honour and integrity, each side proclaiming its own virtue and the double-dealing hypocrisy of the other. The presbyterian notion of honour, conflated with conscience, in the observance of the Covenant was howled down by the regime's apologists. Nedham was most vociferous in this campaign, decrying 'that Qualm called Honour and Conscience'.[131] At the time of the trial of Christopher Love, he wrote that 'It is high time to assert the honour and integrity of the parliament against the passion and proceedings of our malcontents of the ministry'.[132]

A discourse of honour was already being maintained by England's new governors, asserted against foreign powers, and invoked by the regime's agents and agencies as part of the normal course of diplomacy, even administration. That the word 'honour' was forever on their lips did not make them honourable men. A key aspect of what Professor Worden has called the Rump's new 'public morality' was defined in opposition to examples of gross public dishonour – the corruption of Lord Howard, or the adultery of Gregory Clement, the campaigns against which were godly causes championed by Thomas Harrison.[133] What the use of honour discourse does suggest, however, is that the Commonwealth regime took itself seriously enough to expect and demand respect for pretensions voiced in the highest terms of secular morality available to contemporaries. As such, the honour codes of the regime and its members can be read as just another element in the self-consciously dignified political culture of the English Commonwealth. That they were also deferred to, even by the regime's less friendly subjects, suggests that the regime's crude de factoism did not discourage the tactful courtier from employing more subtle strategies in handling the 'Members of the High and Honourable Court of Parliament ... the Supreme Authority of the Three Nations'.[134]

But there was a danger lurking beneath the gilded surface of appearances. As we have seen in the contrast between the Rump's display of captured Scottish regimental colours and the attitude of Colonel Michael Jones after his victory at Dungan Hill in Ireland, there was a tension within the revolutionary coalition over the legitimacy of overt expressions of pride in the achievements of human agency. This was also the case in the matter of titles. Bestowing traditional epithets prompted a number of worried criticisms from radicals. Disdain for the revival of honorific forms was not uncommon, even within Parliament itself. Colonel John Jones MP wrote to his kinsman, Scout-Master General Henry Jones, that

> There be some that doe take notice how you do write your name, and from thence make some conclusions to your prejudice, as the affecting of Titular Dignityes, although empty and scandalous and serving noe end but that of Pride and vain glory, which God in our time beares testimony against or els the opinion of a divine Right in that order which your conscience will not give you leave to lay aside although you fight against the upholder of those kind of order.[135]

In June 1652 Jones also warned Thomas Harrison against 'rising thoughts or desier of great things in the world, which I finde to be close and dangerous snares, attending high Imployments', and the following August wrote that 'I forbeare herein to use the great titular addicions due to you'.[136]

Harrison, for all his vanity, gave every appearance of having resisted at least some of the snares Jones warned against. In his eulogy to the commanders of the republic's armies, Payne Fisher's tribute to Harrison referred to his refusal of 'stollen titles' and his lack of ambition for 'vainer titles, knowing that granted truth, that thou shall get more noble glory, to be good then great'.[137] It may be that this was a form of humility which lacked substance. Lucy Hutchinson derided the Major General's hypocrisy, as when he subjected her husband to a 'harangue' on how he hoped Hutchinson 'would not set his heart upon the augmenting of outward estates', Harrison having himself amassed a personal fortune worth £2,000 per annum, 'besides engrossing great offices, and encroaching upon his under-officers; and maintained his coach and family at a height as if they had been born to a principality'.[138]

Radicals could, however, come up with justifications for a little vainglory. William Hickman, a critic of the civilian regime who thought the revolution had amounted to little more than 'a taking of the head of monarchy and placing upon the body or trunk of it the name or title of a Commonwealth', neverthelesss addressed Cromwell as 'Excellency', and said his title was no more than his just desert, a badge of the honour done to God by the destruction of His enemies.[139] Cromwell, for his part, seems to have managed to appreciate the post's purely honorific aspects. After receiving further lavish reward at the final defeat of the Stuart cause, the Lord Lieutenant felt sufficiently sure of his material base to remit most of his income from the Irish vice-regency. He also allowed the office to be abolished, leaving high and dry 'honest John' Lambert, appointed successor to the lately deceased Lord Deputy, Henry Ireton, whose office now also lapsed with that of its superior at Dublin Castle. Cromwell soothed the aggrieved Lambert by awarding the remainder of his income from that source to defraying the expenses Lambert had run up in preparing to enter on his new appointment in the style befitting a Lord Deputy – no doubt a sweetener which came mixed with a little gall.[140] By then, of course, the titular dignity of Cromwell's own position as commander-in-chief had been assured, once more by mere *fiat*. On 22 July 1650 the Council of State ordered that 'the Lord General ... use such title as he thinks fit, although it was formerly ordered that he should call himself General of the forces of the Commonwealth of England'. Having taken up the dignity of lord lieutenancy on his own initiative, Cromwell clearly was not about to dispense with the lordly epithet.[141]

Ironically, although it was a code which bound up early modern notions of order in society and deferential patterns of social relations, honour also invited dispute. As is illustrated by Richard Cust, it was a competitive language which kept the ruling elite in an almost permanent state of agitation.[142] During the Commonwealth this was all the more true because the regime, with its figureheads in Parliament, in Council, in the courts and in the army, fostered a pluralistic system where no one individual inherently stood out as the chief. A royalist criticism of the revolutionaries' pretensions was supplied by *Mercurius Elencticus*, which said that,

The Rebels having thus made themselves Lords of England ... are very busily imployed to consider whether it will make most for their advantage, to renew the Heptarchie ... dividing the Land by Lot (perhaps) a Province to ... Fairfax, a Duchy to not [Nol?] (surnamed Nasus), a shire to ... Lord President Bradshaw

and so on. The natural corollary of the republic's addiction to titles and honour was a hierarchy headed by a supreme individual. As *Elencticus* pointed out,

the power must be reduced to one ... though never more any kings ... ; but when this madness shall be most prevalent, whoever is most worthy amongst them to be Dominus fac totum, every man being a king in his own conceit, there will be the business.[143]

In a similar vein, *The Moderate* reported the decision to appoint Edmund Prideaux attorney-general by letters patent under the great seal by remarking, 'I thought we had done long since with these things,' warning that 'those that climbe the steps of Honour may catch a fall at last'.[144] By redesigning the same basic edifice of haughty pretension and civic dignity the masters of the republic were courting trouble. Clashes over articles of war had already demonstrated the difficulty of reconciling the honour of Parliament and the honour of its army. There were serious political implications in the apparently insoluble disputes between military and civilian honour. Which was supreme, the laurel or the long robe? After the army had resolved the dispute by sacking its employer, one apologist asked rhetorically,

Is not the High Constable of France above the Chancellor, a knight in the Field before a Doctor in the Law? So should the General of our Army be above any Member in the Commonwealth, and the officers he adjoyneth to him partake of his preeminence.[145]

In 1647 it was the practical imperative of upholding martial honour which had propelled the military into politics. One of the prime catalytic influences in the army's renewed violence against its parliamentary master in 1653 lay once more in an interpretation of its officers' honour, though by then it was no longer an idea expressive of military unity but instead an issue crystallising division.[146] In 1652 the army's leaders came under fire for being

not faithful Commonwealths souliders, [but] worse tyrants and thieves than the king they cast out; and that honor they seemed to get by their Victories over the Commonwealths oppressor they lose again, by breaking a promise and engagement to their friends who did assist them.[147]

Huge pressure for the vindication of martial integrity had built up by the spring of 1653, pressure which only further revolution could ease. In certain other respects, the Rumpers were more obviously responsible for the fate they brought upon themselves. The civilians were ultimately confounded by the very success with which they had recreated a dignified political system. There was little they could do when the notions of honour they had protected and nurtured were turned against them and usurped by men with an honour code of their own and the power to back it up with force. Moreover, many of the Rumpers were themselves soldiers and keen advocates of a sense of military honour. Significantly, when stripping royalists of their peerages and titles, Parliament had permitted soldiers who had served the king (such as Colonel Conquest) to retain their military epithets.[148] The Rump was sunk by the sheer ambiguity of its martial origins, an ambiguity which the mantle of dignity it had bestowed upon itself ultimately failed to conceal.

NOTES

1 Mervyn James, 'English Politics and the Concept of Honour', in *idem, Society, Politics and Culture. Studies in Early Modern England* (Cambridge, 1986); J. G. Marston, 'Gentry Honour and Royalism in Early Stuart England', *Journal of British Studies* 13 (1973–74), 21–43; Anthony Fletcher, 'Honour, Reputation and Office-holding in Elizabethan and Stuart England', in A. J. Fletcher and J. Stevenson eds, *Order and Disorder in Early Modern England* (Cambridge, 1985); Richard Cust, 'Honour, Rhetoric and Political Culture: the Earl of Huntingdon and his Enemies', in Amussen and Kishlansky eds, *Political Culture and Cultural Politics in early modern England*.

2 Letter to Walter Montagu, 8 October 1649, A. Collins ed., *Letters and Memorials of State* (2 vols, 1746) ii, 675–6.

3 J. S. Morrill, 'The Impact on Society', in Morrill ed., *Revolution and Restoration*.

4 James Howell, *Finetti Philoxenis* (1656).

5 *The Parliamentary or Constitutional History of England* xix, 74–5.

6 *A Cat may look upon a King* (1652), pp. 33–4.

7 *Mercurius Politicus* 13–20 June 1650, p. 25.

8 Worden, 'Ben Jonson among the Historians', pp. 67–89.

9 Ian Roy, 'The Profession of Arms' in Wilfred Prest ed., *The Professions in early modern England* (1987), p. 193; Carlton, *Going to the Wars*, pp. 53–4; C. E. L. Philips, *Cromwell's Captains* (1938), p. 68.

10 W. Hunt, 'Civic Chivalry and the English Civil War', in A. Blair and A. Grafton eds, *The Transmission of Culture* (Princeton, 1990). I am grateful to Dr Richard Cust for bringing this article to my attention.

11 Abbott ed., *Writings and Speeches* ii, 54.

12 J. G. Cumming ed., 'A Short Treatise of the Isle of Man', *Manx Society* (Douglas, 1864), pp. 28–9.

13 Richard Elton, *Compleat Body of the Art Military* (1650).

14 *Ibid.*, pp. 8–12.

15 Quoted by Sharpe, *Faction and Parliament*, p. 15.

16 John Milton, *Right and Might Well Met* ([December] 1648), p. 1; *idem*, 'The Tenure of

Kings and Magistrates', M. Y. Hughes ed., *Complete Prose Works of John Milton* (New Haven, 1952) iii, 192, 220.

17 Thomas Manley, *Veni; Vidi; Vici. The Triumphs of the Most Excellent and Illustrious Oliver Cromwell, etc.* (1652), ep. ded.

18 Milton, 'Tenure of Kings and Magistrates', pp. 237–8.

19 *Sergeant Thorpe, Judge of Assize for the Northern Circuit, his Charge, as it was delivered to the Grand Jury at York Assize the 20th of March 1648[9]*, p. 7.

20 *A Disengag'd Survey of the Engagement* (1650).

21 Cumming ed., 'Short Treatise', p. 2.

22 H. Owen and J. B. Blakeway, *A History of Shrewsbury* (8 vols, 1825) i, 467–8.

23 Firth and Rait eds, *Acts and Ordinances* i, 884–5. In April 1646 Parliament questioned Fairfax's right to grant a safe conduct to the countess of Chichester, whose husband had been made earl of Chichester after the annulment of the king's great seal. I. Grimble, *The Harington Family* (1957), pp. 206–7

24 Gardiner, *History of the Commonwealth and Protectorate* i, 10 n.

25 Firth and Rait eds, *Acts and Ordinances* ii, 564–5.

26 Sharpe, *Politics and Ideas in Early Stuart England*, p. 98.

27 *Mercurius Politicus* 4–11 July 1650, p. [79].

28 In *Severall Proposals for the General Good of the Commonwealth with the Grounds and Reasons thereof* ... ([19 February] 1651), p. 12.

29 P.R.O., SP 18/2, 4; *Perfect Diurnall of some Passages in Parliament* 4–11 June 1649, p. [2566]. Seymour prints the text of this draft Act, 'Pro-government Propaganda', pp. 152–3.

30 For the Protector's bestowal of titles of honour, which interestingly was *not* stipulated in the Instrument of Government, see Seymour, 'Pro-government Propaganda', chapter 5.

31 Hirst, *Authority and Conflict*, pp. 13, 96, 100, 122, 131, 152, 156, 162, 242; Worden, 'Ben Jonson among the Historians', pp. 73–4.

32 B. Whitelocke, *Memorials of the English Affairs*, (4 vols, 1682) ii, 527.

33 CJ vi, 135.

34 Barber, 'Irish Undercurrents to the Politics of April 1653', p. 317 n.

35 See above, chapter 3, for the other respects in which the republican Lords Commissioners copied the functions and emulated the behaviour of the king's keepers of the seal.

36 B. Lib., Add. MS 37,344, fo. 307.

37 For the composition of this text see Blair Worden's review of Ruth Spalding's edition of the 'Diary', *English Historical Review* cviii (1993), 122–34.

38 *CJ* vi, 226.

39 P.R.O., SP25/62, 397, 400.

40 See, for example, *The Earl of Pembroke's Farewell to the King at his Departure from the Treaty* ... ([14 December] 1648), in which the 'earl' warned the king that the revolutionaries 'will try ye and you shall have the same play as they desire themselves when they beg to be tried by their peers, and pray, are not those your peers that have won it by the

sword; and if they have won it, by God, I see no reason but they may wear it too ... Let law be what it will; you know might overcomes right.' He greeted the prospect of revolution and subsequent 'Levelling' phlegmatically, saying 'if they deny me my honour, they cannot deny me my age, and that it is makes me honourable'.

41 P.R.O., SP18/1, 4, *Declaration and Protest of the Peers of this Realm of England*. Their protest was made on 8 February 1649, the date under which Whitelocke records the debate about the title to be given the new keepers of the great seal.

42 Whitelocke Papers X, fo. 69.

43 Spalding ed., *Diary of Bulstrode Whitelocke*, p. 240.

44 Whitelocke Papers X, fo. 24.

45 B. Lib., Add. MS 37,345, fo. 2.

46 Whitelocke Papers X, fos 30, 122.

47 *Ibid.*, fo. 111.

48 Spalding ed., *Diary of Bulstrode Whitelocke*, p. 252. The Lady in question was the kinswoman of Sir Henry Mildmay and Whitelocke's fellow Lord Commissioner, John Lisle.

49 *Ibid.*, p. 236.

50 *Ibid.*, pp. 247, 258.

51 Whitelocke Papers X, fo. 148.

52 *Ibid.*, fo. 189. Cf. Spalding ed., *Diary of Bulstrode Whitelocke*, p. 240, where the Lord Commissioner noted the honour done to him in being chosen by the corporation of Oxford to replace the earl of Berkshire as town high steward.

53 *Ibid.*, pp. 247, 250–1.

54 The following is drawn from B. Lib. Add. MS 31,984, Whitelocke's 'History of his 48th Year'. The exact date of the composition of this account requires further clarification, as there are a number of versions. B. Lib. Egerton MS 997, described by the editor of Whitelocke's Swedish Journal as a contemporary record, shares some of the bucolic preoccupations of the Lord Commissioner during his sojourn at the palace; cf. also B. Lib. Add. MSS 4,902 and 4,992. It is not clear that this was an exactly contemporaneous account of his life at this time. It should possibly be seen in the context of Whitelocke's post-Restoration idealisation of the life he led at Chilton Park. K. Thomas, *Man and the Natural World. Changing Attitudes in England, 1500–1800* (1983), p. 252.

55 Folios 3v, 6v–7v.

56 Folios 13–v, 22v, 33v–34, 42–v.

57 Folio 54–v.

58 Folios 61–2.

59 Folios 69v, 102v–104.

60 B. Lib., Egerton MS 997, fo. 39v; Spalding ed., *Diary of Bulstrode Whitelocke*, pp. 292–3.

61 Seymour, 'Pro-government Propaganda', pp. 202–7; *Hosanna: or, A Song of Thanksgiving, Sung by the Children of Zion, and Set forth in three notable Speeches at Grocers Hall* ([12 June] 1649), p. 1.

62 *CJ* vi, 306.

63 See chapter 2; Bachrach and Collmer eds, *Huygens' Journal*, pp. 59–60.

64 Seymour, 'Pro-government Propaganda', pp. 214–17, 248 n. 61.

65 G. Davies, *The Restoration of Charles II* (1955), p. 189.

66 Aylmer, *King's Servants*, p. 16.

67 *CJ* vi, 143; vii, 43; Gardiner, *History of the Commonwealth and Protectorate* i, 6, 12; Worden, *The Rump Parliament*, pp. 182, 249; Seymour, 'Pro-government Propaganda', p. 167. Dr Aylmer states that Bradshaw retained his titular designation, though it should be noted that in legislation passed in September 1652 he was referred to simply as the Chief Justice of Chester. *State's Servants*, p. 135.

68 Stocks ed., *Records of the Borough of Leicester* iv, 400, 412.

69 Worden, *The Rump Parliament*, p. 97.

70 *Mercurius Politicus* 12–19 September 1650, p. 225. Nedham apparently owed his political survival in 1649 to Bradshaw's intervention on his behalf. Worden, *The Rump Parliament*, p. 228.

71 George Walker, *Anglo-Tyrannus, or, The Idea of a Norman Monarch* ... (1650), sig. A2.

72 Manley, *Veni; Vidi; Vici*, sig. Biv.

73 Nickolls ed., *Original Letters and Papers*, pp. 39–40

74 Spalding ed., *Diary of Bulstrode Whitelocke*, p. 234.

75 Carte ed., *Original Letters and Papers* (2 vols, 1739) i, 443–5. Cf. Aylmer, *State's Servants*, p. 15, for the decline of the examinations committee after 1651, as it waned with Bradshaw's star, having been 'very much his committee'.

76 P.R.O., SP64/10, indemnity committee order book, 14 November 1651–9 April 1652, fos 62v–64; *Calendar of the Committee for Advance of Money*, pp. 1191–4; *Calendar of the Committee for Compounding*, pp. 1821; Aylmer, *State's Servants*, p. 15 n.

77 King was one of the deputies serving the Council of State's sergeant, Edward Dendy. *CSPD 1651–52*, pp. 38, 130.

78 Worden, *The Rump Parliament*, pp. 194, 284, 308, 310; Gentles, *The New Model Army*, pp. 421–2.

79 *LJ* x, 310–11.

80 E.g. the army petition of 12 August 1652.

81 Firth and Rait eds, *Acts and Ordinances* ii, 149.

82 *CCC*, pp. 1425 *et seq.*, 3280 *et seq.*, *To the Parliament of the Commonwealth, the Petition of Sir John Stawell* ([September] 1653); *An Act for Confirmation of the Sale of the Lands and Estate of Sir John Stawell* ([October] 1653); *To the Supreme Authority, the Parliament of the Commonwealth, the Lord General Cromwell, and his Councel, the humble Remonstrance of Sir John Stawell* ([October] 1653); *To the Honourable the Referees of His Highnesse most Honourable Councel, in the Cause between Sir John Stowell and the Purchasers. The Petition of William Lawrence of Edenburgh* ([November] 1654); *Reasons for Establishment of Publike Sale. Humbly tendered as well as in behalf of the Commonwealth, as likewise of the Purchasers of the Estate of Sir John Stowel* ([November] 1654); *An Answer of the Purchasers of the Lands late of Sir John Stawel, by Act of Parliament exposed to Sale for his Treason, to a Pamphlet*

intituled, the humble Remonstrancee of Sir John Stawel ([15 February] 1655); The Vindication of Sir John Stawell's Remonstrance against a Pamphlet written by Mr. John Ash ([18 May] 1655).

83 Vindication of Sir John Stowell's Remonstrance, pp. 56, 74.

84 Reasons for Establishment of Publike Sale.

85 An Answer of the Purchasers ... , p. 43, 44–5. Cf. B. Donegan, 'Codes and Conduct in the English Civil War', Past and Present 118 (1988), 65–95.

86 CJ vii, 262.

87 CCC, pp. 1755, 2001–6, 2554; Abbott ed., Writings and Speeches ii, 29.

88 P.R.O., SP25/64, 494; Abbott ed., Writings and Speeches ii, 277.

89 Mercurius Politicus 1–8 August 1650, p. 31.

90 'The Musselburgh Declaration', cited in The Fifth Monarchy Asserted (1659), p. 18.

91 Mercurius Politicus 27 June–4 July 1650, p. 55; Abbott ed., Writings and Speeches iii, 11–12.

92 Mercurius Politicus 22–9 August 1650, p. 182.

93 See above, p. 60.

94 P.R.O., SP18/1, 73.

95 J. Max Patrick ed., 'Miltonic State Papers', Complete Prose Works of John Milton (New Haven, 1969) V ii, 478.

96 CJ vi, 217, 306, 352–3; P.R.O., SP25/63, 564–5.

97 CJ vi, 274.

98 Gardiner, History of the Commonwealth and Protectorate i, 181, 302–5, 309.

99 CSPVen 1647–52, p. 182.

100 Ibid.

101 24–31 December 1650, pp. 3–4; Nickolls ed., Original Letters and Papers, pp. 40–1.

102 CSPVen 1647–52, p. 314, and cf. pp. 265 and 294.

103 Ibid., pp. 225, 294.

104 Ibid., pp. 226–8.

105 Miller, John Milton and the Oldenburg Safeguard.

106 CSPVen 1647–52, pp. 210, 212, 215; CJ vii, 77; Fallon, Milton in Government, p. 40; Miller, John Milton and the Oldenburg Safeguard, p. 170.

107 CSPVen 1647–52, pp. 212, 326; CJ vii, 77, 228; Gardiner, History of the Commonwealth and Protectorate ii, 241; D. Masson, The Life of John Milton (6 vols, reprinted 1965) iv, 382; Fallon, Milton in Government, p. 76.

108 Gardiner, History of the Commonwealth and Protectorate ii, 239–41.

109 CJ vi, 416, 421; Gardiner, History of the Commonwealth and Protectorate i, 318–20.

110 Ibid., ii, 238.

111 P.R.O., SP18/1, 73.

112 P.R.O., SP25/94, 187.

113 S. Pincus, 'England and the World in the 1650s', in Morrill ed., *Revolution and Restoration*, p. 134; Geddes, *De Witt* i, 206, 207, 215. Interestingly, however, Admiral Blake was just as pragmatic in his approach as the Rumpers were in the question of addresses. Flag courtesy was a matter of strength, to be insisted on only when commanders had a naval advantage – precedence was not something to get yourself killed over.

114 Fallon, *Milton in Government*, pp. 38–41.

115 Gardiner, *History of the Commonwealth and Protectorate* i, 324.

116 Bod. Lib., Rawlinson MS C 129, fos 10, 13.

117 Carte ed., *Original Letters and Papers* ii, 1.

118 Worden, *The Rump Parliament*, p. 87.

119 W. R. Jones, *Politics and the Bench. The Judges and the Origins of the English Civil War* (1971), p. 152.

120 Morrill, 'The Making of Oliver Cromwell'.

121 Gardiner, *History of the Great Civil War* iii, 372.

122 Whitelocke Papers X, fo. 1; Underdown, *Pride's Purge*, pp. 183–4 n.; Gardiner, *History of the Great Civil War* iv, 297.

123 P.R.O., SP18/1, 4, *Declaration of the Peers*. Written in French, the style and content of this interesting document, the last assertion of aristocratic political claims for a decade, are the diametric opposite of radical rhetoric about the Norman Yoke.

124 Foster, *House of Lords*, p. 12.

125 Jansson, 'Remembering Marston Moor', pp. 255–6.

126 Hughes, *The Causes of The English Civil War*, p. 81.

127 [Henry Robinson?] *A Short Discourse between Monarchical and Aristocratical Government* (1649), pp. 14–15.

128 *CJ* vi, 318, 321, 322, 517–18, 520; vii, 74; B. Lib., Add. MS 35,864, fo. 1v.

129 See above, chapter 3.

130 ... *the humble Remonstrance of the Sir John Stawell*, pp. 1, 39–40, 41–2; *The Vindication of Sir John Stawells Remonstrance*, p. 42.

131 *Mercurius Politicus* 13–20 June 1650, p. 20.

132 Cited by Worden, *The Rump Parliament*, p. 245.

133 *Ibid.*, pp. 95, 243, 284.

134 Captain J[ames] W[adsworth], *The Civil Wars of Spain ... by Prudencio Sandoval* (1652), ep. ded.

135 Mayer ed., 'Inedited Letters', pp. 7–8.

136 *Ibid.*, pp. 33, 63.

137 Manley, *Veni; Vidi; Vici*, p. 19.

138 Firth ed., *Memoirs of the Life of Colonel Hutchinson* ii, 167–70.

139 Nickolls ed., *Original Letters and Papers*, pp. 29, 31.

140 Abbott ed., *Writings and Speeches* ii, 484–5.

141 *CSPD 1650*, p. 247.

142 Cust, 'Honour, Rhetoric and Political Culture'.

143 *Mercurius Elencticus*, 4–11 April 1649, p. 5.

144 *The Moderate*, 3–10 April 1649, p. [408].

145 Anon, *Reasons why the Supreame Authority of the Three Nations (for the time) is not in the Parliament, But in the new-established Council of State* ([17 May] 1653), pp. 7 and 12.

146 M. Kishlansky, 'Ideology and Politics in the Parliamentary Armies, 1645–9', in Morrill ed., *Reactions to the English Civil War*.

147 *Bloudy Newes from the Barbadoes, being A true Relation of a great and terrible Fight between the Parliaments Navie, commanded by Sir George Ayscue* [25 February] 1652, pp. 6–7.

148 *CJ* vii, 83.

Chapter 5

Politics

Sound the last scene, the Play is done;
The Actors clear the stage.
The People laugh, and homeward run.
This is a merry age![1]

ow that we have described the theatre of Commonwealth politics, its
scenery, set-pieces, props and scripts, this chapter reinterprets the fall
of the Rump in the context of the political culture created during the
Commonwealth. The event itself was, in an age fascinated by the analogy
between politics and theatre, a grand finale of sorts to the years of parliamentary rule. To most, it was evidently a lot less tragic than the scene played out on
the scaffold in 1649. But the civilians' ignominious flight from the stage did
not decrease the amount of interest the event provoked. When the Rump fell
on the morning of 20 April 1653, satirists, royalists and other hostile commentators found great amusement in the spectacle of its demise. The scene was
commemorated graphically by Dutch engravers, just as the regicide had been.[2]
Stories and gossip about England's latest revolutionary twist were relayed back
and forth across London, around Britain and over the seas to Europe and
America. For four and a half years England had been the object of appalled
then admiring attention. Now for the last time the government of the English
Commonwealth achieved notoriety on a global scale.

This chapter describes the dissolution of the Rump as a key moment in the
representation of the regime (albeit one which the Rumpers did not script
themselves) and, historiographically, almost the defining moment.[3] The vivid
story of Cromwell's rant from the floor of the House has not only crystallised
the impression of the frustrations of the godly – it has even passed into the
realm of political folklore. But despite the obvious morality of this tableau, the
dissolution of the Rump was considerably more complex.

First, although the *coup* has been characterised as a last-ditch solution to
the obstruction of reform, public justification and support for the removal of

the Rump also included a great deal of critical comment about the regime's administrative inefficiency and corruption. Returning to the sale of the late king's goods to examine at length a classic case study in the failures of Rump administration, it also becomes apparent that the resentment stoked by the civilian regime was closely connected with the creation of Commonwealth pomp, which in turn contributed to the tensions of Commonwealth politics. The political circus cooked up by the parliamentarians since 1649 could only heighten a sense of superiority on the one hand and of exclusion on the other. While Parliament played its games, it gave artificial cohesion to the rhetoric of those soldiers who sensed most keenly the vast gorge separating 'court and camp', for whom revolution did not necessarily bring power and prestige. By enhancing the position of the civilians and the commanding officers of the army over the soldiers, the political culture of the Commonwealth worked too well. It simply underlined the perception (more apparent than real, but highly affecting) that most of the spoils of war were going to those least worthy.

Secondly, although Cromwell's ire has become famous as an expression of frustration with the parliamentary political system, he himself did everything possible to play down the impression of a violent outburst against morally reprehensible men, and to maintain an appearance of peaceful continuity across the watershed of 20 April 1653. The Commonwealth's topography, spectacle, iconography and language all survived the dissolution. The promises of the military's propagandists that the new regime, committed to radical reform, would do more good, and more quickly, than the Parliament could ever have achieved gave way to the pressing need simply to govern the country and pay the army. The fervent hopes harboured in some quarters that the new revolution would finally sweep away the formalistic 'dross' of governance gave way to the need to govern as respectably as might be.

Finally, although it is claimed that the dissolution was the most popular thing Cromwell ever did, and raised godly optimism to an unprecedented pitch, it was in fact met with a very ambiguous response, even in the least hostile sectors of political opinion. 'Supporters' of the *coup* seemed full of uncertainty. They did not all so much rejoice at the news as remain hopeful that this latest dispensation might yet prove an opportunity for the fulfilment of their dreams. In the event, a wide gap rapidly opened up between the army's professions of good intent and the unfolding reality. To understand why there was a limit to godly optimism, and why it was indeed justified, this chapter also examines the representational quality of the military's involvement in Commonwealth politics, especially in April 1653.

In the 1650s, just as in 1647 and 1648, the army and its partisans used metropolitan printing presses to create a public image, a platform or manifesto for change and reform.[4] This platform was a form of political representation like any other, and can be considered as one more feature of the political culture of the Commonwealth.[5] Like the imagery and appearances of civilian rule, the army's public image embodied imaginary ideals cooked up by a minority. These ideals provided a respectable cover for the seizure of power in the spring of 1653. They masked the material agenda which, in some quarters, were just as important in motivating the *coup* as the demand for a radical reframing of society. The *coup* was not about enacting a strict programme of idealistic reforms so much as about fulfilling all sorts of wishes, both selfless and selfish, cherished by shrewd political operators who had become increasingly frustrated in the face of the success with which the post-revolutionary regime adopted its civilian character.

I

Besides demands for religious freedom and a return to pre-Conquest norms of law and justice, reform of the public finances was a regular feature of the army's radical platform, especially between 1647 and 1649, and then again from 1652.[6] Most specifically, the army command took up the cause (and genuine plight) of public faith creditors and others.[7] This issue lay at the heart of debates about social justice and the political rights of Parliament's poorest supporters in the aftermath of the revolution. By focusing on the failings of the fiscal administration which was supposed to be paying for the army, it was also an effective reply to criticism of the vast expenditure incurred by the military establishment. Radicals in the army demanded that 'the heavy burdens of the people be removed, and all Oppressures and Taxes taken off, that so the poor may no longer be insulted over by the rich'.[8] The Leveller, Samuel Chidley, complained on behalf of those still owed money on the public faith, saying that 'Many of the faces of the poor creditors have been ground away ... as witness their countenances'. Politically explosive, unkept promises made public faith creditors 'weary; and in the bitterness of their hearts ... wish for a new representative, which might make better provision for them'.[9] Immediately prior to the dissolution, one newsbook reported that

> It is the opinion of many wise men that a deliverance draweth near ... Then will ... those faithfull persons who hazarded all for the Parliament, and many of them that spent their whole estates and now lie in prison, not be put to uncover Cathedrals and ransack Monuments of the dead, but be honestly paid with thanks and requittal.[10]

As the champion of the little man the army mined an exceedingly rich vein of popular support. Four days after the abolition of the monarchy in March 1649, Parliament was lobbied by no less a figure than Lord General Thomas Fairfax on behalf of a group of Crown domestic servants seeking satisfaction for wages and salaries owed to them.[11] In negotiations with the court at Oxford during the 1640s, Parliament had taken on responsibility for the subsistence of Crown servants who had remained in London.[12] But by 1649 many had been reduced to a terrible state of debt. In November 1648 John Milton addressed a sonnet to Fairfax, commending him to the 'nobler task' which awaited him once the royalists had been crushed, namely seeing 'public faith cleared from the shameful brand of public fraud'.[13] Now the Lord General took up the challenge with alacrity, and prompted a swift response from Parliament. Within two days of his petition, a parliamentary committee returned a report recommending the appointment of commissioners to inventory, value and sell all the goods of the royal households, excepting anything the Council of State decided was necessary for the use of the government. Most of the proceeds were to be used to pay off the Crown's household debts, i.e. wage and salary arrears and outstanding bills.[14] However, the Rump's vigour and good intentions were soon dissipated. The sale of the late king's goods was a classic example of a widespread phenomenon. It exemplified the administrative logjam which took those who pinned their hopes on Parliament to the very brink of personal disaster, as well as the way administration could be exploited to line the pockets and fuel the self-importance of those who had, in relative terms, ventured so much less.

The Acts passed in 1649 and 1651 for the sale of the royal family's personal property appointed a number of officials to oversee the task.[15] The trustees for the sale located, inventoried and valued goods worth around £185,000, as well as assessing the needs of claimants.[16] The contractors, appointed to arrange the sales, fitted out part of the government bloc at Somerset House as a showroom where they gathered together much of the royal property.[17] The sale was not a success. There was much overseas interest, especially in the dead king's art collection, and Clarendon later recalled bitterly how foreign kings 'assist[ed] Cromwell with very great sums of money while they adorned themselves with the ruins and spoils of the surviving heir'. Nevertheless, two years after the sale began, a huge number of beautiful tapestries and paintings were still lying around gathering dust.[18]

Whilst the contractors were seeing to the sale, the trustees were receiving the representations of those claiming satisfaction. Their first list, containing the 120 most needy creditors and servants, was accepted by Parliament on 14 March 1650, and early in April order was given to make payments totalling £12,800.[19] By May of the same year the treasurers had banked over £35,000 in proceeds, including £4,000 from fines for discoveries and £8,500 from coining the king's plate and regalia.[20] The trustees issued their warrants for the first batch of payments between June and September. These were mostly made to servants of the household, who generally received the full amount awarded to them in the first list.[21] Several payments also went to Crown provisioners such as the pin maker William Ardington and Richard Lyon, 'oatmeal man to ye late king'.[22]

A large number of widows, executors and estate administrators received warrants, suggesting that the 1640s had been a hard decade for the domestic servants left high and dry by the civil wars. Given the necessity of those depending on the trustees, the large number of payments in kind is striking. Occasionally it meant receiving some cash, with the remainder made up in goods. But even small sums, between £10 and £20, were often wholly 'discounted in consideration of goods contracted for'. When cash payments were authorised, they had an air of irregularity about them – in October 1650 the trustees' clerk-register was authorised to instruct the treasurers that, in regard of Mary Coates's warrant for £50, 'upon this poor woman's petition ye committee did order ... that they desire she may have money'.[23] The obvious cash flow problems experienced by the sale's administrators are further evidenced by lengthy delays in turning the warrants into payment. Many were not receipted until years after their issue. One of the earliest warrants signed by the trustees promised the widow Frances Robinson £100 for her late husband's wage arrears. Dated in June 1650, it was not receipted until December 1657, by which time it had been assigned to another party.[24]

The trustees submitted their second list of 970 creditors on 3 January 1651, and had to wait eight months whilst Parliament ignored it, delayed considering it and amended it before ordering the next round of payments.[25] But once again the trustees were able to satisfy the creditors and servants only with payments in kind. Having presented audited claims for a sum of approximately £90,000, the trustees' warrants issued between September and November 1651 authorised cash payments of only £7,500, which were made to less than half those receiving warrants.[26] Furthermore, unlike those of the first list, the creditors and servants on the second usually received only partial satisfaction of their debts. The problems they faced deepened daily; again the committee was inundated with the representations of widows and relicts. But the commissioners were able to do less and less to help, often being able to offer only a 5–10 per cent cash advance on the full sums awarded by their warrant.

For those who did not qualify for cash, the only hope was to join one of the several syndicates set up after July 1651, amongst which goods worth over £70,000 were distributed between October 1651 and January 1652.[27] There were fourteen syndicates, or dividends, each headed by prominent creditors such as Thomas Bagley, the king's glazier, or Edmund Harrison, embroiderer in the king's wardrobe. Each dividend received goods worth about £5,000, which were then split amongst the members, or left with the head of each syndicate with a view to their subsequent sale. In effect many people were simply lumbered with job lots of furniture, household fittings and lesser-quality art works which could be sold only at knockdown prices, leaving the hopeful beneficiaries with a meagre return of a few shillings in the pound.

After suffering for their affection to Parliament for ten years, and having had the hope of satisfaction held out to them, by 1652 many creditors and servants were even more distressed and frustrated, their necessity ever deeper and more pressing. The suffering of the Crown's servants became something of a cliché, subject to stereotype. In 1652 one newswriter reported that 'There is this week a new sect of old counterfeit knaves discovered, they are called Weepers, and have cheated many charitable persons under pretence of Begging for the late kings servants and others that have been in prison and want.'[28]

The atmosphere bred recriminations. Some of the more powerful creditors pursued their grievances through the new corridors of power. The same day the trustees presented their second list, Parliament set up a committee to enquire 'whether any embezzilment hath been made of the said goods; and how the trustees have pursued the rules prescribed to them'.[29] Four months later another committee was examining accusations brought against the contractors, that they had failed to publicise the sales widely enough.[30] Then at the beginning of 1653 a full-blown corruption investigation was set up, principally to examine allegations against the trustees' clerk-register, Thomas Beauchamp, but also to investigate complaints against his employers and their proceedings.[31]

It is extremely difficult to prove or disprove the commissioners' culpability. However, it is clear that certain circumstances leading to the sale's collapse were completely out of their hands.

There was very little they could do about the economic disruption of the previous decade, or the heavy tax burden with which continuing war shouldered the country. With cash in short supply anyway, purchasing property at the Commonwealth sales was not the most obvious way of spending it. The highest returns might have been expected from the king's art collections. But seemingly interminable warfare had also depressed the Continental market for art – the sale served only to create a glut of available pieces and even lower prices. The only people to benefit were the private purchasers in England, who were able to make a killing by selling their acquisitions later. Colonel John Hutchinson paid £600 for Titian's *Venus del Pardo* in 1649 and sold it to the French ambassador, Bordeaux, for £7,000 two years later. By May 1650 the trustees had sold 375 paintings, raising only £700 more than the sum paid for this one picture in 1651.[32]

Economic constraints on the cash raised by the sale were compounded by a possible reluctance in England to be seen to be plundering the Stuart dynasty. The pictures sold in the first eight months of the sale went to just thirty-eight purchasers.[33] It became clear that there were simply insufficient prospective customers willing or able to buy the greater part of the king's effects. And, whilst there were severe restraints on the money available for repaying the royal family's debts, there were also some heavy drains on the funds that the commissioners did scrape together.

First, there was a loan to the navy, charged on the proceeds of the sale under the terms of the first Act, which eventually amounted to £26,500. It was never repaid.

Then there was the sheer expense of the whole operation. The commissioners had to pay their agents, officers and employees. The job of travelling round the country, making inventories, transporting goods and putting them up for sale was a costly one which was sometimes made even more expensive by sharp about-turns in government policy. The trustees' representatives travelled to Tutbury race, for example, inventoried and valued over a hundred horses of the royal stable and returned to London with their list only to be told by Parliament that it was never intended that they 'meddle with the disposal or sale of any the horses belonging to the late King, Queen or Prince'.[34] When they brought one batch of goods from the royal foundry at Vauxhall, Parliament upheld a private petitioner's claim to them, and the trustees had to take them all back again, doubling their transport costs on goods that could not even be offered for sale.[35]

Mistakes and oversights placed further strains on the commissioners' cash flow. On occasion they found themselves unable to deliver the full amount of property that purchasers had contracted for, as items from parcels of goods went astray, and they had to reimburse with cash customers who had exchanged a debt on paper for payment in kind.[36]

With cash leaving the commissioners' coffers faster than it was coming in, they often had to make application to Parliament for allowances to pay their own wages and those of their employees.[37] It is hardly surprising that when it came to doing what they were primarily employed to do, compensating the Crown's creditors and servants, the commissioners were a bit of a let-down. And for the trustees' part, for undergoing the slings and arrows of their supposed beneficiaries' disapprobation, their reward was a measly £80 *per annum* in the estimation of one disgruntled commentator, who defended the trustees, saying they had had 'the worst employment that ever honest men had that acted by authority of parliament'.[38]

As the sales ran out of momentum, as their treasury sprang more and more leaks, and as anxiety to do something mounted, 'growing on by the Scotch king's coming into England', there was little alternative but to hatch the dividends scheme.[39] But joining the syndicates was not an option open to everyone. For many creditors and servants the receipt of an unspecified parcel of goods as payment in kind was not much of a prospect. In consequence, a market in unredeemed warrants developed, judging by the activities of a certain 'Mr. Jackson of the sequestration office who ... bought at a low scale many of the warrants of the creditors'. This was the same Jackson who headed the dividend representing the interests of MPs Sir Gregory Norton and Humphrey Edwards.[40] A number of individuals seem to have taken an interest in this new area of speculation in state securities, not least the commissioners' porter at Somerset House, Thomas Greene.[41]

As an incentive to self-help, Parliament encouraged the prosecution of discoveries – somewhat disingenuously as it turned out, since parliamentary delays in considering many discoveries meant they could not be sold anyway, and so the discoverers went without the 'moiety' of the proceeds they were promised according to the legislation on the matter. In any case, such prosecutions often proved to be more trouble than they were worth, as it seems likely that the willingness of the house to investigate the commissioners and allegations against them may have been related to the desire for revenge of exposed individuals like Sir Henry Mildmay, who was fined £1,800 for goods found in his possession.[42]

Almost inevitably the commissioners, and especially the trustees, ended up taking the fall in expiation of the creditors' anxiety and frustration. But the anonymous author of *A Remonstrance Manifesting the Lamentable Miseries of the Creditors and Servants* pleaded the trustees' innocence in May 1653, stating they had done their best, 'it not being in their power to give either better or speedier satisfaction than they have done from time to time'.[43]

They had certainly been landed with a difficult job, made no easier by the circumstances of the time. Moreover the behaviour of the government hardly lightened the load. Throughout the episode, both Parliament and the Council of State helped to frustrate the interests of those the commissioners were supposed to help: through faults in the legislation; by their exploitation of the trustees; by sacrificing the latter to the private interests of men themselves partly to blame for the sale's failure; and by acting throughout as far from disinterested brokers themselves.

The discussion which had raised the whole issue of Crown debts in the first place was about the plight of the domestic servants and provisioners of the royal households. However, in the course of legislating for their needs, Parliament began to entertain a wider range of interests. The Act passed in 1649 pledged the proceeds of the sale to the satisfaction of Crown debts 'and of such of them especially as were contracted for necessary household expenses'. But the Act's distinction between the provisioners and servants and the Crown's many other creditors signalled that it had also been found prudent to reward or compensate other interests. These were the men who had lent money to the king before 1639, very often for the sake of favour; the men who sought and received compensation for the loss of income caused by the curtailment of Crown-appointed salaries, such as Colonel Downes, who received £1,500, half his salary as auditor-general of the duchy of Cornwall; or who sought compensation for the trouble they had been put to in the 1640s, such as Sir Henry

Mildmay, who claimed £2,000 for money he had been forced to lend his king shortly before the latter left London.[44]

In short, the late king's goods were to be held liable for the debts not only of his private but also, in some instances, of his public person. Paradoxically, Parliament dropped a clause from the second Act which would have made at least some debts owed to the king liable for repayment of his own debts.[45] It was claimed that this denied the trustees access to a potential £100,000, no doubt a heavy exaggeration. But by leaving out, most conspicuously, the king's livestock – his horses at Tutbury, his herds of deer – the legislation certainly denied them access to a few thousand pounds' worth of the most readily vendible property.[46]

When it came to provision for the reservation of Crown property, both Council and Parliament were often lax in their application of the procedures set down in the legislation. Part of the problem lay in the fact that the commissioners were engaged in selling off property which had been assimilated quite rapidly by the new occupants of the palaces and houses the goods furnished and adorned. Rather than waiting for inventories, then making a selection, then seeking parliamentary approval of that selection, the Council became increasingly inclined to reserve by *fiat* miscellaneous parcels of goods in current use any time it liked. In July 1651 the Council brought the whole sale to a halt just so it could pick and choose what it wanted.[47]

The result was often confusion as to what could or could not be sold at any one time. In May 1650 the trustees found themselves in trouble for selling items from apartments in Greenwich which the Council had decided to reserve fully furnished.[48] And procedure was easily bypassed when private interests could be brought to bear – as, for example, the goods brought from Vauxhall, cited above. In that instance the interested party was none other than John Trenchard, MP.[49]

Private interests also seem to have procured the numerous investigations which dogged the hard-pressed commissioners from 1651. In the *Remonstrance* cited above, the author (not impossibly Thomas Beauchamp, the clerk-register accused of corruption) levelled counter-allegations against the trustees' accusers. He claimed that they had themselves frustrated the interests of the servants now starving and languishing in prisons. For a start, some of them had taken advantage of the situation themselves, claiming debts on the basis of the inflated prices they had always charged the royal households for their supplies. Moreover, he argued, what right had these men to complain of the low returns on the goods they received as payment in kind when soldiers of the parliamentary armies were exchanging their warrants for arrears, purchased in blood, for a few shillings in the pound? In contrast with these men, the ultimate state servants, 'several of the said creditors well know how their affections and endeavours have been contrary to the interests of this

Commonwealth as may be particularly made appear if occasion shall offer'. Maybe he was bluffing, but perhaps the trustees' investigations into the political reliability of the creditors had turned up some potentially embarrassing information.[50] It was certainly true that the government itself was using the sale to bail out men of distinctly dubious credentials. For example, the proceeds of the sale were made available to the politically significant caucus of creditors who hounded Randall MacDonnell, marquis of Antrim, for repayment of long-standing debts.[51]

There were many faults in the republican system of government which were exemplified by the administration of the sale of the late king's goods. Isaac Penington junior warned the Rump that 'Multitude of affairs, Prolixity in your motions, ... want of an orderly Government of your own body ... [and] want of a right rule to square and order yourselves in your proceedings may easily draw many things upon you which might be better managed by other hands, and may likewise retard your despatch in what you set about'. Moreover, the cost of attendance on governors too bogged down to help, and the constant 'seeking and waiting' for relief, 'will eat out the sweetnesse of it, if it should come at last'. Diagnosing the political ill-health of the Rumpers, Penington junior reported that 'seeking up and down after them ... is a thing much complained of'.[52] In an enigmatic political parable the trustee for the sale of the king's goods, George Wither, warned his masters that by their actions or inaction on behalf of such groups they courted disaster.

> The causes whence this hazard will arise,
> Are such as this: observe it and be wise.
> The Temple of the Gods, which heretofore
> Stood open to the prayers of the poor,
> Is closed up, and few admitted in,
> But such as are conveyed by a gin,
> Contriv'd so narrow, that the people say
> It was choak'd up, the first, or second day:
> And with distemper they exclaim, that this
> Of all their grievances, the greatest is:
> Because it puts their patience to more trialls,
> Than, if of Justice, they had quick denialls:
> Turnes hopes into despairs, converts their lives
> To living deaths, their blessings to corrosives.
> The Saints likewise, that must propitiate,
> On their behalfs, and offer at the gate
> Of justice and of mercy, their petitions
> Are not so sensible of their conditions;
> Nor from all partiality so free
> As Mediators alwayes ought to be.

If these 'inferior Gods' did not permit greater access, they would soon 'tumble ... / From heav'n like Lucifer, and die like men'. From lack of openness and the restriction of access

> ... doth flow
> Most other grievances, complain'd of now;
> And hence rise those confusions, which increase
> Our troubles, and procrastinate our peace.
> From hence is it, mens suits prolonged are
> Beyond their lives ... [53]

The late king's servants, many of them by then 'late' themselves, would have said amen to Wither's warning.[54]

Another writer complained in similar vein that important business was being left undone, sacrificed to 'the tossing of a feather'; petitions were dealt with slowly, not least because the relevant committees were hidebound by rules and restrictions; public business was dealt with in private, by cabals meeting in the Speaker's chamber, the House then rubber-stamping backroom decisions. Perhaps more important was the sense of partiality in the division of spoils.

> and then came in some motion of an old Grandee who had so much a year given him for resigning up an illegal Office; or stood up some other who brought old arrears (which it may be the poor soldiery was never satisfied for) and for this, he must have such a sum of money ... , by which some countryman or other must be brought into vexation.[55]

Other critics of the regime demanded to know 'why ... we behold fawning, flattering and dissembling persons (who were and still are common enemies to the Government of this Commonwealth) speed better then honest godly and conscientious Christians?'[56] In his no doubt partial analysis of the hounding of the trustees, the author of the *Remonstrance* made clear that the real blame rested with the government, which set the creditors and servants against the commissioners for its own ends. Whether or not there was some kind of conspiracy, it is clear that the trustees were not helped by the way government turned the sale into a series of opportunities to be exploited in its own interests.

The claims of the government's members and its servants on the proceeds of the sale of royal goods do seem to have received preferential treatment. In November 1651 the treasurers to the sale paid out £1,000 in cash for discoveries made by Cornelius Holland, former courtier and now member of the Council of State, even before the goods he had located could be sold, at the same time as the trustees were issuing warrants to the creditors and servants that many of them were unable to cash.[57]

The exclusion of money owed to the Crown from the definition of estate to be held liable for the Crown debts is not surprising, given the way Parliament used these funds for its own purposes. In November 1650 Parliament audited and accepted debts owed to six important servants and provisioners to the royal households owed sums totalling £10,500. One of these was Cornelius Holland, again, who was owed over £2,500 for his salary as a household official to the late king and his son. Others, like the plumber, John Embrey, were also now in the service of the Commonwealth.[58] The sale commissioners were discharged of satisfying these particular debts, which were charged instead on any sums owed to the king since before September 1643 'not heretofore particularly disposed of by the House' that the six could find.

Parliament also added the injunction that 'the monies to be received and recovered by the petitioners ... be raised ... out of such particulars as are least grievous to the People', the quirkily revolutionary tone possibly concealing an injunction not to expose colleagues. If such was the case, it may explain why Embrey was only able to turn up debts to the total of £500, but was allowed to avail himself of paintings worth £500 to make up the remainder of the debt owed to him for which the king's goods were supposedly no longer liable.[59]

Another one of these petitioners, Thomas Smithsby, claimed £3,557 for stable supplies, wages and livery wages. In July 1651 his brother William, who seems to have been sequestered for delinquency in March 1648, was awarded £2,000 from the sale proceeds by Parliament, thanks in part to the intercession of his kinsman, Oliver Cromwell.[60]

In more straightforward exploitation of the sales, funds were diverted in a variety of ways. For instance there were the interesting incidental costs of minting the king's gold and silver plate in the autumn of 1649, which included payments of £225 to Sir John Wollaston and Alderman Noel, appointed to receive the plate from Sir Henry Mildmay, for supposedly 'finding and preparing and fitting ye gold and silver for the Mint', whilst Gurdon, master of the Mint, received £40 for his trouble. In all, the value of the plate fell by £366 between entering and leaving the Mint.[61]

The fate of some of the horses at Tutbury is also interesting. Having taken them off the trustees' hands, the Council, with Parliament's backing, set up a sale of colts from Tutbury at the Mews in Whitehall, and had the makings of a lucrative dealership and stud farm at the race itself, with all the proceeds left at its disposal, denying the creditors another source of compensation.[62]

As Blair Worden has remarked, 'the Rump ... , replacing the Stuart court, had to improvise its own public morality', and the Commonwealth sales certainly played a part in their improvisations. Worden continues, 'any seventeenth century government was bound to centre on a court, to favour those who belonged to it and to deny rewards to those who opposed it ... [The Rump] never challenged the notion that those who worked hardest on the government's behalf were entitled to the pickings of place, patronage and financial opportunity.'[63] It is not helpful to apply modern notions of the probity of public officials to the kind of circumstances which pertained in seventeenth-century government and administration. It comes as no surprise to find the sale was exploited to the advantage of private individuals.

However, the sales do seem to highlight one of the key weaknesses of the Rump regime. After the gargantuan struggle of the 1640s the victorious Parliament emerged so freighted with debts of gratitude to its impoverished supporters that there ensued a struggle over rewards and repayment for services rendered. The sales were one aspect of the conflicting pressures on the Rump. Intended as a means of relieving some of those who had suffered for their loyalty, they were turned into a beanfeast for the members of the new establishment. George Wither was just one of the contemporary commentators who diagnosed the problem. He had his own personal reasons for criticising the jobbery and corruption of Parliament, having spent years trying to recover the public debt owed him for his wartime losses.[64] But perhaps he was reflecting on his experiences as a trustee for the sale of the late king's goods when he wrote in 1653 that the parliamentarians would feel God's wrath 'For turning carelessly, our eyes and ears, / From Widdows prayers and Orphans tears'; and that the day of judgment was not far off, when

> Popinjaies and Parrets, cloath'd and fed
> By what the valour of these purchased,
> (And trim'd with ill got feathers) strutted by,
> Casting upon them a disdainful eye.[65]

This brings us to the government's reservation of Crown property for its own use. The reservation policy was one of the means by which the Rump created for itself a court environment designed to provide a recognisable charismatic centre for the republic, as well as providing the new courtiers with accommodation and the 'office space' in which its myriad executive bodies might go about their business. In so doing, the Rumpers' jackdaw acquisitiveness stoked the hostility which contributed to the regime's demise.

The author of the *Remonstrance* analysed the failure of the sale of Crown property, and, as anonymous authors are wont to do, he blamed the government. The sales had failed because the commissioners had been given only 'a seeming power' to run them effectively. By its delays and pretences Parliament had dashed the hopes of hundreds of needy people. The trustees were set upon by these people because they had been given to understand that the trustees had the power to help them but would not use it. The allegations levelled at the harassed trustees were pure sour grapes on the part of 'divers men then in power'. But the last straw, what had really made it impossible for them to do more for the creditors and servants, was that, instead of working on their behalf, the trustees ended up working for 'men in authority who had both power and occasion to the use of the goods'. That was why 'many of the said goods are still in the use of particular men, whilst [the] creditors and servants beg and starve for want of bread'. In a sense, these were the 'ill got feathers' which Wither's 'Popinjaies and Parrets' had adorned themselves with.

It is not exactly clear what role the reservation policy played in the failure of the sales. On the one hand, maybe it did not matter much, given the trustees' difficulty in selling what they did have. But, on the other, there is the complaint in the *Remonstrance* that, to the commissioners' distress, the goods reserved were very often 'the most vendible' portions of the royal family's effects. And, in any case, the way the Council made its reservations – by *fiat* and without consultation – undoubtedly compounded the problems facing the commissioners.

The government avidly exploited opportunities created by the legislation pertaining to the reservation of Crown property. In the first Act, the Council was empowered to choose goods from the trustees' inventories to a total value of £10,000. A fortnight after the Act was passed, and from then until October 1649, a committee of the Council was considering what to keep.[66] The Council delayed the opening of the sale in September, as it had not yet had a chance to indicate what was to be reserved from amongst the goods at Hampton Court and Whitehall. On the very day Council eventually ordered the sale to go ahead, the committee members were asked to 'lay by what they shall think fit for the use of the Council, though they exceed the value of £10,000'.[67] At this stage the intention may have been to compile a short-list from which goods worth £10,000 might be chosen later. However, by January 1650 it was evident that the Council found the limit imposed in the Act inadequate to its needs, as property to the value of £16,000 had already been reserved.[68] This sum did not include the library at St James's or the collections of books, manuscripts and medals it housed which the Council had reserved, ordering that it should not be counted as part of the permitted £10,000 of goods reserved for the use of the state.[69] The trustees apparently found this decision hard to accept, as a month later the Council had to order them not to sell the collections, and to stop meddling with what did not concern them.[70]

The second Act formalised this improvised distortion of the terms of the first by simply excluding the library 'with all medals, rings, globes and mathematical instruments' therein from the new definition of what 'goods and personal estate' meant. This second piece of legislation also extended the government's reservation facility, doubling it to £20,000. This was an acceptable extension, and prudent, given the ease with which the Council had bust its previous limit. Parliament also sought to reassure those with a wary eye on the government's encroachments into the royal family's personal estate, promising the treasurers repayment for the extra £10,000 so reserved. But since the payment was to come from 'moneys arising by way of discovery', funds which had always been intended for the sale coffers anyway, the offer was less than ingenuous.

Parliament gave the further assurance that the additional reservations were only made 'provided always that all other the said goods shall ... be disposed to the creditors of the late king, queen and prince'. The phrasing is interesting, since the creditors are mentioned alone, and the goods are to be disposed *to* them. The implication is that Parliament passed this Act aware that it was a last opportunity to take what it could from the king's goods before they were dispersed irrevocably amongst the creditors now forming up into dividends.

But the further reservations clearly did not go as far as some people would have liked. A week after the second Act was passed, the Council halted the final break-up of the royal estate, and two months later let it continue, minus goods worth another £30,000. According to the author of the *Remonstrance*, two members of the Council's reserving committee presented their list to the trustees as a *fait accompli* and 'refused to set their hand thereunto'. By now the Council of State was consistently acting in bold contradiction of the rules of engagement laid down in Parliament's legislation. Another turn around came in the spring of 1651, when, as we have seen, the Council wrote to the trustees ordering them not to sell 'certain statues at St James's House that are worthy to be kept for their antiquity and rarity', and which were later set up in the privy garden. But if the governors of the Commonwealth were now showing themselves perfectly capable of appreciating the finer things, it was the creditors who were paying for their tastes. It was later claimed that the tapestry 'suite of 88' set up in the House of Lords had already been assigned as payment in kind for the debts owed to certain royal creditors.[71]

Ultimately, as we have seen already, given their agenda as the restorers of 'normal' civilian rule centred on a court and dramatised by political spectacle, the governors of the parliamentary republic had more important things to worry about than allowing the sale commissioners to do their job. But there was an undoubted political price tag attached to their growing pretensions and the affectation of dignity. Cromwell's *coup* brought hope that the sale might now be extricated from the inefficiency and corruption of Rump politics, and the anonymous author of the *Remonstrance* gave thanks for God's mercy, and charged the supposed beneficiaries of the sale scheme to take up the whole issue with the Lord General.[72] But these hopes, too, were dashed. For it very soon became clear that the dissolution, heralded as 'the greatest of our revolutions', was little more than a palace *coup*.

II

The dissolution of the Rump is one of the great set-pieces in the history of English politics. Cromwell's solution to the inherent difficulties of a parliamentary system of government has become a by-word for pragmatism in the face of perennial problems for generations of Englishmen. The administrations told that they 'have sat long enough for all the good they have done', and commanded to 'go, in the name of God' are almost legion.

Ironically, the reputation Cromwell has earned by his precipitate action on the morning of 20 April 1653 was not one he actively encouraged himself. Of the many versions of the actual event, only five were by eye witnesses, namely Thomas Harrison, Sir Arthur Haselrige, Colonel Robert Reynolds, Algernon Sidney and Bulstrode Whitelocke.[73] These are by no means absolutely reliable accounts. Harrison's was written during a personal political crisis. It is quite likely that Whitelocke was weathering his own political storms whilst composing his version. Sidney's was recounted by his father; Haselrig and Reynolds gave verbal accounts recorded by a diarist, a fellow MP sitting in a Parliament called by the man who had ordered the *coup*. They do not agree in their descriptions of the dissolution. But whereas the precise details of the event are beyond reconstruction, the general thrust of these accounts from men closest to the event is contradicted by all other official versions.

Three – Harrison's, Sidney's and Whitelocke's – described Comwell's 'very sharp language', the personal attacks he made on the loose morals of a few individual members, details which were seized on by gleeful royalists in their newsletters. Sidney told his father that Cromwell had put on his hat, risen from his 'ordinary place' on the benches, and strode about 'the stage or floor in the midst of the House, with his hat on his head, and chid them soundly'. The General himself conceded that his words were 'not parliamentary language'. Haselrig also dwelt on the incivility of the General's proceedings – Cromwell had called in his musketeers, who appeared 'with their hats on their heads and their guns loaden with bullets', and then ordered the reluctant Speaker to be pulled from his chair, 'which was quickly done, without much compliment'. At a stroke, the precious parliamentarianism of the last thirteen years was visibly and violently repudiated. Only Reynolds mitigates the general impression conveyed by the eye witnesses – Speaker Lenthall, he insisted, had been removed from his chair 'sweetly and kindly'. (Harrison also explicitly refuted the allegation that he had manhandled the Speaker.)

The *coup* was greeted by some very public opposition. Lenthall continued to sign himself 'Speaker'; Bradshaw defied the military *coup*, and both he and the judges said they held Parliament's authority to be continuing still.[74] A group of petitioners, including some of the regime's foremost civil servants, demanded the reinstatement of the Rump until such time as it could make provision for a successor. They were faced down by dismissal from state employment, and threatened with the prospect of renewed bloodshed. The military presence in and around London was also increased.[75]

Yet the apparent violence of the dissolution was played down or passed over

entirely in almost all 'official' accounts of the event. Newsbooks, which immediately fell under army supervision, gave accounts of the *coup* which suggested
a peaceful and mutually acceptable conclusion to the thirteen-year reign of the
Long Parliament. According to one, Cromwell had sat in the House that day

> as a member and made a very excellent speech shewing ... why the Parliament
> should forthwith act that which was effectually good for the Commonwealth in
> general, and that no time should be lost therein. After this some other speeches
> were made by Major-General Harrison and others, and some of the soldiery further
> appearing, the Speaker and the rest were desired to depart ... Mr Speaker and some
> few of the other Members seemed unwilling to be dissolved, yet went very orderly
> away, and no symptoms of discontent unto any unless the countenance may be
> blamed for betraying the image of the mind.[76]

More laconic still was the account that reported that 'This day the Lord
General delivered in Parliament divers reasons for the putting a present
period to the sitting of this Parliament, which was accordingly done, the
Speaker and members all departing'.[77]

The *coup* was presented as a straightforward and uncontested change of
government. One propaganda tract described the dissolution as the greatest of
England's recent revolutions, and 'so much the greater as that it was done in a
manner in an instant, without contestation, without effusion of blood, and, for
anything I can perceive, without the least resentment of those whom it generally concerns' – the Rumpers were 'suddenly dispersed like down blown off a
thistle'.[78] It was denied that Cromwell's behaviour had been 'somewhat rough
and barbarous' – Parliament had been eliminated 'civilly, and without noise or
disturbance'.[79] 'People in general seem very well pleased ... as is perceivable by
the facility wherewith so great an action was performed; it being done without
any noise, struggle, or yet discontent but of very few'.[80] The Scottish army was
told that 'the Parliament was dissolved with as little Noyse as can bee imagined'.[81] All this was coupled with repeated assurances that there were no
implications for the normal course of law, justice and administration.[82] Even
foreign relations would continue to be conducted 'though the names
change'.[83]

The reportage and propaganda associated with the dissolution presented it
as little more than an extension, or correction, of the parliamentary process.
As in 1647 and 1648, the army claimed it had felt obliged to lend its support to
the virtuous minority of members. In its public pronouncements the army
repeatedly referred to 'the honest men of the house', and efforts to 'quicken
and incite the best in the House to do themselves what was desired'.[84] The
army protested that it had wanted Parliament to achieve an acceptable settlement itself, 'that by their own means they would bring forth those good things
that had been promised and expected ... so tender were we to preserve them in

the reputation and opinion of the people to the uttermost'; the removal of Parliament was deeply regrettable, 'we [being] very tender and desirous if it were possible that these men might have quit their places with honour'.[85]

In flat contradiction of the political crucifixion many expected, the Rumpers suffered virtually no retribution for their sins.[86] Those who hailed the dissolution as a righteous judgment on the greed and corruption of the ungodly were soon warned that 'those that shall abuse the godly of the late Members of Parliament, without a cause, will not be approved of therein; some being much for piety and worth as probably may be our governors again'.[87] Rumpers were not all to be tarred with the same brush, but rather some were to be honoured for their efforts hitherto 'that they may be righteous and spirited for this government'.[88] In his own justification of the *coup*, John Hall described the Rumpers as 'a people of miracles ... he were a disingenuous man that would not confess that there have been among them as brave men as wise and worthy Patriots as any Nation ever had'.[89] The General had the mayor, Thomas Fowke, suppress a satirical ballad called 'Twelve Parliament Men for a Penny' which received wide circulation in London following the dissolution.[90]

From his subsequent statements, it would seem that few events exercised Cromwell's conscience so much as the dissolution of the Rump. He had lifted his hand against the lesser magistrate, and, perhaps even more than the regicide itself, it was this action that he seems to have found it hardest to forgive himself for.[91] His immediate response in the spring and early summer of 1653 was to ensure, as the Rumpers had done themselves in 1649, that the latest revolution did not open any floodgates to anarchy. The idioms of civil authority which the Rump had so carefully pieced back together since 1649 were preserved intact.

After the dissolution, the city of Westminster petitioned to have government continue from its traditional location 'in regard a great part of the subsistence of that city hath depended on courts, Parliaments etc'.[92] But, despite initial concern brought on by the garrisoning of Westminster, the judges were assured, as in 1649, that there was no intention to obstruct the course of the law, and it soon became clear that there was little intention of either uprooting strong legal traditions or demolishing the charismatic focus painstakingly reassembled by the Rumpers.[93] Throughout the rule of the parliamentary republic, the army had maintained a toehold in Whitehall, despite efforts to demilitarise the palace. After the *coup*, the council of officers consolidated its grip and preserved intact the environment of the Commonwealth court.[94] In May 1653 the interim Council of State set up a new Whitehall committee, comprising Sergeant Dendy, Augustine Garland and 'Mr Emery' (presumably the plumber, Embrey, who replaced Carter as surveyor in 1653) to eject the Rumpers.[95] According to Hyde's informant, people 'conclude much from the orders to purge Whitehall ... and to call for all the late kings Hangings and furniture into the Wardrobe, that the roomes may be well accommodated ... some hereupon inferre that [Cromwell] intends to call home the young king'.[96] This optimism soon proved to be badly misplaced. Cromwell's councillors, the Admiralty committee and all others 'having any other public employment necessarily requiring their attendance at Whitehall' were permitted to remain at Whitehall, Somerset House and the Mews: all others were to remove.[97] Their lodgings were cleared for members of the General's hand-picked assembly.[98] Sir William Masham's apartments were set aside for the treasuries committee. A stable and coach houses at Whitehall were reserved for Walter Strickland. Two secretaries were housed – Walter Frost junior, who got (Augustine?) Skinner's lodgings, and Captain Bishop of the old examinations committee.[99] John Bradshaw had stood up to the General immediately after the coup, and declared Parliament to be still in authority. He was initially thrown out of his Whitehall lodging, departing 'with great displeasure'. But having abased himself, and demonstrated his usefulness in the court for relief on articles of war, of which he was head, he was continued in his office of chancellor of the duchy of Lancaster, and permitted to stay at Whitehall, 'which he rejoyceth at in hope it may give him admission again into the publique business'.[100]

Once again, physical presence at Whitehall equated with proximity to affairs of state, though all were not treated equally. Some of the more obvious grandees of the new order were accommodated very comfortably. Thus Colonel Robert Bennet took over Sir James Harrington's rooms, Philip Jones got alderman Allen's, and Thurloe added alderman Penington's lodgings to his suite.[101] This demonstrates the extent to which the *coup* did indeed have the support of the 'more honest' members of the old order, and that they in turn were rewarded at the expense of former colleagues. But provision for some of the new governors and nominees does not appear to have been quite so generous as that accorded to other nominated Rumpers. Colonel Pyne and (Roger?) Hollister had to share the apartments of Colonel Purefoy, Marsh and Samuel Highland those of Colonel Dixwell. Moreover, whilst Bennet, Jones and Thurloe were admitted to the 'inner circle' after the dissolution, it is not clear that the lodgings prepared for many other members of the new government were intended to reflect their accession to the nation's supreme authority in quite the same way. The order that, if possible, the nominees 'may be disposed of together' at Whitehall suggests there was at least some truth in the rumour that they were being housed in such a way as to be 'neerer to be commanded upon all occasions'.[102]

It was not just the topographical features of the old regime which were maintained. Through the ten weeks of direct military rule between late April and earl July a number of parliamentary idioms of politics survived, preserved for the sake of authenticity. On 28 May a declaration for continuing the six-month assessment was, according to newsbooks, 'twice read and committed' by the council of officers.[103] Even in matters which might be thought more closely associated with the reforming idealism of the dissolution, change was couched in familiar forms. The announcement of the investigation into the corrupt administration of the upper bench prison was announced in newsbooks in gothic 'black letter', as was an order prohibiting the molestation of godly worshippers.[104] Orders of the interim Council were printed with the arms of the Commonwealth at their head. In June the Council began coining a huge haul of Spanish bullion judged as prize in the Admiralty court immediately prior to the dissolution. The fresh currency, which gave the new government an invaluable cash injection, was struck in the style laid down by the Rump.[105]

Business as usual was maintained most visibly in the war with the Dutch, despite backstage efforts to bring about a peace.[106] The victory at Gabbard Sands at the beginning of June was greeted with a traditional thanksgiving. Announcing the intention to solemnise the victory in this way, the government seemed to betray signs of hesitancy about ordering a full-blooded revival of such erastian formalities in the current context, saying that:

> It hath been a custome much exercised, to enjoin Dayes and Duties of Thanksgiving for mercies received from the Lord: the suitableness of which practice with Gospel times and that Gospel Spirit, which is only to bear Rule in the churches of God ... is besides the intent of this paper.

But pious misgivings were clearly outweighed by the hope that this 'mercy at such a time as this, to say no more', will encourage 'establishment and union to all those that fear the Lord amongst us'.[107]

The 'mercy' at Gabbard Sands was a mixed one, as it was there that Admiral Richard Deane died. The interim government had no intention of letting this opportunity pass, either, bringing the admiral's body ashore and transporting it for burial at Westminster amidst some of the most spectacular ceremonial the Commonwealth had ever seen. This event was notable, too, for the prominent involvement of the Lords Commissioners of the great seal, who had recently refused to set the great seal to the writs calling together the nominees who were to sit in Cromwell's new assembly.[108]

High hopes had been entertained of this body by men who looked forward to a period of sanhedral preparation by the saintly elders for the coming of king Jesus. The dissolution, it seemed, had seen the final remnant of the old 'babylonish' constitution discarded at last. Hyde was informed by one of his correspondents that 'You can be assured that title of Parliament will never again be assumed in this nation'.[109] At the time of the *coup* it was suggested that the old moniker should have been dropped years ago in favour of something which did not 'seemeth to savour of malignancy' so much, something sounding a little less like a 'king's great council'. It was even suggested that, since the king was long dead, the Parliament had been a 'non-entitie', and its removal meant that power now rested *de facto* with the General and his hand-picked Council of State.[110]

However, long before the nominees had even been chosen, an army newswriter informed the forces in Scotland that 'The Name of ye new power is to bee a Parliament'.[111] When they did eventually convene in July, Cromwell gave no specific instruction in the matter of title. But he seemed to give a veiled lead to subsequent developments by charging the assembly to sit until 3 November 1654. This was no arbitrary choice of date – it was, of course, the fourteenth anniversary of the sitting of the Long Parliament, as well as the terminal date set by the Rump in 1651, subsequently revised to 3 November 1653.[112] Conscious or otherwise, the nominees took up the General's lead, and before long, the assembly had resumed to itself the full panoply of parliamentary authority.

Having voted to cover their constitutional nakedness by calling themselves a Parliament of the Commonwealth of England, electing a Speaker and sitting in the traditional Westminster seat of Parliaments, Cromwell's nominees reinstated Edmund Birkhead as parliamentary serjeant-at-arms and sent him to St James's to retrieve the mace which the Lord General had removed from Westminster when he dissolved the Rump. The only surviving depiction of the 'fool's bauble' is indeed that which appears in a 1653 portrait of the Speaker of Barebones, Francis Rous. This is doubly ironic, as Rous, a Rumper, had also once enjoined the English people to 'Judge not the appearances but judge righteous judgement' and to render obedience to the *de facto* authorities accordingly.[113] Now he was Speaker, he was treated with all the ceremonial deference with which the Rump had dignified the speakership. The assembly gave order that he was to be escorted by the serjeant who was to carry the mace before him at his coming and going from the 'parliament', as if their nominee were Speaker in the conventional sense.[114]

It was assumed that the initiative in recreating the Commonwealth system was Cromwell's. The earl of Leicester remarked that 'It seems the Lord General hath caused the baubles to be restored again'.[115] In fact, it would seem that some of the more radical members of the assembly were far from unwilling participants in the creation of an *ersatz* parliamentarianism. Opposition to the assumption of the parliamentary title had been led by Sir Gilbert Pickering, one of Cromwell's close associates, whose presence amongst the nominees was one of the General's few concessions to the notion of 'management'.[116] By contrast, in his apology for the assembly, the radical Samuel Highland claimed that 'the lowness and innocency of that title [of Parliament], having little of earthly glory or boasting in it, induced some to give their votes for that'.[117] The new regime kept the image of the parliamentary republic alive in a number of ways. Barebones' July declaration in justification of its authority 'was printed in the darke letter, and with the arms of the Commonwealth before it, like Acts of the late Parliament, and signed "Hen Scobell, Cleric Parliamenti"'.[118] The Rump's great seal continued to be used, and the arms also remained in place over the Speaker's chair.[119]

Why did the outward appearances of rule by the saints become a reprise of the rule of parliaments? Partly, the answer must lie in the fact that the nominated assembly which eventually convened in July 1653 was far from being the disinterested assembly of saints that many in the gathered churches had wanted to see erected.[120] The commitment to some kind of radical restructuring of society on the part of at least some of the nominees cannot be doubted. But the point was that, despite talk of the second coming and an end to all human ordinances, the millenarian vision did not necessarily preclude the notion of a dignified political process. The overwhelming majority of nominees came from the ranks of the judicially active gentry, and there was a limit to the 'other-worldly' anti-traditionalism of even the most saintly amongst them. Not long after the dissolution, John Rogers, one of the fifth monarchists who started log-rolling the idea of a hand-picked assembly of saints, urged that the new representatives 'be solemnly and publicly set apart' as they had been in ancient Israel, where governors had always been annointed with oil.

> These ceremonies are now abolished, and yet the signification of them remains, viz that there be some evidence or other that the Lord hath laid his hands on them ... separating and setting them apart for the worke of this Government, by such a measure of his oyle of grace, as suites with the age wherein we live (i.e. abundantly more than in former ages).[121]

But there was also perhaps an element of wish-fulfilment in the way this new set of gentlemen took up the reins of state. For it was not just the Rump's reluctance to enact reform which had animated its critics. The *coup* had as much to do with appropriating the forms of the Commonwealth and its imagery as with realising the dreams of reformers. A fortnight after the dissolution the radical preacher, Thomas Brooks, who had been in serious trouble with the Rump two years earlier for delivering a somewhat outspoken sermon in the House itself, berated the accounts committee for its impatience with him and his father-in-law, William Bishop, who, Brooks thundered, 'had a businesse of ten thousand times more concernment to the state' than the minor matter in hand. The wax with which he sealed his letter was impressed with a die bearing the cross and harp device of the Commonwealth arms.[122]

III

After the dissolution, graffiti appeared on the door of the Commons which read 'This House to be let, now unfurnished.'[123] Its comic bathos vividly knocked the stuffing out of the jumped-up republic, with its palatial setting, its low-budget but politically high-cost grandeur, and its pretensions to greatness. Elsewhere, it was not all glee. A notice was posted at St Paul's which read 'Thus people make themselves merry with they know not what.'[124]

Such misgivings were common.[125] Indeed, almost all the support for the dissolution was mixed with doubt. From Durham came thanks that God had moved the army to recall its 'former engagements to this poor Nation'. Parliament had failed, 'And that which did very much adde to our sorrow was the Fearing of God's presence withdrawing from You; which Fear was caused by Your long silence.' The letter went on to express the hope that the soldiers

> may be kept low in Your Selves, and that neither Your former Glorious Victories ... nor the Eminent Imployments that God hath now put you upon, may any way take you off from a single looking upon God in it, nor any Oppositions (which we Fear, may be many) may discourage You.[126]

From many quarters came the warning that

> if these soldiers do not deny themselves, and tread their steps very even according to God, but rather grow lordly, lofty, worldly and humoursome, fierce, self-confident, by-ended and touchy, that a man cannot speak to them; Down they also tumble, with all their swords, pikes and cannons.[127]

In other words, if they 'sinned' as the Rumpers had they might expect a similar fate. The prospects were not good, however. One ostensible supporter of the *coup* warned the soldiers that

> Experience hath taught that those that were sometimes famous for their Countrie, as the Earl of Strafford whilst Sir Thomas Wentworth, whom when once poisoned with the ... delicious bait of honour, became presently as bad as ever he was before good.[128]

In its own first declaration after the *coup* the army high command said, 'We have been necessitated, ... to put an end to this Parliament; which yet we have done (*we hope*) out of an honest heart, preferring this Cause above our Names, Lives, Families or Interests, how dear soever'.[129] There was, of course, an implicit modesty in not claiming to know their own mind, being utterly at God's disposal, happy instruments of whatever it was He had in design for the nation. But there was also a subconscious acceptance of the impossibility of a revolution made in humility and forbearance. As 'honest John' Lambert was wont to say, 'The best men are but men at the best.'[130]

Despite its reputation for transcendent religious conviction and clear-eyed political radicalism, the New Model Army was a very human institution.[131] It has been said that '[d]uring the 1650s the continuity of the army's political consciousness rested almost entirely on the permanence of its officer corps'.[132] It is all too rarely acknowledged that the officer corps also provided the backbone of the military's political power and standing within the post-revolutionary state. Reasonable salaries and the opportunities of reward and promotion made military service a professional option for many members of the gentry classes in the mid-seventeenth century.[133] The career opportunities open to leading soldiers are demonstrated perfectly by the well documented examples of Captains Adam Baynes and John Blackwell.[134] Some 449 soldiers acquired Crown land in the 1650s, only 1 per cent of the total standing force in 1648. Almost all were officers, who made up nearly half of all purchasers. Thirty-three officers acquired estates worth £5,000 per annum, twelve of which were worth in excess of £10,000. Many contemporaries on both the right and the left charged that the grandees had 'stuffed themselves with the parks and manors of the late king'.[135] The army was also a power base for its administrators, especially its secretariat.[136] Along with the fighting men, John Rushworth, one-time parliamentary clerk, received his own honorary degree at Oxford in 1649 for his service in the bureau of the commander-in-chief.[137] Dr Clarges, Monk's brother-in-law, received £250 per annum for his services as agent in London for the armies of Scotland and Ireland.[138]

The military world was at least as competitive as any other profession, and the principle of self-denial was often most conspicuous by its absence, crowded out by pride, covetousness and self-seeking. From Scotland in 1651 it was reported that 'Nothing more frequent here than our Officers exhibiting articles against one another: a man must have good footing that stands here.'[139] The ambitious soldier's lot was not helped by the difficulties he faced in trying to remain master of his own fortunes. Officers often resented having to conduct their affairs at great distance from the relevant decision-makers. Colonel John Bright resigned his commission as commander of a foot regiment in Yorkshire because he was denied leave to go to London for a fortnight to deal with private business.[140] Robert Baynes complained to his brother in 1651 that

> Here [at Dundee] are, I believe, many civil employments of advantage here to be disposed of, which, if our regiment had stayed in these parts, I believe I should have found out and procured; but since our quarters is so far off, I shall be prevented both of inquiring into and procuring of such a place as might better that which I have already.[141]

There was some justice in soldiers' resentment of their exclusion from public affairs which affected their own interests. Four days after the miracle at Dunbar, Captain Adam Baynes asked his agent, Cornet Joseph Pease, to finalise the details of his purchase of Crown lands, for 'the General will not permit me to come from my command, so that I hope we shall not suffer for preferring the publick service before our own'.[142] However, many officers, like Captain Baynes, saw the public service as a means of profit anyway, judging from their speculation in the debentures of the men under their command, and resented the difficulties they faced in pursuit of their own business.[143]

Moreover, we should not necessarily accept at face value the commitment of some soldiers to certain idealistic positions on law or religion. Colonel Pride became closely associated with campigns for greater freeedom of the press and further deregulation of the guild-controlled craft of leatherworking, largely owing to his involvement with the relevant professional bodies.[144] In 1650 a lengthy dispute convulsed the officer corps of John Okey's regiment, the colonel himself fomenting a religious conflict with his subordinate, Captain Francis Freeman, which, the latter alleged, was a specious cover for the colonel's nepotistic control over his command.[145] Such instances do not go anywhere near proving the hypocrisy of military attachment to ideals and principles, nor is it my intention so to argue. Material goals did not, do not, mean bare, uninspired profiteering. To the gentleman officer, the prosperity of one's family, friends and associates was an honourable and worthy goal, itself one of the defining features of virtue.[146] I wish only to argue that these examples at least remind us that, since we have learnt to understand the politics of parliamentarianism in the first half of the seventeenth century as a mixture of principle and faction-fighting, the politics of the army should be treated with at least the same kind of subtlety.

Such an endeavour could easily take up a book on its own. However, enough is known already about the military to make the misgivings voiced at the dissolution comprehensible. Given the power and prestige of their position, it is not surprising to find that military leaders could be just as corrupt as Rumpers. Commenting on the paperwork relating to officers' abuses of the army's finance and pay arrangements which passed through his hands in 1651, William Clarke remarked that 'I thinke it is a climacktericall yeare with our army officers, you and others reporte and divers amongst them that have suffered eclipses ... I have at this [time] articles against (I thinke) at least half a dozen officers'.[147] One 'common practice' for which officers were disciplined was the defrauding of wages, either by holding back soldiers' pay or by putting civilians, often connected with military administration, on their muster rolls.[148] The army also suffered from the kind of difficulties most commonly associated with the national church of the early modern period. Its officers often held the command of more than one unit, a situation which led to widespread absenteeism amongst senior commanders and attendant problems of maintaining order in the ranks.[149] Officers absent in London also incurred the resentment of subordinates left without a strong representation within the local command structure, a situation which led to delays in the payment of wages, and the kind of harsh postings which kept them from the pickings of place and office nearer the centre.[150]

Ascent to power through the military organisation encouraged contrasting attitudes, and even those soldiers most often portrayed as repositories of the spirit of zealous radicalism were in truth a mass of contradictions. Colonel John Jones presented himself as a keen advocate of the interests of the soldiery; he also argued against land speculation, preferring to use his interest in Crown lands to ease the fortunes of their sitting tenants.[151] But he also lobbied his London contact (Humfrey Jones) for special treatment which would make the sale of his lands more profitable to him, noting in the process that the debentures of the soldiers under his command were 'in the purchase for 7s in the pound'. We have seen how he acted as remembrancer to colleagues whom he feared had been ensnared by the temptations of power and glory. After the fall of the Commonwealth he acknowledged political realities, and wrote to Henry Cromwell to tell him that he would be happy to serve either him or his father in the conduct of their private business in Ireland, it being 'my snare to be ever ambitious of ye honor of such commands'.[152]

Although he had been teller for those who voted against the abolition of the Lord Lieutenancy of Ireland in 1652, it was said that Major General Thomas Harrison was not one to stand on titles. It is not clear, then, how he felt about the abolition of his post as Lord Lieutenant of the Tower Ordnance in the same year, nor do we know how he reacted to the loss of the massive poundage income he had made from the post. He was still owed £3,431 14s 6d, and, by way of compensation, was awarded inheritance lands worth £500 per annum from those confiscated for treason and put up for sale in 1651. But just a few days later he demanded that Parliament publicise the orders erecting a committee to examine the problem of poverty for which he himself had been made responsible.[153] Harrison seemed to trade office and immensely lucrative remuneration for some land of uncertain title and the infinitely more valuable political capital he could make from publicising his concern for the poor.[154]

Army officers often had considerably more in common with their civilian counterparts, colleagues, friends and relatives than with the mass of soldiery.[155] The poor bloody infantrymen of the army resented their officers' deportment as much as they did the Rumpers'.

> [O]ur officers, who are of as meane birth and breeding as our selves, and of less courage and gallantry then many of us, must be richly cloathed and bedaubed with gold and silver lace whilest we want necessary apparell to cover our nakednesse. And they must be lodged in Noblemens and gentellmens houses whilest we are enforced to take up our lodgings in churches and other empty houses,

where the accommodation was worse than cavalry horses got. And the officers would do nothing about this state of affairs because divers of them are also become parliament men and so by consequence shearrers and deviders of ye wealth and riches of the land ... Let us conforme and governe our selves by ye same rule that is intended and prescribed for the govern-ment of ye kingdome for ye dethroning of ye king and parliament. [I]t is declared that ye absolute power and dominion is in ye people soe that it is their right to call all thos that are there trustees to account for all there actions to devest them of their authoritie when they please and if this rule hold in ye kingdom I know no reason why it should not hold in ye army [for] it is fitt ... that every man be a sharer in the profitt of ye conquest.[156]

Some of the efforts made by the army high command to distance them-selves from their civilian counterparts at the dissolution were a rhetorical sham. This is not to deny the power and influence of the proclaimed reform agenda, especially amongst junior officers. Cromwell explained to the nomi-nees in July 1653 the desire of the officers to 'keep up the reputation of honest men in the world'.[157] Nevertheless, the language of godliness and reform ought perhaps to be seen as the cover for a multitude of agenda, both personal and political, embracing matters of both principle and pragmatism.

One critic of the Rump regime had complained more than a year before its demise in terms which suggest the jealousy prompted by all the effort put into the creation of an independent civilian regime: 'When publique Officers remain long in place of Judicature, they will degenerate from the principle born of humility and honesty' because subject to the human faults of covet-ousness, pride and vain-glory,

> when officers grow proud and full, they will maintain their greatness, tho' it be in the poverty, ruine and hardship of their brethren ... have we not experience in these days, that some officers of the Common-wealth are grown so mossy for want of removing that they will hardly speak to an old acquaintance, if he be an inferiour man, though they were familiar before the wars began? And what hath occasioned this distance among friends and brethren but long continuance in places of honour, greatness and riches? It is good to remove officers every year, that whereas many have their portions to obey, so many have their turns to rule.[158]

To some extent, this was the spirit which informed the dissolution of the Rump. Not long after the event, *The Moderate Publisher* printed a letter from Portsmouth which said that

> the Country are very well satisfied with what is don, and as the State of this Nation now stands who can be so fit to Govern as the Officers of the army, or at least a good part of them, for have not they been the men that have treated with the subtle pollititions of Scotland and Ireland, in times and cases of difficulty, and what the Parliament did afterwards was by way of approbation and ratifying thereof.[159]

John Spittlehouse defended the *coup* on similar grounds, saying that 'the wisdom and policy of the Army hath been very apparent, in point of Treaty with other Nations, as with Scotland and Ireland, in which two places who but the army managed such affairs?' He might have added England, too, where soldiers not only served in local administration after the war, but had also effectively laid the foundations of the wider national settlement by negotiating the terms of surrender by which royalist regions were pacified. Spittlehouse also recommended that soldiers should build on their experience of public affairs by serving in rotation as representatives in the new government, 'by which means a great part of the Officers in the Army will in a short time be as well made politicians as soldiers'.[160]

Despite their experience in public affairs, whilst the Rump was in power soldiers had failed to establish their authority as a proper institutional entity.[161] Disputes over the command of garrisons (such as that involving Algernon Sidney in 1650–51) raised issues of the relationship between martial and civil authority, and invariably left the military feeling affronted.[162] In 1649 Parliament had reacted angrily over the independent initiative shown by George Monk when he came to an accommodation with the confederate Catholic commander in Ulster, Owen Roe O'Neill, despite the manifest good sense he had shown in purchasing a little leeway as his supplies ran out. Despite having connived at Monk's treaty and having kept it secret for three months, the Council of State did nothing to protect him from the censure of the House.[163] In 1651 the army engaged in dispute with the authority of the City of London. Two men of Charles Fleetwood's regiment were arrested and imprisoned. The sheriff, Colonel Tichborne, could not be prevailed upon to let the two men go, claiming they should stand trial by the law whose jurisdiction they had broken. The Court of War wrote to the keeper responsible for the men's incarceration, but Tichborne commanded him not to obey the court's writ. The army claimed 'it is as neccessary and our undoubted jurisdiction to try every member of the army'. In Clarke's newsletter reporting this to the army in Scotland, the author wrote that 'though we are very tender of offering or moving anything that might make differences, yet I think we shall not be so poor spirited as to betray the discipline and necessary jurisdiction of the army'. In 1652 Captain Stoddart's lieutenant was arrested in Scotland, which was thought 'a great dishonour to our army and entrenchment upon our court martial'.[164]

The army was also denied the right to adopt regimental seals which could be used to authenticate self-assessed arrears claims, and only general officers could certify veterans' claims for relief.[165] It had no regular power to influence the settlement of claims on articles of war, apparently creating a situation in which some individuals took direct action. In one of his last directives as commander-in-chief, Lord General Fairfax declared, on 1 June 1650,

> That it is expressly contrary to my Proclamation published throughout the Army, for any Souldiers whatsoever to intermeddle in matters of Title betweene party and

party, either to put in or out of possession; the Law being open for all persons to receive their remedy in that kind.

Aggrieved parties might apply to the Judge Advocate.[166] The issue was not just how to entrench the army as an institution. There were also strong affinities between the army and the 'military middle class' which ran Wales under the commission for the propagation of the gospel, which was as much a branch of civil authority as an evangelist mission.[167] Even Cromwell himself was not entirely secure. He owed his commission and therefore almost everything to the Rump, at least on paper. This was made graphically clear when Parliament voted to take back the palatial residence at Hampton Court granted to the General by a grateful nation. After a lengthy period of withdrawal from Parliament, Cromwell returned on 15 April 1653, and the vote to sell Hampton Court was reversed, an army newswriter reporting that the House had 'cleared some former and vulgar jealousies'.[168]

By the nature of the civilian settlement devised after the regicide, the power of the sword constantly had to insinuate itself into the politics of the Commonwealth by other means. In the winter of 1650–51, with the growth of economic hardship, 'the army became more acutely conscious of its unpopularity, particularly in London ... [;] embarrassed by the immiseration of the populace, it was tempted to recover some of its lost ground by taking up radical demands for the abolition of the excise and tithes, and by supporting the separatists during their tribulations'.[169] But the success of the army was limited. In August 1652 army officers had petitioned Cromwell demanding a new representative 'forthwith'. The Venetian ambassador, Paulucci, thought that part of the reason for their agitation was that the power of the sitting Parliament 'begins to furnish subject for complaint and perhaps jealousy as well ... [since] the present constitution requires others as well to share in the rule and to be acquainted with state affairs'.[170] Little changed, however, and in January 1653, with 'the grandees [in London] fear[ing] a design', a letter which circulated between the regiments around the British Isles, the nearest thing to a military manifesto in the run-up to the dissolution, lamented 'the many inconveniences apparently arising from the long continuance of the same persons in supreme authority'.[171]

After the event, George Wither published what he claimed were his prophetic musings on the night of the twelfth anniversary of the Long Parliament's first sitting, 3 November 1652. He riddled his rhymes, instructing his reader to

> Observe them well, without enquiring, what
> Their Authors meaning was, in this or that,
> Till you your selves have search'd, how they in reason
> Suit our affairs, our persons, and the season,

> According to your judgements: for that shall
> Be somewhat to the purpose, though not all.

Despite the poet's politically well advised reluctance to name names and call a spade a spade, the thrust of his meaning is quite clear. He claimed to have sensed the coming upheaval, to have felt that 'By, and for, envy, jealousy and pride / Shall A. B. C. be laid awhile aside'. Wither may have been too much of a parliamentarian to concede that there was a strongly ideological motive for wanting to replace Rumpers with honest, godly men untainted by pride or covetousness. Yet he also knew how to read between the lines of those who demanded that the Rumpers take a turn at obedience, and leave off commanding to somebody else. At the same time as penning the Rump's epitaph, Wither also expressed the hope

> that I may not have occasion to be as fatall a Remembrancer to them who are now in Throne; lest worse things happen to them, then to their Predecessors, which I am assured will follow, if their proceedings (which I suspect not) be not really design'd and made answerable to their fair pretendings.[172]

The fullest justification of the *coup* was the first one, published two days after the event, which, by its own admission, only 'hinted at' the reasons behind the dissolution. This was the declaration promised by one newswriter as 'a guide or Lanthorn to the people to direct them out of the Labyrinth in which they were travelling'.[173] 'More large and particular' information was promised, but was never forthcoming.[174] One propaganda tract argued that the public should 'wonder not if the account they [the army] may give you be slow, or possibly slower than you expect'.[175] A later communication from the high command in England to their colleagues north of the border claimed they needed 'more time than we have now to spare to give you a particular and full Account of all the grounds and Reasons' for the dissolution.[176] Another apologist excused the delay – 'If the reasons have not as yet been made known, it is because of those worthy Gentleman's being employed about matters of greater moment'.[177] If the reasons given for the dissolution were vague it was because they were meant to be so. Addressing Barebones on 4 July the General made a show of his reluctance to 'rake into sores, and to look backward' before allowing himself 'a word or two' of explanation, as if acknowledging subconsciously the impossibility of telling it straight.[178] The developments of the years 1651–53 were 'a theme ... troublesome to myself'. The General preferred not 'to render things in those colours that would not be very pleasing to any good eye to look upon'. But, addressing his nominees, he allowed himself 'a word or two' by way of 'our own vindication, ... thereby laying some foundation for the making evident the necessity and duty that was incumbent upon us, to make this last great change'.[179] Cromwell acknowledged that the case had 'never yet been fully imparted thoroughly to the nation', and he thought it better to start by explaining the *coup* to his hand-picked representatives, since it was 'more proper for a verbal communication than to have put it in writing'.[180]

This reluctance may well reflect the fact that, as the story has it, having expected to find a Bill which perpetuated the rule of the Rump, Cromwell in fact found no such thing, and so had to climb down from his original vindication of the *coup*. However, as the General's 'verbal communication' made clear, there was more to it than that. He told the nominated assembly in July 1653 of his own frustration with a system in which it was necessary to pull strings, make parties, and all manner of things 'unworthy of a Parliament', not in order to secure this or that *reform*, but 'if anybody were in competition for any place of real and signal trust'. This, he claimed, was 'not as it ought to be in a supreme authority'.[181]

A year before the dissolution, critics were demanding to know 'Why is it that by favor so many Drunkards, Swearers, notorious lyars, etc., are preferred to places of Trust and great concernment, without any desert at all?'[182] When the Rumpers were ejected at the point of passing legislation for elections to a new Parliament, it was alleged that their successors had been provided for in such a way that 'their kingdom may stand, and others sit with them upon the throne', such that 'knowledge of Faces, Acquaintance, Familiarity, and those little intrigues men will make, though they hate one another, will bring all to ruin'.[183] This was the real danger that the army leadership 'hinted at' in struggling to justify its *coup* coherently yet attractively. In his opening speech to the nominees, Cromwell endorsed this sense of grievance at the complexity and inscrutability of the parliamentary political process, and the perceived injustice in sharing out the fruits of victory. But he also told them of the attempts made to influence the Rump from within, 'some of the officers being members, and others having very good acquaintance with, and relations to, divers members of parliament'.[184] Cromwell later described his humble attempts to influence the course of Rump politics after the battle of Worcester, saying that 'though I had not been well skilled in parliamentary affairs, having been ten years in the field, yet in my poor measure my desires did tend to some issue ... I did endeavour to add my mite, which was no more than the interest of one member.'[185] But this was a little disingenuous, to say the least, as Cromwell was one of the leading champions of private causes in Parliament, some of which appear very hard to reconcile with his publicly radical position.[186] Moreover, it was the officers who protested loudest on behalf of dispossessed royalists (on the issue of articles of war, for example), and individual soldiers did more than most as agents for the purchase of confiscated lands on behalf of sequestered royalists.[187] However, they did not all have the institutional influence that parliamentarians had and consequently they did not all have equal access to the fruits of victory. The growing evidence that parliamentarian soldiers no longer had quite the clout they felt they deserved, and the growing sense of frustration this fostered, was all it took to push Cromwell into satisfying their hopes of power.

IV

Traditionally, it is always argued that the Rump's real problems began after the battle of Worcester, when the army turned its mind to the victories of peacetime. One could just as easily say that Worcester seriously eroded what cohesion of opinion there had ever been within the army itself. Whitelocke looked back and saw that 'It is no strange Thing for a gallant Army ... after full Conquest of their Enemies, to grow into Factions and ambitious Designs.'[188] Cromwell seemed to acknowledge as much in his speech to Barebones in which he complained that he had been forced to prevent the passage of electoral legislation which was intended 'to cross the troublesome people of the army, who by now were high enough in their displeasures'.[189]

It has also been argued that the army's righteous indignation at the Rump's 'failure' to enact reform 'was no mere rhetoric' because the officers had pressed for change so tirelessly since the autumn of 1651. Some undoubtedly had. But the reforming impulse did not exactly sweep through the army after Worcester. When it emerged in its final phase a year later with the presentation of the officers' petition of August 1652, it did so as a compromise between the firebrands who wanted immediate dissolution and more cautious counsel to make the existing system work in the army's best interests. The August petition emerged after Cromwell had been lobbied by subordinates demanding the Rump be replaced by a 'new representative', a demand which became the modified but less ambiguous request for the Rump to establish the ground rules for government by successive Parliaments.[190] Already, the agitation in the summer of 1652 had revealed the misgivings of radicals about the army's leadership. Enumerating the burdens of the people, one tract claimed that

> God will find out some way or other of deliverance from [oppressions], but who it is that will be so far honored with the promoting of such a glorious work, we are not yet able to discern ... Whosoever they be that have opportunities in their hands, and makes not use of them, He that knoweth all things will lay such persons aside, and shall make use of others that shall make a better improvement of their Talents which they are betrusted with.[191]

But the containment of more radical impulses was short-lived and even counter productive, as it deepened the gulf between army radicals and some sections of the high command, principally Cromwell. Impatience grew, and in January, when it was reported that 'the Officers have been seeking God two days; the grandees fear a design', the Council of Officers had to set up a

committee to gloss over obvious differences on the question of 'the consistency of the civil authority by successive parliaments and the just and equal
dispensation of justice through the nation for the greatest ease and advantage
of the people'. A small but significant minority seem to have lost all faith in a
parliamentary settlement at least a month before the Rump began to discuss
the future of that cause.[192]

The final months of the Rump saw a great deal of turbulent disagreement
within military counsels. The intense differences of opinion within the army
came out quite clearly in the winter of 1652, when a council of war convened to
issue its response to the heavy sentence imposed by the Rump on John
Lilburne. 'After a large dispute, many declared their ardent affection, To stand
and fall with so great and faithfull an Assertor of Englands Liberties. Others
resolved, To submit their Wills, to the Will of the Power that imposed the
Sentence.' The officers had divided on a fundamental question of power, one
at the heart of the constitutional settlement devised in December 1653 – the
division of legislative and executive functions, the recreation of checks and
balances. So stark a contrast in the officers' response was, however, mitigated
by the latter group's 'declaring, That they will leave no means nor dangers
unattempted, to establish the People in the fulness of their Liberties and
Freedoms', and the whole was glossed as a 'cordial Result'. And Cromwell,
who apparently stood aloof from the specific issue of Lilburne's punishment,
was nevertheless said by *The Faithful Scout* to have 'declared for Liberty and
Freedom, and is resolved to ease the people of their heavy burdens'.[193] This
kind of gloss typified military involvement in civil affairs in the years after
Worcester. Appearances were never as important as they were in the immediate aftermath of the Rump's dissolution.

Military propaganda which appeared in the wake of the *coup* took advantage
of the general dissatisfaction with a long-standing government, as well as
playing up to the great expectations of change being afoot. After the dissolution, the army appealed to the general dissatisfaction with the old fiscal and
financial regime, and did little to damp down expectations of its intention to
enact sweeping reforms. Promises to alleviate taxation and satisfy creditors
were as common in army propaganda as the encouragement it gave to those
who thirsted after godly reform. Many reports claimed that the officers 'are
using all means possible for the taking off Excize and Taxes, and to free the
people from the Tyranny of Oppression etc.'[194] One newspaper prefaced its
account of the dissolution with the headline 'Rouze up, sad hearts, win Gold,
and wear it', and warned, in large type, 'Excise men and Committee men even
your Accounts.'[195]

Petitioners in London and around the country expressed hopes that grasp-
ing officials would now be brought to book. From Essex came the demand that
'Money-Mongers ... be call'd to an account and made to disgorge them-

selves'.[196] In Holland, and even as far afield as the American colonies, it was reported that Cromwell had thrown the Parliament out as punishment for its greed and corruption, and 'To call all those that have cousened the State to an Account'.[197] In Ireland the old Parliament's commissioners warned that 'such as are in the service of the Commonwealth in this Land must expect to be called to a strict account for their neglect therein'.[198]

Despite all the promises and the expectations they fostered, the dissolution had a limited impact on the fiscal regime of the Commonwealth. Tax cuts were still being promised as the council of officers considered the continuation of the old assessment for another six months. When they decided in favour of the measure, the regime's press claimed it had been 'found that the readiest way to ease the people of such burthens for the future is their cheerful contributing to one six moneths assesment more'. However, readers were deflected from pondering this double-speak too deeply by the bland reassurances that 'many worthy things of publick concernment are in preparing, *viz.* 1. The payment of the public faith, 2. The taking away suit and service and base Tenures, 3. a brief regulation of the Law'.[199] Further sops were thrown to public opinion, but they had little substance. Public faith creditors were eventually fobbed off with the mixed blessing of inclusion in the over-subscribed carve-up which characterised the Cromwellian settlement of Ireland.[200] The Rump's investigation into the corrupt administration of the upper bench prison was revived, but there was no wide-scale examination of the state machinery.[201]

Failure to reform these objects of hostility is not surprising, as the intention had never been much more than a pious aspiration which took little account of the practicalities of governing whilst maintaining a huge standing army. Furthermore, although an idealised vision of the army existed in the mind's eye of some of its members and some of the saints, the reality was an army leadership mired in the Gordian complexities of Commonwealth politics which Cromwell's sword had supposedly slashed through. Albert Warren thought it most likely that the common law would survive the spring 1653 *coup* not only because it was the touchstone of property owners, not least the newly wealthy soldiery, but also because it was vital to uphold 'the necessary Art of artificiall reasoning', in which the study and practice of law are essential training: 'hence are men incouraged in the breeding of their sons at our Innes of Courts'. The army again had an interest in seeing that this continued to be so, as 'propping up the sagacity of wits maketh much for, not at all against the Sons of Mars', as it maintains the honour of the nation, '(whereof the Army seemeth very tender)', and will allow 'the presenting of their own issue (when Peace shall triumph in the three Nations joyned happily in one Republick) into places of trust and judicature. But especially, as before hinted, for fixing and establishing their owne possessions.'[202] The underlying agenda of the civilians and the military leadership were too similar for the *coup* to herald a new revolutionary chapter. As John Streater had remarked, pointing out the fallacy on which the military *coup* had been based, 'the army may with more ease and safety change a new elected Parliament than dissolve this, in regard they are wound into an Interest'.[203]

In these circumstances, the little man continued to suffer. The author of the *Remonstrance* had pinned his hopes for the dead king's creditors and servants on this latest revolution. But William Legg, who seems to have taken advantage of events to supplant his former master in the Commonwealth wardrobe, Clement Kynnersley, was soon instructed not to hand over any goods demanded by the trustees.[204] In effect, the Rump's court was preserved intact for the new incumbents. When they too fell by the wayside, their replacement by a constitution much more closely modelled on monarchy spelt the end of any hopes that may still have existed that the Crown's servants would be repaid from the proceeds of the king's goods. A group of household servants petitioned the Protector's Council in July 1654, complaining of the hunger and imprisonment to which they were still prey, begging that the trustees be called to account once more for having 'broken their trust, and disposed of the goods unjustly'. Government patience and sympathy were at a low ebb by then, and the petition elicited only a curt order that the relevant committee dispatch the business as quickly as possible.[205]

It is hardly surprising that the army also failed to deliver on its promises of wide-ranging social, political and religious change. Frustrated zeal for reform made the most compelling copy for publicists and apologists seeking to put a righteous gloss on the *coup*. But there was little prospect of turning the dreams of the godly into reality, given the complex state of military politics by 1653. There had been a notable lack of serious public expressions of intent in the build-up to the *coup*. Compared with the heady days of the summer of 1647 and the winter of 1648, when the army had preceded action with detailed and vigorous polemic, there were no great manifestoes prior to the dissolution, despite the obvious tension and expectation of great things being afoot. Then, in the aftermath of the *coup*, there was a suspicious reluctance to go into detail about the latest dispensation of providence. This created a vacuum which was filled by newsbooks like *Moderate Occurrences*, which summed up the contents of one edition with a precis of 'A Remonstrance of the General Officers of the Army, under the command of his Excellency the L. Cromwell, touching the settling of the Government of this Nation, the removing of all Oppressions and Taxes, and the restoring of the People to their rights and privileges. To be published in all Cities and Market-towns throughout England and Wales' – no such paper had actually been published, let alone appeared in the newsbook itself.[206]

Although the General was portrayed as champion of the radicals in some quarters, it was very often done by insinuation which is unlikely to have convinced much of his supposed constituency.[207] One radical exhortation to the army to live up to its promises berated its leaders as 'Monarchicall souldiers, not Common-wealths souldiers', attacking the hypocrisy of any man who promised freedom in return for blood, sweat and treasure but then 'sits himself down in the Tyrants chair and takes the possession of the land to himself, and calls it his, and none of mine, and tells me he cannot in conscience let me enjoy the freedom of the earth with him, because it is another mans right'.[208] This diatribe against the officers nevertheless carried on its title page an advertisement of 'his Excellencies Resolution, to remove all Burdens and Oppressions from the People; to advance Trading; to pluck down Tyranny; and to purge and cast out all those who are Enemies to the Peace and Freedom of this Nation', tacked on by the printer, George Horton. The text of this supposed 'resolution', like the 'declaration', above, trumpeted by *The Faithful Scout* at the time of Lilburne's banishment, was nowhere in evidence.

In the spring of 1653 London radicals addressed themselves to the General and his officers. 'Our eyes have been upon you,' they said,

> but our hope is in God; and though we be yet clouded, and in the dark, yet deliverance will come and we shall not be deceived ... the good land is before your Excellency; and if you will not enter before us ... yet deliverance shall come, for the spirits anointing caused the people to destroy the yoke of the late king ... for shame, up and be doing.

If he failed, 'we shall be inforced to cease from your Excellency and lift up our eyes to the hills, and expect deliverance some other way'.[209] Cromwell must have seen (he cannot have missed the point – it was made forcefully and repeatedly by his own radical 'supporters' right up to the dissolution) that he and most of his colleagues in the military high command were guilty of everything the Rumpers stood accused of. They had themselves dragged babylonish garments from the ruins of the palace, had wrapped themselves in the finery of royalty and stuffed themselves with the lands, manors, parks and orchards of their enemies. They, too, had grown mossy for want of removing, were equally inaccessible to their one-time friends, and were obsessed with the little intrigues that men will make, though they hate one another. It was not surprising that they did not succeed where the Rumpers had 'failed'. At the dissolution, a radical supporter of the army claimed 'this business was butt to pull downe the father and to sett up the son, that the father should weare worsted and the son silk stockings'.[210]

The manner of the dissolution is not uncommonly cited as evidence for its causes.[211] Cromwell appeared in the House on 20 April 1653 'clad in plain black clothes, with grey worsted stockings'. In some accounts, the apparel in which the Lord General came to Westminster is seen as 'another proof – if proof were still necessary – that his action was not premeditated', and there-fore of crucial significance for explaining the dissolution of the Rump in terms of the Rumpers' treachery and evil designs. It is argued that, after his conference with MPs the evening before, Cromwell believed that Parliament would not pass the election Bill that day, and that his plain dress that morning attested to the fact that he had rushed to the House having been caught on the hop.[212]

Alternatively, his appearance may in fact lend more weight to the specula-tion in London about the conflict within the ranks between Cromwell and Harrison, each bidding to be the saints' champion; or at any rate the sugges-tion that Cromwell dissolved the Rump in order to preserve his leadership of a united army.[213] Haranguing the drunkards and whoremasters, the corrupt, unjust and scandalous membership, he appropriated the fire and brimstone of the officer who had led the campaigns against the corruption of Lord Howard and the moral turpitude of Gregory Clement. In happier times the General himself had been caught up in scandalous allegations involving a prostitute. Whether true or not, the story was passed from one senior secretary in the army, Thomas Margetts, to another, William Clarke, 'only to make thee merry and to be used at discretion'.[214] Now, with religious radicals breathing down his neck, the Lord General had recourse, in Blair Worden's phrase, to 'the histrionics of the fifth monarchists'.[215] His appearance in the House on the morning of the 20th could be taken as the visual equivalent of the 'language of the saints' that he used against the Rumpers.[216] It confirmed that the Lord General had been 'capture[d] ... by the chosen'.[217] Thereafter, the Barebones period did witness something of a fad for plainness, and it is tempting to see the General pandering to the saints by aping a godly appear-ance.[218] But his adoption of the ways of the zealots after months and months of hard slog on Parliament's behalf, the morning after he had once again dis-suaded the hotheads from acting too precipitately, whether or not it was 'an act of spiritual intoxication', was absolutely not 'apolitical', as has been claimed.[219]

The dissolution testified as much to military disunity as to radical dissatis-faction with the Rump. In spite of these tensions, as the events of 1659 would eventually prove, the success of the army in politics depended on maintaining at least the appearance of unity. And it is quite clear that whatever unity the army did have depended largely on presentation. Cromwell's *coup* did not end his troubles. The gathered churches rapidly cooled towards him. Junior offic-ers burst into a Council meeting at Whitehall, symbolically mounting their own assault on the citadel and demanding representation for their views in the new regime.[220] After the dissolution, some officers were not happy, 'conceiv-ing that the way they were now going tended to ruin and confusion', but Cromwell professed himself resolved to do much more good, and with more expedition than could be expected from the Parliament: which professions from him put most of them to silence, and moved them to a resolution of waiting for a further discovery of his design, before they would proceed to a breach and division from him.[221]

According to the dissident major, John Streater, Cromwell told his officers immediately afterwards that 'when he went into the House, he intended not to do it; but the spirit was so upon him, that he was overruled by it; and he consulted not with flesh and blood at all'. 'Now they must go hand in hand with him, and justify what was done to the utmost hazard of all.'[222] Thereafter, he had to work hard to manufacture the consensus on which his new-found lease of leadership would depend. The propaganda of the army used the rhetoric of spiritual unity and reforming mission to project the required image.

The army was made up of a thousand politicians, who had at their disposal a convenient rhetoric of unity which they could use to create the impression that they were in fact part of one huge political organism. Not without reason has it been said that the army was the nearest thing to an end-of-century political party to be found at the mid-century.[223] Apologists were keen to stress that the dissolution 'was no more his [Cromwell's] action than it is the action of the Head moved by Tendons and Muscles which are parts of the Body and without which the Head itself could not possibly at all move'; the *coup* 'was not a rash precipitate Act of his, but a Trust, and Result of those under him'.[224] A month later, when confronted with a deputation of civil servants, citizens and divines who petitioned for the restoration of the Rump, Cromwell took the opportunity to affirm his leadership, telling the petitioners that 'he took it ill that they should go about to obstruct the proceedings for the good of the people, that himself and those about him (turning to the officers) would make good what was done with their bloods etc'.[225] Cromwell's bloody threat (itself possibly exaggerated for the consumption of some of the more hot-headed elements within the army) was glossed elsewhere as 'a very modest answer', in which he said

> to this purpose, That the Councel of State and Officers of the Army were all unanimously of one mind. That it was the duty of such as were in place of civil government to attend their duties at home, That it was well known who were the first contrivers and promoters of this Petition etc.[226]

One news report claimed that the petitioners had completely failed to enlist military support for their position, for 'the Officers, blessed be God, are exceeding unanimous'.[227] Declarations of support from the authorities in Scotland and Ireland were prefaced by the remark that 'It is very observable how forward the Nations are to comply with this present Government ... [and] with my Lord General and the Council of the Army in the present management of affairs'.[228]

Despite the presentation of a black-and-white world in which soldiers rose up as one to put down the betrayers of the cause, the line between officers and civilians was very often an extremely hazy one in the matter of Westminster politics. What Cromwell was increasingly concerned by, and what he was eventually forced to deal with by acting in a way the thought of which had 'made his hair stand on end' not two months earlier, was the invisible line dividing men of broadly similar backgrounds, beliefs and experiences when-ever the main source of pressure for change was seen to derive from outside the hallowed confines of the civilian state.[229]

In 1657 Cromwell reflected once more on the decision to dissolve the Rump. Quite simply he felt justified in the matter because the Rump's plans for settlement 'did not satisfy a company of poor men that had ventured their lives ... men that had wives and children in the nation, and therefore might a litle look after satisfaction in what would be the issue of the business'.[230] The whole history of the army's involvement in politics hitherto had included an element of material interest. At Putney, in 1647, Cromwell and his son-in-law Henry Ireton corrected the Levellers who demanded votes for soldiers, saying they had not fought for that, but for the limitation of prerogative, the right to parliamentary government and 'freedom of trading to get money to get estates by'.[231] When Bulstrode Whitelocke wrote his fictitious account of his 1652 conversation with Cromwell in St James's park, the words he put in the Lord General's mouth to express the discontent of his subordinates indicated the impression Whitelocke had of that army's real priorities. The Rumpers were at fault for their 'Pride, and Ambition, and Self-seeking, [and] ingrossing all Places of Honour and Profit to themselves and their Friends'. Conversely, Cromwell stated, the soldiers complained that 'they are not rewarded accord-ing to their Deserts, [they complain] that others, who have adventured least have gained most; and they have neither Profit nor Preferment, nor Place in Government, which others hold, who have undergone no Hardships nor Hazards for the Commonwealth; and herein they have too much of Truth'.[232] Whitelocke's authorial licence made the issue clearer than it had ever really been. It has also been remarked that those soldiers who doubled as officers and gentlemen of the administration were in a far stronger financial position than those lesser MPs with no lucrative administrative posts at their disposal, no garrison commands to draw pay from, and few contacts and networks worth exploiting for political and financial gain. Some of the most senior soldiers had the greatest stake in the post-revolutionary settlement. But this should not deflect us from acknowledging that Whitelocke too 'had too much of Truth'. For it was precisely those senior soldiers – each one 'a monarch in his regiment' – who had most to lose, in the medium and long term, from the 'civilianisation' of the settlement.[233]

NOTES

1 *Mercurius Democritus* 20–7 April 1653, p. 420.

2 Both are reproduced in Morrill ed., *Revolution and Restoration*, pp. 15, 18.

3 Second only to the even greater ignominy of its final departures, like ante-curtain calls, in 1659 and 1660.

4 Non-metropolitan presses were also of considerable importance. See the *Declaration of the Army of England upon their March into Scotland*, printed at Newcastle in July 1650, in Abbott ed., *Writings and Speeches* ii, 283–9; D. Stevenson, 'A Revolutionary Regime and the Press: the Scottish Covenanters and their Printers, 1638–1651', *The Library* vii (1985), 334; J. D. Ogilvie, 'Papers from an Army Press, 1650', *Edinburgh Bibliographic Society Transactions* 2 (1938–45), 420–3.

5 It did not entirely depend on the press, as evidenced by the 'circular letter' of January 1653, for example, and the letters sent to the commanders of the Scottish and Irish forces after the dissolution. However, other devices, such as the major petition of August 1652, were printed.

6 Worden, *The Rump Parliament*, pp. 168, 193–4, 308, 315, 318–19; Gentles, *The New Model Army*, p. 415; *A Declaration of the Army to his Excellency ... for the Dissolving of this present Parliament, and chusing of a New Representative* ([10 August] 1652).

7 Samuel Chidley, *Remonstrance to the Valiant and well deserving Soldier and the rest of the Creditors of the Commonwealth* ([23 April] 1653); *A Declaration of the Army to his Excellency*.

8 *A Declaration of the Army*, p. 6.

9 *Remonstrance to the Valiant and well deserving Soldier*, also printed in *The Faithful Post* 22–9 April 1653, pp. 722–4. For Chidley and his co-operation with Colonel Pride in pressing for the payment of the public faith see Worden, *The Rump Parliament*, pp. 318–19.

10 *The Moderate Publisher of Everydays Intelligence from the Parliaments Army ...* 15–22 April 1653, p. 809.

11 *CJ* vi, 170.

12 *Ibid.*, 264.

13 John Milton, *On the Lord General Fairfax, at the Siege of Colchester*.

14 *CJ* vii, 171–2.

15 Firth and Rait eds, *Acts and Ordinances* ii, 160–8, 546–7.

16 Millar ed., 'Inventories'.

17 P.R.O., SP25/62, 547; SP28/282, 11.

18 Clarendon, *History of the Great Rebellion* (Oxford, 1712) xi, 251; Bachrach and Collmer eds, *Huygens' Journal*, p. 61.

19 *CJ* vi, 382; *Remonstrance ... of the Creditors and Servants*, p. 2.

20 P.R.O., SP28/282, 13; W. L .F. Nuttall, 'King Charles I's Pictures and the Commonwealth Sale', *Apollo* 82 (1965), 303.

21 P.R.O., SP28/282, *passim*.

22 Ibid., 75, 77.

23 Ibid., 79.

24 Ibid., 66.

25 Remonstrance ... of the Creditors and Servants, p. 2; CJ vi, 545, 551, 553, 605, 606.

26 P.R.O., SP28/283, passim; Remonstrance ... of the Creditors and Servants, pp. 4–5

27 Nuttall, 'King Charles I's Pictures', pp. 302–9.

28 Mercurius Democritus 25 May–2 June 1652, pp. 66–7.

29 CJ vi, 519.

30 Ibid., 563.

31 CJ vii, 250–1.

32 MacGregor ed., The Late King's Goods, pp. 73–113, 203–31; Nuttall, 'King Charles I's Pictures', p. 303.

33 Ibid.

34 P.R.O., SP25/88, 15.

35 Remonstrance ... of the Creditors and Servants, p. 6.

36 P.R.O., SP28/282, 32.

37 Ibid., 18, 21.

38 Remonstrance ... of the Creditors and Servants, preface.

39 Ibid., p. 5.

40 MacGregor ed., The Late King's Goods, p. 17; Nuttall, 'King Charles I's Pictures'; P.R.O., SP28/283, 79, 100.

41 A remarkably large number of warrants in SP28/282 and 283 had been assigned to Greene by the time they were redeemed.

42 Firth and Rait eds, Acts and Ordinances ii, 546; Remonstrance ... of the Creditors and Servants, pp. 6 and 9; P.R.O., SP28/282, 13; H.M.C. Seventh Report, Appendix p. 595.

43 Preface.

44 CJ vi, 261.

45 Ibid., 389.

46 Firth and Rait eds, Acts and Ordinances ii, 546; Remonstrance ... of the Creditors and Servants, p. 3.

47 CSPD 1651, p. 295.

48 P.R.O., SP25/64, 331.

49 Millar ed., 'Inventories', Appendix pp. 424–5.

50 Remonstrance ... of the Creditors and Servants, p. 10.

51 Jane H. Ohlmeyer, Civil War and Restoration in the three Stuart Kingdoms. The Career of Randall MacDonnell, Marquis of Antrim, 1609–1683 (Cambridge, 1993), p. 252.

52 Isaac Penington junior, A Word for the Common Weale ([15 February] 1650), pp. 2–3, 16.

53 Wither, Perpetuall Parliament, pp. 13–14.

54 Worden, *The Rump Parliament*, pp. 88–92.

55 [John Hall], *A Letter Written to a Gentleman in the Country touching the Dissolution of the late Parliament and the Reasons thereof* ([3 May] 1653), p. 6.

56 *The Anti-Levellers Antidote against the most Venomous of the Serpents, the Subtillest Monopolizers* ([7 August] 1652), p. 42.

57 P.R.O., SP28/283, 11.

58 MacGregor ed., *The Late King's Goods*, p. 227; *H.M.C. Seventh Report*, Appendix p. 88.

59 *CJ* vi, 496–7.

60 *Ibid.*, 605; *CCC*, p. 95.

61 P.R.O., SP28/282, 13.

62 P.R.O., SP25/64, 502; SP25/8, 7; SP25/14, 59 and 77; *CSPD 1651*, p. 4; Firth and Rait eds, *Acts and Ordinances* ii, 546; *Remonstrance ... of the Creditors and Servants*, p. 3.

63 Worden, *The Rump Parliament*, p. 93.

64 *CJ* vi, 104, 298, 518–19.

65 Wither, *Perpetuall Parliament*, pp. 6, 24.

66 P.R.O., SP25/62, 544, appointment of Sir James Harrington, Cornelius Holland, alderman Isaac Penington and Sir Henry Mildmay; *ibid.*, 624, Sir Gilbert Pickering, Colonel John Hutchinson, and Thomas Scot added; SP25/63, 91 and 115, earl of Denbigh and William Heveningham added.

67 P.R.O., SP25/63, 115.

68 *Remonstrance ... of the Creditors and Servants*, p. 2.

69 P.R.O., SP25/63, 33.

70 P.R.O., SP25/94, 460.

71 *Remonstrance ... of the Creditors and Servants*, p. 4; *CSPD 1651*, pp. 295, 449.

72 *Remonstrance ... of the Creditors and Servants*, p. 11.

73 *The Speeches and Prayers of some of the Late Kings Judges* (1660); J. T. Rutt ed., *The Diary of Thomas Burton* (4 vols, 1828) iii, 209; R. W. Blencowe ed., *The Sydney Papers* (1825), pp. 139–41; Spalding ed., *The Diary of Bulstrode Whitelocke*, p. 286; Firth ed., *Memoirs of Edmund Ludlow* ii, 352–3; *idem*, 'Cromwell and the Expulsion of the Long Parliament', p. 532; *idem*, 'The Expulsion of the Long Parliament' I, pp. 133–5.

74 D. A. Johnson and D. G. Vaisey eds, *Staffordshire and the Great Rebellion* (Stafford, 1965), p. 72; C. H. Firth ed., *The Clarke Papers*, Camden Society and Royal Historical Society (London, 1891–1901) iii, 3–4; *Calendar of Clarendon State Papers*, letter no. 1121; *The Army no Usurpers, or, The late Parliament not Almighty and Everlasting* ([20 May] 1653), p. 1; J.W., *A Mite to the Treasury*, appended 'Declaration of the Esquire at Arms', Thomas Elsliot, p. 19, 7 May 1653.

75 Bod. Lib., Tanner MS lii, fo. 13; Firth ed., *Clarke Papers* iii, viii and n., 6–7.

76 *The Moderate Publisher of Everydays Intelligence from the Parliaments Army* ... 15–22 April 1653, p. [813].

77 *The Perfect Diurnall of some Passages and Proceedings of and in relation to the Armies in England, Ireland and Scotland* 18–25 April 1653, p. 2661.

78 [Hall], *A Letter Written to a Gentleman in the Country*, pp. 1–2.

79 *Ibid.*, pp. 14, 15.

80 *Reasons why the Supreme Authority of the Three Nations (for the time) is not in the Parliament*, p. 12.

81 Worcester College, Clarke MS XXV, fo. 12.

82 *A Declaration of the Lord General Cromwell and his Council of Officers* ([23 April] 1653), pp. 10–11; *The Moderate Publisher of Everydays Intelligence from the Parliaments Army ...* 15–22 April 1653, p. 813, 22–9 April 1653, p. 1034; *The Perfect Diurnall of some Passages and Proceedings of and in relation to the Armies in England, Ireland and Scotland* 18–25 April 1653, p. 2663; *The Faithfull Post impartially communicating the Proceedings of the Parliaments forces in England, Scotland and Ireland* 15–27 April 1653, p. [716]; Worcester College, Clarke MS XXV, fo. 13v.

83 [Hall], *A Letter Written to a Gentleman in the Country*, pp. 18–19.

84 *Several Proceedings of State Affairs* 21–8 April 1653, pp. 2957–9.

85 *A Declaration of the Lord General and his Council of Officers*; Abbott ed., *Writings and Speeches* iii, 56.

86 It was said that Alderman Allen was temporarily imprisoned.

87 *Several Proceedings of State Affairs* 21–8 April 1653, p. 2945.

88 *The Armies Scout. Impartially communicating to the People the Faithful Proceedings of the Lord General Cromwell and his Council of Officers* 23–30 April 1653, p. 899.

89 [Hall], *A Letter Written to a Gentleman in the Country*, pp. 4, 6.

90 B. Lib., 669 f. 17 (12); T. Wright ed., *Political Ballads published in England during the Commonwealth* (Percy Society, 1841), pp. 126–31; Firth ed., *Clarke Papers* iii, 3–4.

91 John Adamson, 'Oliver Cromwell and the Long Parliament', in Morrill ed., *Oliver Cromwell and the English Revolution*, pp. 49–92.

92 *The Moderate Publisher* 6–13 May 1653, p. 1055.

93 Bod. Lib., Clarendon MS 46, fo. 8; Johnson and Vaisey eds, *Staffordshire and the Great Rebellion*, p. 76.

94 *CSPD 1652–53*, pp. 336, 369, 377, 454; Firth, 'Cromwell and the Expulsion of the Long Parliament', p. 534; Johnson and Vaisey eds, *Staffordshire and the Great Rebellion*, p. 74.

95 Worcester College, Clarke MS XXV, fo. 69v; *CSPD 1652–53*, pp. 336, 377; *The Moderate Publisher* 10–17 June 1653, p. 1093; M. Whinney, 'John Webb's drawings for Whitehall Palace', *Walpole Society* 31 (1942–43), 50.

96 Bod. Lib., Clarendon MS 45, fo. 483.

97 *CSPD 1652–53*, pp. 369, 377.

98 Bod. Lib., Clarendon MS 45, fos 400v, 483; Johnson and Vaisey eds, *Staffordshire and the Great Rebellion*, p. 74.

99 *CSPD 1652–53*, pp. 397, 402, 405.

100 Bod. Lib., Clarendon MS 45, fos 356, 381, 483, 486v; Johnson and Vaisey eds, *Staffordshire and the Great Rebellion*, p. 72; Firth ed., *Clarke Papers* iii, 3–4.

101 *CSPD 1652–53*, p. 394.

102 *Ibid.*, pp. 412, 415, 442, 445, 452, 454, 455, and *CSPD 1653–54*, pp. 3, 5, 61, 66; Johnson and Vaisey eds, *Staffordshire and the Great Rebellion*, p. 76.

103 *The Perfect Account* 25 May–1 June 1653, pp. 995–6.

104 *Perfect Diurnall of some Passages and Proceedings in relation to the Armies in England, Ireland and Scotland* 25 April–2 May 1653, p. 2684; *The Faithful Post* 22–9 April 1653, p. 722.

105 Worcester College, Clarke MS XXV, fo. 77v; Bod. Lib., Clarendon MS 45, fos 269–70; Thomas Violet, *A True Narrative of some Remarkable Proceedings concerning the ships Samson, Salvador and George* ... (1653); Henfrey, *Numismata Cromwelliana*, pp. 31–2. £275,000 of bullion was coined in this way between June 1653 and May 1654.

106 Woolrych, *Commonwealth to Protectorate*, p. 281.

107 *Several Proceedings of State Affairs* 9–16 June 1653, pp. 3064–6.

108 Seymour, 'Pro-government Propaganda', pp. 225–7.

109 *Calendar of Clarendon State Papers*, no. 1121.

110 *Reasons why the Supreme Authority of the Three Nations (for the time) is not in the Parliament*, p. 4.

111 Worcester College, Clarke MS XXV, fo. 61.

112 Worden, *The Rump Parliament*, pp. 267, 313.

113 See above, chapter 3 and plate 4.

114 *CJ* vii, 282–4; Worcester College, Clarke MS XXV, fo. 83; Woolrych, *Commonwealth to Protectorate*, pp. 151–4.

115 Blencowe ed., *The Sydney Papers*, p. 151.

116 Woolrych, *Commonwealth to Protectorate*, p. 153.

117 Cited by Gardiner, *History of the Commonwealth and Protectorate* ii, 288.

118 Blencowe ed., *Sydney Papers*, pp. 152–3.

119 See plate 9.

120 Woolrych, *Commonwealth to Protectorate*.

121 John Rogers, *A Few Proposals, relating to Civil Government* ([25 April] 1653).

122 P.R.O., SP28/260, 431; Worden, *The Rump Parliament*, pp. 120–1, 237, 326.

123 *Several Proceedings of State Affairs* 21–8 April 1653, p. 2945.

124 *The Moderate Publisher* 22–9 April 1653, p. 1037.

125 Woolrych, *Commonwealth to Protectorate*, pp. 104, 133.

126 *Several Proceedings of State Affairs* 28 April–5 May 1653, pp. [2975–6]; Worden, *The Rump Parliament*, p. 380.

127 *A Warning Seriously Offered to the Officers of the Army and others in Power* ([18 May] 1653); cf. *Mercurius Britannicus* 16–23 May 1653, pp. 14–15; *The Faithful Post*, p. 1060.

128 John Spittlehouse, *A Warning Piece Discharged* ([19 May] 1653), pp. 12, [14].

129 *A Declaration of the Lord General and his Council of Officers*, p. 8. The emphasis is mine.

130 O. L. Dick ed., *Aubrey's Brief Lives* (1962).

131 There is a long tradition of scepticism about the motives of the military, which began within the army itself. See John Streater, *Ten Queries: by a ffrend of ye new disolved Parlement* (1653); *idem, Secret Reasons of State* (1659); Firth ed., *Memoirs of the Life of Colonel Hutchinson* ii, 190; Godwin, *History of the Commonwealth* iii, 400; Abbott ed., *Writings and Speeches* ii, 652–3. Even Gardiner rejected the notion of the New Model Army as a saintly host, e.g. *History of the Great Civil War* iii, 228. Modern revision of the New Model's reputation is now well advanced. See J. P. Kenyon, *The Stuart Constitution* (Cambridge, 1965), p. 289; Ian Gentles, 'The Sale of Crown Lands during the English Revolution', *Economic History Review* second series, 26 (1973), 614–35; Morrill, 'The Army Revolt of 1647'; Kishlansky, *The Rise of the New Model Army*; *idem*, 'Ideology and Politics', p. 179; D. Massarella, 'The Politics of the Army and the Quest for Settlement', in I. Roots ed., *'Into another Mould'. Aspects of the Interregnum* (Exeter, 1981); H. M. Reece, 'The Military Presence in England, 1649–1660' (Oxford D.Phil., 1981).

132 Gentles, *The New Model Army*, p. 413.

133 Ashley, *Cromwell's General's*, Appendix.

134 Aylmer, *State's Servants*, pp. 233–4, 243–6.

135 Ian Gentles, 'The Sale of Crown Lands during the English Revolution'.

136 Aylmer, *State's Servants*, pp. 260–3.

137 See above, chapter 2.

138 Aylmer, *State's Servants*, p. 126.

139 Akerman ed., *Letters from Roundhead Officers*, p. 28.

140 Ashley, *Cromwell's Generals*, p. 28. Bright resigned in July 1650, immediately prior to the invasion of Scotland, his regiment thereafter being commanded by John Lambert (by popular demand of the rank and file. Gentles, *New Model Army*, p. 367). Firth and Davis suggest that Bright was a covert supporter of the royalist cause. It was certainly claimed that he opposed putting Charles I on trial in 1649 (B. Lib., Add. MS 21,417, fo. 28). If Bright shared Fairfax's scruples over the invasion, it is interesting that his reluctance to march against the Scottish king should have been glossed in terms of a 'professional dispute' of this nature.

141 Akerman ed., *Letters from Roundhead Officers*, pp. 40–1.

142 *Ibid.*, pp. 3, 11.

143 Gentles, 'The Sale of Crown Lands'; cf. M. Kishlansky, 'The Sales of Crown Lands and the Spirit of the Revolution', and Ian Gentles, 'The Sale of Crown Lands: a Rejoinder', *Economic History Review* second series, 29 (1976), 125–35.

144 Worden, *The Rump Parliament*, pp. 310, 318.

145 H. G. Tibbutt, 'Colonel John Okey, 1606–1662', *Publications of the Bedfordshire Historical Records Society* 35 (1955), 50–6.

146 Fletcher, 'Honour, Reputation and Office-holding'.

147 Aylmer, *State's Servants*, pp. 155–6. Cf. Akerman ed., *Letters from Roundhead Officers*, pp. 26–8.

148 Firth and Davies, *Regimental History* i, 196.

149 See for example *CSPD 1649–50*, pp. 154, 160, 204; Ashley, *Cromwell's Generals*, p. 247; F. D. Dow, *Cromwellian Scotland, 1651–1660* (Edinburgh, 1979), p. 23.

150 Akerman ed., *Letters from Roundhead Officers*, p. 45.

151 Mayer ed., 'Inedited Letters', pp. 6, 47–8.

152 *Ibid.*, pp. 54–5.

153 CJ vi, 436; vii, 126, 129; Ashley, *Cromwell's Generals*, p. 248.

154 Amongst other parcels of land, Harrison initially contracted for the manor of Auler in Somerset, formerly in the possession of Sir John Stowell. *CCC*, p. 1430; and cf. chapter 4, above.

155 Massarella, 'The Politics of the Army', pp. 65–9; Reece, 'Military Presence', p. 9.

156 B. Lib., E537 (8), 'Pay, provision and good accommodation for ye privat souldiers' ([4 January] 1649).

157 Abbott ed., *Writings and Speeches* ii, 55.

158 *The French Intelligencer* 11–18 February 1652, pp. 90–1.

159 22–9 April 1653, p. 1033.

160 *The Army Vindicated in the Late Dissolution of the Parliament* ([24 April] 1653), pp. 8–9, 13.

161 Gentles, *The New Model Army*, p. 436; Massarella, 'The Politics of the Army', p. 69.

162 J. Scott, *Algernon Sidney and the English Republic, 1623–1677* (Cambridge, 1988), p. 98.

163 *CSPD 1649–50*, pp. 263–4; *CJ* vi, 277; Gardiner, *History of the Commonwealth and Protectorate* i, 83–4.

164 Akerman ed., *Letters from Roundhead Officers*, p. 50.

165 *CJ* vii, 22.

166 *A Perfect Diurnall* 3–10 June 1650, p. 289.

167 C. Hill, 'Propagating the Gospel', in H. E. Bell and R. Ollard eds, *Historical Essays, 1600–1750, presented to David Ogg* (1963), pp. 35–59; T. Rees, *History of Protestant Nonconformity in Wales* (1883), pp. 73–83; T. Richards, *A History of the Puritan Movement in Wales, 1639–1653* (1920), pp. 90–9, 248–9; Stephen Roberts, 'Godliness and Government in Glamorgan, 1647–1660', in Colin Jones, Malyn Newitt and Stephen Roberts eds, *Politics and People in Revolutionary England. Essays in Honour of Ivan Roots* (Oxford, 1986), pp. 225–51.

168 Firth ed., *Memoirs of Edmund Ludlow* ii, 347; Godwin, *History of the Commonwealth* iii, 275, 432–3; Gentles, *The New Model Army*, p. 423.

169 *Ibid.*, p. 415.

170 *Ibid.*, p. 419.

171 Worden, *The Rump Parliament*, p. 317.

172 Wither, *Perpetuall Parliament*, Introduction 'To the Reader'.

173 *The Moderate Publisher of Everydays Intelligence from the Parliaments Army* 15–22 April 1653, p. [813].

174 *A Declaration of the Lord General and his Council of Officers*, p. 10; *The Moderate Publisher of Everydays Intelligence from the Parliaments Army* 22–29 April 1653, p. 1034; Firth ed., *Clarke Papers* iii, 5; Worden, *The Rump Parliament*, pp. 352–3.

175 [Hall], *Letter Written to a Gentleman in the Country*, p. 19.

176 Worcester College, Clarke MS XXV, fo. 48.

177 *Reasons why the Supreme Authority of the Three Nations (for the time) is not in the Parliament*, p. [16].

178 Abbott ed., *Writings and Speeches* iii, 54–5; cf. *Ibid.*, p. 435.

179 *Ibid.*, pp. 54–5.

180 *Ibid.*, pp. 56–7.

181 *Ibid.*, p. 57; cf. Worden, *The Rump Parliament*, p. 383; Woolrych, *Commonwealth to Protectorate*, p. 9.

182 *The Anti-Levellers Antidote*, p. 42.

183 [Hall], *Letter Written to a Gentleman in the Country*, p. 10.

184 Abbott ed., *Writings and Speeches* iii, 55.

185 *Ibid.* iv, 485.

186 Worden, *The Rump Parliament*, p. 312.

187 Joan Thirsk, 'The Sales of Royalist Land during the Interregnum', *Economic History Review* 2 (1952–53), 188–207; P. G. Holiday, 'Land Sales and Repurchases in Yorkshire, 1650–1670', *Northern History* 5 (1970), 77; C. R. Markham, *A Life of the Great Lord Fairfax* (1870), p. 362; David Farr, 'Kinship, Catholics and Cavaliers in the Career of John Lambert', paper given at the Institute of Historical Research, London, May 1995. Cf. also Hugh Peters's intercession on behalf of the duke of Hamilton at the latter's trial in 1649. Stearns, *Strenuous Puritan*, pp. 339–41.

188 Abbott ed., *Writings and Speeches* ii, 588.

189 *Ibid.* iii, 56.

190 *A Declaration of the Army to his Excellency*; B. Lib., 669 f. 16 (58); Worden, *The Rump Parliament*, p. 307.

191 *The Anti-Levellers Antidote*, p. 43.

192 Firth, 'Cromwell and the Expulsion of the Long Parliament', p. 527; cf. Abbott ed., *Writings and Speeches* iii, 56.

193 *A Declaration of the Armie concerning Lieutenant Collonel John Lilburn* ([14 February] 1652), pp. 3–4 (cf. Akerman ed., *Letters from Roundhead Officers*, p. 30); Worden, *The Rump Parliament*, pp. 274–5, 282–3; *The Faithful Scout* 20–7 February 1652, p. 456.

194 *The Faithful Post* 22–9 April 1653, p. 724; *Moderate Occurrences* 26 April–3 May 1653, p. 38.

195 *The Moderate Publisher of Everydays Intelligence from the Parliaments Army* 15–22 April 1653, p. [813].

196 *Ibid.*, 20 May–3 June 1653, pp. 1072, 1074–6.

197 *Several Proceedings of State Affairs* 12–19 May 1653, p. 3007; *Collections of the Massachusetts Historical Society* fourth series, vii (1865), p. 463.

198 *Mercurius Politicus* 5–12 May 1653, pp. 2426–7.

199 *The Moderate Publisher* 10–17 June 1653, pp. 1091, 1093; Blencowe ed., *Sydney Papers*,

pp. 141–2. The earl of Leicester noted that tax policy was dictated by Cromwell and the officers at the same time as another supposedly supreme authority, the Council of State, was dealing with the allotment of lands in Ireland.

200 Firth and Rait eds, *Acts and Ordinances* ii, 73; K. S. Bottigheimer, *English Money and Irish Land* (Oxford, 1971), p. 134. This was first proposed by the Rump – *CJ* vii, 152.

201 *Moderate Occurrences* 26 April–3 May 1653, p. 37; *The Weekly Intelligencer* 26 April–3 May 1653, p. 828; *A Perfect Account* 27 April–4 May 1653, pp. 967–8.

202 Albert Warren, *Eight Reasons Categoricall: ... That its Probable the Law-Common will stand and continue at London and Westminster* (1653), p. 7.

203 [Streater,] *Ten Queries*.

204 *Remonstrance ... of the Creditors and Servants*, p. 11; *CSPD 1652–53*, pp. 336, 369, 377, 454. Legg may have become Wardrobe Keeper after the dissolution, especially in the light of Kynnersley's difficulties in 1653. See P.R.O., SP18/26, 20.

205 P.R.O., SP25/75, 434; *CSPD 1654*, p. 255.

206 *Moderate Occurrences* 10–17 May, p. [56].

207 Worden, *The Rump Parliament*, pp. 274–5, 278; Gentles, *The New Model Army*, p. 417.

208 *A Declaration of the Commoners of England to his Excellency the Lord General Cromwell* ([13 February] 1652), pp. 4–5.

209 *To His Excellency the Lord General Cromwell and all the honest Officers and Soldiers of the Army ... The Humble Remonstrance of Many Thousands in and about the City of London, on behalf of all the Free-Commoners of England* ([21 April] 1653), pp. 2, 4.

210 Spalding ed., *Diary of Bulstrode Whitelocke*, p. 287.

211 Worden, *The Rump Parliament*, p. 379.

212 Gardiner, *History of the Commonwealth and Protectorate* ii, 261 n.; Woolrych, *Commonwealth to Protectorate*, pp. 65, 71; Gentles, *The New Model Army*, p. 432.

213 Worden, *The Rump Parliament*, pp. 380–1.

214 *H.M.C.R.*, Leybourne-Popham (1899), p. 79.

215 *The Rump Parliament*, p. 381.

216 *Ibid.*, p. 383.

217 *Ibid.*, pp. 380, 383.

218 Akerman ed., *Letters from Roundhead Officers*, p. 63.

219 Worden, *The Rump Parliament*, pp. 381, 383.

220 Johnson and Vaisey eds, *Staffordshire and the Great Rebellion*, pp. 73, 74; Woolrych, *Commonwealth to Protectorate*, p. 134.

221 Firth ed., *The Memoirs of Edmund Ludlow* ii, 356.

222 John Streater, *Secret Reasons of State ... at the Interruption of this present Parliament: Anno 1653, Discovered* (1659), p. 3.

223 Massarella, 'The Politics of the Army', p. 64.

224 [Hall], *A Letter Written to a Gentleman in the Country*, p. 15.

225 Bod. Lib.,Tanner MS lii, fo. 13; Abbott ed., *Writings and Speeches* iii, 29; *Mercurius*

Britannicus 23–30 May 1653, p. 24; Woolrych, *Commonwealth to Protectorate*, pp. 124–5.

226 *The Moderate Publisher* 20–7 May 1653, pp. 1065–6.

227 *The Moderate Intelligencer* 23–30 May 1653, pp. 25–6.

228 *The Weekly Intelligencer* 10–17 May 1653, p. 841.

229 Worden, *The Rump Parliament*, p. 321.

230 Abbott ed., *Writings and Speeches* iv, 486.

231 Cited by E. P. Thompson, *The Making of the English Working Class* (1965), p. 23.

232 Abbott ed., *Writings and Speeches* ii, 588–9.

233 Whitelocke, *Memorials* iii, 374. Cf. the observation that 'in a sense the regiments were constituencies represented by their colonels', Firth and Davies, *Regimental History* i, xiii.

Conclusion

Inventing
a republic

CCOUNTS of Commonwealth politics which focus on the battles over reform after the revolution tend to characterise the civilian regime as a 'stagnant millpond' by comparison with the army's torrid stream. In fact, between 1649 and 1653 Whitehall and Westminster were both hives of activity which throbbed with life. The republican regime strove to create a dignified focus of government in the two palaces. In the one, civilians and soldiers lived amidst a certain degree of luxury, in suites decorated from government stocks of furniture, found spiritual refreshment in the chapel royal, and physical nourishment from the palace kitchens, and enjoyed privileged access to the newly restored privy garden. In the other, ceremonies of state and the rituals of both public and personal pride and dignity were enacted with great formality and a degree of splendour learnt from the past yet inescapably novel. The imagery and language of state were reshaped to fit the consequences of revolution, and rewritten to reflect the honour and dignity of Parliament and nation.

Each of these elements of the Commonwealth's political culture was designed to adorn *de facto* authority with the mantle of *de jure* legitimacy. But, as it became more grandiose, this new culture became politically more and more expensive, creating arguments which helped to bury deeper the wedge being driven between supporters of the Commonwealth by the settlement issues of power, patronage and policy. The court of the Commonwealth provided much of the hierarchy and division of authority that the court had always provided of old. But under the Commonwealth there were so many more avenues open for the politics of intrigue and faction, or at least it was far less clear that all such routes led ultimately to one single source of authority. Real problems remained in the lack of definition of jurisdictional boundaries – authority still derived from too broad a range of sources (Council, commission, committee; parliamentary enactment, declaration or resolve) – and in the risk that any real, lasting resolution of the confusion would inevitably turn many of the routes by which individuals might have recourse to authority into dead-ends.

By its sheer complexity, England's court without a king became a court in need of a protector. Given all that had gone before, it is not so surprising that he eventually manifested himself in the form of a Lord Protector.

The course steered at the end of 1653 fixed the military interest more securely than a lasting parliamentary settlement could ever have been relied on to do, a priority more significant to the upper reaches of the military hierarchy, at least in the short term, than a radical reordering of society. Conflict over reform was not just the cause but also a consequence of the fatal tension within the republic over the division of the spoils of victory. This was not an issue from which the military command stood aloof. Long before Cromwell vaccillated over the title of king, he and his colleagues were tainted by the sin of Achan – they had dragged garments, curtains, carpets, beds, bolsters, pots, pans and close-stools from the ruins of Jerico. The creation of a Commonwealth court culture illustrates graphically the organic inter-mingling of interests which makes the polarity between civic and martial politicians less than satisfactory as a framework for analysing Commonwealth politics. In that enterprise civilians and soldiers were colleagues in com-petition.

These complex features of the Commonwealth political scene may be addressed, for the moment, only as new beginnings, rather than inspiring definitive conclusions. To draw a line under the present study, I shall argue that the political culture of the Commonwealth takes us beyond conventional accounts of the period principally because it can be said to have constituted a vernacular language of republicanism. Since the English state became repub-lican by default rather than by design, it has generally been accepted that Englishmen, aside from the devotees of a cultish concoction of classical history and ideology, were incapable of fostering any kind of intellectual or spiritual conviction about the status of the new polity, let alone their status within it, which had any kind of positive force. It is my contention not only that this is untrue, but also that Englishmen were perfectly adequately equipped to turn the unprecedented circumstance of kinglessness into a set of convictions based upon ideas already long since dominant in early modern English political culture. I propose that, for at least as long as Englishmen had spoken to one another of the primacy of the common good, and of the priority of service to this 'commonwealth', they had in their hands an ideology, based on an abstracted notion of the state-in-society, of at least equal significance to any monarchical or absolute ideal. The codes of honour and prestige which cemented the culture of the early modern gentry republic derived in approxi-mately equal measure from the humanist, neo-classical notion of service to the wider community, on the one hand, and pedigree, on the other. The Commonwealth, in practice, and for some in theory, too, was the finest hour of this ideology of service. It was certainly the most explicit expression it achieved until that point at which, under threat from would-be domestic and actual Continental absolutism, the political nation set up that fiscal–military entity which, with its parties, ministries and majorities, would become the 'hidden republic' of England's constitutional monarchy.

As I have sought to demonstrate, a variety of discursive strategies elevated the English Commonwealth to heights far above the grim determinism of kingless circumstance. These strategies drew on fairly conventional notions of magisterial aristocratism (epitomised by the palatial occupations in London, or the titles of regime officials), military virtue and nationalism (advertised in martial display, and the imagery and language of coins, medals, maces and seals), all bound up by an overarching formalism (exemplified by the prominence of spectacle and other forms of ritualised display). Taken together as an idiom of sovereignty, the several strands of Commonwealth political culture I have described can also be interpreted as indications of the radical mutability of early modern English conservatism. Each implied continuity, even across a divide so deep as regicide – a continuity of status, honour and degree; of law, magistracy and civic grandeur. Maintaining order in society by maintaining the respectable outward appearances of its governors and institutions was quite visibly demonstrated to be entirely independent of regality, or at least far from reliant upon it. Even amongst those most hostile, the forms of government were largely respected, when it was desirable, convenient or imperative, arguably the same kind of provisional respect they had commanded in the days of the monarchy.

Vernacular, or Commonwealth, republicanism was not some kind of unspoken or subconscious political agenda which had been lurking at the heart of early modern English politics, waiting for the right moment to embody its devilish schemes. We need not worry about tracing its antecedents to smoky back rooms filled with Elizabethan, Jacobean or Caroline conspirators plotting the downfall of the monarchy. Many of its forms (and certainly the more iconic ones) were devised in 1649 by that small hard core generally held to be the 'real' republicans – dogmatically opposed to the hereditary authority of an individual. But Commonwealth republicanism depended a lot less on such explicit positions. Anti-monarchism was by no means its defining characteristic – it was certainly not a condition of accommodation at Whitehall, or the adoption of some grand title to denote government office. Neither was it an innately progressive creed, untenable to men of conservative political tendencies. For most, both inside government and without, it was the epitome of their conservatism; of their preference, not for any mythical or visionary ideal about a time before or after kingship, but for stability in the here-and-now, and the safe and orderly conduct of the *res publica*.

I

It has been said that Englishmen lacked a theory of republicanism, and that, finding themselves kingless in 1649, they jerry-built one from the materials to hand, creating a *post facto* ideology aphoristically described as 'a language, not a programme'. The materials most readily to hand were mined from the rich vein of European classical republicanism opened up by the Renaissance humanist revolution in letters. In the hands of men like John Milton, Marchamont Nedham and Algernon Sidney these materials were shaped into a vibrant ideology linking liberty, meritocratic citizenship and the responsibilities of self-rule. The effects of their concoctions on contemporaries are hard to gauge, but they proved highly influential amongst a generation of eighteenth-century revolutionaries on either side of the Atlantic.[1]

Examining the republicanism of the Commonwealth era through the texts of propagandists and theorists runs the risk of mistaking 'avowedly short-term political polemic, in which tactical considerations were strongly present' for political belief.[2] In a sense, also, this approach is almost as limiting as it has been fruitful, not least because it tends to tell us a lot more about a very small handful of republican authors than about their readers, but also because it focuses very specifically on a fairly elevated, metropolitan, even cosmopolitan plane of cultural formation. The roots of literary republicanism can be traced to an interest in the classical world which broadened significantly as a consequence of the growth of humanist patterns of education from the middle of the sixteenth century. Travel also brought men into contact with republics, living and dead, in the form of the United Provinces, Venice and Switzerland, Rome, Athens and Sparta. But it has been well said that there were many more routes to republicanism than familiarity with the classical world, the study of which by no means demanded one single conclusion.[3] English literary 'classicism' emerged long before the mid-seventeenth century. David Norbrook, Malcolm Smuts and Blair Worden have all described how early modern Englishmen used Roman histories and classical forms to develop covertly an oppositionist line of thought and argument.[4] Moreover, their strategies were moulded by men possessed of 'the common-law mind' far more than a classicist mind-set, and were complementary to the actual politics of faction, which came increasingly to exploit English theoretical peculiarities such as the 'country' interpretation of ancient constitutionalism.[5] They were also considerably more intellectually elevated, but possibly therefore considerably less meaningful to most, than the much more popular strategies of the 'rayling rhymers' and the propaganda of the stage associated with factionalism.[6]

The focus on the classical roots of Commonwealth republicanism has in some sense distracted attention from the amount of traditional English ideology which went into justifying civil wars and manufacturing the revolution, as well as the experiential significance of the *de facto* existence of republican institutions. One of the chief criticisms of the Rump is the assertion that the regime it erected was a republic in name only, a mere expedient designed to fill the gap left by the abolition of the monarchy at a time when it was more important simply to have a government of sorts than to have a particular sort of government.[7] There is an irresistible force to this argument. Englishmen had not wanted a war with their king, let alone a republic, and had it not been for Charles I's intransigence they would not have had to resign themselves to that fate. However, once they did so, traditional ideas about the common good embodied in fundamental laws and Englishmen's liberties justified and sustained war against the person of the king, as well as the trial and execution of his most trusted advisers. And, as the king's own trial showed, there was an almost overwhelming amount of theory, both biblical and constitutional, as well as precedent, ancient and contemporary, justifying the unthinkable – regicide itself. Ideas about the contract between kings and subjects had never been used to kill a monarch publicly before, but they had most certainly served for decades as political counterweights to more absolutist voices in the ears of successive rulers.[8] Only a relatively short distance had to be traversed in order to pass from contemporary ideas about parliamentary representation to the concept of popular sovereignty.[9] The 'duplex' theory of constitutionalism and absolutism described by Glenn Burgess which characterised the 'fruitful tension' in early Stuart politics created so many combinations and intersections of legal spheres – common law, prerogative, natural law, reason of state and necessity – that the radical potential for a destruction of old bonds, albeit firmly within the old bounds of the ancient constituion, was latent long before the crises of the 1640s. Ultimately, their complex political philosophy was a well stocked toolbox for justifying or disputing the particular condition of the times in which Englishmen found themselves.

Above all, resignation to the necessity of abolishing monarchy clearly did not translate into the diffident or half-hearted creation of an alternative regime merely by default. The various strands of the political culture devised during the parliamentary Commonwealth were, to a greater or lesser extent, cast from old ideas played with a new spin. Whilst the regime's propagandists assembled an eclectic assortment of classical *bon mots* from the dusty pages of antiquity, the government itself busily scavenged ideals such as the rule of law and the role of necessity, the political activism of a (parliamentarian) minority, and providential nationalism from the corpses of 'country' ideology and the ancient constitution. It constructed a government not patterned on any other, but based on contemporary English practice – both its inadequacies (the failure to separate powers) and its aspirations (the goal of an accountable executive). In the hands of men responsible for governing, judging and taxing the subjects of the state, and for conquering neighbours and dealing with foreign governments, the ideals and practice of English civil governance were revived and lived once more in the very being of a highly visible gentry republic.

Blair Worden has argued that 'the republicanism of the Rump in 1649 was ... a mere improvisation, triumphant by default, unconvinced and largely unprofessed'.[10] But it is possible to miss the wood for the trees by looking for a specific kind of republicanism – an avowedly king-hating, dogmatically anti-monarchical idealism. We may more profitably concentrate on a far more practical Commonwealth republicanism – a positive capacity for embracing the challenges posed to the leaders of a polity when their monarch is intent on self-destruction and on taking the tranquillity of his subjects with him. This kind of republicanism, perhaps only tangentially anti-monarchical but quite undoubtedly *pro bono res publica*, was expressed over and over again in the very heartbeat of a kingdom surviving (and ultimately thriving) in the absence of its king. By keeping the central courts open, holding assizes and entrusting the course of legal process to a quasi-mystical body, the Keepers of English Liberties, the Rumpers erected a kind of common law republic.[11] As has hopefully become clear, however, it was a regime which felt in no sense restricted merely to getting on with the job in hand. Republican imagery and spectacle consistently and repeatedly expressed some very big ideas, and made some very bold claims, many of which became reality. The imagery of the great seal, agreed upon even before the king was tried and executed and the monarchy abolished, symbolised a sense of liberty through the collective responsibility of a few patriots, matched the Commons' claim to sovereignty and anticipated the military, maritime and mercantile successes from which the Commonwealth's apologists made so much capital. The new coinage, whose design was formally adopted in April 1649, a month before England was declared a free state, was 'an expensive earnest of intent'.[12] The republic would be no meaningless interlude in the seamless regal tale. The conjunction of the harp of Erin with the cross of St George in the arms of the English Commonwealth which appeared on these coins confidently predicted the total annihilation of opposition in, and the comprehensive resettlement of Ireland. It was also a dramatic appropriation of Crown prerogative authority over that kingdom. When he returned to England in 1660 Charles II remarked that he found the incorporation of the harp into the arms of the English Common-wealth highly offensive.[13] In a period so sensitive to title and nomenclature, contemporaries *may* have detected a difference between calling England a free state and Commonwealth, rather than an out-and-out republic.[14] But by adopt-ing the title and formality not of a general assembly, representative, senate, states-general or Convention, but of a Parliament, the Rumpers pinned their colours to the mast quite unmistakably, and made sure everybody saluted accordingly. When Parliament called the tune to which foreign diplomats danced, when the Commonwealth's representatives held forth the honour and dignity of their state and nation, and when its navy precipitated war with a disrespectful Dutch admiral, the fusion of nationalistic pride with institutional arrogance was unmistakable. There was nothing at all 'unprofessed' about the Commonwealth's *de facto* republicanism, or the status and power of the republic, the manner of whose exaltation constantly advertised the complete absence of shame or guilt for the destruction of the monarchy.

There was a lot more to Commonwealth republicanism than the 'negative' circumstance of kinglessness. It has been argued that, whilst classical republican doctrine was never very popular amongst Rumpers, they were a lot more committed to the idea of Commons supremacy.[15] But too sharp a distinction has been drawn between 'proper' republicanism and 'political convictions about parliament's superiority over prerogative which had hardened long ago'.[16] There may have been relatively few explicit avowals of the superiority of a commonwealth over a monarchy (though it is unclear exactly how many such statements are required to satisfy those searching for a positive commitment to kinglessness). More significantly, as Professor Collinson has pointed out, the conventional conception of theoretical republicanism has 'underestimated ... quasi-republican modes of political reflection and action within the intellectual and active reach of existing modes of consciousness and established constitutional parameters'.[17] Professor Collinson resisted the temptation to extend his thesis beyond the bounds of his immediate concern with the Tudor polity. But in considering the political theory of the English revolution Professor Tuck has also identified the significance of a 'true' republicanism – 'in which a monarch is only at best the chairman of a board of oligarchs' – an idea with 'deeper roots in England than is often realised'.[18] The ancient constitutionalism underpinning Englishmen's notion of a mixed monarchy may have had relatively little radical potential – but then the idea of a mixed monarchy is not in itself particularly monarchical. The Tudor ideology of the state from which it derived had erected the notion of an abstract entity – the commonwealth, or 'common good' – as the touchstone of policy, an ideal to which Crown and subjects alike must submit. In order to preserve the socio-political peace and extend its own authority, the English monarchy had already learned to abase itself before this mythical notion of legitimate power embodied in the parliamentary high court. The political culture of the English Commonwealth made its own explicit expressions of a quasi-republicanism that was already part and parcel of English political life.

It did not take a revolution to prove the point. The coming of war in 1641–42 had made perfectly clear how the ideology of mixed monarchy could become a weapon in the hands of those hostile to a particular monarch. And as men took up arms against the king in the name of the Crown, they self-consciously exploited their quasi-republican heritage. In 1584 a bond of association had been formed by leading councillors and courtiers in response to fears of a succession crisis should Queen Elizabeth be assassinated. This arrangement had expressed a sense of the 'collective responsibility' among the early modern English political elite. In effect, if not in reality, it claimed emergency powers for an 'acephalous' body politic.[19] It was deliberately re-prised in May 1641, in response to the army plot, when it was proposed to create by oath a bond and association, 'as was in the 27th year of Queen Elizabeth', for the defence of the Crown, Parliament, Protestantism and the union and peace between the three kingdoms, the principal objects of the Protestation.[20]

Contingency plans such as these were hardly common in early modern England. But the kind of pragmatic flexibility they evidenced was a remarkably *regular* feature of the age, equally closely associated with the greatest constitu-tional 'triumphs' (the Conventions of 1660 and 1689) and 'disasters' (the High Court of Justice). Furthermore, they were only the most naked expression of the broader political arrangements of a nation far more comfortable than many others in Europe with the kind of constitutional relativism most suitably matched to its institutional and jurisdictional diversity. Some of the most totalitarian and libertarian creeds of the age emerged amidst war, religious strife and civil chaos on the Continent. Most English contemporaries man-aged to preserve an illusion of agreeing that their realm was a mixed polity, made up of several kinds of authority, each with its own interlocking yet distinct jurisdictional rights and reciprocal obligations. Regal prerogative au-thority was only one element in a highly integrated system of government and self-government which enshrined the rule of a law perfectly suited by adapta-tion to circumstance, and called on a remarkably large proportion of the population to serve at some level of office in order to uphold and enforce it.[21]

The pinnacle of this mixed polity was the assembly of king, Lords and Commons in Parliament, not least because it fostered a sense of nationhood which made England quite unique amongst the monarchies of early modern Europe.[22] In the early seventeenth century, historians (albeit the more esoteric ones) were cultivating a 'living myth' of Parliaments, a feature of the political culture of representation indispensable to its survival as a living entity.[23] Whatever men's ideological beliefs about the institution itself, in England, unlike many of the Continental kingdoms, the representative assembly was cherished as the focus (or launch-pad) of ambition and a political career on a national scale.

Active participation in the life of the community and the politics of the nation, together with the idea of a godly magistracy with responsibilities and obligations, was an integral feature of early modern English civic thinking. It had clear classical and humanist Renaissance antecedents. It was the back-bone of the Ciceronian civicism described by Richard Tuck as 'old humanism', and even the *raison d'état* of 'new humanism' made room for the moral imperative of serving one's nation.[24] But there was no need to 'import' such ideas into England, where civic humanism was a matter of domestic experience and its literature became popular not because it was exotic but because it reflected English life. It was all of a piece with the 'country' ideology of the early seventeenth century, which stressed the active role of a better sort.[25] Classical culture was one voice in which to express that which every village or parochial assembly, every urban corporation or craft guild, every grand jury and county sessions gave vital expression to – the active involvement of a society whose members, far more than those of any other in Europe, themselves partook of, gloried in and manipulated a notional unitary authority. In the words of Nathaniel Bacon, this was a polity which 'affarre off ... seems a Monarchy, but in approach discovers more of a Democracy'.[26]

After the regicide, it was their overwhelming sense of responsibility for the interests of their families, friends, neighbours, locality, region and perhaps above all their nation which drew so many of the members of the Long Parliament back to the political cockpit. On the whole, they returned not to serve the needs of some military junta but to shore up the House of Commons itself, the last vestige of this tradition of polymorphous political activism. The imagery of their great seal bore eloquent testimony to their parliamentarianism, to the sense some of them obviously had of the evolution of the Commons into a national forum. Subsequently, leading Rumpers dignified every aspect of their authority in an effort to make the one-time great 'event', already changed beyond recognition by the experience of running a country at war, into a grand institution.

The principles of classical republicanism may not have been positively espoused at every turn by members of the Rump, but the fact remains that the Commonwealth depended for its very existence on the principle of virtuous self-government under law. At the trials of the king and a number of aristocrats in 1649, state counsel repeatedly made a case for the prosecution which rested on the collective authority of a morally superior minority to uphold fundamental liberties by judging what was in the nation's interests. In his charges to the northern assizes in 1649 the circuit judge, sergeant Francis Thorpe, described the Crown as merely one rubric under which authority might be organised, giving a name to matters of general public interest – 'the name and word "king" ... is frequently used to set forth the publique interest of the People, so we call it "The King's Peace, the King's Coyne, the King's High-way", etc'. By fighting for Charles in the 1640s royalists, therefore, 'catcht at the shadow, but let go the substance, and so under colour of fighting for the king, they fought against him'. He told the jury that Parliament 'will no more trust the crown upon the Head of any one person' and 'resolve[s] to keep the crown within its proper place, the Cabinet of the Law'; 'If we place the Law in the Throne, the Law will preserve and protect us'.[27]

The essence of this piece of on-the-spot theorising, far from being 'largely unprofessed', was to be found in all areas of Commonwealth political life. Political authority was embodied in an ideal far better than in the person of a less than ideal individual. It was service to the ideal that created legitimacy. The regime's supporters often referred to 'the patriots' of the parliamentary cause, in much the same way as pre-war 'country' leaders were hailed as the guardians of the national interest.[28] Having taken over all aspects of government, the active members of the regime, civilian and soldier alike, laboured ceaselessly in the preservation and administration of the nation. They ran the chief departments of central government, dispensed justice at Westminster and around the country, administered taxation and the militia and headed the judicial benches in the counties. They negotiated with foreign diplomats and even served in that capacity themselves, accepting postings to Continental courts long before it was safe to do so. The range of their responsibilities encompassed other aspects of the political nation's traditional duties and obligations. They were appointed as chancellors of the universities, served on or on behalf of corporations in towns and cities, as recorders, high stewards, mayors and aldermen, and devoted a great deal of attention to the management of schools, hospitals and almshouses, for which many also acted as governors.[29] In short, they fulfilled all the responsibilities of the morally worthy political life.

The peculiar morality of this sense of civic responsibility amongst the members of the government was evident in the refusal of diplomatic gifts, or the avoidance of toasts and suchlike 'cup skirmishes'. Its moral continence, not to say abstinence, was manifested by the lack of boasting coupled with pre-eminent self-assurance of the regime's titular formulae, the muted yet almost animistic reverence for state ceremonial. It is apparent in instructions for the distibution of scraps from the tables of state banquets, or the frequently repeated injunction to avoid conspicuous expenditure in the repair and adornment of the palace of Whitehall. Whereas frugality was dictated by current circumstances such as the shortage of money, this was also a period when Englishmen were taxed more heavily and more regularly, and more often extraordinarily, than ever before in order to pay for military expenditure not overtopped until the time of 'the second Hundred Years' War' which ensued upon the next great revolutionary reshuffling of the board. Frugality at court was dictated not just by cash constraints but also by some kind of ethical imperative. Clearly, criteria had to be met to justify spending public money. The virtuous man knew that the proper exercise of his God-given reason meant avoiding superfluity, it meant the liberty of rational restraint. The Whitehall privy garden was in some sense the measure of the governors' achievement. A garden was the symbol of how man ordered the natural world at the centre of which he had been placed. To men like Sir John Danvers, who popularised Italian horticulture in England, or Lord Commissioner Whitelocke, with his sense of the bucolic, the military men who loved to cultivate roses and the faddish tulip bulbs which came from the Netherlands, the associates of Andrew Marvell, whose green thought in a green shade was shared no doubt by the Frosts, by Thurloe, Milton and the rest of the secretariat, it must have been a delight to see the privy garden resurrected. The pleasure of restoration was all the greater for the relative parsimony with which it had been achieved.

The profligacy (both financial and sexual) of Henry Marten and one or two other Rumpers was at odds with a simple conservative idealism about the responsible management of affairs which a great many English families had clung to, lived by and prospered on throughout the inflationary cycles and the rapidly shifting financial fortunes which influenced early modern European society and politics so deeply.[30] More like Elizabeth's government, perhaps, than the thorough reforming intent of the Caroline 'cabinet', the administration of the Commonwealth leaked a lot but knew how to cut corners in order to maintain commitments on tight budgets. On the morning of its first meeting in 1640, and every morning thereafter, the Speaker of the Commons had read a prayer which called on God to lend to the assembled servants of the king and the public good as great a care in their management of the nation's business as He had blessed them with in overseeing their own.[31]

During the great kinglessness, the Protestant gentry of the English republic did not need classical models to ponder. They adapted England's rich and varied political culture. This was a cloth woven out of deeply religious and nationalistic fatalism, to a pattern shaped by strong commitments to languages of political collectivism and patrician scruple, cut to size then wrapped around a skeleton fashioned from the bones of due legal process and the sinews of fiscal bureaucracy. The deeper memories of history and the surface legacies of a turbulent half-century terminated by violence were the meat and drink of the new magistrates. This sustenance was provided by kinship, blood and loyalty, by rivalry, expediency and belief, by the genes, nurture and experience of the men who occupied the centres of Commonwealth politics. For the present, kingship had been discarded as untrustworthy and unworkable, but it was not just imperative therefore to rely on catch phrases about the rule of law and the rights of property, the necessity of justice and the duty of obedience – it was basically instinctive.

Although its essentially conservative nature did indeed preclude sweeping social reform and blanket religious toleration, this attitude of virtuous responsibility also had its goals and ideals. Notably, what progress the Rump made in electoral reform was designed to put the emphasis back on the representation of the shires. Parliament's plan to reduce borough representation was a direct assault on the system which gave influence over a preponderance of seats in the House to the great political magnates of the nation. This was in part 'a revolt by the "country gentry" against the "borough gentry"', the latter being 'a more cosmopolitan breed through whom courtiers and magnates had customarily established networks of electoral clientage'. But more prominent members of the regime, themselves great electoral magnates, sought reform because the old system 'compromised the independence of the men elected'.[32] Like Sir Richard Grosvenor earlier in the century, many Rumpers apparently believed in encouraging voters to elect those who would look to the good of their 'country'.[33] This was a commitment to a social revolution of sorts. Rumpers may have had no wish whatsoever to do away with inherited wealth and title. But neither did they feel duty-bound to lift their social superiors into the saddle. Commoners in Parliament had changed from being aristocrats' to the nation's 'men of business'.

All the while, their gaze was most surely fixed on England. Classicism was expressed at times in their behaviour and the tropes of its description – the Commonwealth was still in some senses a Renaissance state. Cromwell presented the parliamentary deputation sent to greet him on his return from Worcester with a pair of captured Scotsmen each. Certainly Lord Commissioner Whitelocke took the opportunity to exercise the virtue of his magisterial mercy by granting his pair (one of whom was of 'good quality and extraordinary parts', he was pleased to note) their freedom, perhaps in conscious emulation of Roman manumission.[34] We have seen elsewhere how Whitelocke gave his own form to the literary trope of country retreat. In this rich political culture, others, too, shaped their description of events to fit classically sanctioned forms. But whereas republicans chose, on occasion, to honour the style of antiquity, Englishmen did not depend on classicism to express the republican experience. Long before Milton would have considered himself a republican, he believed that 'as wine and oil are imported to us from abroad, so must ripe understanding and many civil virtues be imported into our minds from foreign writings and examples of best ages'.[35] After his elevation to the heights of state propagandist for the republican regime he proudly declared that 'We are our own exemplars'.[36]

The importance of classical republican thought should not be underestimated. However, its glories and imaginative potency emerged from a milieu of active political life which did not so much need prescriptive theory as inspire it. The English republican imagination began with the basics. In contemporary terms, functioning courts, legal writs and a great seal came before a theory of liberty and civic responsibility. Once theorising began, and propagandists started to look beyond the rough-and-ready *raison d'état* of de factoism, classical republicanism became the cultural shadow cast by the Commonwealth's practical model of active magistracy. The classical republicanism of the 1650s was characteristically English, devised by men deeply involved in the ordinary business of the republican state. The civil servant Andrew Marvell subverted the Horatian genre by stripping it of indolence, not so much emulating classicism as rescuing it from its Augustan decline. The secretary for foreign tongues, John Milton, contrasted the servility promoted by monarchy with the bracing freedom of a republic 'wherein they who are greatest ... are not elevated above their brethren ... walk the streets as other men, may be spoken to freely, familiarly, friendly, without adoration', things only a wistful former 'secretary of state' who had lived at Whitehall for part of his service could genuinely believe to be the case.[37] Milton and Wither picked up the Sidneian legacy, extolling the virtues of the active political life, spreading what Milton called 'the natural heat of government'.[38] It is already fully understood that the English republicans used classical ideas in combination with theories of contract, resistance and natural rights, ideas just as 'Protestant' (or indeed 'Catholic') as they were 'classical'. It has also been well said that there was a 'classicism of the household' which formed an 'intellectual and imaginative inheritance' passed down the bloodline, through the ancestral memory of families like the Sidneys.[39] It may be difficult indeed to prove that classical republican writers turned for inspiration to the example of their political masters, peers, colleagues, compatriots and forebears, building their understanding of republican political theory on their familiarity with existing republican political forms. But the suggestion, were it to be advanced, that their ideas came solely from books would command little credibility.

The overwhelming tone of Commonwealth political culture was its providential nationalism. The classicism of certain republicans was just one function of that sense of English destiny. There was no question of emulation when Payne Fisher eulogised Cromwell's glory. There was simply nobody with whom he might adequately be compared:

> Let fame forget each ancient Roman wighte ...
> Neither let Greece in all her height of pride,
> Brag of her Heroes that were deify'd ...
> For why? The vertues of our Generall
> Equall the Trophies of these worthies all.[40]

In 1652 Hugh Peters tried to alter school curricula, suggesting that pupils need no longer trouble their heads with Virgil, whom he thought 'outdated and fanciful', when they could study the heroic eulogy written by Fisher. Apparently he 'almost succeeded in carrying his point'.[41]

But the anglicism of republican culture was not just about a sense of history. It was also about linguistic nationalism. The panegyric which Fisher wrote in Latin, in a classical heroic style, was translated shortly afterwards by Thomas Manley. In his dedication of the translation to Cromwell he explained that,

Latine [is] a language too high for the greatest part of our Nation to understand: and considering it [Fisher's poem] was a jewell exposed only to the view, not to the understandings of all, made me presume to render it into English, that even the meanest of our Natives might be able in their hearts with joy and thankfulness to confess the greatness of their obligations to your Excellency.[42]

In a commendatory verse Samuel Sheppard praised Fisher but reserved his greatest praise for the translator 'who mak'st his song to vail it's Bonnet to our English Tongue'.[43]

In the 1640s the poet Waller wrote that 'Poets that lasting marble seek / Must carve in Latin or in Greek', and that he who wrote in English built on shifting sands. Not until the eighteenth century and the publication of Dr Johnson's *Dictionary* was the English language properly considered a reliable literary foundation. But English republican culture erected its own important landmarks down this long road to modernity.[44] Most notable was the Rump's abolition of law French, one of its few positive reforms of the legal system, designed to make the law more accessible. The contrast with the declaration of the peerage which followed the abolition of the Lords is instructive. Almost in explicit avowal of the system of authority some described as a 'Norman Yoke', the Lords couched their impotent protest in French.[45] The Rump also adopted English mottoes for the design of the republic's new coinage.[46] In 1650 it was decreed that henceforth judicial pardons granted by the mercy of the state were to be couched in the English tongue.[47] From 1651, entries in the Rump's *Journal* were written up under English days, rather than Latin. And there were individual initiatives such as that of the Gloucester town clerk, John Dorney, who translated the city's royal charters from Latin into English.[48]

In its justly famous motto the great seal of the Commonwealth proclaimed, in English, the restoration of England's 'freedome' (eschewing the latinate fancy of 'liberty'). When American and French revolutionaries set about inventing republics for themselves in the following century, they self-consciously plundered the motifs of classicism for images of pyramids, eagles clutching arrows, fasces and phrygian bonnets, Hercules and pulchritudinous Liberty. England's revolutionaries could have done likewise. They could have used sources such as Cesare Ripa's *Iconologie*, just one of many catalogues of classical motifs published in the fifty years before the revolution, or the popular emblem and heraldic source books.[49] They could have followed the leading seventeenth century exponent of the art of personal and political iconography, Henri Estienne, who published in 1645 his *Art of Making Devices*, in which he advocated the use of obscure visual metaphors and Latin tags, saying that 'by how much this way of expression is much lesse usuall with the common people, by so much is it the more excellent'.[50] But they did no such thing. They chose clarity and aimed at universal comprehension. They did so partly because England was already a nation welded together by a common tongue and a shared political institution with deep roots in the way neither the American colonies nor France were when they set about instilling their new states with republican imagery. The rulers of the English Commonwealth knew already, in a way that neither their American nor their French counterparts could, that there were the foundations of a republic already, in the hearts and minds of their countrymen. Their invention was not so much the creation of novelty as a discovery, an act of revelation.

II

The intellectual heritage of republicanism was brought to life during the Commonwealth. Following Machiavelli, Nedham argued that responsibility for national security lay more safely in the hands of men who made their own laws than in those of paid mercenaries. But the soldier-civilian was a very real entity already by the time he wrote. It is beyond the scope of this book to gauge the full extent of popular participation in the militias which played such a crucial role during the 1651 emergency. But what has been touched upon is the central role played by soldiers, not only within Commonwealth political culture, but also across the very 'canvas' of politics which that culture framed.

The rule of the Rump having ensured that 'constitutional forms [were] preserved', after the defeat of the royalists in 1651 it became 'increasingly clear that the prime conflict was now between the respective proponents of parliamentary and military rule. However disreputable the Rump's constitutional credentials, its tenure of power was infinitely preferable to the prospect of government by the sword.'[51] Yet the contrast between the two needs to be defined more carefully than it has been hitherto if it is to retain any justification.

There are significant problems in pinning the explanation for the political difficulties of the Commonwealth on the division between two different cultures – 'the spirit of the camp and the spirit of the palace of Westminster'.[52] The essence of this division and its political implications was that 'men who had experienced fire and the sword were estranged from the arts of backroom politics, power-broking, compromise and deals which now aroused their disgust'.[53] Clearly, there would always be a large gulf separating some aspects of the experience of soldiers and that of civilian politicians. Indeed, anybody who had spent time on the camp side of the divide, fighting Parliament's British wars, would have been affected in a way not experienced by most people. The experience could forge the strongest possible convictions and beliefs (though perhaps the same experience was the best available instruction in the art of the possible; it undoubtedly gave pay disputes a particularly keen edge). Cromwell argued that the Rump's haste with the Bill for elections showed a spirit 'not according to God', or 'the whole weight of this cause – which must needs be very dear unto us who had so often adventured our lives for it'.[54] After Worcester the army had hoped that the Rump would 'give peace and rest to [God's] people and especially those who had bled more than others in the carrying on of the military affairs'.[55] As we have seen, elements of republican political culture served to dramatise the gulf between soldiers and civilians. The Council of State battled to preserve its dignity at Whitehall whilst also maintaining a military presence there. The government kept a tight rein on the stock of furniture in its wardrobe, guarding against 'embezzlement' by soldiers and the damage they caused to the goods of the Commonwealth. Codes of honour stoked antagonisms within the ruling coalition, and affronts to the dignity of individuals such as John Lambert, over the lord deputyship, and to Cromwell himself, in the matter of Hampton Court, probably did little to calm the atmosphere. The court and camp divide was real enough. But the officer and the civilian classes of politicians were basically contiguous, their conflicts fought out within a shared culture. Many had one foot in both 'camps'. We may even say that some had one foot in both 'courts', for the army high command, wherever it camped, comprised a court in the same way as Whitehall and Westminster were the *loci* of the civilian court. In 1642 one commentator remarked on how tragically strange it was 'That the Feild should be turn'd to Court, and the Court into a desert'.[56] This inversion continued to resonate throughout the mid-century crisis. Cromwell's campaigns had a certain element of the royal progress about them, the business of war going hand in hand with civic receptions and similar junketings, not to mention the General's own entertainment of guests and the reception of visitors with suits to press.[57] On his return from Ireland in 1650 he held court at Windsor and it was reported that 'he shews himself very affable, and courteous unto all, and as time will afford, admitteth any man that hath business, to speak with him'.[58] A few months later, the General went to Scotland with a train which included four tents, one for his lodging, as well as one each for a kitchen, a buttery and a stable.[59] Town corporations frequently entertained military guests of much less stature than the commander-in-chief. Expense was spared. From 1649 to 1651 the mayor of Shrewsbury's total expenditure on 'Parliamente men, Justices of Peace, Colonells and other persons of wor[shi]pp that came to this towne' did not reach double figures.[60] And yet, where once the town might have feted the grandees of local society, now it was soldiers and MPs who received the honours.

Conversely, the metropolitan centres would have been stripped of a fair amount of their glory and grandeur had there been no military parades and guards of honour. Military endeavour provided the regime with something to celebrate (be it in the manner of victory or of something a little more valedictory). Moreover, without military success the regime would have remained totally isolated, and diplomats would have seen little need to court the pretensions of its members. The military were the source of a significant section of the administrative personnel of the regime. Obviously, soldiers also sat as MPs, many having been recruited into Parliament in the place of defectors in the 1640s.[61] Many others served in the Commonwealth's civil service, and were practically responsible for running local administration in many areas.[62] Officers of the Commonwealth court itself often had a martial background. George Vaux, the head of the Whitehall household, was known as Captain Vaux, although it is not clear whether he and other household servants such as Captain Henry Middleton (who apparently also doubled as sergeant-at-mace to the Lords Commissioners of the great seal) had actively shouldered arms. Major George Wither, poet and trustee for the sale of the king's goods, certainly had seen active service, as had his colleagues, Colonel John Humphreys and Captain Anthony Mildmay. Militarism is a long-standing feature of English political culture, and a characteristic colonial export. The first thanksgiving in Plymouth colony, 1621, was celebrated with prayer and a muster of the militia.[63] The letter to England describing that day's joyous events had been written by Edward Winslow, cousin of Sir Arthur Haselrige, close ally of Sir Henry Vane junior, sequestration commissioner and yet another trustee for the sale of the late king's goods.[64]

The honorary degrees awarded to leading soldiers in 1649 may seem to have been intended as a means of 'civilising' them, but that is not to deny that they were quite naturally inclined to the preservation of civilian life already. Indeed, they were ostensibly rewarded for putting down the Leveller menace to society. However, their civilian credentials needed to be advertised to the world at large, and their own pretensions pandered to. On the other side of the coin, many civilian MPs had military experience from the 1640s, even such unlikely characters as Sir James Harrington, who proudly asserted his military background despite having himself suffered at the hands of pillaging soldiery in 1649.[65] In the final months of the Rump's life Harrington had a medal struck on which he was depicted in bust profile, wearing armour. On the reverse the medal bore the legend:

THE.EFFIGIES.OF.SIR.JAMES.HARRINGTON.OF.SWEAKLEY.IN.YE.COV.OF.MID.KN+BAR:
MAI.GEN.OF.YE.FORCES.OF.YE.CITTIES.OF.LONDON+WESTMINSTER.AT.YE.BATTELL.OF.
NEWBERY.IN.1644:A.MEMBER.OF.PARLIAMENT.FOR.YE.COV.OF.RUTLAND.AND.
ONE.OF.YE.COUNCELL.OF.STATE.AGED.45.1653.[66]

Harrington had commanded about 3,000 men in 1644, five regiments, and overseen the fortification and defence of Henley, where a number of City units were stationed after the second battle of Newbury. His ancestors had a long history of military activity, his namesakes having held the bridge at Fisherton on the eve of Agincourt, another fighting for Richard III at Bosworth.[67]

Some Rumpers were important as local military governors (Colonel John Hutchinson, Colonel Herbert Morley, Colonel Algernon Sidney, Colonel John Moore), and a great many more partook of the common martial culture of the times. A remarkably high proportion of MPs were referred to in the Rump's *Journal* by their military titles on one or more occasion, possibly reflecting their service in the Commonwealth's militias, another entity which spread the military ethos into the fabric of English provincial society.[68] Rowland Wilson's funeral in 1650 was dignified by many companies of the City militia which he had commanded.[69] Blood ties and marriage united all strands of the gentry republic. Whitelocke was probably not the only MP who took pride in the military service of a son.[70] To some extent, hard-and-fast distinctions between the military and civilian orders were drawn largely to rhetorical effect. Behind the sabre-rattling posturings lay another indispensable ingredient of the Commonwealth's vernacular republicanism – men connected by common endeavour and united by a culture held in common. They might argue over the land settlement, or their relative jurisdiction *vis-à-vis* one another, but they did so in the same language of honour. The political battles which led to the dissolution of the Rump were fought between men of very diverse outlook yet broadly similar background, who agreed that there could be no return to the old monarchy for the present, nor yet any compromise with the new monarch, but who came to disagree about who should run the country instead, and how. This difference of opinion became ever sharper as the practical arrangements of the republic became more and more complex, until the shaky foundations on which it was built broke under the pressure of its byzantine bulk. The structural features of government and politics under the Commonwealth also contributed considerably to the quality of its political culture.

The revolution had ushered in a practical constitutional revolution. The institutional relations between Parliament, the Council of State and their committees, and between Parliament and the army, were in some senses a replacement for the ancient constitution. In the absence of the Crown, the Privy Council, the royal prerogative (especially control of the armed forces, but also of course the church), the Lords, the bishops, their courts and jurisdctions, the new institutional relations were all the constitution there was. In as much as this study has been concerned with them, it is quite clear that they were mediated, in part, through features of the contemporary political culture. Issues such as control of the precincts and occupants of the palace of Whitehall, or the interpretation of the principal spectacular, iconic and linguistic discursive fields help illustrate how Commonwealth politics navigated a sophisticated political landscape whose major failing was its polymorphous complexity rather than its monomaniacal devotion to stifling real change. The republican constitution was what made the free state a living, breathing political organism; its political cultural media were what made that organism such a vivid, rare bird, and 'the republican' a species of infinite variety.

Far too much variety, to some. The Rump was attacked, in military propaganda, for its factional divisiveness, just as the Long Parliament had been criticised for similar reasons each time the military had felt bound to save the parliamentarians from themselves. In December 1648 the army justified the purge as the only resort left, 'having with others for a long while sadly beheld and tasted, in your proceedings, the miserable fruits of councils divided by faction and personal interest, even to the neglecting betraying and casting away all public good', and justified the dissolution in similar terms.[71] But the republic was built on, and helped foster, notions of political pluralism, and factional 'janglings' were certainly not considered morally inferior to some self-serving theocratic dogma. Diversity was thought wholesome by Nedham, especially because 'it is ... unavoidable ... that while the world stands there will be differences of opinion' which should be managed, not violently beaten into a strained uniformity.[72] John Hall made the case for a dash of disorder as a means of strengthening any political system – 'among many joynt Causes, there may be some jarring, yet like cross wheels in an Engine, they tend to the regulation of the whole'.[73] Isaac Penington junior saw something to be gained, too, from orchestrating divergent voices: 'Surely methinks both that variety and contrariety that is amongst us, might be better ordered: true wisdom could so dispose of it, as it should no longer thus harshly jarre but make up a sweete harmony.'[74] The sentiment was echoed widely, one civic functionary using the speech he gave annually at the election of Gloucester's corporation to ask, 'May not many sounds in musick being well modelled make a good consort?'[75] In his shrouded poetic analysis of the regime George Wither described how

> In that Catholicon, or Mithridate [i.e. panacea],
> Which Providence confected hath of late,
> To temper or dispell, what hath diseas'd
> The Body Politike; it hath been pleas'd
> (As finding it a mixture requisite)
> Vipers and mortall poysons to unite
> With wholesome things; yea, minerals and mettle,
> Sulphur and Steel, fixt matter, to unsettle:
> The Serpents brains, with faithfull Turtles hearts:
> Of Lions, Lambs and Foxes some choice parts:
> Somewhat of Hares that swift and fearful be:
> Somewhat of Snailes, in whom we nothing see,
> But slownesse, and, by compounding these,
> A cure preparing is, for our disease ...
> Fire, Water, Earth and Ayr, (though disagreeing
> In qualities) if well mixt, give a being
> To that, which cannot be by any one

Or, any two, or three of these alone:
And, so, at last, shall ev'ry contradiction
Among us add some Dos to our perfection:
Yea, they who pull down and they who erect
Shall in the close concur in one effect;
That, he, who's all in all may have due praise
By ev'ry contradiction in our wayes ... [76]

The sheer complexity of this hybrid body politic much better explains the internal tensions afflicting the regime than the suggestion that they exemplified the internal ideological and psychological contradictions of one man. After the creation of a regime defined by the variety of its members' opinions, Hugh Peters argued that 'Republics sow the seed of their ruin in faction: which wise men say cannot be cured but by frequent elections, and clear and plain dealings betwixt men in place'.[77] Unfortunately, there was a distinct lack of clarity in Commonwealth political relations. Isaac Penington junior wanted to see the establishment of clear 'bounds', an 'exact Rule' as to the manner of governing, which should be 'carefully look'd to at the beginning, while things are in constitution, and may more easily be molded then after things are setled'. That done, men might see that 'there is no such great matter in the change of Government as many conceive'.[78] But as anyone wanting or needing the assistance of the government found out, the revolution had created a state of labrynthine complexity. This was of crucial significance for the long-term survival of the parliamentary republic. James Harrington believed that 'The reasons why the Nations that have Commonwealths use them so well and cherish them so much, and yet that so few nations have Commonwealths, is that in using a Commonwealth it is not necessary that it should be understood, but in making a Commonwealth that it should be understood is of absolute necessity.'[79]

On the other hand, by making the equation of might and right only too clear the English revolution made politics all too comprehensible. In accounting for the intellectual roots of that revolution, an ill-defined and elusive scepticism has been blamed for its corrosive influence on traditional beliefs and structures in early modern England. If not a cause of the English revolution, it at least did not hinder it.[80] It is open to debate how much 'stability' may derive from English traditions of constitutional relativism. The civil war certainly did nothing to stabilise belief in a politics of permanence. In his famous letter to Colonel Robert Hammond of 25 November 1648 Cromwell claimed that authority itself was ordained by God – the powers that be *must* be – but 'this or that species is of human institution' only, conveniently demonstrating the awesome destabilising potential of radical Protestant theocracy.[81] Visions of godhead were not the only means of sustaining this kind of political relativism. A sense of history would suffice:

It is apparent that many times power and power alone, without legall title, hath been many times the supporter of the Royall arms; yet in thos times I find in our Law-books, That obedience to the powers De Facto was approved of, and disobedience was in those times accounted a crime not a vertue.[82]

After the revolution, in order to justify its authority, supporters of the Rump dug even deeper beneath the foundations of order. Politics, it was alleged, did not follow 'the absolute order of nature'.[83] 'Let us therefore forget these things which are impossible to be helped and fall on to those which are possible and necessary ... We are now (through Providence) on a new Foundation, and have time to consider our own good'; 'Prudence and Reason that teacheth men to make vertues of necessities, may well make men ingenious in improving advantages and conveniences'.[84] 'Whatever mens affections may be to one government more then another ... there is no Divine Character of respect more on one then another.'[85] Oaths to support king and Crown had been nullified by revolution, 'especially when the matter about which the Oath [was] made is civil and changeable'.[86] Similarly, George Wither criticised those who would accept

[no] truths ... which have not been entailed on [them] by ... their Grandsires: Religious and civill Government must be a Gentleman of three descents, like a Knight of Malta, or it must not be admitted into their order ... But say they, our Fore-Fathers were wiser than we, and we will follow them: we grant they were, for they embraced the Truth, and would not be scared by the bug-bear of Novelty ... the new light appearing was embraced not scorned.[87]

The point of the revolution was that, as Sergeant Thorpe told the northern assizes in 1649, the people 'being not tyed to any one Forme of Government, they choose againe and take some other Form ... whereby they will avoid the evils they suffered under their former choice'. The Stuarts' title was based, ultimately, on the Norman conquest, and 'therefore may bee again as justly regained, as it was gained at First by Force, and by the stronger Arm and sharper sword'.[88]

It would have been surprising if such talk had not had a detrimental effect on the idea of political absolutes. According to one apologist for the dissolution, the Rump's election Bill's qualifications were inadequate because 'who can discover a man's heart? ... Who can judge that a convert is real?' This was a line of argument which allowed no possibility of anything but despotism of the strongest will.[89] But that was the inevitable concomitant of a state which had made a virtue out of contingency. Members of 'a Publique State', it was argued, 'are more open to the view of the World, and are but themselves in power "quam diu bene gesserint"'.[90]

The inveterate opponent of the Rump, Clement Walker, criticised its members for having 'cast all the mysteries and secrets of government before the vulgar, and taught the soldiery and the people to look into them and ravel back all governments to the first principles of nature'.[91] Many believed that here indeed was the beginning of wisdom, and that the Commonwealth's greatest strength lay in its involvement of people in the regulation of their own lives. Many Rumpers believed no such thing. Figuratively, and in reality, they repaired the gates to the palace, reglazed its windows and policed entry thereunto. But, for all the effort it made subsequently to shore up the ruins of the ancient constitution by hiding them beneath piles of rich tapestry, it was still the case, as Sir Henry Vane junior noted some years later, that 'the parliament showed that ... shackles were broken. It did not oblige further.'[92] Light had been let in on the mystery. At the leading edge of political scepticism the Rump's efforts to weave an elaborate political culture probably seemed risible. Wither's recommendations as to the dignity of his imaginary parliamentary republican regime were prefaced with the advice to 'Mark them, if they be worth your heed; if not, let them be passed over as forgot'.[93] Of his visions he said, 'Much more I saw, which would I here relate, / Would yet appear, things worthy laughing at; / (As these declar'd already do to some).'[94] In some sense, the political culture of the Commonwealth was largely dispensable. There was certainly something supremely ironic in the fate of Anthony Ascham, a leading *de facto* theorist, who fell prey to his own arguments, assassinated by English royalists just hours after complaining that his suite at the Prado did not become the dignity of his mission as resident on behalf of the Parliament of the Commonwealth of England.[95]

But clearly, arguing for their *de facto* authority did not preclude a sense of dignity and the preservation of an honourable magistracy on the part of many members of the regime. The problem faced by the Rump was that it had been created by a revolution which privileged action over precedent. Its dissolution was greeted in some quarters by concern that the military lacked the education and experience of the former governors, and so would simply reduce government to the sword, for the dissolution was 'rash, unlawfull and strange: and that so much the more, that those Parliamentary men were accounted the refuge and sanctuary of the People, the Representatives of the Nation, the braines of that politick body, whereof the Army is but the hands'.[96] But it was argued in reply that the greater learning of the civil governors (manifested as 'quaint expressions and flourishes of rhetorick', used for 'gilding a bad cause') made them inferior to the men of action, whose 'practical industry make[s] the Theory of the former useful to the furtherance of the benefit of this Commonwealth'. The honest soldiery were devoid of the dissimulation and deceit which masqueraded behind a facade of intellect.[97]

There is a risk inherent in exposing to popular view the contingency of political forms, when myths of continuity are the obvious and necessary preconditions of order, and it is firmly maintained that 'that commonwealth is best that is framed for all time', even if the ship of state, to adapt Selden's common law analogy, was patched so often that, though the structure remained the same, it contained none of the original fabric. The revolutionaries of 1648–49 dared to proclaim publicly that means could be justified by ends. Thereafter they tried to limit the impact of this disastrously undermining revelation by building the Rump as grandly and pompously as they could; they adorned it, gave its civil institutions symbolic forms. Political thinkers like Harrington, and lesser mortals like the Leaches, strove to invent ways of bringing permanence into the polity; even poets, like Wither and Milton, had a go. But none of this was enough to forestall the whirlwind's harvest. Before long the Rump fell to assailants who said 'parliament' was just a name, not essential in itself, just as Rumpers had said the word 'king' was just that – a word. Power was all. Colonel John Jones went to the scaffold in October 1660 saying

> That it was the power that made the Law, for that some years ago they [the regicides] had the power in their hands, and whatsoever they did at that time was accounted Law and executed accordingly; That now the king had executed the Law upon them, and that the king did nothing but what he would have done himself, were he in the king's case.[98]

III

Revolution had had a dramatic impact on the style of English politics. At the time of the Restoration, the Convention voted from a sense of continuity and legitimacy to continue using the great seal of the Commonwealth, and had its own mace made. Antiquaries have argued over whether the 'fools' bauble' was melted down and the metal used to make the Convention's mace.[99] The assembly also committed the Declaration of Breda to preservation amongst the records of the House of Commons. After Charles II's return, members of the Commons retained the 'MP' moniker, which came to denote a member of the lower House exclusively in 1650.[100] These events symbolise some of the changes which the experience of the 1650s had wrought in the nature of English Parliaments. It would demand a separate study in its own right to test the claim that that experience changed Parliaments for ever. A few comments may be made, however, about locating the Commonwealth in the story of the emerging impersonal state; and how the experience of the 1650s changed aspects of the public face of English monarchism.

Historians continue to argue as to whether the 'political sphere' was a discrete phenomenon before 1640. What seems clear, however, is that already by then there was an emerging notion of the state, both as an object of allegiance and as a source of employment. Civil war and the on-going militarisation of the 1650s massively expanded the bureaucracy of the state, creating machinery which clearly no longer had anything to do with royal household administration. Some of the features of Commonwealth political culture I have described also contributed significantly to overlaying that machinery with linguistic conceits designed to conjure the ideal of an abstract source of authority. However, as we have seen in the case of the honour of the Commonwealth, the language of interest could still be discerned clearly just beneath the surface. Paradoxically, the impersonal state was being brought to life through the agency of highly personalised politics.

English monarchy learned a great deal from the usurpation. Charles II became a great patron of charities, and of the arts and sciences, the original founder of the 'welfare monarchy'. The Royal Hospital at Chelsea turned the veteran soldiers of the republic into grateful royal pensioners. The Royal Society picked up the various loose threads of Interregnum intellectual endeavour and welded them into a royal institution.

Maces adopted by town corporations during the republic were altered back into regal ones. In the case of Congleton the motto now read THE FREEDOME OF ENGLAND BY GODS BLESSING RESTORED TO C R 1661.[101] This example symbolises the way in which monarchy was both reinstated by and regrafted on to the gentry republic of the 1650s. Most obviously, the financial and constitutional elements of the 'Restoration settlement' left little doubt that the king's unconditional return did not mean reinstatement of an unconditional prerogative authority. Attitudes towards the key emblems of state showed how the monarchy assiduously adapted to post-regicidal politics rather than cling to *ante bellum* forms. Before 1649 all royal maces had been provided at their bearers' expense. Thereafter the state footed the bill. Before 1651 no English ruler had sent maces to dignify his or her officers in Ireland. Following the precedent set by the Commonwealth, the restored Charles II sent two.[102] To expunge its republican potential, the symbolism of the English oak, so prominent in the iconography of the Commonwealth, was rapidly 'reappropriated' to the monarchy, and the republicans' use of it castigated as 'pagan'. In a discourse on English natural history John Aubrey asked, 'Was not the oak abused by the Druides to superstition? And yet our late Reformers gave order (which was universally observed accordingly) for the Acorn, the fruit of the oak, to be set upon their maces or crowns, instead of the cross.'[103] But Charles II deliberately fostered his own oak cult after the Restoration, elevating his escapades in Boscobel forest during his flight after Worcester to an important iconic element of his reign. The Caroline cult was celebrated every year on the anniversary of Charles II's official restoration, 29 May, and still celebrated annually, for example in Northampton, where a statue of the king is garlanded with oak and flowers, or at Chelsea, where the pensioners of the Royal Hospital still wear oak in their lapels and give three cheers in honour of their founder. Thus Charles successfully reappropriated the myth of ancient British wisdom and liberty by drawing on the Renaissance literary trope of the oak as monarch or sovereign of the forest, as used by Petrarch, Spenser and Herrick. But perhaps Charles appropriated the oak's druidic connotations to symbolise the magical or priestly role of a monarch restored to a kingdom where so many of his subjects had held him and his office in such loathing and contempt.[104]

In 1660 it was only the regal form of government which was restored, not the formalism of governing itself, a phenomenon which had continued to flourish and find expression in a host of new ways during the Interregnum. The Rump Parliament is often taken for a squalid affair, with 'little obvious attraction for scholars of any particular political persuasion'.[105] Rumpers' retrospective self-justifications, even glorifications, 'tempt us', it has been argued, 'to misunderstand [their] attitude ... towards the Parliament at the time of its sitting' because they have 'disguised the limits of its members' earlier enthusiasm for their government'.[106] This book presents graphic evidence for the contention that at least some Rumpers were proud of their creation at the time, rather than afterwards, and that submissive republicanism, connivance in the novel formalities of the few, was an acceptable option for most, possibly explaining the curious manner in which the Restoration regime adapted some of the features of Commonwealth political culture. Others were far less readily incorporated into the new regal political culture. In particular, the rising tide of the English language, so prominent a feature of Commonwealth republicanism, was firmly turned back. Until the revolution, Gloucester's corporation minutes had always been headed with a formula which dated meetings, in Latin, according to the regnal year. Throughout the Interregnum a simple calendrical note was taken in English. Then, in June 1660, on the day the corporation ordered the alteration of their Maundy maces in line with the restoration of the old dynasty, the regnal date was once more incorporated. The following year, the king was referred to for the first time as *Caroli secundi*. In a city which paid such a heavy price politically for its resistance to the royalist cause, it may seem somewhat marginal to note that from 22 December 1662 the English language had entirely disappeared from this linguistic convention. But the phenomenon is wholly characteristic of the way that, after the Restoration, the mists once more slowly descended over the life of the body politic.[107]

Rumpers were aware that the regime invented in 1649 was an improvisation. As Sir Arthur Haselrige argued a decade later, 'force was much upon us. What should we do? We turned ourselves into the Commonwealth.'[108] But that does not necessarily mean they were shamefaced about their constitutional status. This is just as evident from the circumstances surrounding the demise of the institution as it is from the political culture which characterised its short life. The Rump was committed to a civilian constitutional settlement.[109] Fresh elections, it has been claimed, would return to the House those members purged in December 1648 – hence Worden's conclusion that the Rump, by proceeding to general elections, was motivated by a desire for 'revenge for Pride's purge'. But by preparing for elections, he also claimed, 'the rumpers were jeopardising the Commonwealth's survival. That they were prepared to do so is a reminder of their continuing lack of commitment to the form of government which had emerged after the execution of the king.'[110]

On the contrary, I would argue that the Bill for elections showed just how committed to the parliamentary republic the Rump had become, and that their commitment is illustrated, and partly explained, by the vibrant form in which English government was recast between 1649 and 1653. The greatest threat to the survival of the parliamentary republic was posed, not by royalist reaction in the nation at large, but by the fact that a majority in the army needed convincing, by January 1653, that there could indeed be a 'consistency of the civil authority by successive parliaments and the just and equal dispensation of justice through the nation'.[111] The Bill was passed, not as a revenge measure, but out of a desperate sense that the expected radical assault which the military leadership could no longer be seen to oppose could therefore no longer be fended off. The best that might be expected was to pass an electoral Bill of the utmost integrity so that the army might be seen to have acted from deliberate and obvious self-interest. The Bill was testament to the conviction that a civil settlement by successive Parliaments was not only possible but, in the circumstances, positively desirable. Had not Cromwell desecrated the tomb, it would have served as the headstone to John Cook's ideal of 'elective aristocracie'.[112]

By building a court, mounting spectacle, inventing icons and endowing the whole panoply of parliamentary rule with the dignity of executive authority the Rump had put as much distance as possible between itself and the moment of its inception. An active minority, presumably many of them present in the House on the morning of 20 April 1653, spent four and a half years imaginatively moulding a new state (albeit within quite unimaginative constitutional parameters), and were now prepared to send the ship of the Commonwealth sailing off on a course to be set by its electors. This was not 'throwing away the cause'. The wheel would have been quite firmly tied, not only by the likely return of those very republicans who had plucked up the courage to seek a popular mandate, but also by the simple, inescapable and politically defining fact that the army would still be around to 'poyze the affairs of the whole Nation'.[113] Moreover, it is hard to believe that, after all their efforts to push the power of the sword at least into the background, the Rumpers would have envisaged a return to monarchy in any way which would have certainly led to fresh civil war. We should remain suspicious of the claims made by the military that the Rump's Bill for elections made insufficient provision for excluding royalists. By their actions on behalf of dispossessed royalists, military commanders had already done more than most to re-enfranchise malignants, and were criticised accordingly by radicals who warned them that 'lenity doth break more hearts than sequestration'.

John Morrill has observed that

> Many – perhaps most – of those who exercised authority in the 1650s saw the Revolution of 1649 not as a beginning but as an end, not as a dawn of liberty but as a desperate expedient to prevent the loss of traditional liberties either to a vengeful king or to social visionaries like the Levellers ... In most respects there was a rush to restoration: of the old familiar forms of central and local government (exchequer, quarter sessions etc.) and of gentry power in the localities ... There was just enough about Cromwell's concern for the existing social order ... to permit some of those to whom the 1650s were based on a politics of regret to work alongside him.[114]

This book has argued that restoration did not just mean reaction, and that 'the politics of regret' could invite a response far more positive than remorseful. The revolution of 1649 had indeed heralded the beginning of a new kind of politics in a new kind of state. Such a statement, as with much of the material in this book on which it is based, is so very *obvious* that the failure properly to assay the significance of the situation it describes, barring a handful of notable exceptions, is almost inexplicable. Historians clearly appreciate the long-term impact of the mid-seventeenth century on the underlying structures of Brtish politics. The fiscal and administrative innovations associated with the mobilisation of the revolutionary armed forces is credited as a key staging post along the road to military professionalisation, the fundamental reordering of state finance by the end of the seventeenth century and the emergence of a military-industrial complex capable of imperial pretensions on a global scale. The political theory of the interregnum has never been treated as respectfully and intellectually honestly as it is by modern scholars. Yet the institutions of the Commonwealth period remain the object of scorn, and, by comparison with the early Stuart court, the Parliaments of that period, and the relationship between centre and localities, they continue to languish in a historirgraphical blind spot. Their apparent contingency and obvious ephemerality have made it harder to perceive them as living political entities. But they are also often judged 'inferior' in some sense (morally? Certainly *constitutionally*) to a monarchy which was in fact no less prone to an instability of form than the fledgling republic. The novelty of the latter denies the provisional nature of its forms any substantive cover behind which to hide. Unmistakable improvisation is a necessity embraced by any revolutionary government seeking to navigate its way back to political stability. But it is just as important to, and manifested just as obviously by, more long-standing political establishments, which derive much of their ideological force from a continuity which has to be improvised to conceal discontinuity in policy and personnel, even dynasty. Monarchs are forever 'making up' monarchy as they go along. The accession of a Scottish dynasty may have made this more obvious than it had been prior to the seventeenth century. But the ability to improvise, to innovate and to assume a creative initiative was perhaps one of the strengths of the incoming line. Flexible, at least initially, in the arrangments of the household (a virtual revolution themselves in the shift from an unmarried childless queen – a prime example of how radical change is implicit in the most orderly succession) or the form of conciliar government, espying opportunities in the interpretation of traditional patterns of ceremony, from the novelty of Henry's investiture as Prince of Wales to the subtle revision of the sacramental en-thronement of his brother Charles, innovators in the political culture of monarchy as much as its aesthetic, the Stuarts did not so much depart from a script as write their own. There is no hard-and-fast distinction, other than age and the patina of authenticity it bestows, between 'real' forms of government based on belief and ideals and 'pretend' ones which are conjured out of necessity. Although we may legitimately *describe* it as a pragmatic solution to dire circumstances, there is neither justice nor intellectual reason in *marginalising* the Rump Parliament from the mainstream of English history on the basis of its constitutional expediency. For British constitutional history may best be summed up in a phrase which the Commonwealth exemplified – contingent creativity.

In February 1651 Secretary Nicholas wrote to the marquis of Ormond, telling him that 'In my judgement, the rebels in England are not founding their Common Wealth as if they intended it should subsist long: but what will come in the place of it God knows.'[15] The secretary, for all his experience and insight, knew not whereof he spoke. By 1651 the regime had started to bed down into the fabric of authority, had set its roots into the political landscape. The confidence of parliamentary pretensions took time to develop, but there existed right from day one a confidence about their direction. Whitehall would be colonised, and the honour of its inhabitants asserted; the supremacy of the Commons would be visibly proclaimed and upheld in the face of world opinion, and the cross and harp, by land and sea, would guide the way. Survival depended entirely on the successful armed defence of the Common-wealth, and the shift in attitudes it forced both upon its subjects at home and on the foreign powers of Europe. It also depended on entrenching civilian authority, and acclimatisation to the supreme novelty of the situation. The evolution of dignified civilian rule helped take England further and further away from her regal past. In just under four and a half years a remarkable distance was covered.

NOTES

1 J. G. A. Pocock, *The Machiavellian Moment. Florentine Political Thought and the Atlantic Republican Tradition* (Princeton, 1975); Worden, 'Classical Republicanism and the Puritan Revolution'; *idem*, 'English Classical Republicanism', in Burns with Goldie eds, *Cambridge History of Political Thought*, pp. 443–75; Z. Fink, *The Classical Republicans* (Urbana, 1945); Scott, *Algernon Sidney and the English Republic*; *idem*, 'The English Republican Imagination'; *idem*, 'The Rapture of Motion: James Harrington's Republicanism'.

2 Tuck, *Philosophy and Government*.

3 Worden, 'Classical Republicanism and the Puritan Revolution', p. 183; Scott, 'Rapture of Motion'.

4 Smuts, 'Court-centred Politics and the Uses of Roman Historians'; D. Norbrook, 'Lucan, Thomas May, and the Creation of a Republican Literary Culture'; Worden, 'Ben Jonson among the Historians'; all in Sharpe and Lake eds, *Culture and Politics in Early Stuart England*.

5 What passes hereafter for an understanding of the political theory of early modern Englishmen is entirely dependent on the brilliant elucidations of others, principally Richard Tuck and Glenn Burgess, and principally their *Philosophy and Government* and *The Politics of the Ancient Constitution. An Introduction to English Political Thought, 1603– 1642* (1992), respectively.

6 Alastair Bellany, '"Rayling Rymes and Vaunting Verse"'; Butler, *Theatre in Crisis* (Cambridge, 1984).

7 See for example I. Roots, *The Great Rebellion 1642–1660* (1966), p. 138.

8 J. P. Sommerville, *Politics and Ideology in England, 1603–1640* (1986).

9 Morgan, *Inventing the People*.

10 Worden, *The Rump Parliament*, p. 173.

11 See for example the Act of February 1649 altering the wording of all manner of legal writs, substituting the Keepers of the English Liberties by Authority of Parliament for the Crown, Firth and Rait eds, *Acts and Ordinances* ii, 6–9.

12 Seymour, 'Pro-government Propaganda', p. 424.

13 Latham and Matthews eds, *The Diary of Samuel Pepys* i, 136–7.

14 Possibly not enough credit is given to the ambiguity of contemporary usages, especially as so many of the recognised republican constitutions of the day incorporated Doges, Stadtholders and Grand Dukes.

15 Worden, *The Rump Parliament*, pp. 174–5, 341.

16 Woolrych, *Commonwealth to Protectorate*, p. 6.

17 P. Collinson, *De Republica Anglorum, or, History with the Politics put back*, given at his inauguration as Regius Professor of Modern History, Cambridge University, 9 November 1989 (Cambridge, 1990), p. 23; *idem*, 'The Monarchical Republic of Queen Elizabeth I'.

18 Tuck, *Philosophy and Government*, p. 204; cf. pp. 230, 238–40.

19 Collinson, 'Monarchical Republic', pp. 416–18.

20 Quoted by Adamson, 'Oliver Cromwell and the Long Parliament', p. 53.

21 Collinson, 'Monarchical Republic', pp. 396–7; Barry Coward, *Social Change and Continuity in Early Modern England, 1550–1750* (1988), p. 26; Cynthia Herrup, *The Common Peace* (Cambridge, 1987).

22 Hughes, *Causes of the English Civil War*, pp. 158–62.

23 Pauline Croft, 'Sir John Doddridge, the Society of Antiquaries, and the Antiquity of Parliament', *Parliaments, Estates, and Representatives* 12 (1992), 95–107.

24 Tuck, *Philosophy and Government*. Cf. H. A. L Fisher, *The Republican Tradition in Europe* (1911).

25 Hughes, *Causes of the English Civil War*, pp. 69–76; 87–9, 102, 105–6, 167.

26 Nathaniel Bacon, *Historical Discourse* (1647), cited by Burgess, *Politics of the Ancient Constitution*, p. 97.

27 *Sergeant Thorpe, Judge of Assize for the Northern Circuit, his Charge*, pp. 13, 15, 33. Cf. [Robinson?], *A Short Discourse between Monarchical and Aristocraticall Government*, p. 14

28 Peters, *Good Work for a Good Magistrate*, ep. ded.; Manley, *Veni; Vidi; Vici*, ep. ded.; Hughes, *Causes of the English Civil War*, pp. 89, 159.

29 *CJ* vi, 113, 131, 139, 150, 147, 155, 157–8, 178, 217–18, 227, 231, 246, 292, 299, 384, 403, 416, 435, 437, 440, 544–5, 561, 569–70; vii, 134, 190, 172, 210, 262–3; Abbott ed., *Writings and Speeches* ii, 276 n., 386 n., 391, 580–2, 582–3, 593; *H.M.C. Eighth Report* (1880), Appendix II, 64; Worden, *The Rump Parliament*, p. 47 n. 3; Stocks ed., *Records of the Borough of Leicester* iv, 397–8, 400, 412; Ackerman, *The History of the Colleges*, pp. 18, 23; Quick, *Charterhouse*, pp. 18–21; J. Sargeaunt, *Annals of Westminster School* (1898), pp. 82–8; L. E. Tanner, *Westminster School* (1934), pp. 13–14; W. Urwick, *The Early History of Trinity College, Dublin, 1591–1660* (London and Dublin, 1892), pp. 54–71.

30 I am very grateful to Sarah Barber for letting me read an early draft of her study of Marten which places his reputation in context of his battle with creditors and scandaleers alike.

31 Harleian MS 162, fo. 4*v, 'A praier read by the Speaker of the House of Commons each morning; and in the afternoone alsoe during the Earle of Straffords Triall during this Parl'.

32 Worden, *The Rump Parliament*, chapter 8, especially pp. 153–4.

33 R. Cust and P. Lake, 'Sir Richard Grosvenor and the Rhetoric of Magistracy', *Bulletin of the Institute of Historical Research* 54 (1981), 40–53; Hughes, *Causes of the English Civil War*, pp. 73–4.

34 Spalding ed., *Diary of Bulstrode Whitelocke*, p. 271.

35 French Fogle ed., *Complete Works of John Milton* V i (New Haven, 1971), 450.

36 Don M. Wolfe ed., *Complete Prose of John Milton* IV i (New Haven, 1966), 656.

37 S. Orgel and J. Goldberg, *John Milton* (Oxford, 1991), p. 336. Cf. [Robinson?] *A Short Discourse between Monarchical and Aristocraticall Government*, p. 15.

38 Norbrook, 'Marvell's *Horatian Ode* and the Politics of Genre'; *idem, Poetry and Politics* (1984); John Milton, 'The Ready and Easy Way', in Orgel and Goldberg, *John Milton*, p. 351.

39 Worden, 'Classical Republicanism and the Puritan Revolution', pp. 188–90; Scott, *Algernon Sidney and the English Republic*, pp. 43–58.

40 Quotation from Thomas Manley's translation, *Veni; Vidi; Vici*, pp. 25–6.

41 Bachrach and Collmer eds, *Huygens' Journal*, p. 19.

42 Manley *Veni; Vidi; Vici*, ep. ded.

43 *Ibid.*

44 R. McCrum, W. Cran and R. MacNeil, *The Story of English* (BBC, 1982), especially chapter 2, for the connection between governance, politics and the rise of the vernacular as the language of administration in the Middle Ages.

45 *CSPD 1649–50*, pp. 2–3. The declaration also appeared in English, but it has been suggested that this was a translation of the original document. See I. Ward, 'The English Peerage, 1649–1660: Government, Authority and Estates' (Cambridge Ph.D., 1989), p. 16 n.

46 House of Lords Record Office, MS Journal of the House of Commons, September 1648–June 1649, p. 957.

47 *CJ* vi, 468.

48 Roy, 'The English Republic'; Worden, *The Rump Parliament*, pp. 111, 117; *CJ* vi, 563.

49 Thomas, *Man and the Natural World*, pp. 52, 64, 67.

50 Translated by Thomas Blount, 1646, p. 13.

51 Worden, *The Rump Parliament*, pp. 78, 325, 378–9.

52 Woolrych, *Commonwealth to Protectorate*, p. 9.

53 Gentles, *The New Model Army*, p. 416.

54 Abbott ed., *Writings and Speeches* iii, 56.

55 *Ibid*, p. 452.

56 *Miseries of the Pallace*, sig. A2.

57 For Cromwell's departure and return from Ireland see Seymour, 'Pro-government Propaganda', and Abbott ed., *Writings and Speeches* ii, 88, 92–3, 260–1. For his progress to Scotland in 1650 see Abbott ed., pp. 281–2, 289; *Mercurius Politicus* 4–25 July 1650, pp. 74, 87, 100; Ashley, *Cromwell's Generals* p. 28; Stocks ed., *Records of the Borough of Leicester* iv, 378, 393. The remarkable detail of P. Gaunt's *Cromwellian Gazetteer* (Stroud, 1992) provides a thorough itinerary for almost the entire span of Cromwell's career in the saddle.

58 *A Speech or Declaration of the Declared King of Scots upon the Death of Montrose*, p. 5.

59 Abbott ed., *Writings and Speeches* ii, 400 and n.

60 Shropshire Record Office, 3365/595–7: 1649, £4 4s 2d; 1649–50, £1 7s 10d; 1651, £2 13s 10d.

61 D. Underdown, 'Party Management in the Recruiter Elections', *English Historical Review* 83 (1968), 235–64.

62 *CJ* vi, 105; vii, 91, 97, 182; Aylmer, *State's Servants*, p. 59; Reece, 'Military Presence'.

63 M. L. Ahearn, *The Rhetoric of War* (New York and London, 1989), p. 1.

64 Aylmer, *State's Servants*, p. 15.

65 Carlton, *Going to the Wars*, pp. 5, 41, 51, 128; *CSPD 1649–50*, pp. 162–3; Stowe MS 184, fos [159], 161–2.

66 Hawkins *et al.* eds, *Medallic Illustrations* i, 408.

67 Grimble, *The Harington Family*, pp. 199–202. The dating suggests that the medal must have been struck in the final month or so of the Rump's life. Sir James appears to have been making a particularly forthright point about his military experience in the teeth of growing hostility to the civilian regime.

68 Use of military titles for men also denoted as civilians, first reference only: *CJ* vi, 98 (Captain [Augustine?] Skynner), 111 (Colonel Henry Marten), 129 (Colonel Francis Bingham), 131 (Colonel George Thompson), 137 (Colonels John Moore and Alexander Rigby), 125 (Captain John Fry), 146 (Colonel Algernon Sidney), 224 (Colonel Francis Russell), 272–3 (Captain Henry Smith, MP?), 294 (Colonel William Purefoy), 311 (Colonel Thomas Birch), 350 (Colonel John Venn), 499 (Colonel Hugh Rogers), 506 (Colonel John Fielder), 534 (Colonel Peter Temple), 566 (Colonel Herbert Morley); *CJ* vii, 44 (Colonel Richard Norton), 55 (Colonel George Fenwick), 119 (Colonel Thomas Wogan), 92 (Major Lister).

69 B. Lib., Add. MS 37, 345, fos 54–v.

70 Spalding ed., *Diary of Bulstrode Whitelocke, passim* (though the father was just as likely to lament his son's prodigality with money); Abbott ed., *Writings and Speeches* ii, 98.

71 Cited by Kishlansky, 'Ideology and Politics', p. 179.

72 Knachel ed., *Case of the Commonwealth*, pp. 123–5.

73 Cited by Norbrook, 'Marvell's *Horatian Ode* and the Politics of Genre', pp. 157–8.

74 Penington junior, *A Word for the Common Weale*, p. 4.

75 John Dorney, *Certain Speeches made upon the Day of the Yearly Election of Officers in the City of Gloucester* (1653), p. 55–6.

76 Wither, *Perpetuall Parliament*, pp. 10–11. Wither did not, however, commend the delays which these 'contradictions in our wayes' promoted – pp. 13–14.

77 Peters, *Good Work for a Good Magistrate*, sig. A4v.

78 Penington junior, *A Word for the Common Weale*, pp. 7–9, 12–13.

79 Cited by Fisher, *The Republican Tradition in Europe*, p. 34.

80 L. Stone, *The Causes of the English Revolution* (1972), pp. 98, 108–9.

81 Abbott ed., *Writings and Speeches* i, 697

82 Dorney, *Certain Speeches* p. 50.

83 [Robinson?], *A Short Discourse Between Monarchical and Aristocraticall Government*, p. 3.

84 *Ibid.*, p. 7.

85 *Ibid.*, pp. 8–9.

86 *Ibid.*, p. 10.

87 Wither, *Respublica Anglicana*, pp. 3–4.

88 *Sergeant Thorpe, Judge of Assize for the Northern Circuit, his Charge*, pp. 7, 13.

89 [Hall], *Letter Written to a Gentleman in the Country*, p. 11.

90 [Robinson?], *A Short Discourse between Monarchical and Aristocraticall Government*, p. 12.

91 Clement Walker, *History of Independency* (1661), cited by M. James, *Social Problems and Policy during the Puritan Revolution, 1640–1660* (1966), p. 1.

92 Cited by Worden, *The Rump Parliament*, p. 87.

93 Wither, *Perpetuall Parliament*, p. 68.

94 *Ibid.*, p. 71.

95 *The Process and Pleadings in the Court of Spain upon the Death of Anthonie Ascham, Resident for the Parliament of England, and of John Baptista Riva his Interpreter*, p. 3; Glenn Burgess, 'Usurpation, Obligation and Obedience in the Thought of the Engagement Controversy', *Historical Journal* 29 (1986), 515–36.

96 *Reasons why the Supreme Authority of the Three Nations (for the time) is not in the Parliament*, p. 1.

97 *Ibid.*, pp. 14–15.

98 G. Bate, *The Lives, Actions and Execution of the prime Actors, and principle Contrivers of the horrid Murder of our late pious and Sacred Sovereign, King Charles I* (1661), pp. 29–30.

99 Sitwell, 'Royal Sergeants-at-Arms and the Royal Maces', pp. 216–19.

100 S. R. Gardiner, 'Note', *English Historical Review* 8 (1893), 525.

101 Jewitt and St John Hope, *Corporation Plate* I i, liv and 67–8.

102 Sitwell, 'Royal Sergeants-at-Arms and the Royal Maces', p. 219.

103 J. Britten ed., 'Remaines of Gentilisme and Judaisme', *Publications of the Folklore Society* 4 (1881).

104 Brooks-Davies, *The Mercurian Monarch*.

105 Worden, *The Rump Parliament*, p. 87.

106 *Ibid.*, p. 86.

107 G.R.O., GBR B3/3, pp. 136, 179, 250.

108 Rutt ed., *Diary of Thomas Burton* iii, 27. Cited by Worden, *The Rump Parliament*, pp. 86–7.

109 *The Rump Parliament*, p. 376.

110 *Ibid.*, p. 377.

111 Firth, 'Cromwell and the Expulsion of the Long Parliament', p. 527.

112 Cook, *Monarchy no Creature of Gods making*, cited by Tuck, *Philosophy and Government*, p. 240; cf. *Ibid.*, pp. 238–40.

113 [Streater], *Ten Queries*.

114 Editor's 'Introduction', Morrill ed., *Oliver Cromwell and the English Revolution*, p. 16.

115 Carte ed., *Original Letters and Papers* i, 407.

Bibliography

PRIMARY SOURCES

BODLEIAN LIBRARY

Clarendon MSS 34, 37, 45, 46 (miscellaneous royalist letters)

Rawlinson MS C129 (Journal of the embassy to the United Provinces)

Tanner MSS 52, 53, 54 (miscellaneous state papers)

BRITISH LIBRARY

Additional MSS:

    10,114 (Diary of John Harington)

    29,547 fo. 28 (Testimony of Patrick Young, Keeper of the late King's Antiquities)

    31,984 (Whitelocke's 'History of his 48th year')

    35,863 (Hale Commission minute book)

    35,864 (Minutes of parliamentary negotiations with the Scottish deputies, 1652–3)

    36,792 (Presentations to benefices by Lords Commissioners of the Great Seal)

    37, 344–5 (Whitelocke's 'Annales')

Harley MSS 163, 164 (Sir Simond D'Ewes' Journal of the House of Commons)

Stowe MSS 184, 189

Thomason Tracts

GLOUCESTERSHIRE RECORD OFFICE

GBR B3/3 (Common Council order book)

GUILDHALL RECORD OFFICE, LONDON

Journal of the Common Council, vols 40 and 41

Journal of the Court of Aldermen, vol. 59

HOUSE OF LORDS RECORD OFFICE

MS Journal of the House of Commons, September 1648–June 1649

INSTITUTE OF HISTORICAL RESEARCH, SENATE HOUSE, LONDON

Whitelocke Papers X (microfilm)

Bibliography

PUBLIC RECORD OFFICE, CHANCERY LANE, LONDON

C231/6 (Crown Office docquet book, 1643–60)

Commonwealth Exchequer Papers:

SP18 (Letters and Papers)

SP25 (Council of State Order books)

SP28/242 (Somerset Militia Committee)

SP28/258–260 (Committee of Accounts)

SP28/282–285, SP28/350/9, SP28/447/24 (Records of the Commissioners for the Sale of the late King's Goods)

SP64/10 (Indemnity Committee)

SHROPSHIRE RECORD OFFICE

3365/595–7 (Mayor of Shrewsbury's accounts, 1649–51)

WORCESTER COLLEGE, OXFORD

Clarke MSS XXIV, XXV

PRINTED SOURCES

W. C. Abbott ed., *The Writings and Speeches of Oliver Cromwell* (4 vols, Oxford, 1988)

J. Y. Akerman ed., *Letters from Roundhead Officers written from Scotland ... 1650–1660* (Edinburgh, 1856)

A. G. H. Bachrach and R. G. Collmer trans. and eds, *Lodewijck Huygens: The English Journal 1651–1652* (Leiden, 1982)

W. de G. Birch, *Catalogue of Seals in the Department of Manuscripts in the British Museum* (1887)

R. W. Blencowe ed., *The Sydney Papers* (1825)

M. F. Bond ed., *Sir Edward Dering's Convention Diary* (1976)

Calendars of State Papers, Domestic Series

Calendars of State Papers, Venetian Series

Calendars of the Clarendon Manuscripts

Calendars of the Committee for Compounding

T. Carte ed., *A Collection of Original Letters and Papers concerning the Affairs of England from the year 1641 to 1660* (2 vols, 1739)

W. H. Coates ed., *The Journal of Sir Simonds D'Ewes, from the first Recess of the Long Parliament to the Withdrawal of King Charles I from London* (New Haven, 1942)

A. Collins ed., *Letters and Memorials of State* (2 vols, 1746)

C. H. Firth ed., *Memoirs of the Life of Colonel Hutchinson, Governor of Nottingham* (2 vols, 1885)

— ed., *The Clarke Papers*, Camden Society and Royal Historical Society (1891–1901)

— ed., *The Memoirs of Edmund Ludlow* (2 vols, Oxford, 1894)

C. H. Firth and R. S. Rait eds, *Acts and Ordinances of the Interregnum* (3 vols, 1911)

French Fogle ed., *Complete Works of John Milton* V (New Haven, 1971)

E. Hawkins, A. W. Franks and H. A. Grueber eds, *Medallic Illustrations* (2 vols, 1885; reprinted 1969)

Historical Manuscripts Commission Seventh Report (1879)

Historical Manuscripts Commission Eighth Report (1880)

Historical Manuscripts Commission, Leybourne-Popham (1899)

T. B. Howell, *A Complete Collection of State Trials* iv (1816)

M. Y. Hughes ed., *Complete Prose Works of John Milton* (8 vols, New Haven, 1953–82)

D. A. Johnson and D. G. Vaisey eds, *Staffordshire and the Great Rebellion* (1965)

P. A. Knachel ed., *The Case of the Commonwealth of England, Stated* (Charlottesville, 1969)

J. Mayer ed., 'Inedited Letters of Cromwell, Colonel Jones, Bradshaw and other regicides', *Transactions of the Historical Society of Lancashire and Cheshire* 13 (1861)

O. Millar ed., *The Inventories and Valuations of the King's Goods, 1649–1651*, Walpole Society 43 (Glasgow, 1970–72)

J. Nickolls ed., *Original Letters and Papers of State, Addressed to Oliver Cromwell ... 1649–1658* (1743)

The Parliamentary or Constitutional History of England (second edition, 24 vols, 1761–63), vols 18 and 19

J. Max Patrick ed., 'Miltonic State Papers', *Complete Prose Works of John Milton* V (New Haven, 1969)

J. T. Rutt ed., *The Diary of Tomas Burton* (4 vols, 1828)

W. Scott ed., *A Collection of Scarce and Valuable Tracts ... of the Late Lord Somers* (13 vols, 1809–15)

Ruth Spalding ed., *The Diary of Bulstrode Whitelocke* (Oxford, 1990)

H. Stocks ed., *Records of the Borough of Leicester* (4 vols, Cambridge, 1923)

G. Vertue, *Medals, Coins, Great Seals, and other Works of Thomas Simon* (second edition, 1780)

Bulstrode Whitelocke, *Memorials of the English Affairs* (4 vols, 1682)

Don M. Wolfe ed., *Complete Prose of John Milton* IV (New Haven, 1966)

T. Wright ed., *Political Ballads published in England during the Commonwealth* , Percy Society (1841)

A. B. and A. Wyon, *The Great Seals of England* (1887)

Bibliography

SECONDARY TEXTS

Unless otherwise stated the place of publication is London.

ABBREVIATIONS

BIHR – *Bulletin of the Institute of Historical Research*

EHR – *English Historical Review*

HJ – *Historical Journal*

TRHS – *Transactions of the Royal Historical Society*

R. Ackerman, *The History of the Colleges of Winchester, Eton and Westminster, with the Charterhouse, the Schools of St Paul's, Merchant Taylors, Harrow and Rugby, and the Free-school of Christ's Hospital* (1816)

J. H. Adamson and H. F. Holland, *Sir Harry Vane. His Life and Times, 1613–1662* (1973)

J. S. A. Adamson, 'Oliver Cromwell and the Long Parliament', in J. S. Morrill ed., *Oliver Cromwell and the English Revolution* (1990)

— 'Chivalry and Political Culture in Caroline England', in K. Sharpe and P. Lake eds, *Culture and Politics in Early Stuart England* (1994)

M. Agulhon, *Marianne into Battle. Republican Imagery and Symbolism in France, 1789–1880* (Cambridge, 1979)

M. L. Ahearn, *The Rhetoric of War* (1989)

L. Alston, ed., *De Republica Anglorum* (Cambridge, 1906)

S. Anglo, *Spectacle, Pageant and Early Tudor Policy* (Oxford, 1969)

J. Arlott ed., *John Speed's England* (1953)

M. Ashley, *Cromwell's Generals* (1954)

P. Aubrey, *Mr Secretary Thurloe. Cromwell's Secretary of State, 1652–1660* (1990)

G. E. Aylmer, *The King's Servants. The Civil Service of Charles I, 1625–1642* (1961)

— *The State's Servants. The Civil Service of the English Republic, 1649–1660* (1973)

S. Barber, 'The Engagement for the Council of State and the Establishment of the Commonwealth Government', *Historical Research* 63 (1990), 44–57.

— 'Irish Undercurrents to the Politics of April 1653', *Historical Research* 65 (1992), 315–35

I. F. W. Beckett, *The Amateur Military Tradition, 1558–1945* (Manchester, 1991)

H. E. Bell and R. Ollard eds, *Historical Essays, 1600–1750, presented to David Ogg* (1963)

Alistair Bellany, '"Rayling Rymes and Vaunting Verse": Libellous Politics in early Stuart England, 1603–1628', in K. Sharpe and P. Lake eds, *Culture and Politics in Early Stuart England* (1994)

G. H. Bishop, *The History and Legend of the Oak* (Batley, 1975)

M. F. Bond, 'The Formation of the Archives of Parliament, 1497–1691', *Journal of the Society of Archivists* 1 (1955), 151–8

K. S. Bottigheimer, *English Money and Irish Land* (Oxford, 1971)

C. M. L. Bouch, *The Lady Anne, Hereditary High Sherifess of the County of Westmorland and Lady of the Honour of Skipton-in-Craven* (Penrith, 1954)

L. Boynton, *The Elizabethan Militia, 1558–1638* (1967)

Robert Brenner, *Merchants and Revolution. Commercial Change, Political Conflict and London's Overseas Trade, 1550–1653* (Princeton, 1993)

J. Britten ed., *Remaines of Gentilisme and Judaisme*, Publications of the Folklore Society 4 (1881)

D. Brookes-Davies, *The Mercurian Monarch* (Manchester, 1983)

G. Burgess, 'Usurpation, Obligation and Obedience in the Thought of the Engagement Controversy', *Historical Journal* 29 (1986), 515–36

Glenn Burgess, *The Politics of the Ancient Constitution. An Introduction to English Political Thought, 1603–1642* (1992)

M. Butler, *Theatre and Crisis, 1632–42* (Cambridge, 1984)

B. Capp, *The Fifth Monarchy Men. A Study in Seventeenth-Century Millenarianism* (1972)

— *Cromwell's Navy. The Fleet and the English Revolution, 1648–1660* (Oxford, 1989)

Norah Carlin, 'Extreme or Mainstream? The English Independent and the Cromwellian Reconquest of Ireland', in B. Bradshaw, A. Hadfield and W. Maley eds, *Representing Ireland. Literature and the Origins of Conflict, 1534–1600* (Cambridge, 1993)

C. Carlton, *Going to the Wars. The Experience of the British Civil Wars, 1638–1651* (1994)

G. Chettle, *The Queen's House, Greenwich* (1935)

M. T. Clanchy, *From Memory to Written Record. England 1066–1307* (second edition, Cambridge, Mass.; Oxford, 1993)

Clarendon, *History of the Great Rebellion* (Oxford, 1712)

R. A. Clarke, A. Wright and R. Barnett, *The Blasted Oak. The Oak Tree: Natural History, Art and Myth in European Culture* (Batley, 1987)

M. Coate, *Cornwall in the Great Civil War and Interregnum* (Oxford, 1933)

A. Coleby, 'Military–Civilian Relations on the Solent, 1651–1689', *Historical Journal* 29 (1986), 949–61

P. Collinson, 'The Monarchical Republic of Queen Elizabeth I', *Bulletin of the John Rylands Library* 69 (1986), 394–424

— *De Republica Anglorum, or, History with the Politics put back* (Cambridge, 1990)

M. Corbett and M. Norton eds, *Engraving in England* (Cambridge, 1964)

A. N. B. Cotton, 'London Newsbooks in the Civil War. Their Political Attitudes and Sources of Information' (Oxford D.Phil., 1971)

Barry Coward, *Social Change and Continuity in Early Modern England, 1550–1750* (1988)

Pauline Croft, 'Sir John Doddridge, the Society of Antiquaries, and the Antiquity of Parliament', *Parliaments, Estates, and Representatives* 12 (1992), 95–107

Alan Cromartie, 'The Rule of Law', in J. Morrill ed., *Revolution and Restoration. England in the 1650s* (1992), pp. 55–69

J. G. Cumming ed., *A Short Treatise of the Isle of Man*, Manx Society (Douglas, 1864)

Bibliography

Richard Cust, 'Honour, Rhetoric and Political culture: the Earl of Huntingdon and his Enemies', in S. D. Amussen and M. A. Kishlansky eds, *Political Culture and Cultural Politics in Early Modern England. Essays presented to David Underdown* (Manchester, 1995), pp. 84–111

R. Cust and A. Hughes eds, *Conflict in Early Stuart England. Studies in Religion and Politics, 1603–1642* (1989)

R. Cust and P. Lake, 'Sir Richard Grosvenor and the Rhetoric of Magistracy', *BIHR* 54 (1981), 40–53

G. Davies, *The Restoration of Charles II* (1955)

W. H. Dawson, *Cromwell's Understudy. The Life and Times of General John Lambert* (1938)

David Dean, 'Representations of Parliament', in D. Hoak ed., *Tudor Political Culture* (Cambridge, 1995)

E. S. de Beer ed., *The Diary of John Evelyn* (6 vols, Oxford, 1955)

B. Donegan, 'Codes and Conduct in the English Civil War', *Past and Present* 118 (1988), 65–95

F. D. Dow, *Cromwellian Scotland, 1651–1660* (Edinburgh, 1979)

G. S. Dugdale, *Whitehall through the Centuries* (1950)

R. T. Fallon, 'Filling the Gaps: New Perspectives on Mr. Secretary Milton', *Milton Studies* 12 (1978), 165–95

— *Milton in Government* (1993)

J. E. Farnell, 'The Usurpation of Honest London Householders: Barebones' Parliament', *English Historical Review* 82 (1967), 24–46

H. Farquhar, 'New Light on Thomas Simon', *Numismatic Chronicle*, fifth series, xvi (1936), 229–30

Z. Fink, *The Classical Republicans* (Urbana, 1945)

C. H. Firth, 'Cromwell and the Expulsion of the Long Parliament in 1653', *English Historical Review* 8 (1893), 526–34

— 'The Expulsion of the Long Parliament' I, *History*, new series 2 (October 1917), 129–43, and II, *ibid.* 3 (January 1918), 193–206

— *Cromwell's Army. A History of the English Soldier during the Civil Wars, Commonwealth and Protectorate* (third edition, 1921)

— 'London during the Civil War', *History* 11 (1926), 25–36

C. H. Firth and G. Davies, *The Regimental History of Cromwell's Army* (2 vols, Oxford, 1940)

H. A. L. Fisher, *The Republican Tradition in Europe* (1911)

Anthony Fletcher, 'Honour, Reputation and Office-holding in Elizabethan and Stuart England', in A. J. Fletcher and J. Stevenson eds. *Order and Disorder in Early Modern England* (Cambridge, 1985)

A. J. Fletcher and J. Stevenson eds, *Order and Disorder in Early Modern England* (Cambridge, 1985)

D. Foskett ed., *Samuel Cooper and his Contemporaries* (1974)

E. R. Foster, *The House of Lords, 1603–1649. Structure, Procedure and Nature of its Business* (1983)

J. J. Foster, *Samuel Cooper and the English Miniature Painters of the Seventeenth Century* (1914–16)

Joseph Frank, *The Beginnings of the English Newspaper, 1620–1660* (Cambridge, Mass., 1961)

A. Fraser, *Cromwell, Our Chief of Men* (1973)

S. R. Gardiner, *History of the Great Civil War* (4 vols, Moreton-in-Marsh, 1987)

— *History of the Commonwealth and Protectorate* (4 vols, Moreton-in-Marsh, 1988)

— 'Note', *English Historical Review* 8 (1893), 525

P. Gaunt, *Cromwellian Gazetteer* (Stroud, 1992)

I. Gentles, 'The Management of Crown Lands, 1649–1660', *Agricultural History Review* 19 (1971), 25–41

— 'The Sale of Crown Lands during the English Revolution', *Economic History Review* second series 26 (1973), 614–35

— 'The Purchasers of Northamptonshire Crown Lands, 1649–1660', *Midland History* 3 (1976), 206–32

— *The New Model Army in England, Ireland and Scotland, 1645–1653* (Oxford, 1992)

A. Globe, *Peter Stent. London Printseller, c. 1642–1665* (Vancouver, 1985)

Walter H. Godfrey, *Swakeleys, Ickenham* (1993)

W. Godwin, *History of the Commonwealth of England from its Commencement to the Restoration of Charles II* (4 vols, 1824–28)

I. Grimble, *The Harington Family* (1957)

E. O. G. Haitsema Mulier, *The Myth of Venice and Dutch Republican Thought in the Seventeenth Century*, trans. G. T. Moran (Assen, 1980)

A. W. Hakewill, *Thorpe Hall* (1852)

Henry Hallam, *The Constitutional History of England from Henry VII to George II* (1872)

P. H. Hardacre, *The Royalists during the Puritan Revolution* (The Hague, 1956)

A. Hast, 'State Treason Trials during the Puritan Revolution', *HJ* 15 (1972), 37–53

E. Hellmuth ed., *The Transformation of Political Culture. England and Germany in the late Eighteenth Century* (Oxford, 1990)

B. L. K. Henderson, 'The Commonwealth Charters', *TRHS* third series, vi (1912)

H. W. Henfrey, *Numismata Cromwelliana* (1877)

Thomas Herbert, *Memoirs* (1702)

Cynthia Herrup, *The Common Peace* (Cambridge, 1987)

C. Hill, 'Propagating the Gospel', in H. E. Bell and R. Ollard eds, *Historical Essays, 1600–1750, presented to David Ogg* (1963), pp. 35–59

D. Hirst, *Authority and Conflict. England 1603–1658* (1986)

D. Hoak ed., *Tudor Political Culture* (Cambridge, 1995)

P. G. Holiday, 'Land Sales and Repurchases in Yorkshire, 1650–1670', *Northern History* 5 (1970), 67–92

M. Holmes and H. D. W. Sitwell, *The English Regalia. Their History, Custody and Display* (1972)

Bibliography

D. and R. Hook, 'More Light on John Davies of Kidwelly', *Carmarthenshire Antiquary* 15 (1979), 57–64

Roger Howell junior, '"Who nees another Cromwell?" The Nineteenth-century Image of Oliver Cromwell', in R. C. Richardson ed., *Images of Oliver Cromwell. Essays by and for Roger Howell* (Manchester, 1993)

Ann Hughes, 'Parliamentary Tyranny? Indemnity Proceedings and the Impact of the Civil War: a Case Study from Warwickshire', *Midland History* 11 (1986), 49–78

— *Politics, Society and Civil War in Warwickshire, 1620–1660* (Cambridge, 1987)

— *The Causes of the English Civil War* (1991)

— 'Coventry and the English Revolution', in R. C. Richardson ed., *Town and Countryside in the English Revolution* (Manchester, 1992)

W. Hunt, 'Civic Chivalry and the English Civil War', in A. Blair and A. Grafton eds, *The Transmission of Culture* (Princeton, 1990)

R. Hutton, *The Restoration. A Political and Religious History of England and Wales, 1658–1667* (Oxford, 1985)

— *The British Republic, 1649–1660* (1990)

F. A. Inderwick, *Sidelights on the Stuarts* (1888)

— 'Rye under the Commonwealth' and 'The Rye Engagement', *Sussex Archaeological Collections* 39 (1894), 1–27

J. G. A. Ive, 'The Local Dimensions of Defence. The Standing Army and the Militia in Norfolk, Suffolk and Essex, 1649–1660' (Cambridge Ph.D., 1986)

M. James, *Social Problems and Policy during the Puritan Revolution, 1640–1660* (1966)

— 'English Politics and the Concept of Honour', in *Society, Politics and Culture. Studies in Early Modern England* (Cambridge, 1986), pp. 308–415

Maija Jansson, 'Remembering Marston Moor: the Politics of Culture', in S. D. Amussen and M. A. Kishlansky eds, *Political Culture and Cultural Politics in Early Modern England. Essays presented to David Underdown* (Manchester, 1995), pp. 255–76

L. Jewitt and W. H. St John Hope eds, *The Corporation Plate and Insignia of Office of the Cities and Towns of England and Wales* (2 vols, London and Derby, 1895)

D. A. Johnson and D. G. Vaisey eds, *Staffordshire and the Great Rebellion* (Stafford, 1965)

W. R. Jones, *Politics and the Bench. The Judges and the Origins of the English Civil War* (1971)

J. P. Kenyon, *The Stuart Constitution* (Cambridge, 1965)

M. Kishlansky, 'The Sale of Crown Lands and the Spirit of the Revolution', *Economic History Review* second series, 29 (1976), 125–35

— *The Rise of the New Model Army* (Cambridge, 1979)

— 'Ideology and Politics in the Parliamentary Armies, 1645–9', in J. S. Morrill ed., *Reactions to the English Civil War, 1642–1649* (1982), pp. 163–184

S. Lambert, 'The Clerks and the Records of the House of Commons, 1600–1640', *BIHR* 43 (1970), 215–31

— 'Procedure in the House of Commons in the Early Stuart Period', *EHR* 95 (1980), 753–81

— 'The Beginning of Printing for the House of Commons, 1640–1642', *The Library* sixth series, 3 (1981), 43–61

— *Printing for Parliament, 1641–1700*, List and Index Society special series, 20 (Cambridge and New York, 1984)

R. Latham and W. Matthews eds, *The Diary of Samuel Pepys* (9 vols, 1970)

A. L. Le Quesne, *Carlyle* (Oxford, 1982)

R. Lightbown, 'The King's Regalia, Insignia and Jewellery', in A. MacGregor ed., *The Late King's Goods. Collections, Possessions and Patronage of Charles I in the Light of the Commonwealth Sale Inventories* (Oxford, 1989)

Thomas Babington Macaulay, *History of England* (Everyman edition, 1906)

A. MacGregor ed., *The Late King's Goods. Collections, Possessions and Patronage of Charles I in the Light of the Commonwealth Sale Inventories* (Oxford, 1989)

B. Manning, *1649: Crisis of the English revolution* (1993)

C. R. Markham, *A Life of the Great Lord Fairfax* (1870)

J. G. Marston, 'Gentry, Honour and Royalism in early Stuart England', *Journal of British Studies* 13 (1973–74), 26

D. Massarella, 'The Politics of the Army and the Quest for Settlement', in I. Roots ed., *'Into Another Mould'. Aspects of the Interregnum* (Exeter, 1981), pp. 42–69

D. Masson, *The Life of John Milton* (6 vols, reprinted 1965)

H. C. Maxwell-Lyte, *Historical Notes on the Use of the Great Seal of England* (1926)

R. McCrum, W. Cran and R. MacNeil, *The Story of English* (BBC, 1982)

O. Millar, *Rubens and the Whitehall Ceiling* (1958)

— *Sir Peter Lely, 1618–1680*, National Gallery exhibition catalogue (1978)

L. Miller, *John Milton and the Oldenburg Safeguard* (New York, 1985)

— 'Before Milton was Famous: January 8, 1649/50', *Milton Quarterly* 21 (1987), 1–6

— *John Milton's Writings in the Anglo-Dutch Negotiations, 1651–54* (Pittsburgh, 1992)

E. S. Morgan, *Inventing the People* (1988)

Victor Morgan, 'The Cartographic Image of the Country in Early Modern England', *Transactions of the Royal Historical Society* fifth series, 29 (1979), 129–54

J. S. Morrill, 'The Army Revolt of 1647', in C. A. Tamse and A. C. Duke eds, *Britain and the Netherlands* (1977)

— 'The Impact on Society', in *idem* ed., *Revolution and Restoration. England in the 1650s* (1992)

J. S. Morrill ed., *Reactions to the English Civil War, 1642–1649* (1982)

— ed., *Oliver Cromwell and the English Revolution* (Cambridge, 1990)

— ed., *Revolution and Restoration. England in the 1650s* (1992)

J. Morrow, 'Republicanism and Public Virtue: William Godwin's *History of the Commonwealth*', *HJ* 34 (1991), 645–64

— 'Heroes and Constitutionalists: the Ideological Significance of Thomas Carlyle's Treatment of the English Revolution', *History of Political Thought* 14 (1993), 205–23

Bibliography

A. J. Nathanson, *Thomas Simon. His Life and Work, 1618–1665* (1975)

J. Newman, 'Inigo Jones and the Politics of Architecture', in K. Sharpe and P. Lake eds, *Culture and Politics in Early Stuart England* (1994)

David Norbrook, 'Lucan, Thomas May, and the Creation of a Republican Literary Culture'

— 'Marvell's *Horatian Ode* and the Politics of Genre', in T. Healy and J. Sawday eds, *Literature and the English Civil War* (Cambridge, 1990)

— 'Levelling Poetry: George Wither and the English Revolution, 1642–1649', *English Literary Renaissance* 21 (1991), 217–56

Wallace Notestein, *The Winning of the Initiative by the House of Commons* (1924)

W. L. F. Nuttall, 'King Charles I's Pictures and the Commonwealth Sale', *Apollo* 82 (1965), 302–9

Jane H. Ohlmeyer, *Civil War and Restoration in the three Stuart Kingdoms. The Career of Randall MacDonnell, Marquis of Antrim, 1609–1683* (Cambridge, 1993)

S. Orgel and J. Goldberg, *John Milton* (Oxford, 1991)

H. Owen and J. B. Blakeway, *A History of Shrewsbury* (8 vols, 1825)

E. H. Pearce, *Sion College and Library* (Cambridge, 1913)

C. E. L. Philips, *Cromwell's Captains* (1938)

S. Pincus, 'England and the World in the 1650s', in J. S. Morrill ed., *Revolution and Restoration. England in the 1650s* (1992)

J. G. A. Pocock, *The Machiavellian Moment. Florentine Political Thought and the Atlantic Republican Tradition* (Princeton, 1975)

R. B. Pugh, 'The Patent Rolls of the Interregnum', *BIHR* 22 (1950), 178–81

A. Quick, *Charterhouse* (1990)

Joad Raymond, *Making the News. An Anthology of the Newsbooks of Revolutionary England, 1641–1660* (Moreton-in-Marsh, 1993)

H. M. Reece, 'The Military Presence in England, 1649–1660' (Oxford D.Phil., 1981)

T. Rees, *History of Protestant Nonconformity in Wales* (1883)

T. Richards, *A History of the Puritan Movement in Wales, 1639–1653* (1920)

R. L. Rickard ed., 'A Brief Collection of the Queens Majesties High and Most Honourable Courtes of Recordes', *Camden Miscellany* 20 (1953)

Stephen Roberts, 'Local Government Reform in England and Wales during the Interregnum: a Survey', in I. Roots ed., *'Into Another Mould'. Aspects of the Interregnum* (Exeter, 1981), pp. 24–41

— 'Godliness and Government in Glamorgan, 1647–1660', in C. Jones, M. Newitt and S. Roberts eds, *Politics and People in Revolutionary England. Essays in Honour of Ivan Roots* (Oxford, 1986), pp. 225–51

J. C. Robertson, 'Caroline Culture: Bridging Court and Country?', *History* 75 (1990), 388–416

I. Roots, *The Great Rebellion, 1642–1660* (1966)

Ian Roy, 'The English Republic, 1649–1660: the View from the Town Hall', *Schriften des Historischen Kollegs Kolloquien* II, *Republiken und Republikanismus im Europa der frühen Neuzeit* (Oldenburg, 1983), pp. 213–37

— 'The Profession of Arms', in Wilfred Prest ed., *The Professions in early modern England* (1987), pp. 181–219

W. Noel Sainsbury, *Original Unpublished Papers illustrative of the Life of Sir Peter Paul Rubens* (1859)

J. Sargeaunt, *Annals of Westminster School* (1898)

Jonathon Scott, *Algernon Sidney and the English Republic, 1623–1677* (Cambridge, 1988)

— 'The English Republican Imagination', in J. Morrill ed., *Revolution and Restoration. England in the 1650s* (1992), pp. 35–54

Graham Seel, 'Cromwell's Trailblazer: Reinterpreting the Earl of Essex', *History Today* 45/4 (1995), 24

M. J. Seymour, 'Aspects of Pro-government Propaganda during the Interregnum' (Cambridge Ph.D., 1986)

Kevin Sharpe, 'Parliamentary History: in or out of Perspective?', in *idem* ed., *Faction and Parliament* (Oxford, 1978)

— '"The Image of Virtue": the Court and Household of Charles I, 1625–1642', in *idem*, *Politics and Ideas in Early Stuart England* (1989), pp. 147–73

— 'The King's Writ: Royal Authors and Royal Authority in Early Modern England', in K. Sharpe and P. Lake eds, *Culture and Politics in Early Stuart England* (1994), pp. 117–38

K. Sharpe and P. Lake eds., *Culture and Politics in Early Stuart England* (1994)

Roy Sherwood, *The Court of Oliver Cromwell* (second edition, Cambridge, 1989)

C. H. Simpkinson, *Thomas Harrison, Regicide and Major-General* (1905)

H. D. W. Sitwell, 'Royal Sergeants-at-Arms and the Royal Maces', *Archaeologia* 102 (1969), 203–50

Nigel Smith, *Literature and Revolution in England, 1640–1660* (New Haven, 1994)

R. M. Smuts, 'Public Ceremony and Royal Charisma', in A. L. Beier, D. Cannadine and J. M. Rosenheim eds, *The First Modern Society. Essays in Honour of Lawrence Stone* (Cambridge, 1989)

— 'Court-centred Politics and the Uses of Roman Historians, c. 1590–1630', in K. Sharpe and P. Lake eds, *Culture and Politics in Early Stuart England* (1994)

J. P. Sommerville, *Politics and Ideology in England 1603–1640* (1986)

Ruth Spalding, *The Improbable Puritan* (1975)

D. Starkey, D. A. L. Morgan, John Murphy, Pam Wright, Neil Cuddy and Kevin Sharpe, *The English Court: from the Wars of the Roses to the English Civil War* (1987)

R. P. Stearns, *The Strenuous Puritan* (Urbana, 1954)

D. Stevenson, 'A Revolutionary Regime and the Press: the Scottish Covenanters and their Printers, 1638–1651', *The Library* vii (1985), 334

J. Douglas Stewart, 'Samuel Cooper: an English Baroque "Man of his Century"', in D. Foskett ed., *Samuel Cooper and his Contemporaries* (1974)

L. Stone, *The Causes of the English Revolution* (1972)

Roy Strong, *The English Renaissance Miniature* (1983)

L. E. Tanner, *Westminster School* (1934)

Bibliography

K. Thomas, *Man and the Natural World. Changing Attitudes in England, 1500–1800* (1983)

H. G. Tibbutt, *Colonel John Okey, 1606–1662*, Publications of the Bedfordshire Historical Records Society 35 (1955)

J. Thirsk, 'The Sales of Royalist Land during the Interregnum', *Economic History Review* 2 (1952–53), 188–207

P. Thorne, *Ceremonial and the Royal Mace in the House of Commons*, House of Commons Library Document 11 (London, 1980)

— *The Royal Mace*, House of Commons Library Document 18 (London, 1990)

Richard Tuck, *Philosophy and Government, 1572–1651* (Cambridge, 1993)

David Underdown, 'Party Management in the Recruiter Elections, 1645–1648', *EHR* 83 (1968), 235–64

— *Pride's Purge. Politics in the Puritan Revolution* (Oxford, 1971)

W. Urwick, *The Early History of Trinity College, Dublin, 1591–1660* (London and Dublin, 1892)

M. Walzer, *Regicide and Revolution*, trans. Marian Rothstein (1974)

I. Ward, 'The English Peerage, 1649–1660: Government, Authority and Estates' (Ph.D. thesis, Cambridge, 1989)

G. F. Warner and J. P. Gilson, *Catalogue of Western Manuscripts in the Old Royal and King's Collections in the British Museum* (4 vols, 1921)

S. J. Weyman, 'Oliver Cromwell's Kinsfolk', *EHR* 6 (1891), 48–60

M. Whinney, *John Webb's Drawings for Whitehall Palace*, Walpole Society 31 (1942–43)

M. Whinney and O. Millar, *English Art, 1625–1714* (Oxford, 1957)

C. M. Williams, 'Extremist Tactics in the Long Parliament, 1642–3', *[Australian] Historical Studies* 15 (1971–73), 136–50

— 'The Anatomy of a Radical Gentleman: Henry Marten', in D. Pennington and K. Thomas eds, *Puritans and Revolutionaries. Essays in Honour of Christopher Hill* (Oxford, 1982), pp. 118–38

A. H. Woolrych, 'The Calling of Barebones' Parliament', *EHR* 80 (1965), 492–513

— *From Commonwealth to Protectorate* (Oxford, 1982)

A. B. Worden, *The Rump Parliament, 1648–1653* (Cambridge, 1974)

— 'Classical Republicanism and the Puritan Revolution', in H. Lloyd-Jones, V. Pearl and B. Worden eds, *History and Imagination. Essays in Honour of H. R. Trevor-Roper* (1981), pp. 182–200

— 'The Politics of Marvell's *Horatian Ode*', *HJ* 27 (1984), 525–47

— 'English Classical Republicanism', in J. H. Burns with M. Goldie, *Cambridge History of Political Thought* (1991), pp. 443–75

— review of Spalding ed., *The Diary of Bulstrode Whitelocke*, in *English Historical Review* 108 (1993), 122–34

— 'Ben Jonson among the Historians', in K. Sharpe and P. Lake eds, *Culture and Politics in Early Stuart England* (1994)

Index

Note: 'n' after a page number refers to the number of a note on that page.

Index

Wollaston, Sir John 101, 162
Worcester, battle of 2, 223
   regimental colours captured at 17,
      58
Worden, Blair 4–5, 13, 141, 162–3, 187,
      203, 205
writs *see* legal system

York 92, 95, 121
Young, Peter 39–40

Zanchy, Jerome *see* Sankey, Jerome
Zeeland 65